The Law of Global Custody

The Law of Global Custody

Second edition

Dr Joanna Benjamin

Reader in law
London School of Economics

Madeleine Yates

Solicitor, Clifford Chance Limited Liability Partnership

Gerald Montagu

Solicitor, Clifford Chance Limited Liability Partnership

Butterworths
LexisNexis™

Members of the LexisNexis Group worldwide

United Kingdom	LexisNexis Butterworths Tolley, a Division of Reed Elsevier (UK) Ltd, Halsbury House, 35 Chancery Lane, LONDON, WC2A 1EL, and 4 Hill Street, EDINBURGH EH2 3JZ
Argentina	LexisNexis Argentina, BUENOS AIRES
Australia	LexisNexis Butterworths, CHATSWOOD, New South Wales
Austria	LexisNexis Verlag ARD Orac GmbH & Co KG, VIENNA
Canada	LexisNexis Butterworths, MARKHAM, Ontario
Chile	LexisNexis Chile Ltda, SANTIAGO DE CHILE
Czech Republic	Nakladatelství Orac sro, PRAGUE
France	Editions du Juris-Classeur SA, PARIS
Hong Kong	LexisNexis Butterworths, HONG KONG
Hungary	HVG Orac, BUDAPEST
India	LexisNexis Butterworths India, NEW DELHI
Ireland	Butterworths (Ireland) Ltd, DUBLIN
Italy	Giuffrè Editore, MILAN
Malaysia	Malayan Law Journal Sdn Bhd, KUALA LUMPUR
New Zealand	LexisNexis Butterworths, WELLINGTON
Poland	Wydawnictwo Prawnicze LexisNexis , WARSAW
Singapore	LexisNexis Butterworths, SINGAPORE
South Africa	Butterworths SA, DURBAN
Switzerland	Stämpfli Verlag AG, BERNE
USA	LexisNexis, Dayton, Ohio

A CIP Catalogue record for this book is available from the British Library.

ISBN 0 406 94721 X

Typeset by B & J Whitcombe, Nr Diss, Norfolk, IP22 2LP
Printed and bound in Great Britain by Antony Rowe Ltd, Chippenham, Wilts

To Nina Farhi

Preface

This second edition of *The Law of Global Custody* is overdue; its delivery was inconveniently but happily delayed by the earlier than expected arrival of Benjamin Reiner.

There have been such profound operational and legal changes in the global custody industry that the book has been largely rewritten. This was an enormous task, to which I alone was unequal. This edition has therefore been generally co-authored by myself and Madeleine Yates, with Gerald Montagu providing the chapter on taxation. The book has been very significantly improved by their practice-based expertise. I am very grateful to them (not least because it is not clear that a mother of a young child is busier than a successful practitioner).

All three of us are indebted to many colleagues who have generously helped in the preparation of this edition, as indicated in the relevant sections of this book. We are also grateful to Butterworths for their patience and competence in managing this project.

Joanna Benjamin
London School of Economics
November 2002

Contents

Table of statutes

Paragraph references in **bold** type indicate where the legislation is set out in part or in full.

References in this table to *Statutes* are to Halsbury's Statutes of England (Fourth Edition) showing the volume number and page at which the annotated text of the Act will be found.

Table of statutory instruments

Paragraph references in **bold** type indicate where the legislation is set out in part or in full.

Table of EU legislation

Paragraph references in **bold** type indicate where the legislation is set out in part or in full.

Table of cases

PARA

L

M

N

P

Q

PARA

Y

Chapter 1

Introduction

Overview

1.1 Global custody[1] is a service whereby a financial institution assumes responsibility for the safekeeping and administration of its client's international portfolio of securities.

1 The term global custody was developed in the early 1990s. In many cases today it is referred to as global securities services.

International securities portfolios

1.2 A number of different types of institution invest in large international portfolios of investment securities. These include pension funds, insurance companies, managed funds (both wholesale and retail), building societies, banks, and commercial companies acting through their corporate treasury operations[1]. Over the years ahead, the size of these institutions' portfolios is projected to grow[2], and to become increasingly international, as opportunities for domestic investment fail to keep pace with demand[3].

International investors need access to local facilities, so that they are able to liaise with the issuers of their securities in relation to corporate actions, and relevant tax authorities in relation to withholding tax. Such liaison is traditionally achieved through banks operating in the issuer's jurisdiction. In addition, where securities are bought and sold, the processing of such transactions increasingly takes place through domestic and international electronic systems[4]. Direct access to these systems is often restricted[5].

1 See also the *Myners Report, Institutional Investment in the United Kingdom, A Review*, 2001, p 18: 'The main types of institutional investor are:
- occupational pension funds;
- insurance companies;
- pooled investment vehicles, such as unit trusts, open-ended investment companies (oeics) and investment trusts; and
- other financial institutions, such as charities, endowments and educational institutions.'

2 Pension funds must continue to grow in the years ahead because 'The population is relentlessly ageing': letter from Paul Myners to the Chancellor, 6 March 2001, presenting the *Myners Review*. Non-pension managed funds also constitute a growth industry requiring custody services.

3 See Chapter 5 for a discussion of other factors leading to increases in cross-border investment.

4 These include clearing, settlement and straight through processing systems. See Chapter 8.

5 Whether on financial or operational criteria. See CPSS/IOSCO Joint Task Force *Recommendations for Securities Settlement Systems*, 2001, p 21.

Global custody

1.3 It is often impracticable and in some cases impossible for the investor itself to access all the facilities and systems necessary for the administration and settlement of its international portfolio. Rather than instruct each local bank and electronic system directly, the client appoints a global custodian to do so on its behalf, or to act through the global custodian's own local branches. The client's contractual relationship and dealings are with the custodian only, which keeps the global network behind the scenes. This offers the convenience of 'one stop shopping' to the client.

In theory, it might be possible for each local bank and electronic system to hold and/or process the assets in the client's name, dealing with the global custodian as agent. However, this is not generally the position. In most cases, the counterparty wishes to deal with the global custodian as principal, and not to take note of the identity of the ultimate clients. Reasons for this include desire to achieve administrative convenience and to limit levels of regulatory and civil law duty. Thus, the account with the local bank or electronic system is generally maintained in the name of the global custodian, perhaps with a general client designation. The individual entitlements of the global custodian's clients are recorded only on the records of the global custodian. Thus, the global custodian holds or controls title to the assets and, in addition to administration and settlement, the global custody service (as its name suggests) involves safekeeping.

The global custody industry

Background

1.4 Global custody was first developed in the United States, in response to the regulatory needs of pension funds, including the obligation to have independent custodians. The service was developed in London in the 1980s, and today many of the leading global custodians operating in London are the UK branches of US banks. More recently, global custody has been developed on continental Europe, with several continental banks taking a leading position in the industry.

Challenges and opportunities

1.5 Since the mid-1990s, global custodians have been under pressure from a number of sources. Over-provision served to drive down fees, and led to significant withdrawals from the industry. A number of mergers and business transfers have also served to reduce the number of global custodians. Establishing and maintaining the electronic systems required to provide a global custody service involves a very significant investment. Depressed market conditions in recent years have reduced the enthusiasm of some global custodians for this. Meanwhile, enhancements to the post-trade infrastructure are reducing the inefficiencies to which global custody is the traditional solution[1].

More recently and in other respects, however, the industry is going through a very dynamic period. The new millennium has seen growth in the industry, with a number of smaller players entering the field[2]. Particularly following *The Myners Review* of 2001[3], institutional investors are increasingly appointing multiple fund managers, and looking for accurate measurements of their respective performances. As indicated below, global custodians are able to meet this need by presenting organised portfolio information, that enables clients to compare like with like. In an associated development, demand has grown for the performance enhancing financial services that global custodians are able to offer, including cash management and securities lending[4]. Another major trend is the outsourcing by fund managers of their middle and back office functions[5] to global custodians[6]. While not part of traditional global custody, outsourcing services may be provided by financial institutions from within the same business divisions as global custody services, which they may naturally complement[7]. With an ageing population across Europe, the institutional investment industry which forms the client base of global custodians is expected to grow very significantly. Legal and operational risk analysis associated with global custody is reaching new levels of sophistication and a number of new initiatives serve to enhance the operational standards in the industry[8]. A measure of the operational robustness of the major global custodians is provided by the aftermath of September 11. While the New York Stock Exchange was closed for a week, global custody operations in general continued business without significant disruption[9].

1 See Chapter 8. Indeed, international settlement systems are enhancing their services so as to rival global custody. See The European Securities Forum *Contribution on the Joint CESR/ECB Consultation on Clearing and Settlement*, 2002, ESF comment on consultation question 2.3.

2 Some industry commentators have suggested that these new smaller global custodians serve the smaller institutional investors. These may be less attractive to the major established global custodians, who may impose minimum account sizes on their client base.

3 *The Myners Report: Institutional Investment in the United Kingdom; A Review*, 2001. In the 2000 Budget, the Chancellor Gordon Brown asked Paul Myners, the Chairman of Gartmore Investment Management, to investigate possible distortions in institutional investment decision-making. The background to this request is understood to have been concerns relating to the under-performance of UK pension funds and other institutional investors in comparison with their US equivalents, and the underdevelopment of the private equity industry in the UK in comparison with the US private equity industry. Myners carried out a consultation exercise between May and July 2000, and his report was published on 4 March 2001. The key recommendations of the report were accepted by Gordon Brown in his 2001 Budget.

The report identified a number of distortions affecting decision-making by institutional investors in general, and occupational pension funds in particular, with the result that '... savers' money is too often being invested in ways that do not maximise their interests. It is likely to follow too that capital is being inefficiently allocated in the economy.' The key recommendation of the Review is the drawing up of Principles of Institutional Investment. These include performance measurement: broadly, trustees should measure fund performance, assess their own procedures and decisions, and assess procedures and decisions delegated to advisers and managers.

4 'The Maxwell effect is beginning to subside, but the Myners review sent a jolt through the fund manager and pensions manager market': 'Global Custody Survey' Pensions Management, Sept 2001, p 33. In the Maxwell scandal of November 1991, pension fund assets were stolen using transactions that purported to be securities loans.

5 These terms are used in the industry with a range of meanings: usually middle office is taken to mean post-trade and pre-settlement functions including matching, allocation and reporting, while back office is taken to mean settlement and post-settlement functions.

6 With a view to improving efficiency and saving costs by concentrating on management, and in particular sharing development costs with the outsourcing service provider. The massive investment required by global custodians to meet the challenge of T+1 settlement, discussed in Chapter 8, is beyond the budget of many thinly-capitalised fund managers.

See Chapter 7 for regulatory issues surrounding outsourcing. The authors are grateful to Rob Price, Senior Associate, Clifford Chance, for his comments about outsourcing.

7 In some cases, fund managers will choose as their global custodian the institution which is able to provide outsourcing services for the middle office.

8 See Chapter 8.

9 Jonathan Brown 'Recovery wakes up to extreme risk' Euromoney, November 2001, 82 at 84–5.

Development of the service

1.6 Traditional global custody comprises the core services of safekeeping and settlement[1]. Customarily associated with these are basic portfolio administration[2] together with foreign exchange services[3]. In addition, as global custodians compete to retain and expand their client base, value-added services are developed. Without these, global custodians may be unable to win new mandates. These include the cross-selling of financial products[4]; information and accounting services[5]; (crucially) collateral management[6]; tax advice[7]; reporting; and compliance monitoring and other supervisory services[8]. Global custodians have traditionally provided access to electronic settlement systems; as the post-trade infrastructure for securities develops, clients may also be provided with access to clearing[9] and straight through processing[10]. Thus, the larger global custodians are able to offer comprehensive investor services to their clients.

1 That is, the receipt and delivery of securities and cash to settle client trades, as discussed below and in Chapter 8).
2 That is, income and dividend collection and withholding tax reclamation, proxy voting, handling corporate actions and trade portfolio reporting.
3 For example, converting sale proceeds from one currency into another to finance a purchase.
4 These include cash management, cash lending, stock lending, repos (repurchase agreements), and derivatives. With contractual settlement, cash and (more rarely) securities are credited to the client's account on the date they should have been received, irrespective of the date of actual receipt.
5 Including consolidated and multi-currency record keeping, valuation and portfolio analysis including value at risk calculations and performance measurement. In recent years, and particularly following the *Myner's Review*, pension funds in particular are appointing multiple managers, and 'investment accounting' enables them to compare managers' performance across the whole of their portfolio.
As discussed in Chapter 8, the development of straight through processing may increase the potential for information management services. 'Data aggregators by nature, custodian banks are ideally placed to sit between the investment manager and the trustee, collating, filtering, enriching and shaping these strands of information . . .': Pensions Management, September 2001, p 34.
6 Assisting the client in developing the potential of its portfolio to collateralise credit exposures and thereby raise finance, whether from third parties or from the global custodian, as discussed in Chapter 4.
7 In practice, global custodians may provide significant guidance and assistance to clients in relation to withholding tax. However, they may not wish to assume legal responsibility for giving tax advice. See Chapter 10 for a discussion of withholding tax.
8 For example, the custodian may agree to monitor a fund manager's compliance with a fund's investment powers, or (less commonly) assume express responsibility to a fund client for monitoring the compliance of the investment manager with investment powers and guidelines. It is crucial clearly to define the scope of any such duties: see the discussion in Chapter 7 and (in relation to straight through processing) Chapter 8.
9 Access to clearing would often be provided by a broker associated with the global custodian.
10 By global custodians acting as 'concentrators': see the discussion in Chapter 8.

Other custody functions

1.7 Financial institutions may hold securities and related assets for clients in contexts other than global custody. Very large sections of the securities markets involve repackaging, whereby new securities are issued on the economic basis of other underlying securities. Important examples include depositary receipts (in which a depositary holds legal title to underlying shares[1] on behalf of the holders of depositary receipts issued by it); and structured notes (in which a custodian holds underlying assets on behalf of a special purpose vehicle issuing notes)[2]. Safekeeping of securities portfolios may also arise in the context of investment fund[3] and collateral structures[4].

A very rudimentary analysis of the current service providers involved in the safekeeping of securities and related assets might divide the players into the (primarily) large bank entities (often providing a full global custody service); small custodians historically offering chiefly intra-group services[5]; and trustee entities used in the context of capital market issues. Thus, the introduction of custodial intermediaries serves a range of operational functions beyond the portfolio administration traditionally associated with global custody. In any case, it is important to note that such intermediation also fundamentally changes the nature of the client's asset, as discussed in Chapters 2 and 3.

1 Or, more rarely, debt securities.
2 See Joanna Benjamin *Interests in Securities* (2000, OUP), chs 11 and 12 for more detail. However, this function is reduced by the growth of synthetic structures, where in place of underlying assets held in custody, credit derivatives and other derivatives are used to back the new notes.
3 Joanna Benjamin *Interests in Securities* (2000, OUP), ch 11.
4 See Chapter 4.
5 Non-bank custodians also include brokers and a small number of fund managers providing custody in-house for their clients. As indicated above, smaller institutions are now also offering global custody services.

The legal analysis

Electronic, intermediated, cross-border securities markets

1.8 As discussed in Chapters 2 and 3, global custodians and the systems which they use operate in an electronic, intermediated and cross-border environment. A major source of legal risk here is legal anachronism. While banks have provided investment custody services for centuries, the traditional legal analysis of such arrangements is outdated. Many of the relevant cases date from an era when banker's custody meant promissory notes in strong boxes. The ideas judicially developed in those cases (relating to the ownership, safekeeping, transfer and use as collateral of such securities) rested on the assumption that paper documentation, and therefore physical possession, were involved.

Today, physical assets have been replaced by electronic records[1]. This alters the traditional analysis of the nature of the investor's asset, her relationship with the custodian, and the duties of the custodian to the client[2]. Moreover, '[c]ross-border holdings of securities often involve several layers of intermediaries acting as custodians'[3]. Thus, the asset in which the investor has an interest may generate credit entries in accounts maintained by a number of intermediaries. In turn, these intermediaries may operate in different jurisdictions. This multiplication of databases has raised questions concerning the true nature of the investor's asset, and where it is legally located. It is necessary to answer these questions in order to address legal risk in cross-border securities collateral arrangements[4].

1 See Chapter 2.
2 See Chapters 2, 3 and 6 respectively.
3 'For example, an institutional investor may hold its securities through a global custodian, which, in turn, holds securities in a sub-custodian that is a member of the local CSD. Or a broker-dealer may hold its securities through its hold country CSD or an international CSD, which, in turn, holds its securities through a cross-border link with the local CSD or a local custodian' (CPSS/IOSCO *Recommendations for Securities Settlement Systems*, 2001, p 20).
4 See Chapter 5.

Analytic and law reform context

1.9 The first edition of this book was written at a time[1] when the legal analysis of the above issues in this jurisdiction was limited, although in the US an important debate had surrounded the 1994 revision of Pt 8 of the Uniform Commercial Code[2]. Since that time, tremendous international and UK industry, public sector and academic attention has turned to the subject, generating a considerable literature. There have also been important law reform initiatives seeking to address insolvency risk and to clarify the applicable conflict of laws rules[3]. At the time of writing, discussions are taking place in London with a view to preparing a UK investment securities code. This would serve to clarify many of the issues discussed in this work, and enhance the competitive position of London as an international financial centre. It may inform a future European securities code.

1 More recently, see Austen Peters *Custody of Investments* (2000, Oxford University Press). Like the first edition, this book was based on a PhD thesis, drawing on the author's experience in practice.
2 See, for example, CW Mooney *Beyond Negotiability* (1990) Cardozo Law Review; J Rogers 'Policy Perspective on the Revised UCC Article 8' UCLALR, June 1996, 1413.
3 These are discussed in Chapters 4 and 5, and include the Hague Convention on Indirectly Held Securities.

Scope

1.10 It is assumed throughout that the global custodian operates in London and that English law governs the global custody contract. The impact of the electronic environment on securities is considered in Chapter 2, and on the custody relationship in Chapter 3. Chapter 4 discusses the use of the custody portfolio as collateral. Chapter 5 considers cross-border issues, particularly in relation to collateral and sub-custodian insolvency. The custodian's duties at general law are discussed in Chapter 6, and under the regulatory regime established under the Financial Services and Markets Act 2000 in Chapter 7. Chapter 8 gives an overview of the post-trade infrastructure, while Chapter 9 considers CREST and the CMO. Taxation is discussed in Chapter 10; conclusions are given in Chapter 11.

Changes from the first edition

1.11 The first edition of *The Law of Global Custody* was published in 1996. As already indicated, there have been very significant legal and operational changes since that time, in response to which this work has been almost entirely rewritten. Chapter 4 (collateral), Chapter 7 (regulation), Chapter 8 (post-trade infrastructure) and Chapter 10 (taxation) are wholly new. The remaining chapters have been extensively revised. While the first edition was written by Joanna Benjamin alone, the task of the second was shared with Joanna's practitioner colleagues, Madeleine Yates (who was primarily responsible for Chapter 7 (regulation), Chapter 9 (settlement systems) and, jointly with Joanna, for Chapter 6 (duties)) and Gerald Montagu (who was responsible for Chapter 10 (taxation).

Fundamental concepts[1]

1.12 The legal analysis of international securities settlement, clearing, custody and collateral is sometimes regarded as a highly technical specialised area, impenetrable to outsiders. The authors would prefer to dispel this myth. Half the battle is mastering the jargon and, in order to assist the non-specialist reader, this section will consider the key operational and legal concepts that inform this area. As a brief introduction to these concepts, this section is necessarily simplistic. It will not assist the experienced reader, and does not do justice to the subtlety of many of the issues involved. However, it may prove useful to the beginner as a basis from which to go on to further reading, some of which is indicated in the footnotes.

This section will briefly consider the following: the nature of securities; securities trading, clearing and settlement; personal rights, property rights and insolvency; securities collateral; possession; and legal categories of assets.

1 The authors are grateful to Dr Sarah Worthington and Dr Eva Micheler of the London School of Economics for kindly reviewing this section. Any errors are the authors' own.

The nature of securities[1]

1.13 The services, products and arrangements discussed in this book all concern securities; this discussion will therefore start with the nature of securities. Securities are a form of transferable financial asset, of which equities and bonds are the most common examples[2]. When a company, government agency or other institution wishes to raise capital, it may consider borrowing from a bank. However, bank lending is in general comparatively expensive and short term. An alternative is to raise capital by issuing securities. In this case, new assets in the form of intangible rights, known as securities, are issued (ie created) and delivered either to members of the public (in a public offer) or selected investors (in a private placement) in exchange for cash. The issuer obtains a large sum of capital in the form of the aggregate issue price of the securities.

1 For a more detailed discussion of the nature of securities and the securities markets, see, P Wood *Comparative Financial Law* (1995, Sweet & Maxwell); R Tennekoon *The Law and Regulation of International Finance* (2000, Butterworths) (2nd edn awaited); S Valdez *An Introduction to the Global Financial Markets* (1997, 2nd edn, Macmillan); D Adams *Corporate Finance: Banking and Capital Markets*, LPC (Jordans, 2002–03) and J Benjamin *Interests in Securities* (2000, Oxford University Press), chs 1 and 2.

2 For a note of the historic development of the meaning of the term 'securities', see J Benjamin *Interests in Securities* (2000, Oxford University Press), p 4.

Debt and equity

1.14 In terms of holders' rights, securities are divided into two broad categories, namely debt and equity[1]. In the case of debt securities, investors are owed a debt by the issuer, and the relationship between the holder and the issuer is that of creditor and debtor. The terms of issue of the securities characteristically entitle the holders to the repayment of the principal sum (usually at a specified maturity date) and also to regular interest payments. In addition, depending on the terms of issue of the debt securities, holders are usually entitled to other rights, including the right to vote at holders' meetings and to receive information from the issuer.

Equity securities (also known as shares) may only be issued by companies. The holder of equities is an ordinary shareholder in the issuing company. Ordinary shareholders are entitled to a return of their capital only on the company's winding up, and are paid only after all creditors of the company have been paid first, and then only to the extent that sufficient assets are available. Shareholders do not have an automatic right to income, and are paid income in the form of dividends at the discretion of the directors of the company in accordance with company law, depending on the company's profitability. However, if the value of the company increases over time, this will be reflected in the value of the shares, so that shareholders may have the prospect of capital growth. Also, shareholders generally have voting rights, and other rights protected by company law[2]. From an issuer's perspective a significant difference between debt and equity funding is that a tax deduction may be available with respect to interest paid on a debt security, whereas dividends on equity are paid out of post-tax profits.

1 Certain types of securities have characteristics of both debt and equity. Examples of such 'hybrid' securities are preference shares, convertible bonds and equity warrants.

2 'A share is an item of intangible property. It is itself a "bundle of rights", giving the shareholder neither ownership of the company's assets nor ownership of the company as a "thing", but attracting to itself the protection of the law to a degree that warrants the label "property" ': Sarah Worthington 'Shares and Shareholders: Property, Power and Entitlement, Part 1' (2001) Comp Law 22(9) at 258.

Bearer and registered securities

1.15 Securities are also categorised according to another basic distinction, namely that between bearer and registered securities. This distinction relates to the manner in which securities are traditionally evidenced and transferred. In the case of a security in bearer form, the issuer creates a physical instrument (ie a formal document), which in legal theory constitutes the security. The security is held by whoever holds the instrument from time to time, and the security is transferred simply by transferring possession of the instrument. In the case of registered securities, the issuer (or, more commonly, a registrar acting as its agent) maintains a database (known as a register) in which the names of the holders from time to time are recorded. In order to transfer registered securities, it is necessary for the register to be amended, so as to show the name of the transferee in the place of the name of the transferor in respect of the securities in question.

Computerisation

1.16 The practice of evidencing and transferring holdings of securities has been radically altered by the computerisation of the securities markets. Chapter 2 considers this development, and its implications for the legal nature of securities.

Securities trading, clearing, settlement and custody[1]

Trading

1.17 The issue of new securities is known as primary market activity. Of course, the first holder of securities may decide to hold them indefinitely or to maturity. However, in many cases, the holders of securities wish to realise their investment by sale. The securities are transferred to the third party, who becomes their holder in place of the original holder. In exchange for this, the third party pays the original holder a purchase price. The sale of securities from holder to holder is known as securities trading, and occurs in the secondary markets. Much secondary market activity takes place on organised and officially recognised markets known as stock exchanges. However, an important and growing trend is for securities to be bought and sold away from stock exchanges. Such secondary market activity is known as 'over the counter' or 'OTC' trading. The increasing trend is for OTC trading to take place through electronic networks.

1 For more detail, see J Benjamin *Interests in Securities* (2000, Oxford University Press), chs 1, 4, 8 and 9.

Clearing

1.18 Clearing is a function that has recently been introduced into a number of securities markets[1]. Where clearing is provided, it operates after trading and before delivery (or settlement, as discussed below). Broadly, clearing generally involves techniques designed to address the risk of counterparty default after trading and before settlement, primarily through the netting of obligations, and the use of a well capitalised intermediary, known as a clearing house. The clearing house assumes the contractual obligations of each party (ie it is bound both as buyer to the seller, and seller to the buyer) to settle the trade. This means that, even if one party defaults post-trade and pre-settlement, settlement will still go ahead. Clearing is discussed in detail in Chapter 8.

1 Clearing has long been a feature of the derivatives markets.

Settlement

1.19 Settlement means delivery (usually against payment). Once a trade has taken place, the buyer is contractually bound to deliver the securities to the seller, and the seller is contractually bound to pay the purchase price to the seller. It is then necessary to arrange for delivery and payment to take place, in order to discharge these contractual obligations. Whereas securities trades generally take place on markets, securities settlement generally takes place through electronic systems known as settlement systems, which are designed to avoid the delays and inconvenience of paper-based settlement, and to synchronise the payment and delivery side of each transaction ('delivery versus payment'). Settlement is discussed in detail in Chapter 8.

Personal rights, property rights and insolvency[1]

1.20 The following is an extremely brief discussion of a complex area of law, and is intended for elementary guidance only. Private legal rights are divided into two fundamental categories, namely personal rights and property rights. In the financial markets, the main practical importance of the difference between personal and property rights relates to insolvency.

1 For excellent commercial discussions of these issues, see R M Goode 'Ownership and Obligation in Commercial Transactions' (1987) 103 LQR 433 and *Legal Problems of Credit and Security* (1988, 2nd edn, Sweet & Maxwell) (new edition forthcoming); S Worthington *Proprietary Interests in Commercial Transactions* (1996, Clarendon Press). Highly recommended also is S Worthington *Personal Property Law; Text and Materials* (2000, Hart Publishing). A huge theoretical literature exists in this area. Particularly recommended are K Gray 'Property in Thin Air' (1991) CLJ 252 and Hohfeld *Fundamental Legal Conceptions* (1964, Yale University Press) (first printed 1919). For a discussion of property rights in relation to securities and interests in securities, see J Benjamin *Interests in Securities* (2000, Oxford University Press), ch 13.

Personal rights

1.21 A personal right, as its name suggests, is a right which is enforceable against a person (whether a natural person or a legal person such as an incorporated company). An example of a personal right is a debt. In commercial practice, a personal right is only as good as one's ability successfully to enforce it against the person who owes it (known as the obligor)[1]. Crucially, if the obligor becomes insolvent, the value of a personal right in general[2] is reduced and may become worthless. The holder of the personal right (the obligee) may be paid late, only in part, or indeed not at all, depending on the outcome of the insolvency proceedings. The risk that personal rights may lose their value in the obligor's insolvency is known as credit risk.

1 Of course, the obligee may seek to sell its personal right to a third party, but the purchase price she is able to obtain will in practice reflect the prospects of successful enforcement.
2 However, rights of insolvency set off may be available in some circumstances.

Property rights

1.22 In contrast, a property right is a right which is enforceable directly against an asset. An example of a property right is ownership; another example is a mortgage. In the financial markets, the great advantage of property rights is that they are not subject to credit risk, and are not in general affected by the insolvency of third parties. For example, if I *own* 100 bonds which you hold on my behalf, my rights to the bonds are proprietary, and should not be affected by your insolvency[1]. On the other hand, if you *owe* me 100 bonds (eg under an unsettled trade), my rights are merely personal, and may be defeated by your insolvency[2].

In the securities markets, two contexts in which the successful assertion of property rights is crucial, are custody and settlement. The custody client is not willing to take the credit risk of the custodian in relation to its portfolio of securities. For this reason, it is important that, as against the custodian, the rights of the client are proprietary. This is discussed in detail in Chapter 3. In the context of settlement, it is important for the purchaser to be confident that the insolvency of the vendor will not affect her rights in the settled securities[3]. For this reason, it is crucial that, as against the vendor, the rights of the purchaser of securities are, upon settlement, proprietary[4].

Another context in which property rights are of central important is securities collateral.

1 Client assets do not form part of an insolvent's estate, and are not available to creditors. See, for example, *Barclays Bank Ltd v Quistclose Investments Ltd* [1970] AC 567, [1968] 3 WLR 1097, [1968] 3 All ER 651; and *Re Kayford Ltd* [1975] 1 WLR 279, [1975] 1 All ER 604. In the case of a bankrupt individual, see Insolvency Act 1986, s 283(3)(a).
2 In this example, I have property rights against you in relation to the bonds. However, the issuer of the bonds owes only personal rights under their terms of issue: this is discussed further below and in Chapter 5.
3 Particularly if the price of those securities has risen since the trade was concluded, so that the trade is profitable for the purchaser.
4 See Chapter 8.

Securities collateral

1.23 Collateralisation is a technique which is designed to address credit risk. Where A owes B a personal obligation, B bears A's credit risk. B may address this by requiring A to deliver to B property rights in identified assets which serve as collateral. In the event that A becomes insolvent or otherwise defaults, B will be able to enforce her property rights against the assets, and thereby avoid suffering loss through A's default. Thus collateralisation involves the use of property rights to support personal rights, and thereby address credit risk.

The question arises, what assets should serve as collateral? Securities are an important and increasingly popular form of collateral, as they are easy to value and highly liquid (ie easy to deliver). Securities collateral is discussed in detail in Chapter 4.

Possession[1]

1.24 Possession is a legal concept which is related to property, but distinct from it[2]. As indicated above, property comprises legal rights in relation to assets, such as rights of ownership. In contrast, possession is (broadly speaking) physical control of a tangible asset (ie an asset which one can touch). Whereas property is a question of law, possession is (in part) a question of fact. For example, if Madeleine lends Joanna her watch, Madeleine remains the owner of the watch, but Joanna has possession. If Joanna places Madeleine's watch on her own wrist, Joanna has physical control. Because Madeleine retains the right to call for the return of her watch at any time[3], she has the ability to recover possession. In legal terms, while Joanna has *actual* possession, Madeleine has *constructive* possession. Another example of constructive possession is where goods are stored in a warehouse, and the warehouse keeper (who has actual possession) acknowledges[4] that she holds the goods for a client: in this case, the client has constructive possession[5].

As discussed in Chapter 3, the traditional legal analysis of custody was based on possession, as were many important securities delivery and collateral arrangements (particularly negotiation and pledge). However, as Chapters 2 and 3 will argue, the computerisation of the securities markets has in many cases replaced physical instruments (which may be subject to possession) with electronic records (which may not)[6]. This has very significantly reduced the importance of possession in these markets, and altered the legal nature of relationships between market participants and their assets. Failure to appreciate this is a source of legal risk.

1 For old but unsurpassed discussion of possession, see Pollock *An Essay on Possession in the Common Law* (1888, Clarendon Press).
2 For a recent discussion of the relationship between possession and property, see N Palmer 'Possessory Title' in Palmer and McKendrick *Interests in Goods* (1998, 2nd edn, LLP).
3 But not otherwise
4 Such acknowledgment is known as attornment.
5 'A person has actual possession (*de facto* possession, possession in fact) of a thing when he exercises physical control over it . . . A person has constructive possession . . . when someone representing him has actual possession of the thing': *Jowitt's Dictionary of English Law* (2nd edn, 1985, Sweet & Maxwell) under 'Possession'.
6 The proposition that an intangible may not be subject to possession is developed in Chapter 3.

Legal categories of assets

1.25 Assets are divided into broad legal categories. Roughly speaking, *real* assets comprise freehold land and related assets[1], and *personal* assets comprise all other asset types. Personal assets are in turn sub-divided into tangible personal assets (known as goods, or 'choses in possession') and intangible personal assets (known as claims, or 'choses in action')[2]. The key point here is that the computerisation of the securities markets has converted clients' investment assets from (in the case of traditional bearer securities) choses in possession into choses in action.

It is important to note that any type of asset may be the subject of property rights[3]. Some commentators have questioned whether claims may be subject to property rights. Of course, as against the obligor, a claim confers only personal rights. However, a wide variety of commercial structures involve intermediation, whereby claims are held through third parties. For example, an investor may hold her debt securities through a custodian. She does not take the credit risk of the custodian because, *as against it*, her rights are proprietary. This is developed in Chapter 3. Also, the investor may borrow money from a bank and collateralise that debt by granting a security interest in her bond portfolio. In her insolvency, the bank is able to enforce its rights against the portfolio because *as against the investor*, its rights are proprietary. This is developed in Chapter 4.

1 Such as certain rights of way.
2 Tangible personal assets are called choses in possession because rights in them can be enforced by physically seizing the assets, or taking possession. Intangible personal assets are called choses in action, because the normal way to enforce them is to sue, or take legal action.
3 Things of value which may not be subject to property rights, such as human lives or clean air, are not assets.

Chapter 2

Securities in the electronic environment*

2.1 In the late twentieth century and the new millennium, securities and related assets have seen a growing trend towards computerisation. Paper instruments and certificates have been replaced by electronic records. Because these records are in general maintained by intermediaries and not by issuers, increased computerisation means increased intermediation.

The trend towards computerisation is driven by the new efficiencies offered by electronic technology. However, it has far-reaching legal consequences. In the absence of clarifying legislation and case law, these consequences have not always been fully analysed[1].

Two types of legal consequence are considered in this book. These are changes to the legal nature of the investors' assets (which are discussed in this chapter); and changes to the legal nature of the relationship between investors and their custodians (which are discussed in the following chapter).

Commercial arrangements relating to computerised securities often operate cross-border, and a legal analysis of them necessarily involves a consideration of private international law. However, the starting point of this analysis is the position under English domestic law, and the following discussion is made on the basis that English domestic law governs the commercial arrangements relating to computerised securities. While somewhat artificial, it is a necessary preliminary to a consideration of the position under English private international law, which will follow in Chapter 4.

* The authors are grateful to Ed Bradley, Partner, Clifford Chance, for kindly reviewing this chapter. Any errors are their own.

1 See J Benjamin 'Negotiability and Computerisation' (1995) 10 JIBFL 253 to 357; RM Goode 'The Nature and Transfer of Rights in Dematerialised and Immobilised Securities' (1996) 10 JIBFL 167; J Benjamin *Interests in Securities* (2000, Oxford University Press), chs 2 and 3; and S L Schwarcz 'Intermediary Risk in a Global Economy' (2001) 50 Duke LJ 1541; and E Micheler 'Farewell Quasi-Negotiability' (2002) JBL 358.

Immobilisation and dematerialisation

2.2 The original cause of the computerisation of securities and related assets is the need for efficient settlement. As discussed in Chapter 8, the settlement of securities used to involve the physical movement of paper instruments[1], certificates[2] and transfer forms. By the late twentieth century the delays and other inefficiencies associated with paper-based settlement became intolerable to the developed securities markets, and the transition to electronic settlement gathered pace. The original terms of the debate concerning electronic settlement were set by a seminal report of the Group of 30 entitled *Clearance and Settlement in the World's Securities Markets* ('The 1989 G30 Report'). This identified two broad models of electronic settlement, namely immobilisation and dematerialisation[3]. A feature shared by both immobilisation and dematerialisation is book entry transfer.

1 As discussed below, instruments are the formal legal documents which constitute bearer securities in traditional form.

2 As discussed below, certificates are the documents which evidence, but do not constitute, registered securities in traditional form.

3 Chapter 8 considers this together with subsequent developments in the post trade infrastructure.

Book entry transfer

2.3 Book entry transfer involves an electronic system known as a settlement system. The settlement system maintains accounts in favour of market participants (and/or their nominees and custodians). When participant 1 wishes to transfer assets to participant 2, both participants send matching electronic instructions to the settlement system. Provided sufficient assets are available in the relevant accounts, the settlement system then debits the account of participant 1 and credits that of participant 2. Account entries are colloquially known as 'book entries', and because the legal effect of such debits and credits is to transfer property rights in relation to the assets from participant 1 to participant 2, this arrangement is known as book entry transfer.

Immobilisation

2.4 The 1989 G30 Report defined immobilisation as 'The storage of securities certificates in a vault in order to eliminate physical movement of certificates/documents on transfer of ownership.' With immobilisation, paper instruments and/or certificates exist, but they no longer move from person to person in the secondary markets. Instead, they are retained by a depositary which is linked to a settlement system. Property rights in relation to the immobilised securities move between participants in the settlement system by book entry transfer.

The majority of immobilised securities are issued in global form. This means that a single paper instrument or certificate exists in respect of the entire issue of securities. Such 'globals' are distinguished from 'definitives', ie individual securities in traditional form.

The original reason for issuing globals instead of definitives was the desire to avoid adverse US taxation and regulatory consequences in the international securities markets. It used to be customary, in the case of *temporary* global securities, for definitives to be issued to the depositary at the end of a 40-day 'lock up' period, upon certification by the settlement system (in practice, Euroclear and/or Clearstream) that the participants for whom definitives were to be issued have in turn certified that the investments were not beneficially owned by US persons. Further, while definitives were security printed, globals are not. Because of the expense and delay involved in security printing, international debt securities are today generally issued in *permanent* global form. This means that, in the absence of issuer or settlement system default, definitives are never issued. A *temporary* global would be exchangeable wholly or in part at the request of the holder for definitives, and would be reduced in value pro rata by the value of definitives issued in exchange. Partial exchanges were endorsed on the global, which would be cancelled when it was exchanged in full. In contrast, a *permanent* global is generally only exchangeable for definitives upon default[1].

1 If the issuer fails to issue definitives on default, the following enforcement problem arises. Investors generally have no locus standi against the issuer, as they are not the holders of the securities which are held through intermediaries standing between them and the issuer. Their rights under the global may be enforced through a trustee (in cases where a trustee is appointed). However, where no trustee is appointed, their rights under the global can only be enforced through the depositary; in practice depositaries are unwilling to enforce on behalf of investors, as they do not consider this to be part of their role; indeed they do not regard enforcement as part of their role as conduit and may have a customer relationship with the issuer.
To overcome this problem, it is usually provided that, if the issuer fails to issue definitives within 30 days of default, the obligations of the issuer under the global will become void; in their place, new obligations on the issuer arise under a deed poll executed directly in favour of investors (ie participants in Euroclear and Clearstream having entitlements under the global credited to their accounts). The effect of such provision is sometimes referred to as 'the disappearing global'.

Dematerialisation

2.5 Dematerialisation is defined as follows in the 1989 G30 Report:

> 'The elimination of physical certificates or documents of title which represent ownership of securities so that securities exist only as computer records.'

In the UK, examples of dematerialised registered securities are equities and gilts within CREST.

Securities may be held through a chain of intermediaries with a large number of links. For the sake of simplicity, the term 'investor' will be taken here to mean an investor whose interest is as direct as possible, ie the participant in the settlement system to whose account the assets are credited.

This chapter will seek to establish the effect of computerisation on the legal nature of investors' interests in securities. The issue falls naturally into two parts, as securities fall into two categories: bearer securities and registered securities. As indicated in Chapter 1, the difference between them may be summarised as relating to the procedure for their legal transfer. A bearer security promises on its face to pay the bearer (ie the holder) of the instrument, and the chose in action (ie the claim) against the issuer is considered at law to be locked up in the instrument. Because they consist of tangible instruments, bearer securities are categorised as choses in possession. In general, whoever possesses the instrument legally owns the bearer security, which is transferable by delivery of the instrument. In this sense, bearer instruments are like paper money. Examples of bearer securities are bearer bonds and certificates of deposit. In contrast, legal ownership of registered securities is determined prima facie by the register of holders maintained by or on behalf of the issuer[1]. In order legally to transfer a registered security, it is necessary for the register to be amended in favour of the transferee. Examples of registered securities are equities[2] and gilts[3]. Bearer securities will be considered briefly in paras **2.6–2.15** and registered securities in para **2.16**.

1 *Société Générale de Paris v Walker* (1885) 11 App Cas 20. While certificates may be issued, they are not documents of title, but merely documents evidencing title.
2 That is, ordinary shares of companies.
3 That is, registered debt securities issued by the government of the United Kingdom.

Bearer securities in the electronic environment

2.6 The most important example of bearer securities in the electronic environment is in the eurobond markets, where most securities are both immobilised and issued in global form. The major impact of computerisation on investors' interests in bearer securities appears to be the loss of negotiable status. In this discussion the term 'computerised bearer securities' will mean the assets of investors (being participants in a settlement system) which are derived from bearer securities[1] and bearer securities not in electronic form will be referred to as traditional bearer securities.

1 Derived because (in the case of immobilised securities) the underlying securities are in bearer form or (in the case of global securities) the definitive securities are, or would if issued be, in bearer form. As explained at para **2.17**, it is assumed for the purposes of this discussion that the arrangements are fungible, in the sense that there is no allocation between a particular participant and a particular underlying instrument. Non-fungible arrangements are less common today, but still exist, for example in the Central Moneymarkets Office ('CMO') as discussed in Chapter 9. Whereas physical instruments in the CMO retain their negotiable status, fungible computerised bearer securities, it is argued, do not. It is proposed to merge the CMO with CREST, as discussed in Chapter 9.

Negotiability

2.7 The secondary markets in bearer securities have traditionally benefited from the doctrine of negotiability. A negotiable instrument has two attractive features. First, it is transferable without formalities[1]. Second, honest acquisition confers good title (even if the transferor did not have good title)[2]. Thus, market transfers are informal and reliable. The holder in due course[3] takes the instrument free from prior equities or defects in the title of the transferor. The general view is that these benefits are not available to securities which are not negotiable instruments[4].

An instrument may acquire negotiable status either by statute or by commercial usage, as reflected in the law merchant. It is generally[5] established that traditional bearer securities in the secondary markets are negotiable instruments[6].

1 By physical delivery, or by endorsement and delivery in the case of certain instruments requiring endorsement, such as cheques.
2 Provided the instrument is negotiated (ie transferred) prior to maturity: see *Brown v Davies* (1789) 100 ER 466.
3 That is, broadly, the good faith purchaser. See Bills of Exchange Act 1882, s 29(1).
4 See, however, E Micheler 'Farewell Quasi-Negotiability; Legal Title and Transfer of Shares in a Paperless World' (2002) Journal of Business Law 358–78.
5 Certain provisions that have been incorporated in commercial paper have been considered adversely to affect their status as promissory notes negotiable under s 83 of the Bills of Exchange Act 1882. Such provisions include withholding tax grossing up provisions (having the result that the note is not a promise to pay a sum certain); restrictions (driven by US regulatory requirements) on negotiation of the instrument to nationals of certain countries (so that the note is not an unconditional promise to pay); and the enfacement of guarantees on the instrument. These provisions must be considered on a case by case basis.
6 Domestic corporate bonds: *Re General Estates* (1868) 3 Ch App 758; *Higgs v Northern Assam Tea Co Ltd* (1869) LR 4 Exch 387; *Re Imperial Land Co of Marseilles* (1870) LR 11 Eq 478; *Bechuanaland Exploration Co v London Trading Bank* [1898] 2 QB 658.

Foreign government and corporate bonds: *Gorgier v Mieville* (1824) 3 B & C 45; *Simmons v London Joint Stock Bank* [1891] 1 Ch 270; *Bentinck v London Joint Stock Bank* [1893] 2 Ch 120; *Venables v Baring* [1892] 3 Ch 527.

Scrip for bonds (ie certificates acknowledging the holder's entitlement to be issued with bonds): *Goodwin v Robarts* (1875) LR 10 Exch 337.

Secured bearer bonds: *Webb v Herne Bay* (1870) LR 5 QB 642.

The above references are quoted in Ewart 'Negotiability and Estoppel' (1900) 14 LQR 135 at 156. See also the following:

Bearer bonds, whether foreign or domestic, corporate or government: *Edelstein v Schuler* [1900–3] All ER Rep 884.

Certificates of deposit: *Customs and Excise Comrs v Guy Butler (International) Ltd* [1977] QB 377 at 382; *Libyan Arab Foreign Bank v Bankers Trust Co* [1988] 1 Lloyd's Rep 259 at 276 (quoted in *Encyclopedia of Banking Law* (1994, Butterworths), F(116) n1).

The more recent introduction of Euro-notes and Euro-commercial paper to the London secondary markets raised the question of whether these new forms of bearer security were negotiable in the absence of clear statutory or judicial authority. The general consensus in the legal community is that these physical instruments have become negotiable on the basis of commercial custom in London.

A new class of negotiable instrument?

2.8 In the UK there is no statutory basis for claiming negotiable status for bearer computerised securities. Therefore, to show that bearer computerised securities are negotiable, it would be necessary to argue that they have been recognised under the law merchant as a new class of negotiable instrument. There is ample authority that the law merchant is a dynamic branch of law, evolving to reflect changing commercial practice from time to time. Thus, in principle, the law merchant is capable of recognising bearer computerised securities as negotiable. The question is whether it has in fact done so.

Arguments against negotiability

Indirect

2.9 One obstacle to treating bearer computerised securities as negotiable is their indirect nature, in the following sense. The ability of the holder from time to time of an instrument to enforce it in her own name against its issuer has generally been taken to be an essential criterion of negotiability[1]. In general, an investor in computerised securities does not have directly enforceable rights against the issuer[2].

However, an alternative view has been expressed. In the past the London legal community considered this question in relation to physical Eurodollar bonds constituted under a trust deed which imposed limitations on bondholders' rights to sue the issuer, so that generally only the trustee had rights of enforcement, and bondholders were able to sue the issuer only if the trustee failed in its duties on their behalf. One leading counsel argued that the instruments were not negotiable because on the face of the bonds the person holding them for the time being was prevented from suing on them in her own name. Another leading counsel argued that the instruments were negotiable, and that the requirement of negotiability was not that the holder should have an unrestricted right to sue, but that in circumstances where she is given such a right, she should not need to sue in the names of prior holders. For this reason, the absence of direct rights of enforcement under bearer computerised securities may not necessarily be incompatible with negotiable status.

1 See *London and County Banking Co Ltd v London and River Plate Bank Ltd* (1887) 20 QBD 232 at 236. See also *Crouch v Crédit Foncier of England* (1873) LR 8 QB 374 per Blackburn J.

2 Any direct rights arising on default under 'disappearing global' arrangements are not rights under a negotiable instrument, because they arise under a deed poll.

Intangible

2.10 The stronger argument against bearer computerised securities being treated as negotiable is their intangibility. Bearer computerised securities comprise intangible assets on the following basis. In the case of dematerialised securities, no tangible asset exists to which the investor's property rights relate. In the case of immobilised securities, provided the underlying instrument is in global form, the investor's property rights do not attach to any particular definitive instruments, for none exist. Rather, the investor's rights relate to an unallocated share of the global. In the absence of attachment, the investor cannot be said to hold a tangible asset. Her co-proprietary rights form a distinct intangible asset which relates to the underlying global, but does not exhaust it. This argument is continued at para **2.17**[1].

The early negotiable instruments (bills of exchange and promissory notes) were recognised as negotiable because they were like paper money, and used by merchants as an alternative method of payment for goods[2]. Indeed, the test of negotiability has been held to be that the instrument should pass from hand to hand like money[3]. 'Money passes with good title because it is money; and notes because they are like money'[4].

The general rule with paper money is that property passes with possession. Equally, 'For the purpose of rendering bills of exchange negotiable, the rights of property in them pass with the bills . . . The property and the possession are inseparable'[5]. Thus property is with the holder, or the person having possession. For this reason, a negotiable instrument must be capable of possession. If it were incapable of possession, it could not confer upon its possessor (a holder) the status of holder in due course.

There is no clear authority for treating an intangible as a negotiable instrument, and it may be legally impossible to do so. To extend the concept of negotiability to intangibles would be a major departure from the existing law merchant, and perhaps only achievable by statute[6].

It is true that in the case of immobilised securities, there are tangible instruments (and directly enforceable rights) in the hands of an intermediary depositary[7]. This does not, however, render the interest of the investor a negotiable instrument, because all negotiable instruments 'are intended to be ambulatory'[8]. The physical securities underlying the immobilised securities are (as the term suggests) immobilised with depositaries acting for Euroclear or Clearstream. Thus the indicia of negotiability are distributed between the asset held by the depositary and the investor. The physical instrument (expressed to be negotiable) and directly enforceable rights are held by the depositary, and the 'ambulatory' assets are held by the investors.

1 Investors may have the right to call for underlying physical securities; however, if they do so, they convert their investment from computerised securities to physical securities.

2 'A Bill of exchange is a security, originally invented among merchants in different countries, for the more easy remittance of money from the one to the other, which since spread itself into almost all pecuniary transactions': Blackstone *Commentaries*, Book II, at 466.

3 See *Lang v Smyth* (1831) 7 Bing 284; *Miller v Race* (1758) 1 Burr 452 and *Friedlander v Texas* 130 US 416 (1889).

4 Ewart 'Negotiability and Estoppel' (1900) 14 LQR 135 at 152.

5 *Collins v Martin* (1797) 1 Bos & P 648 at 651, per Eyre CJ.

6 Section 8 of the Electronic Communications Act 2000 arguably provides an opportunity for extending negotiable status to computerised bearer securities. However, consultation among bankers and practitioners conducted by Hugh Pigott and Joanna Benjamin through The Centre for Law Reform on behalf of the Law Commission during 1999 and 2000 indicated that there was little appetite in London for such provision.

7 These underlying physical securities will also be expressed on their face to be negotiable; this is also a necessary (but not sufficient) criterion of negotiability: *London and County Banking Co v London and River Plate Bank Ltd* (1887) 20 QBD 232; *Jones & Co v Coventry* [1909] 2 KB 1029, quoted in Prime *International Bonds and Certificates of Deposit* (1990, Butterworths), p 242.

8 Ewart 'Negotiability and Estoppel' (1900) 14 LQR 135 at 155.

Conclusion

2.11 In the absence of authority to the contrary, the features of negotiability appear to remain first, that an instrument should be transferable, like cash, by delivery and second (subject to the comments at para **2.9**) that the instrument should be capable of being sued upon by the holder from time to time[1].

Delivery is the transfer of possession. As an intangible a computerised bearer security is incapable of possession and therefore of delivery in the technical legal sense of that term. It would therefore seem that computerised bearer securities cannot be negotiable instruments.

Nor would it be commercially helpful to seek to argue that, on the contrary, bearer computerised securities are negotiable instruments. This is because the existing law merchant assumes that negotiable instruments are capable of physical delivery, signature and endorsement. In the absence of legislation, the application of the law relating to such matters to intangible assets would be uncertain and unpredictable.

In crossing into the electronic era, the secondary markets in bearer securities have (it is argued) crossed an important legal boundary, and left the law merchant.

1 'It may therefore be laid down as a safe rule that where an instrument is by the custom of trade transferable, like cash, by delivery, and is also capable of being sued upon by the person holding it pro tempore, then it is entitled to the name of a *negotiable instrument*, and the property in it passes to a bona fide transferee for value, though the transfer may not have taken place in market overt. But that if either of the above requisites be wanting, ie, if it be either not accustomably transferable, or, though it be accustomably transferable, yet, if its nature be such as to render it incapable of being put in suit by the party holding it pro tempore, it is not a *negotiable instrument*, nor will delivery of it pass the property of it to a vendee, however bona fide, if the transferor himself have not a good title to it, and the transfer be made out of market overt', per Blackburn J in *Crouch v Crédit Foncier* (1873) LR 8 QB 374 at 381, quoting from the notes to *Miller v Race* (1758) 1 Burr 452.

The benefits of negotiability

2.12 The chief benefits of negotiability are ease[1] and security[2] of transfer[3]. It is argued below that such benefits may also be enjoyed by bearer computerised securities, not under the law merchant, but by statute.

1 That is, no need for written transfers or notice to the issuer.
2 That is, the general inability of the trade to be reversed due to defects in the transferor's title.
3 For a full discussion of the benefits of negotiability, see Bank of England *The Future of Money Market Instruments*, November 1999, Appendix II.

Ease of transfer

2.13 At the time of writing the major international settlement systems for computerised bearer securities (Euroclear and Clearstream) are located on continental Europe. Book entry transfers within such systems are not governed by English law, but rather by local statutory regimes. However, the London-based settlement system, CREST, is actively developing its cross-border links as discussed in Chapter 9. Where book entry transfers of computerised bearer securities take place under English law, the position would be as follows.

Transfers of intangible assets are, at the time of writing, subject to statutory formalities under ss 136 and 53(1)(c) of the Law of Property Act 1925. There is legislative power to disapply such provisions under s 8 of the Electronic Communications Act

2000, and such general disapplications may in due course be made in favour of electronic securities settlement. Moreover, a number of technical legal arguments are available that these statutory formalities do not apply to electronic securities settlement[1]. Nevertheless, Uncertificated Securities Regulations 2001, which provide a statutory regime for book entry transfers through CREST, expressly disapply ss 136 and 53(1)(c)[2].

1 See ch 3, section C of J Benjamin *Interests in Securities* (2000, Oxford University Press).
2 Regulation 38(5).

Security of transfer[1]

2.14 A transfer is secure if the good faith purchaser is able to retain the transferred assets free from adverse claims. It is arguable that, by removing negotiable status, the computerisation of securities has reduced security of transfer under the general principles of English law. However, CREST operates under a statutory regime. Opinion of leading counsel has been obtained to the general effect that reg 29 of the Uncertificated Securities Regulations 1995 (now incorporated in reg 35 of the Uncertificated Securities Regulations 2001) provides security of transfer comparable to that enjoyed by negotiable instruments.

In Luxembourg, art 7 of the Grand Ducal Regulation of 17 February 1971 Modifying the Circulation of Securities has the effect of transferring the risk of adverse claims from the purchaser to Clearstream. The Belgian Royal Decree of 1962 has the effect of defeating unpublished adverse claims once securities have entered Euroclear.

1 This same concept is also called 'security of receipt'. See Peter Birks in P Birks (ed) *Overview: Tracing, Claiming and Defences, Laundering and Tracing* (1995, Clarendon).

Conclusion

2.15 In conclusion, because they are intangible, bearer computerised securities are not negotiable instruments. In the UK and elsewhere, the traditional benefits of negotiability (ease and security of transfer) therefore require to be replicated by statute.

Registered computerised securities[1]

2.16 Securities held through CREST are computerised registered securities[2], ie unlike traditional registered securities they are evidenced and transferred without paper certificates or instruments of transfer.

The impact of computerisation on the legal nature of registered securities is much less extensive that its impact on the legal nature of bearer securities. This is because traditional registered securities have never enjoyed negotiable status and (like computerised registered securities) are intangible assets[3].

1 Registered securities in electronic form will be referred to as registered computerised securities, and registered securities not in electronic form as traditional registered securities.
2 They are known as uncertificated securities, as discussed in Chapter 9.
3 A share is a chose in action: *Colonial Bank v Whinney* (1886) 11 App Cas 426. A registered share is not the same as a share certificate, which is not a document of title but a document evidencing title.

Interests in securities

2.17 This chapter has considered the consequences of computerisation for the legal nature of investors' interests in securities. It was shown that, for bearer securities, computerisation has cost negotiability. However, in practice the secondary markets should not be affected, as the benefits of negotiability are arguably provided by statute.

In contrast, because traditional registered securities have never enjoyed negotiable status, and are intangible, computerisation has not significantly altered the legal nature of investors' assets.

The preceding discussion has considered computerisation in the narrow sense of the replacement of paper instruments and certificates with the electronic records associated with electronic settlement. In practice, the introduction of electronic settlement has been accompanied by two other related developments. These are intermediation and commingling. Because direct participation in electronic settlement systems is not always possible and/or practicable for many clients, it is common for them to gain access to electronic settlement through custodians. Thus in many cases the custodian, and not the client, has a direct relationship with the settlement system, and the title of the client to the underlying assets is asserted through the custodian. As discussed in the following chapter, the natural legal characterisation of such a custody relationship is as a trust, so that the rights of the client are equitable and not legal. Moreover, it is customary for the custodian to commingle the like assets of its different custody clients, which are held together in a commingled pool. As also discussed in the following chapter, the combined effect of such intermediation and pooling is to render the interest of the client equitable and co-proprietary. In technical terms, this interest arises under an equitable tenancy in common.

Such equitable tenancies in common are called 'interests in securities' and are discussed in detail by Joanna Benjamin in her book having that title[1]. The key significance of the market participant's asset comprising interests in securities, as opposed to securities in their traditional form, relates to the legal requirements of creating effective cross-border collateral arrangements, as discussed in Chapter 5 of this work. Another consequence is as follows. Traditional bearer securities are physical, allocated assets, where the root of title is possession, and which are transferred by delivery. In contrast, traditional registered securities are intangible, unallocated assets[2], where the root of title is a register entry, and which are transferred by amending the register. On the basis that interests in securities are intangible, unallocated assets, where the root of title is an entry in the custodian's accounts, and which are transferred by amending those accounts, interests in securities are arguably a form of registered security. The key relevance of this analysis is in the conflict of laws, in attributing a situs or legal location to such assets, as discussed in Chapter 5. For ease of reference, this book will in general refer to the assets of custody clients as securities.

1 J Benjamin *Interests in Securities* (2000, Oxford University Press).

2 'There is no identity in stock': *Bank of England v Cutler* [1907] 1 KB 889 at 909, per Lawrence J. See also *Ind's Case* (1872) 7 Ch App 485 at 487, per Mellish LJ and, more recently, *Hunter v Moss* [1993] 1 WLR 934; affd [1994] 1 WLR 452, [1994] 3 All ER 215; *Re Harvard Securities Ltd (in liquidation)* [1997] 2 BCLC 369.

Chapter 3*

The custody relationship in the electronic environment**

3.1 The impact of the electronic environment on the legal nature of investors' assets was considered in the previous chapter. Its effect on the legal nature of the custody relationship will now be assessed.

* The authors are grateful to Professor D J Hayton of King's College, London, for kindly reviewing this chapter. Any errors are their own.

** See also J Benjamin 'Custody: an English Law Analysis' (1994) 9 JIBFL 121 at 188; A O Austen-Peters *Custody of Investments* (2000, OUP), ch 2; and Joanna Benjamin *Interests in Securities* (2000, OUP), chs 2 and 10.

The accounts

3.2 The custodian maintains both cash accounts and securities accounts in the name of the client. The cash from time to time credited to the cash accounts may represent the proceeds of sale of custody assets and/or dividends and other income received in respect of them. The securities accounts record the securities held by or through the custodian for the client. The legal nature of the asset recorded in each type of account will be considered in turn.

Cash

The debtor/creditor principle

3.3 Custodians have traditionally been banks. It is a clear principle of banking law that the deposit of cash with a bank establishes the relationship of debtor and creditor between the bank and the depositor ('the debtor/creditor principle')[1]. Depositors' money is not held by the bank by way of trust[2]. The bank is free to use the deposited money as it pleases[3], and so the money is available to the bank's creditors on its insolvency. The depositor's rights of repayment are contractual and not proprietary[4]. On the bank's insolvency, therefore, the depositor must prove as an unsecured creditor[5] (subject to any available deposit protection scheme)[6].

It has generally been assumed that the debtor/creditor principle applies to custodians in respect of clients' cash accounts[7]. Custodians generally conduct their business on the basis of that principle, using the money credited to the custody cash accounts for their own purposes, and not segregating it as trust money. While this approach is, in the authors' view, correct, two points arise. First, the debtor/creditor principle applies to money deposited with banks, and may not apply to non-bank custodians. Second, the credit balance of the custody cash accounts may not represent deposits.

1 *Carr v Carr* (1811) 1 Mer 541n.
2 *Foley v Hill* (1848) 2 HL Cas 28.
3 *South Australian Insurance Co v Randell* (1869) 16 ER 775 at 759.
4 'True it is that in the case of money paid into the banker's account it is converted into a debt, while in the case of money placed in a special repository it remains in specie': *Re Halletts Estate, Knatchbull v Hallett* (1880) 13 Ch D 696 at 746 per Thesiger LJ.
5 *Space Investments Ltd v Canadian Imperial Bank of Commerce Trust Co (Bahamas) Ltd* [1986] 1 WLR 1072, [1986] 3 All ER 75.
6 This principle creates an exposure for the global custodian in respect of foreign currency cash balances. Where, for example, the global custodian maintains a US dollar account in favour of the client with a balance of $10,000, the global custodian remains liable to pay that sum even if the New York correspondent bank with which the global custodian holds its dollar assets becomes insolvent. While in theory a global custodian might draft 'limited recourse' wording into its contract with the client to provide that its obligation to pay the client was dependent on the solvency of its New York correspondent, such a provision does not reflect normal banking practice and may be unacceptable to clients.
7 Barings Brothers & Co Ltd acted as a global custodian. In March 1995, after the company went into administration and before the announcement of the agreement of ING Bank to buy the Barings group and take over its debts, it was generally assumed in the City of London that the balance of the cash accounts held by the company for pension fund custody clients was at risk. This cash amounted to some £100 million.

Trust over cash

3.4 The credit balances of the cash accounts may represent the proceeds of sale of custody assets or income derived from custody assets. Paragraphs **3.5–3.7** below will argue that, in a computerised environment, custody assets are in most cases held by the custodian for the client as trustee. The proceeds of sale of trust property[1] and income derived from trust property[2] are generally subject to the same trusts as the property to which they relate. This raises the risk for custodians of a duty to segregate cash.

The answer to this problem for the bank custodian is provided by *Space Investments*[3]. In this case it was held that, where a bank trustee lawfully deposits trust money with itself *as banker*, it becomes beneficially entitled to that money, and owes only a contractual duty of repayment. In order to be certain of benefiting from this rule, bank custodians should include express wording in their custody agreements, authorising them to deposit any monies credited to the cash accounts with themselves as banker.

However, some clients do not wish to take the credit risk of their custodians as banker in respect of their cash balances. In order to avoid such credit risk, it is necessary to establish a trust over the cash in the hands of the custodian. As discussed in more detail later in this chapter, a valid trust requires certainty of subject matter. Therefore, it is necessary to identify a particular asset in the hands of the custodian, corresponding to the cash balance, which will be subject to the trust[4]. If the account is a sterling account, a particular sterling sum in the hands of the custodian must be segregated in order for the trust to take effect. In practice, this is achieved by the custodian placing a sterling sum on deposit with a third party bank, and declaring a trust over its rights of repayment from that bank. For commercial and operational reasons, custodian banks may be reluctant to place client cash with their rival banks. A pragmatic alternative is for the greater part of client cash balances to be regularly invested in 'near cash', ie highly liquid debt instruments such as CDs, or units in 'cash funds', ie collective investment schemes investing in near cash. Because they are highly liquid, these assets enable the custodian promptly to meet payment obligations arising on the client's account. Because they comprise securities (and not merely the payment obligation of the custodian to the client) they may be the subject of a trust in the hands of the custodian[5].

For custodians regulated under the Financial Services and Markets Act 2000, the Client Money Rules[6] ('CMR') generally apply (broadly) to money received or held from or on behalf of a client in the course of 'designated investment business'[7], which in practice will include custody services[8]. The general effect of the CMR is to create a statutory trust over client money[9], thus protecting it from the insolvency of the custodian. However, an exemption is available for 'approved banks'[10], which will include most bank custodians[11]. The approved bank exemption relates to money held by an approved bank in an account with itself. It requires that the approved bank gives written notice to the client, (broadly) warning it that the money is held by it as banker and not as trustee, and will not be held in accordance with the CMR.

A minority of the firms offering custody in London are not banks, and are not authorised to carry on the business of accepting deposits[12]. Such custodians are not permitted generally to treat the credit balances of custody cash accounts as debts owed by them to their clients, but instead must hold such credit balances on trust for their clients, for a number of reasons. First, non-banks will not benefit from the debtor/creditor principle as a matter of general law. Second, it is prudent to assume that the operation of a custody cash account otherwise than on a trust basis would amount to accepting deposits. Third, as firms receiving or holding client money in the course of designated investment business, such custodians will generally be subject to the CMR[13]. However, they will not be exempt from the CMR as approved banks (although custody clients who are either market counterparties[14] or intermediate customers[15] may opt out of client money protection)[16]. In practice, such non-bank custodians usually maintain custody cash accounts as client money accounts with third party banks, and operate those accounts as trustees on their clients' behalf.

1 See *Re Hallett's Estate, Knatchbull v Hallett* (1880) 13 Ch D 696.
2 *Swain v Law Society* [1981] 3 All ER 797 at 813, CA per Oliver LJ.
3 *Space Investments Ltd v Canadian Imperial Bank of Commerce Trust Co (Bahamas) Ltd* [1986] 3 All ER 75.
4 Of course, the cash account itself cannot serve as the trust asset, as it records the liability of the custodian to pay the client, and under English law a liability as opposed to an asset cannot be subject to a trust.
5 After the 1995 failure of Barings Brothers, the appetite of UK clients for custodian credit risk was reduced, and greater use was made of such 'near cash' arrangements.
6 The CMR comprise section 9.3 of the Conduct of Business section of the Financial Services Authority's Handbook.
7 See the definition in the Handbook's Glossary of Definitions ('the Glossary').
8 Designated investment business includes safeguarding and administering investments for the purposes of art 40 of the Financial Services and Markets Act 2000 (Regulated Activities) Order 2001 (SI 2001/544) ('The Regulated Activities Order') provided (broadly) the assets include designated investments as defined in the Glossary. For further discussion, see Chapter 7 below.
9 CMR 9.3.31.
10 CMR 9.3.2(3).
11 See the definition of 'approved bank' in the Glossary.
12 For the purposes of art 5 of the Regulated Activities Order.
13 CMR 9.3.1.
14 See the definition in the Glossary, and the discussion in Chapter 10 below.
15 See n 14 above.
16 CMR 9.3.9.

Interests in securities, trust and bailment

3.5 Whereas custody clients are generally willing to take custodian credit risk in respect of their cash accounts, it is imperative to ensure that assets credited to client securities accounts are not at risk in the custodian's insolvency, or otherwise[1] available to its creditors[2]. The traditional characterisation of the custodian in respect of traditional bearer securities[3] (and other non-cash assets such as bullion[4]) is as the bailee of the client. This characterisation is based on physical possession[5].

The essence of bailment is the delivery of possession, or physical control (as opposed to the delivery of title, or ownership) by the bailor to the bailee[6]. Thus, the bailee custodian has possession of the physical custody securities, but they remain owned by the client and are unavailable to the creditors of the custodian upon its insolvency.

This traditional view of the custody relationship is challenged by computerisation. Chapter 2 argued that, in the electronic environment, the assets in the hands of the custodian in general comprise, not physical instruments, but intangibles. It will be argued below that intangibles cannot be the subject of possession, nor therefore of bailment, and that for these reasons the natural characterisation of the contemporary custody relationship is as a trust.

1 For example, following execution by a judgment creditor.

2 'Local laws and regulations should ensure that there is segregation of client assets from the principal assets of their custodian; and no possible claim on client assets in the event of custodian bankruptcy or a similar event.' 1995 G30/ISSA Recommendations, recommendation 8. See the G30 website at www.group30.org.

3 'These bonds are her bonds deposited with Mr Hallett according to the receipt, for safe custody, which would make him, no doubt, an ordinary bailee': *Re Hallett's Estates, Knatchbull v Hallett* (1880) 13 Ch D 696 at 708, per Jessell MR. See also *Kahler v Midland Bank* [1950] AC 24, [1949] 2 All ER 621, HL.

4 See *Dollfus Mieg v Bank of England* [1949] Ch 369, [1949] 1 All ER 946.

5 '"Custody" here clearly relates to the possession or control of the certificates as physical objects': *Swiss Bank Corpn v Lloyds Bank Ltd* [1980] 2 All ER 419 at 431, CA, per Buckley LJ.

6 'A bailment arises whenever specific goods are delivered into the possession of someone other than the person immediately entitled to them, on condition that those identical goods are returned to the deliveror or disposed of in accordance with his instructions when the purpose of the bailment is fulfilled': N E Palmer *Liability of Bankers as Custodians of Client Property* (1979), p 1. See also the famous classification of bailments in the judgment of Holt CJ in *Coggs v Bernard* (1703) 2 Ld Raym 909.

Possession

3.6 The common law recognises both physical (or actual) and legal (or civil) possession. Legal possession has been described as the right to possess. However, the ultimate basis of possession is always fact rather than law because 'the existence of the *de facto* relation of control or apparent dominion [is] required as the foundation of the alleged right'[1]. The concept of constructive possession (discussed in Chapter 1) enables possession to arise without direct physical control[2]. However, constructive possession (like legal possession) is derived from actual possession, and therefore cannot apply to intangible assets[3].

As indicated above, the bailor client retains ownership of the bailed assets, which are not available to the creditors of the bailee in its insolvency. If the computerisation of the securities markets precludes the characterisation of the custodian as bailee, it is necessary to identify another basis on which to protect the client from the credit risk of the custodian. Under English law, the only available alternative is trust. While 'the essence of bailment is possession . . . without possession there can be no relationship of bailor and bailee'[4], trust property may be intangible for '. . . any property may be held in trust'[5]. The role of the custodian has evolved far beyond its traditional status as a bailee. The question arises, has it taken the law relating to bailment with it, so that bailment may now relate to intangibles? Or has it left bailment behind so that now the custodian is a trustee? In the absence of direct judicial authority, it would be prudent to assume that the custodian, by moving into the electronic environment, has moved into a new legal category, and is a trustee[6].

1 Pollock *An Essay on Possession in the Common Law* (1888, Clarendon Press, Oxford), p 10.
2 Relevant case law concerning constructive possession is mainly concerned with matters such as keys to rooms and boxes in which physical assets are contained.
3 Moreover, it is '. . . improbable that the courts will develop the . . . supposition that there may be a bailment of an intangible thing': *Palmer on Bailment* (1991, 2nd edn, Sweet & Maxwell), p 13.
4 *Palmer on Bailment* (1991, 2nd edn, Sweet & Maxwell), p 192.
5 *Snell's Equity* (2000, 30th edn, Sweet & Maxwell), p 113. See also *Lewin On Trust* (2000, 17th edn, Sweet & Maxwell), para 2–35; and *Underhill & Hayton on the Law relating to Trusts and Trustees* (1995, 15th edn, Butterworths), Art 10.
6 For a supporting analysis, see A O Austen-Peters *Custody of Investments* (2000, OUP), ch 2. For a contrary view, see A Beaves 'Global Custody – A Tentative Analysis of Property and Contract' in N Palmer and E McEndrick (eds) *Interests in Goods* (1998, 2nd edn, Lloyd's of London Press). See also Hayton & Marshall *Cases and commentary on the law of Trusts and Equitable Remedies* (2001, 11th edn, Sweet & Maxwell), paras 3–07 and 3–90 to 3–93.
The bailment analysis will still, of course, be available where physical instruments are directly held by the custodian.
For a discussion of custodian insolvency risk under US law, see Steven L Schwarcz *Intermediary Risk in a Global Economy* (2001) Duke Law Journal, 50 1541.
Interestingly, the bailment analysis was laid aside in the US in the preparation of the revised art 8 of the Uniform Commercial Code: 'Relatively early in the drafting process, the decision was reached to eschew the approach of trying to squeeze the analysis of the property interest of a person who holds securities through an intermediary into old legal concepts, such as bailment': J S Rogers *Policy Perspectives on Revised UCC Article 8*, UCLA Law Rev, June 1996, p 1431 at 1496.
Custodians who are trustees should not be confused with custodian trustees for the purposes of s 4(3) of the Public Trustee Act 1906. Statutory custodian trustees hold trust property while leaving the administration and management of the trust to managing trustees. Custodian trustees may be appointed in connection with a debenture issue.

Trust

3.7 A trust is a legal relationship in respect of assets (known as 'trust assets') between (i) one or more persons each known as trustee and (ii) one or more persons each known as beneficiary. The trustee holds the trust assets on trust for (ie for the benefit of) the beneficiary. While the trustee has technical or legal ownership of the trust assets, the beneficiary has the economic or beneficial ownership.

Trust assets are not available to the creditors of the trustee, and are thus protected from its credit risk[1]. This insolvency protection is the reason why it is necessary to characterise the custodian in the electronic environment as a trustee. However, trustee status has other legal consequences including, importantly, the following.

First, under the general law the trustee is subject to a high level of implied fiduciary duties towards the beneficiary, and it follows that the custodian will wish carefully to limit the level of its fiduciary duties by contract[2].

Second, English law distinguishes between two types of property interest:

(1) Property interests recognised by the general body of English law (common law) are known as legal interests.

(2) Equitable interests are those interests recognised by the branch of English law known as Equity.

The law of trusts forms part of the law of equity, and the interests of beneficiaries under a trust in the trust assets are equitable and not legal. On this basis, the property rights in the custody portfolio of the client are equitable. This contrasts with the property rights of a bailor client, which are legal.

Equitable ownership is as effective as legal ownership in addressing the custodian's credit risk. However, where competing interests in the custody portfolio arise (in the event of fraud or double dealing), the priority of an equitable interest is in some circumstances weaker than that of a legal interest[3].

Third, a technical requirement arises concerning the establishment of a valid trust; this is discussed in the following paragraphs.

1 In the case of the bankruptcy of an individual, assets held by the individual on trust are excluded from her estate by s 283(3)(a) of the Insolvency Act 1986. In the case of a corporate insolvency, the authority for the exclusion of trust assets lies in the general principle that only assets owned by the company form part of its estate, as reflected in case law. See, for example, *Barclays Bank Ltd v Quistclose Investments Ltd* [1970] AC 567, [1968] 3 WLR 1097, [1968] 3 All ER 651; and *Re Kayford Ltd* [1975] 1 WLR 279, [1975] 1 All ER 604, as well as cases discussed in relation to the allocation question below.

2 For a discussion of contractual limitation of implied fiduciary duty, see Chapter 6 below.

3 The general principle is that a person acquiring a legal interest in good faith, for value and without notice of a prior equitable interest, takes the disputed asset free from the prior equitable interest. See Joanna Benjamin *Interests in Securities* (2000, OUP), ch 2, pp 51 and 52 and ch 4.

The allocation question[1]

3.8 The allocation question is a technical issue associated with the customary practice among custodians of holding client securities on an unallocated or fungible basis.

1 There is now a large critical literature on this legal question. Particularly recommended are D Hayton 'Uncertainty of Subject-Matter of Trusts' (1994) 110 LQR 335; S Worthington 'Sorting out ownership interests in a Bulk: Gifts, Sales and Trusts' [1999] JBL 1; and P Birks 'Mixtures' in Palmer and McKendrick (eds) *Interests in Goods* (1998, 2nd edn, LLP). In relation to custody, see J Benjamin *Custody: an English Law Analysis* (1994) 9 JIBFL 188 and Joanna Benjamin *Interests in Securities* (2000, OUP), ch 2, section B.3 as well as A O Austen-Peters *Custody of Investments* (2000, OUP), ch 3.

Fungible custody and equivalent redelivery

3.9 Custodial arrangements in respect of securities are in most cases fungible, in the following sense. The custodian aggregates the holdings in securities of a particular issue which it holds for its various clients into one commingled holding ('client holding'). In the case of securities held through a sub-custodian, the client holding will usually be represented in the books of the sub-custodian by a designated client account in the name of the custodian. The client holding in securities held through a settlement system in which the custodian is a participant will usually also be held in a designated client account in the name of the custodian. In cases where a sub-custodian or settlement system is not employed, the client holding in registrable securities will be registered (with a client designation) in the name of the custodian or its nominee and physical bearer securities will be physically held (and earmarked for clients) by the custodian or its nominee. While the custodian's house position[1] in any security will be segregated from the client holding, there will in general be no record of any allocation between clients in the books of the relevant sub-custodian, settlement system, register or in the physical holding, as the case may be. The only note of the respective entitlements of the individual clients within the client holding will be in the books of the custodian. This arrangement will be referred to as 'fungible custody'[2].

Thus, while it is possible at any time to determine how many of the individual securities comprised in the client holding are attributable to a particular client, it is not possible to determine which ones. A corollary of fungible custody is that the redelivery obligation owed by the custodian to each client is not an obligation to return the assets originally delivered in specie, but merely an obligation to return assets equivalent to those originally delivered.

During the 1990s a line of case law prompted a debate in the London legal community concerning the impact of fungible custody on the trust relationship between the client and the custodian, which debate will be referred to as 'the allocation question'. The allocation question concerns the possible legal difficulty in asserting proprietary rights over assets forming part of the commingled pool or bulk, in circumstances where one cannot identify which particular assets within the pool are subject to such purported proprietary rights.

1 The house position is any holding by the custodian for its own account, beneficially owned by it.
2 Reasons for fungible custody include economies of scale, administrative convenience and accounting facility.

The requirement for allocation

3.10 The allocation question concerns '. . . the law's insistence that proprietary rights cannot be acquired in fungibles forming an unidentified part of a bulk until they have been separated by some suitable act of appropriation'[1]. This requirement applies both at law and in equity. The common law rule is well established in case law concerning the sale of goods[2], and is given statutory force in s 16 of the Sale of Goods Act 1979[3]. The rule in equity is based on the principle that a trust cannot be validly established without certainty of subject matter[4]. As Lord Mustill stated in *Re Goldcorp Exchange*[5]:

> 'It makes no difference what the parties intended if what they intend is impossible as is the case with an immediate transfer of [legal and equitable] title to goods whose identity is not yet known.'

Accordingly, a trust cannot be created by the legal owner of a commingled pool of goods who purports to transfer to another person equitable ownership of an unallocated amount of that pool[6].

Because, in fungible custody, the particular securities are not allocated to particular clients, some commentators have argued that the rights of clients may be confined (broadly) to a contractual right against the custodian, arising under the custody agreement, to call for redelivery of securities equivalent to those originally deposited[7]. If this were the position, the implications would be serious, both for the clients and for the custodian. The client's assets would be available to general creditors in the custodian's insolvency. Further, the value of the portfolio as collateral would be reduced[8]. Fortunately, in the light of recent case law, the general view is that fungible custody is compatible with the protection of clients' property rights in the custody portfolio under a trust relationship with the custodian, as discussed below.

1 RM Goode 'Ownership and Obligation in Commercial Transactions' LQR 103, July 1987, 433 at 436.
2 See, for example, *Healy v Howlett & Sons* [1917] 1 KB 337; *Re Wait* [1927] 1 Ch 606; *Carlos Federspiel & Co SA v Charles Twigg & Co Ltd* [1957] 1 Lloyd's Rep 240; *Re London Wine Co (Shippers) Ltd* [1986] PCC 121; *Re Goldcorp Exchange Ltd (in receivership)* [1995] 1 AC 74, [1994] 3 WLR 199, [1994] 2 All ER 806 and, more recently, *Glencore International AG v Metro Trading Inc* [2001] Lloyd's Rep 284.
3 This provides as follows: 'Subject to section 20A below, where there is a contract for the sale of unascertained goods no property in the goods is transferred to the buyer unless and until the goods are ascertained.'
Section 20A (inserted by the Sale of Goods (Amendment) Act 1994, s 1(1) in response to Law Commission paper No 215) provides for title in ex-bulk goods to pass under a tenancy in common, where the purchase price has been paid.
This provision relates to goods, and securities are not goods but (generally) choses in action. Goods are defined in s 61(1) of the Sale of Goods Act 1979 to exclude things in action.
4 *Knight v Knight* (1840) 3 Beav 148.
5 [1994] 2 All ER 806 at 814.
6 See *Re Wait* [1927] 1 Ch 606. A trust of six of my cases of Château Lafite 1961 where I own 12 cases is void for uncertainty, while a trust of half of my cases of Château Lafite 61 is valid.
7 See Robert Ryan 'Taking Security Over Investment Portfolios held in Global Custody' [1990] 10 JIBL 404.
8 If the client has no proprietary rights in the custody assets, the value of such collateral to any third party will depend upon the credit risk of the custodian, as well as that of the issuer of the underlying securities.

The cases

3.11 Debate about the allocation question has focused on the following line of cases.

Re London Wine (Shippers) Ltd[1]

3.12 This case concerned a wine importing company to which a receiver had been appointed pursuant to a floating charge in favour of a bank. The company held wine in various warehouses. Most of the wine had been sold to clients who left the wine in the possession of the company's warehouse agent. There was no segregation of any wine crates or cases in favour of clients generally or any particular client. The clients claimed that they had proprietary interests in the wine. The receiver argued that they had merely personal claims against the company for delivery of wine.

Judgment was given in favour of the receiver. This was on the basis that there had been no allocation to the clients: proprietary rights could not pass at law for want of allocation or under a trust for want of certainty of subject matter.

1 *Re London Wine (Shippers) Ltd* [1986] PCC 121.

Re Stapylton Fletcher Ltd[1]

3.13 The facts of this case were similar to those of *Re London Wine*[2], except that the wine intended for customers was segregated from the trading stock of the company. This difference was held to be crucial[3] and judgment was given in favour of the claimants from the liquidators: 'They will take as tenants in common'[4].

As custodians segregate their house positions from client holdings, this case supports a robust approach to the allocation question. However, it would be prudent to note that, unlike *Re (London Wine)*, *Stapylton Fletcher* related only to legal interests arising in the sale of goods and not to interests under a trust[5].

1 *Re Stapylton Fletcher Ltd; Re Ellis, Son & Vidler Ltd* [1994] 1 WLR 1181, [1995] 1 All ER 192.
2 *Re London Wine (Shippers) Ltd* [1986] PCC 121.
3 'I do not regard that decision [in *Re London Wine*] as inevitably governing the case before me. One obvious difference in the present case is the segregation of the wine purchased by the customers in a separate part of the warehouse and the careful maintenance of records within the company. Further as the London Wine Company was free to sell its stock and satisfy the customers from any other available source, there was no ascertainable bulk in that case', per Judge Paul Baker QC at 1194.
4 [1994] 1 WLR 1181 at 1200.
5 'As I have found for the first four claimants in the case relating to ESV on the basis of the passing of property at law, I do not have to consider the alternative lines of argument based on trusts, fiduciary relationships or other equitable principles in relation to these claims' ([1994] 1 WLR 1181 at 1201).

Re Goldcorp Exchange Ltd (in receivership)[1]

3.14 Goldcorp, a dealer in precious metals, agreed with certain customers ('the unallocated customers') to sell gold to them and to hold it for them on an unallocated basis. It represented that it would set aside and hold a pool of gold sufficient to meet the claims of the unallocated customers, but did not do so. Goldcorp became insolvent and its stock of gold was insufficient to meet the claims of the unallocated customers. In a dispute between receivers appointed pursuant to a floating charge and unallocated customers, judgment was given in favour of the receivers. The claims of the unallocated customers were held to be merely contractual.

The judgment distinguishes between 'generic' goods (the source of which is not specified) and 'ex-bulk' goods (which must come from a specified source)[2]. The case for the claimants failed (both at law and in equity) because on the facts *Goldcorp* related to generic goods[3]. If it had been a question of ex-bulk goods, the position might have been different[4]. Thus, it could be argued that, because custodians segregate house position from client holdings, fungible custody falls outside the scope of the decision in *Goldcorp*. However, the judgment remains unclear on this point. Nowhere is it unequivocally stated that if client and house assets had been segregated, the interest of unallocated clients would have been proprietary. As Cooke P understated in the court below, '. . . it is a difficult area of law'[5].

1 [1994] 2 All ER 806.
2 [1994] 2 All ER 806 at 814.
3 [1994] 2 All ER 806 at 814.
4 [1994] 2 All ER 806 at 820.
5 *Liggett v Kensington* [1993] 1 NZLR 257 at 268.

Hunter v Moss[1]

3.15 The custody industry was therefore grateful for the decision in *Hunter v Moss*. The facts of this case were as follows. Moss was the registered holder of 950 shares in a company with 1,000 shares in issue. Moss made a declaration of trust over 5 per cent of the company's issued share capital in favour of Hunter. A valid trust was held by Colin Rimer QC, a deputy judge, to have arisen from the intention to create a trust over 50 of Moss's shares. Moss applied by motion for the judgment to be recalled to deal with the overlooked point that the trust failed for want of certainty of subject matter.

However, Rimer QC held that, in a trust over intangibles, the requirement for certainty of subject matter does not apply.

> 'The defendant did not identify any particular 50 shares for the plaintiff because to do so was unnecessary and irrelevant. All 950 of his shares carried identical rights . . . Any suggested uncertainty as to subject matter appears to me to be theoretical and conceptual rather than real and practical'[2].

The Court of Appeal dismissed the appeal on the erroneous ground that, just as a person can by will give a specific number of her shares in a particular company, so equally she can declare herself a trustee of 50 of her shares in a particular company. However, on death the settlor is divested of all legal and beneficial ownership of her shares. In life she can only divest herself of the beneficial interest in shares when she has done everything necessary to identify those shares to which she has relinquished beneficial entitlement, viz when she has segregated 50 from those of which she retains beneficial ownership.

This decision has been treated with some caution in the legal community[3]. In particular, in the Court of Appeal, inter vivos transfers are not distinguished from testamentary transfers. On the particular facts of the case, it was clearly in the interests of justice that a valid trust should be found in the absence of a contractual entitlement. The judgment, which was pragmatic, focused more on the merits of the dispute before the court than the wider principles of equity. There is plenty of authority that certainty of subject matter is essential to a trust over a type of intangible asset, namely cash at bank, which is not adequately dealt with in this case[4].

However, in spite of these problems, *Hunter v Moss* has now been followed in *Re Harvard Securities*[5] and the Hong Kong case of *CA Pacific*[6], and may appear to be good law.

1 [1993] 1 WLR 934; affd [1994] 1 WLR 452, [1994] 3 All ER 215, CA.
2 [1993] 1 WLR 934 at 946, per Colin Rimer QC (sitting as deputy High Court judge). But in these days of mass production, many tangibles are identical.
3 See David Hayton 'Uncertainty of Subject-Matter of Trusts' (1994) 110 LQR 335.
4 See, for example, *Mac-Jordan Construction Ltd v Brookmount Erostin Ltd* [1992] BCLC 350. See also *Re Jartray Development Ltd* (1982) 22 BLR 134; *Rayack Construction v Lampeter Meat Co Ltd* (1979) 12 BLR 30; *Neste Oy v Lloyds Bank plc* [1983] 2 Lloyd's Rep 658; and *Concorde Constructions Co Ltd v Colgan Ltd* (1984) 29 BLR 120. However, these cases may be distinguishable on the basis that they relate to generic and not ex bulk assets.
A purported trust created for value over an unallocated part of a pool of intangibles may create a mere charge if by way of security for payment of a debt: *Swiss Bank v Lloyds Bank* [1979] Ch 548, [1979] 3 WLR 201, [1979] 2 All ER 853; revsd [1982] AC 584, [1980] 3 WLR 457, [1980] 2 All ER 419; affd [1982] AC 584, [1981] 2 WLR 893, [1981] 2 All ER 449.
5 *Re Harvard Securities (in liquidation)* [1997] 2 BCLC 369. Neither this case nor the Hong Kong case should be cited in court proceedings covered by *Hunter v Moss*: see *Practice Note* [2001] 2 All ER 510.
6 *Re CA Pacific Finance Ltd (in Liquidation)* [2000] 1 BCLC 494.

Equitable tenancy in common

3.16 In the authors' view, *Hunter v Moss*[1] may be (roughly) reconciled with *Mac-Jordan*[2] and the other cases referred to above relating to trusts over cash accounts, by taking the current position to be as follows. In fungible custody arrangements, provided client assets are segregated from house assets, the requirement for certainty of subject matter is not inapplicable; however, it is automatically satisfied by an implied co-ownership arrangement, whereby the custodian holds the client holding under a single trust for all clients to whose accounts it has credited the relevant security, as equitable tenants in common. This analysis is consistent with the decision in *Re Stapylton Fletcher*[3], but not with that in *CA Pacific*[4]. It is submitted that the latter is unreliable. It is also submitted that it should not be assumed that clients enjoy property rights unless the client holding is segregated from the house position[5]. Thus, in collateral arrangements where the custodian is permitted to credit client securities to its house account[6], it should be assumed that the client's rights are merely contractual, so that she takes the credit risk of the custodian[7].

1 [1993] 1 WLR 934; affd [1994] 1 WLR 452, [1994] 3 AllER 215, CA.
2 *Mac-Jordan Construction Ltd v Brookmount Erostin Ltd* [1992] BCLC 350.
3 *Re Stapylton Fletcher Ltd; Re Ellis, Son & Vidler Ltd* [1994] 1 WLR 1181, [1995] 1 All ER 192.
4 *Re CA Pacific Finance Ltd (in Liquidation)* [2000] 1 BCLC 494.
5 Without such segregation, the assets would be generic and not ex bulk, and therefore outside the scope of *Re Stapylton Fletcher* and related cases.
6 For example, under prime brokerage arrangements.
7 See Hayton and Marshall *Cases and commentary on the law of Trusts and Equitable Remedies* (2001, 11th edn, Sweet & Maxwell), para 3–90.

Two lines of cases

3.17 An advantage of the above 'tenancy in common' approach is that it reconciles the cases relating to the allocation question with another line of cases, relating to mixing.

The issue under consideration in the allocation cases discussed above was the acquisition, by the purchasers, of proprietary interests in assets forming part of a fungible pool. In all these cases the mixing of the whole *antedates* the possible ownership of part.

Another line of cases establishes the principle, based on Roman law, that where the goods of different owners are mixed together so that they cannot be separated, the owners will hold the commingled goods as tenants in common[1]. In these cases, the mixing of the whole *predates* the possible ownership of part. These cases concern the preservation of existing proprietary rights, as opposed to the creation of new ones.

In practice, the operational complexities of settlement are such that it may not be possible to determine which part of a client's custody portfolio is governed by which line of case law. It is therefore helpful to conclude that such determination is unnecessary, on the basis that the position will be the same in any event, and that the client enjoys property rights under an equitable tenancy in common.

1 See *Buckley v Gross* (1863) 3 B & S 566, 122 ER 213; *Spence v Union Marine Insurance Co Ltd* (1868) LR 3 CP 427; *Indian Oil Corpn Ltd v Greenstone Shipping SA, The Ypatianna* [1988] QB 345, [1987] 3 WLR 869, [1987] 3 All ER 893; and *Glencore International AG v Metro Trading Inc* [2001] 1 Lloyd's Rep 284.

Conclusions

3.18 In relation to the custody securities portfolio, it is necessary to protect the client from the credit risk of the custodian. The traditional legal technique for achieving this, by characterising the custodian as a bailee, is ineffective in an electronic environment. It is therefore necessary to establish a trust. With fungible custody, the lack of allocation between any particular client and particular underlying securities raises the allocation question: is there sufficient certainty of subject matter in order to establish a valid trust? As discussed above, the natural answer to the allocation problem is co-ownership. Rather than seek to identify a trust in favour of each client over their unallocated portion of the client securities, one may identify one global trust over all the client securities of a particular type in favour of all relevant clients as tenants in common[1].

In the interests of legal clarity, it may be prudent to include express wording in the custody documentation to confirm the existence of such equitable tenancies in common among the custody clients over the commingled client holdings.

1 A separate tenancy in common exists in relation to each type of security from time to time comprised in clients' portfolios. This is because, in practice, it will not be the case that each client's portfolio includes the same range of securities in the same proportions. A necessary feature of a tenancy in common is unity of possession. Megarry and Wade *The Law of Real Property* (6th edn, Sweet & Maxwell), p 481.

This multiplication of tenancies in common should not create any administrative difficulty, because their existence is notional and automatic, and does not require any practical step to be taken.

Shortfalls

3.19 Even if a trust or similar arrangement is recognised in the insolvency of the custodian, the client will still suffer loss if there is a shortfall in the securities held for it by the custodian.

> 'Shortfalls in custodial holdings may develop for a number of reasons, including the failure of trades to settle as anticipated, poor accounting controls, or intentional fraud. The shortfalls may be temporary or long-standing. Allocation of the risk of loss from a shortfall will vary depending on the circumstances under which the shortfall arose. Of course, if the custodian is solvent, no real problems arise; it may either replace the missing securities, or pay damages, or both. However, if the custodian is insolvent, or the shortfall arises from fraud or insolvency on the part of a sub-custodian or CSD, the investor's risk of loss may be severe.'[1]

1 Bank for International Settlements *Cross-Border Securities Settlement* (May 1995, Basle), p 20.

Shortfalls and commingled accounts

3.20 A risk associated with commingled custody accounts is that shortfalls attributable to the business of one client may be borne by other clients sharing the account. Where client-specific segregation is not offered, therefore, clients may wish to know whether the custodian engages in practices which heighten the risk of shortfall.

One source of shortfall risk is presented by security interests in favour of intermediaries in the global custody chain, such as sub-custodians and settlement systems. For example, if a global custodian becomes insolvent, a sub-custodian may enforce a lien over the client assets it holds for the global custodian in respect of unpaid fees[1].

A further source of shortfall risk is liquidator's costs. The case of *Berkeley Applegate (Investment Consultants) Ltd*[2] established the principle that, where the assets of the insolvent company are insufficient to meet the liquidator's costs in administering property held on trust by the company for its clients, the court has discretion to award those costs out of the trust assets[3]. This principle may pose a threat to the assets of custody clients where the custodian does not have substantial assets of its own, and where adequate records of the custody business have not been kept, so that significant work is required to clarify the entitlements of clients.

1 In Chapter 9.1 of the Financial Services Authority's Conduct of Business Sourcebook, Rule 9.1.51 requires custodians to agree in writing with private customers (or to notify intermediate customers or market counterparties) where a lien or security interest is taken over the custody assets by the custodian (or a third party) 'except in respect of any charges relating to the administration or safekeeping of the custody assets'. This would have the result that the custodian should agree in writing with the client (or notify as appropriate) any lien or similar claim of a sub-custodian (and in principle any sub-delegate of the sub-custodian) unless such lien or other claim only relates to administration and safekeeping charges. Similarly, Rule 9.1.69 in the same chapter requires that where a custodian delegates the holding of assets to a sub-custodian, it must agree with the sub-custodian that the sub-custodian will not exercise a 'lien, right of retention or sale' over custody assets unless the custodian has notified the sub-custodian that the custody client has given written consent (note that this does not entirely reflect the requirements of Rule 9.1.51 where written consent is not required from intermediate customers or market counterparties) or the rights are only exercised in respect of administration of safekeeping charges.

2 [1988] 3 All ER 71.

3 [1988] 3 All ER 71 at 76, 82.

Contractual settlement

3.21 An example of such a practice is the contractual settlement of securities. Contractual settlement is a service offered by some global custodians in relation to cash or (more rarely) securities. It is agreed that, where moneys or securities are due to be received under a trade, those assets will be credited to the client's account on the date agreed for settlement with the counterparty, whether or not they are actually received on that date by the custodian. The custodian reserves the right to reverse the credit entry if the assets do not arrive within a reasonable period[1]. Contractual settlement amounts to the lending of cash and/or securities[2]. Where contractual settlement is offered in connection with a commingled securities account, the following risk arise. If a purchase of bonds is contractually settled, the client is free to sell them to a third party. If such a sale leaves the client's holding at zero and the original trade fails, the custodian cannot reverse the credit entry without causing a shortfall. Further, as the contractual settlement of securities amounts to securities lending, the question arises, from whom is the client borrowing? It will only be borrowing from the custodian if the custodian transfers new securities into the commingled account to support the transaction. If the custodian does not do this, the client is borrowing securities from the other clients of the custodian, possibly without their consent or knowledge. Such arrangements may well be unlawful.

1 Custodians only offer contractual settlement in markets where they are confident of timely settlement.

2 This raises issues of authority to lend and borrow such assets, as well as taxation issues.

Allocation of shortfall

3.22 Where there is a shortfall in the pooled client securities account of an insolvent custodian, the question arises how the shortfall will be borne by the respective clients. Where the account has been very active, it seem likely that the loss would be borne pro rata among all the affected clients[1]. However, the position would be less clear in the unlikely event that the account was inactive, so that as a matter evidence it was relatively easy to identify the transactions which had caused the shortfall. In such a case, the courts might apply the traditional tracing rules to attribute the 'missing' securities to a particular client or clients[2].

1 See *Barlow Clowes International v Vaughan* [1992] 4 All ER 22. The risk warnings required to be given to commingled clients by the FSA assume that shortfalls will be pro rated: see the Financial Services Authority's Conduct of Business Sourcebook:

> 'When explaining the meaning of pooling to a private customer, firms are expected to advise the private customer that . . . in the event of an unreconcilable shortfall after the failure of a custodian, clients may share in that shortfall in proportion to their original share of the assets in the pool.'

2 In *Barlow Clowes*, the loss was pro rated because the accounts had been so active that the application of the traditional tracing rules would have been unduly complex.

Chapter 4*

The use of the custody portfolio as collateral**

4.1 This chapter will consider the growing use of the custody portfolio as collateral. This is a commercially important development, for a number of reasons. Firstly, the provision of a global custodial service can involve significant credit exposures for the global custodian, which the global custodian will wish to collateralise as effectively as possible against the custody portfolio. Secondly, in the light of the increasing competitive pressures to which the global custody industry is subject, successful global custodians must continue to develop and offer 'value added' services in order to retain and extend their client bases. Arguably, the most important potential area for the development of such value added services is collateral management. As collateral manager, the global custodian either assists the client in offering the custody portfolio as collateral to third parties, or alternatively itself offers credit facilities to the client, collateralising these exposures against the custody portfolio. An important example of the latter type of arrangement is prime brokerage, discussed below. Some industry commentators have argued that the future of global custody lies in such collateral management services.

* The authors are grateful to Peter Taylor, Partner, Clifford Chance, for kindly reviewing this chapter. Any errors are their own.

** See also Bank for International Settlements *Collateral in Wholesale Financial Markets: Recent Trends* (March 2001) Basle.

Overview

Nature of collateralisation

4.2 Collateralisation is a technique for managing credit risk. Chapter 2 discussed the difference between personal rights (which are enforceable against persons) and property rights (which are enforceable against assets). Because a personal right such as a debt is enforceable only against the person who owes it (the debtor), it may become valueless if for any reason the creditor's ability successfully to enforce is affected. In the financial markets, the most commercially significant reason why debts and other personal rights may become valueless is insolvency. When a debtor becomes insolvent, the debt generally cannot be successfully enforced in the normal way, and the debtor must prove in the insolvency proceedings as an unsecured creditor. Depending on the outcome of the insolvency proceedings, the debtor is likely to face delay in payment, and may receive only a fraction of the sum owed, or indeed nothing at all. This exposure to a counterparty's insolvency is called credit risk.

In order to manage credit risk, creditors and other persons who are owed a personal obligation[1] may require that their counterparties collateralise these exposures. Collateralisation involves the delivery from the debtor[2] to the creditor[3] of property rights in identified assets. If the collateral giver defaults, the collateral taker is able to satisfy its claims out of the collateral assets.

1 Such as, for example, a right to the redelivery of loaned securities under a securities lending agreement.
2 Or other obligor.
3 Or other obligee.

Financial institutions as collateral takers

4.3 Throughout the 1990s and into the new millennium, there has been a significant growth in the use of collateral by financial institutions. The market turbulence of 1998 focused attention on the need carefully to manage credit exposures. Further, regulated institutions are subject to regulatory capital requirements in respect of their credit exposures, and such requirements are very significantly relieved by collateralisation. The need to demonstrate a good return on capital in an increasingly competitive environment has encouraged regulated institutions to seek ever greater capital efficiencies, by collateralising their credit exposures to the greatest possible extent.

A number of other developments in the securities markets are causing a significant increase in the use of collateral. These include the continuing development of the securities lending and repo markets; the introduction of central counterparties[1]; and the use of central bank money in securities settlement[2].

Another factor which may increase the use of collateral by global custodians and other financial institutions extending credit to insurance companies is the implementation of the Insurance Winding Up Directive[3]. Article 10 provides for the priority of insurance claims over the claims of other unsecured creditors[4]. Because the priority provisions serve to subordinate unsecured claims which do not arise under insurance contracts, the credit standing of insurance companies in the financial markets may be reduced, and the cost of credit for them may increase[5]. Because these provisions significantly reduce the value of an unsecured debt or other personal claim against an insurance company, custodians may wish to negotiate to secure exposures to insurance company clients.

However, it is also important to appreciate the limits of collateral. This is arguably the most important lesson to be drawn from the near collapse in 1998 of the hedge fund, Long-Term Capital Management, which is discussed briefly below[6]. Collateralisation should complement, but should never substitute, effective credit control.

1 See Chapter 8.
2 See Chapter 8.
3 Directive No 2001/17/EC on the reorganisation and winding up of insurance undertakings. The Insurance Winding Up Directive applies to reorganisation measures and winding up proceedings. These terms are (widely) defined in arts 2(c) and (d) respectively. Insurance undertaking is defined in art 2(a) so as to include direct insurance business, but not reinsurance.
4 For this purpose, the term 'insurance claims' is defined in art 2(k) as 'Any amount which is owed by an insurance undertaking to insured persons, policyholders, beneficiaries or to any injured party having a direct right of action against the insurance undertaking and which arises from an insurance contract . . . in direct insurance business . . .' This clearly excludes reinsurance.
Two options are available for the implementation of the priority of insurance claims. Firstly, there may be absolute precedence of insurance claims with respect to insurers' assets representing technical provisions; alternatively, insurance claims may take precedence with respect to all the assets of the insurers, with the possible exception of certain preferential claims.
5 Also, financial counterparties may seek to restructure their credit arrangements so as to bring them within the definition of insurance claims, and therefore the priority provisions of the Directive.

6 'A related concern is whether the LTCM Fund's counterparties were lulled into a false sense of security based solely upon their collateral arrangements with the Fund. Counterparties' current credit exposures were in most cases covered by collateral. However, their potential future exposures were likely not adequately assessed, priced, or collateralised relative to the potential price shocks the markets were facing at the end of September 1998, and relative to the creditworthiness of the LTCM Fund at that time. Further, expectations about the ability to collect on collateral calls were probably unrealistic for an entity like the LTCM Fund, particularly in the market environment of last Fall. Thus, counterparties that were relying on variation margin to manage credit risk were left with the unsatisfactory prospect of liquidating collateral and closing out exposures in a declining market': *Hedge Funds, Leverage, and the Lessons of Long-Term Capital Management*, Report of the President's Working Group on Financial Markets, April 1999, p 15.

Financial assets as collateral

4.4 Any type of asset may in theory serve as collateral. However, it is important for the collateral taker that collateral assets should be capable of being readily valued and, upon enforcement of the collateral arrangement, readily sold. For these reasons, financial assets such as cash at bank (and in particular US dollars) and securities (and in particular US Treasuries) are highly sought after by collateral takers. As the demand for financial collateral increases, other forms of financial collateral, including corporate debt securities and, in some cases, equities[1], are increasingly used to collateralise financial exposures.

1 Equities have traditionally been regarded as unattractive collateral, primarily because of their volatility.

Collateral and the global custodian

4.5 As indicated above, the use of the custody portfolio as collateral is important for the global custodian, both to collateralise its own settlement exposures to the client, and also in the development of collateral management products, where the collateral taker is either itself or a third party.

The global custodian's settlement exposures

4.6 The provision of a settlement service to clients may involve the global custodian in significant and unpredictable exposures. Many global custodians extend credit to clients in order to facilitate settlement. For example, the global custodian may settle a client's purchase instruction out of its own funds where the client has not pre-funded the transaction. As discussed in Chapter 3, many global custodians offer a service called 'contractual settlement', in relation to cash or (more rarely) securities accounts. It is agreed with the client that, where moneys or securities are due to be received on the settlement of a trade, those assets will be credited to the client's account[1] by the global custodian on the date agreed for settlement with the counterparty, whether or not they are actually received on that date by the global custodian. The global custodian reserves the right to reverse the credit entry if the assets do not arrive within a reasonable period. In practice, this service is only offered in markets where global custodians are generally confident of timely settlement. Contractual settlement amounts to the lending of cash and/or securities[2], and exposes the custodian to the credit risk of the client.

Possible credit and liquidity problems associated with the settlement systems[3] with which the global custodian deals present a further source of potential credit risk. The global custodian will customarily contract as principal with settlement systems. Under standard terms of participation, these counterparties take indemnities from the global custodian in respect of exposures associated with the global custodian's business. Suppose the client instructs the global custodian to settle a purchase of 1,000 ABC securities through a settlement system, and subsequently instructs the global custodian to settle a sale of the same securities, leaving the ABC client account at the settlement system at zero. The next day it transpires that the initial credit to the account reflected a bad delivery (perhaps under insolvency avoidance provisions affecting the vendor to the client), and the credit is reversed, so that the account has a negative balance. Under its terms of participation in the settlement system, the global custodian will be contractually required to deliver 1,000 ABC securities into the account, at its own expense if necessary. Clearly, under its own global custody agreement with the client, the global custodian will have a contractual right to recover the associated costs from the client under an indemnity. However, an indemnity confers only a personal right against the client, and hence involves credit risk. If the client is insolvent, the indemnity may be worthless.

Standard global custody agreements contain provisions whereby the global custodian may use the custody portfolio to collateralise such exposures. Because such client settlement exposures may be very significant indeed, it is important to ensure that these provisions are robust. A number of sensitivities arise, as discussed at paras **4.12–4.35**.

1 So that they are available to the client for delivery to third parties.
2 It is important to establish that the client has authority to borrow such assets, and to consider the taxation implications of the arrangements.
3 Equivalent issues arise in relation to sub-custodians.

Collateral management products

IN FAVOUR OF THIRD PARTIES

4.7 In many cases, global custody clients incur credit exposures to third party financial institutions, and wish to offer assets within the custody portfolio as collateral to such third parties. One possibility is that the global custodian acts as agent of the custody client in entering into collateralised transactions with third parties, for example under agency securities lending arrangements.

Another possibility is that the assets to be delivered by the client as collateral remain with the custodian, which (thereafter) holds them on behalf of the collateral taker. In this case, the collateral taker must satisfy itself that the custody arrangements, as well as the collateral arrangements, are legally robust[1]. Bespoke collateral arrangements may be drafted to support particular credit facilities in favour of the client. Importantly, global custodians may develop collateral netting services in order to enable their clients to make the most efficient use of available collateral assets. These services may range from cross-product netting arrangements with particular counterparties of the custody client, to cross-market collateral netting services for central counterparties, as indicated in Chapter 8[2].

Under such arrangements, in addition to providing a custody service to the custody client, the global custodian provides services to the collateral taker, monitoring and administering the whole or part of the custody portfolio that comprises the collateral on its behalf. It is important to consider potential conflicts of interest that may arise between the global custody client and the collateral taker. As discussed in Chapter 6, the global custodian owes implied fiduciary duties of undivided loyalty, so that in general it must not allow its duties to one client to conflict with its duties to another client. Implied fiduciary duties may be effectively modified by contract, provided the contractual relieving provisions are sufficiently clear and detailed. Thus, it is important that in the documentation supporting these arrangements, potential conflicts are disclosed and permitted. Also, for commercial reasons, it is obviously important to clarify the rights and duties of the global custodian in the event of conflict between the custody client and the collateral taker, for example upon default and enforcement.

1 See for example Basel Committee on Banking Supervision, Bank for International Settlements *Consultative Document, The New Basel Capital Accord* (January 2001, Basel), p 16: 'Collateral is effective only if the legal mechanism by which collateral is given is robust and ensures that the lender has clear rights over the collateral, and may liquidate or retain it in the event of the default . . . of the obligor and where applicable the custodian holding the collateral . . . Where the collateral is held by a custodian, banks must seek to ensure that the custodian ensures adequate segregation of the collateral instruments and the custodian's own assets.'

2 With the development of central counterparty arrangements in the securities markets (discussed in Chapter 8), significant commercial demand is developing to achieve the greatest possible netting efficiencies in the collateralisation of such arrangements, so that surplus collateral available in relation to one market can be applied without delay to meet collateral needs arising in another market. The long term answer will undoubtedly be the evolution of a single central counterparty to serve as many markets as possible. However, in the medium term global custodians may be well placed to meet this demand by offering cross-market collateral netting services, as agent for central counterparties. 'No efficient mechanism exists today to identify excess collateral and move it where and when it is needed': Patricia Tsien 'Present Problems and Future Possibilities for Central Counterparties' in Marcus Evans Conference Proceedings *Trading in Europe: Assessing the Future for Central Counterparties*, 1 and 2 October 2001, p 13.

IN FAVOUR OF THE GLOBAL CUSTODIAN – PRIME BROKERAGE

4.8 Another way in which global custodians can assist their clients to develop the potential of the custody portfolio as a collateral pool is through services such as prime brokerage, where the global custodian is both collateral manager and collateral taker.

Prime brokerage is a service which has been developed, somewhat controversially, by financial institutions (including global custodians) in favour of hedge fund clients. Hedge funds are a type of unregulated collective investment scheme offering a high risk/high reward investment to sophisticated investors[1]. A key characteristic of hedge funds is that they are often highly geared, ie their borrowings are extremely large relative to their net assets[2]. This enables hedge funds, which may raise a relatively small sum from investor's subscriptions, to gain a very large exposure to the financial markets. In turn, this permits spectacular profits when the portfolio management strategy is successful and, unfortunately, equally spectacular failures when it is not[3].

The prime broker enters into complex contractual arrangements with the client, which include (in simplified form) the following provisions[4]. The prime broker purchases securities on behalf of the client, itself lending the purchase price. The prime broker then holds the purchased securities in custody for the client, subject to collateral arrangements in its favour. These collateral arrangements characteristically fall into two parts. Firstly, the client grants a security interest to the prime broker over the securities. As a quid pro quo for permitting the client to pay a discounted rate of interest on the loan, the prime broker has the power at any time to transfer securities out of the client's custody account and into its own account, subject to a contractual obligation to redeliver equivalent securities to the client. This enables the prime broker to use the securities in its own business with third parties, as collateral or as loaned securities, itself retaining associated profits.

Under these arrangements, it is important to consider a second type of potential conflict of interest. The previous section discussed potential conflicts between two clients of the global custodian. In contrast, it is necessary here to consider potential conflicts between the client as collateral giver and the global custodian as collateral taker. Because there is a general implied fiduciary duty of avoiding such conflicts (discussed in Chapter 6), clear and detailed relieving provision in the client documentation is necessary.

These arrangements raise certain other legal sensitivities, discussed at paras **4.12–4.35**.

1 'The term "hedge fund" is commonly used to describe a variety of different types of investment vehicles that share some similar characteristics. Although it is not statutorily defined, the term encompasses any pooled investment vehicle that is privately organised, administered by professional investment managers, and not widely available to the public. The primary investors in hedge funds are wealthy individuals and institutional investors': Report of the President's Working Group on Financial Markets *Hedge Funds, Leverage, and the Lessons of Long-Term Capital Management*, April 1999, p 2. For a further discussion of legal aspects of prime brokerage and hedge funds, see J Benjamin *Interests in Securities* (2000, OUP), ch 10, section B.

2 Leverage may be thirty times capital: see The Report of the President's Working Group, p 5.

3 A major hedge fund, Long Term Capital Management, notoriously nearly failed in 1998, threatening the stability of the New York financial markets.

4 The following is a brief summary of customary provisions; in practice, however, prime brokerage terms are complex and vary from case to case. See also Report of the President's Working Group, p 17: 'Like most hedge funds, LTCM centralised much of its custodial, recordkeeping, clearance, and financing services with a single firm. This bundle of services is typically referred to as prime brokerage and generally includes the following: providing intraday credit to facilitate foreign exchange payments and securities transactions; providing margin credit to finance purchases of equity securities; and borrowing securities from investment fund managers on behalf of hedge funds to support the hedge funds' short positions (thus allowing investment funds to avoid direct exposure to hedge funds). LTCM's prime broker was, and still is, Bear Stearns.'

Legal structures of collateral[1]

4.9 In order to understand the legal sensitivities surrounding collateral arrangements, it is necessary briefly to consider the different legal structures that are available. These fall into two broad categories, namely security interests (which are recognised in all systems of commercial law) and outright collateral transfers (which are in origin Anglo-Saxon structures, and historically less widely recognised in civil law jurisdictions). The difference between them relates to the nature of the property interest received by the collateral taker in the collateral assets prior to enforcement. As discussed below, the implementation of the Settlement Finality Directive will reduce the difference between the two structures.

1 The following is a very brief summary of a complex area of law. For more detail, see J Benjamin *Interests in Securities* (2000, OUP), chs 4, 5 and 6.

Security interests

4.10 Under a security interest, the collateral giver delivers to the collateral taker a limited property right or interest. This limited interest (the security interest) confers certain rights on the collateral taker, including (crucially) the right upon the default of the collateral giver to sell the collateral assets and apply the proceeds of sale to discharge the collateralised obligation[1].

However, in the absence of default, the collateral taker is in general not free to deal with the collateral assets. This is because the non-defaulting collateral giver retains a residual property right in them, which is known as the equity of redemption. This is the right, upon the discharge of the secured obligation, to the return of the particular assets that were originally delivered as collateral. Because it is a property right, the equity of redemption is not at risk in the insolvency of the collateral taker. Thus, the collateral giver who discharges its collateralised debt can recover the collateral assets from the collateral taker's insolvency official. Where the value of the collateral assets exceeds the value of the debt by a significant margin, the equity of redemption has a correspondingly significant value to the collateral giver in managing its credit exposure to the collateral taker. (However, as discussed below, the Financial Collateral Directive, when implemented, will confer a right of use on the collateral taker in wholesale financial collateral arrangements, which cuts across the equity of redemption.)

Many systems of law have only one form of security interest, often known as a pledge. However –

> 'There are . . . four kinds of consensual security known to English law: (i) pledge; (ii) contractual lien; (iii) equitable charge and (iv) mortgage. A pledge and a contractual lien both depend on the delivery of possession to the creditor as security. The difference between them is that in the case of a pledge the owner delivers possession to the creditor as security, whereas in the case of a lien the creditor retains possession of goods previously delivered to him for some other purpose. Neither a mortgage nor a charge depends on the delivery of possession.'[2]

It was argued in Chapter 2 that custody assets are intangible and therefore cannot be subject to possession. On this basis, security interests in relation to the custody portfolio cannot take effect either as pledge or as lien[3].

A mortgage may be either legal (where legal ownership is delivered by way of security, subject to the equity of redemption) or equitable (where equitable ownership is delivered by way of security, subject again to the equity of redemption). Chapter 3 argued that the custody relationship involves a trust, and therefore the asset of the client in the custody portfolio is equitable and not legal. On this basis, if the collateral assets remain in the hands of the global custodian, the interest of a third party[4] collateral taker in the client's custody assets can only take effect in equity[5]. Such a security interest could be characterised as an equitable mortgage, or alternatively as a charge.

A charge can only take effect in equity and not at law[6]. There are two types of charge, namely fixed charges and floating charges.

> 'The essence of a floating charge is that it is a charge, not on any particular asset, but on a fluctuating body of assets which remain under the management and control of the chargor, and which the chargor has the right to withdraw from the security despite the existence of the charge. The essence of a fixed charge is that the charge is on a particular asset or class of assets which the chargor cannot deal with free from the charge without the consent of the chargee.'[7]

1 Any surplus must be returned to the collateral giver (or, if it is insolvent, its insolvency official). Exceptionally, a lien does not generally confer a power of sale, but only a right of retention, as discussed below.

2 *Re Cosslett (Contractors) Ltd* [1997] 4 All ER 115 at 125, per Millett LJJ.

3 This is notwithstanding the fact that traditional global custody agreements routinely refer to the security interest of the global custodian as a lien; see the discussion below.

4 It is arguable that a security interest in favour of the custodian (either as principal or as agent) may effect as a legal mortgage, on the basis that the global custodian holds legal title to the assets. The

counter argument (indicating an equitable mortgage or charge) is that the global custodian acquired legal title as trustee, and not as mortgagee; a legal mortgage involves the delivery of legal title *by way of security* (and not by way of custody).

5 It is not possible to acquire a legal interest in an equitable asset. This is because an equitable asset is an asset recognised by equity, but not by the common law. The law will not recognise a property right where the asset to which it relates is not also recognised by it.

6 The exception is a charge over land. See Roy Goode *Legal Problems of Credit and Security* (2nd edn, Sweet & Maxwell), pp 14–15.

7 *Re Cosslett (Contractors) Ltd* [1997] 4 All ER 115 at 143, per Millett LJJ. While the floating charge has never been judicially defined, the classic description of the floating charge is given by Romer J in *Re Yorkshire Woolcombers Association Ltd* [1903] 2 Ch 284 at 295: 'I certainly do not intend to attempt to give an exact definition of the term "floating charge," nor am I prepared to say that there will not be a floating charge within the meaning of the Act, which does not contain all the three characteristics that I am about to mention, but I certainly think that if a charge has the three characteristics I am about to mention it is a floating charge. (1) If it is a charge on a class of assets of a company present and future; (2) if that class is one which, in the ordinary course of the business of the company, would be changing from time to time; and (3) if you find that by the charge it is contemplated that, until some future step is taken by or on behalf of those interested in the charge, the company may carry on its business in the ordinary way as far as concerns the particular class of assets I am dealing with.' See also Lord Macnaghten in *Illingsworth v Houldsworth* [1904] AC 355 at 358. A very interesting recent discussion of the floating charge is contained in the judgment of Millett LJ in *Agnew v IRC* [2001] UKPC 28, [2001] 2 AC 710, [2001] 3 WLR 454.

Outright collateral transfers

4.11 Whereas, under a security interest, the collateral giver retains residual property rights in the collateral assets, which it continues to enjoy concurrently with the security interest of the collateral taker, an outright collateral transfer (as its name suggests) involves the transfer of the entirety of the interest of the collateral giver to the collateral taker. This means that the collateral giver retains no property rights in the collateral assets. Obviously, the non-defaulting collateral giver expects to receive assets back upon the discharge of the collateralised obligation. However, these rights of redelivery are personal (enforceable against the collateral taker) and not proprietary (enforceable against the collateral assets). Moreover, these redelivery rights are fungible, in the following sense. Rather than being able to call for the return of the particular securities originally delivered as collateral, the collateral giver's right is to the redelivery of *equivalent* securities. This means that it is entitled to the return of the same number and type of securities as were originally delivered, but not the same ones.

It follows from this that the collateral taker is free, from the moment it receives the collateral securities, to deal with them as it pleases. Its only obligation is to meet its equivalent redelivery obligation; as a practical matter, this may involve getting in the relevant type of securities just in time. Because the financial institutions which receive collateral under certain transactions are also obliged to deliver collateral under other transactions, this right of use has great commercial value. Indeed, it is generally regarded as the chief advantage of an outright collateral transfer over a security interest. As discussed below, the implementation of the Financial Collateral Directive will extend the right of use to security interests over financial assets in wholesale arrangements.

In the event that either party defaults, set off applies[1]. This means that collateralised obligation of the collateral giver to the collateral taker, and the redelivery obligation of the collateral taker to the collateral giver, are valued, automatically converted into debts to pay their respective values, and then set off one against the other, so that only a net sum is payable. Repos[2] and, in London, securities loans are structured as outright collateral transfers, as are the collateral arrangements supporting many swaps[3].

1 Such transactions are generally entered into as part of a programme involving many transactions under master agreements. The default provision of such master agreements provides for close out netting as a preliminary to set off. As discussed below, close out netting reduces all the outstanding obligations of each party to a single net obligation. These net obligations of each party are then set off against each other. See art 2.1(n) of the Financial Collateral Directive for a definition of close out netting.
2 See para **10.35** for the taxation treatment of repos and para **10.43** for that of manufactured payments.
3 See J Benjamin *Interests in Securities* (2000, OUP), ch 6 for more details.

Sensitivities

4.12 This section briefly considers some of the legal sensitivities for the collateral taker. Sensitivities associated with all types of collateral assets, and also sensitivities particularly associated with the use of a custody portfolio as collateral will be considered in turn. It should be emphasised that this discussion gives an overview only of key sensitivities, and is not intended to be relied on in practice or to address all relevant legal issues. Legal advice should be sought in relation to any particular proposed collateral arrangements.

A fundamental principle of insolvency law is that all creditors who have the misfortune to be owed money by the insolvent should be treated equally[1]. This is known as the pari passu principle. Notwithstanding the pari passu principle, the effect of successful collateralisation is to remove the collateral taker from the ranks of unsecured creditors, ensuring that it is paid before them. This depletes the pool of assets available for unsecured creditors. All systems of commercial law known to the authors permit some form of collateralisation. However, because collateralisation cuts across the pari passu principle, the circumstances in which collateralisation is permitted to succeed in the insolvency of the collateral giver are restricted. The sensitivities discussed below generally reflect such restrictions. Law reform initiatives such as the Financial Collateral Directive[2], the Insolvency Regulation[3] and the Winding Up Directive[4], discussed briefly below, seek to address many of these sensitivities within the EU.

1 For an interesting contrary view, see R J Mokal 'Priority as Pathology: The Pari Passu Myth' (2001) 69(3) CLJ 581–621.
2 2002/47/EC.
3 1346/2000/EC.
4 2001/24/EC.

For all types of collateral assets

4.13 The following points arise irrespective of the nature of the collateral assets. Sensitivities associated with all collateral structures, with security interests, and with outright collateral transfers will be considered in turn.

All collateral structures

4.14 This section will consider sensitivities that may arise irrespective of the collateral structure.

INSOLVENCY DISPLACEMENT

4.15 If the collateral giver is affected by insolvency at the time of the collateral transaction, or shortly thereafter, its insolvency official may be able to claim back the collateral assets, displacing the interest of the collateral taker. This reflects a concern of insolvency law that the assets available to general creditors should not be unfairly depleted. Insolvency displacement provisions are included in all systems of developed commercial law, and broadly speaking fall into two categories. First, the giving of collateral at a time when the collateral giver is insolvent is, in general, automatically void as a post-insolvency disposition[1]. (A further risk in some jurisdictions is presented by 'zero hour' rules, which may have the effect of moving the commencement of insolvency to the beginning of the 24-hour day.) Second, transactions concluded prior to insolvency but close enough to it to fall within the statutory 'suspect period'[2] may, at the option of the insolvency official, be avoided if they offend rules designed to protect general creditors against unfair prejudice, such as rules against preferences[3]. Collateral arrangements that are put in place in respect of pre-existing and originally unsecured debts, may be particularly vulnerable[4].

As a general principle, it is not possible to contract out of the mandatory provisions of insolvency law[5], and in order to address the risk of insolvency displacement, well advised collateral takers will always undertake counterparty credit assessment, and avoid doing business with an actually or potentially insolvent counterparty. However, unforeseen insolvency is a fact of commercial life. Therefore it is customary for collateral takers to seek legal opinions to the effect that, should the collateral giver be affected by insolvency, the transaction would not fall foul of insolvency displacement rules, as a preference or otherwise. Under English law, very broadly speaking, the risk of insolvency displacement is generally remote in the case of bona fide arm's length collateral arrangements with solvent counterparties for new money (ie where the collateralised exposure did not predate the delivery of the collateral).

With foreign counterparties, insolvency displacement risk should always be assessed under the law that would govern the counterparty's insolvency. The conflict of laws rules for cross-border insolvency are complex, as discussed in Chapter 5. As a broad generalisation[6], it is prudent for the collateral taker to consider the law of the collateral giver's organisation and, if different, the law of the branch through which it entered into the transaction. Recent EU measures have altered the position within Europe, as discussed in Chapter 5. Very broadly, the Insolvency Regulation applies to individuals and companies other than credit institutions, insurance companies, investment services firms and retail collective investment schemes. It provides in general that insolvency is handled by the courts and governed by the laws of the member state where the insolvent's centre of main interests is located; in the case of a company, the registered office is presumed to be the centre of main interests. Although pre-existing property rights arising under foreign law collateral arrangements will be respected, they are subject to the insolvency displacement rules of the law of the centre of main interests. The cross-border insolvency of banks and insurance companies is governed by the Banking Winding Up Directive and the Insurance Winding Up Directive respectively. The position under these measures, which are due to be implemented in 2004 and 2003 respectively, is in some respects similar to that under the Insolvency Regulation, except that the relevant jurisdiction is the home member state in which the bank or insurance company is authorised, rather than the centre of main interests.

1 Under English law, see s 123 of the Insolvency Act 1986. Note that the Insolvency Regulation provides that the validity of post insolvency dispositions of registered securities is governed by the law of the member state where the register is kept (art 14). In relation to the insolvency of banks, the

equivalent provisions in the Banking Winding Up Directive are contained in art 31, and are drafted more widely. They relate to 'instruments or rights in such instruments the existence or transfer of which presupposes their being recorded in a register, an account or a centralised deposit system held or located in a Member State'. The provisions of art 14 the Insolvency Regulation may not be sufficiently widely drafted to cover bonds or interests in bonds held through Clearstream or Euroclear.

2 Also known as the 'hardening period', because transactions made within it are 'soft', or potentially avoidable.

3 Under English law, see s 238 (transactions at an undervalue); s 239 (preferences); and s 245 (avoidance of floating charges). Section 240 defines the hardening periods.

4 In the UK, see the provisions for the avoidance of floating charges under s 245.

5 In the UK, see *British Eagle International Airlines Ltd v Compagnie International Air France* [1975] 1 WLR 758, [1975] 2 All ER 390.

6 The following is a very rough summary; please see Chapter 5 for more detail.

MARGINING OR MARKING TO MARKET[1]

4.16 Many collateralised transactions are subject to margining, or marking to market. It is customary for the value of the collateral assets to exceed the value of the collateralised exposure by an agreed margin. The value of the financial assets serving as collateral, and in some cases also the collateralised exposure, may vary from time to time, either enlarging or reducing the margin from that originally agreed. In order to restore the agreed margin, cash and/or other collateral assets are delivered between the parties to eliminate collateral shortfalls and excesses that arise from time to time. Such margining or marking to market may take place several times a day, and is helpful in enabling the parties to manage their credit exposures[2]. However, a number of sensitivities may arise. First, where collateral shortfalls are eliminated under marking to market arrangements, the result is that part of the collateral pool has been delivered at a later time than the original collateral delivery. As well as possible priority problems[3], this may raise the risk of insolvency displacement[4]. As discussed below, the Financial Collateral Directive offers protection in relation to wholesale financial collateral arrangements within the EU. A further possible risk relates to recharacterisation as a floating charge. As discussed in more detail below, floating charges suffer from a number of disadvantages, including the requirement for registration. If margining provisions are so drafted as to confer on the collateral giver an unqualified right to the release of particular types of collateral asset to eliminate a collateral excess, this might be interpreted as conferring on the collateral giver freedom to deal in the collateral assets. As discussed below, this is the hallmark of a floating charge. Care is taken in drafting margining provisions to minimise this risk, often by having the collateral taker and not the collateral giver select the asset type to be returned.

1 The near failure of LTCM in 1998 illustrated how margining can turn a liquidity problem into a credit problem. Many financial firms fail because of their inability to meet margin calls.

2 'This discipline is useful for preventing the concealment of losses and for encouraging the timing resolution of problems': Report of the President's Working Group on Financial Markets *Hedge Funds, Leverage, and the Lessons of Long-Term Capital Management*, April 1999, US Dept of the Treasury, pp 4, 5.

3 It is important to ensure that the new assets are treated as being subject to the original security interest, in order that the interest of the collateral taker should not be postponed to any security interests created after the original security interest but prior to the top up delivery.

4 This might be for various reasons. The later delivery (but not the original delivery) might amount to a post insolvency disposition, or fall within the hardening period. The later delivery might also be treated as the collateralisation of a pre-existing debt.

SUBSTITUTION

4.17 The general principle is that the collateral giver retains a position in the collateral assets, having the risks and rewards of ownership[1], and may therefore wish to actively manage these assets during the collateral transaction. For example, if the value of the collateral assets is falling, the collateral giver may wish to cut its losses by selling them; if it is rising, the collateral giver may wish to take the profits, again by selling them. For this reason, it is customary in collateralised transactions to provide for substitution, whereby original collateral assets are returned to the collateral giver upon the delivery of new assets of equal value.

This raises similar priority, insolvency displacement and recharacterisation sensitivities to margining, discussed above. Again, the Financial Collateral Directive provides protection against insolvency displacement. Recharacterisation risk is often addressed by making substitution subject to the consent of the collateral taker[2].

1 This is because, in the absence of default, the collateral assets will be returned to the collateral giver. Even upon default, any excess in the value of the collateral over the debt will be returned to the collateral giver, who remains liable to the collateral taker in respect of any shortfall. Thus, increases in value of the collateral involve a capital gain for the collateral giver, and falls in value involve a capital loss.

2 Interestingly, art 2(2) of the Financial Collateral Directive may address the recharacterisation risk potentially associated with both rights of substitution and marking-to-market: 'Any right of substitution or to withdraw excess financial collateral in favour of the collateral provider shall not prejudice the financial collateral having been provided to the collateral taker as mentioned in this Directive.'

PRIORITIES

4.18 Questions of priorities arise where third parties are able to assert property rights in the collateral assets, which compete with the property rights of the collateral taker. If the value of the collateral assets is insufficient to meet all the property claims that arise against them, it is crucial to determine the order in which these claims will be met. This is a question of priorities, and the collateral taker will wish to ensure that, in the event that it faces competing claims to the collateral assets, its claims have the highest possible priority. Such competing rights may arise for a range of reasons. The collateral giver may improperly deliver client assets to the collateral taker in respect of its own exposures, leaving the collateral taker vulnerable to competing claims from the defrauded clients[1]. The collateral giver may properly[2] or improperly engage in double dealing, and purport to deliver the same assets as collateral to more than one collateral taker.

Many systems of commercial law have rules which generally favour good faith purchasers over holders of prior interests, in order to protect the smooth operation of commercial markets. Such rules may benefit the collateral taker where it is challenged by a holder of a prior competing interest, and disadvantage the collateral taker where it is challenged by the holder of a subsequent competing interest.

In the UK, the rules governing priorities are complex and their application highly sensitive to the facts of each particular case. However, the following principles generally apply:

(1) The general rule at common law is that the priority of competing interests in the same asset is determined by the order in which such interests were created. This means that, where two interests are granted in the same asset, the first in time prevails. This general rule is displaced in certain circumstances by the following special rules.
(2) The good faith purchaser[3] (or collateral taker) of a negotiable instrument generally has priority over earlier claims. Chapter 2 argued that the electronic nature of most assets currently held in global custody is incompatible with negotiable status.
(3) A subsequent legal interest will take priority over an earlier equitable interest,

provided the subsequent interest holder is the bona fide purchaser of the legal interest for value without notice of the earlier claim, otherwise known as 'equity's darling'[4].

(4) Where the collateral asset comprises a debt or (by analogy) other intangible financial asset, priority depends, not on the order of creation of the competing interests, but the order in which they were notified in writing to the debtor or other obligor[5].

(5) A fixed charge in general takes priority over a prior floating charge, unless the prior floating charge included a negative pledge of which the fixed chargee had notice.

The law relating to priorities would be significantly altered by the proposals of the Law Commission to reform the law relating to the registration of security interests[6].

1 It is customary for the collateral taker to require a warranty of beneficial ownership, but this does not eliminate the risk that client assets may be fraudulently delivered in breach of warranty.

2 The parties may have agreed that the collateral giver may grant successive security interests in the same collateral assets.

3 Known as the holder in due course. See s 29(1) of the Bills of Exchange Act 1882.

4 *Pilcher v Rawlins* (1872) 7 Ch App 259. It was argued in Chapter 3 that the global custodial relationship is a trust, so that the asset of the custody client is equitable and not legal. This means that the equitable priority rules in (3) above may apply. Where, for example, a collateral taker receives securities collateral from a global custodian, which proves to have been delivered without the authority of the custody client, the collateral taker faces the risk of competing claims from the defrauded client. Because the defrauded client will be claiming back her equitable interest, the equitable rules of priority will apply. The outcome of the dispute will generally depend on the nature of the interest acquired by the collateral taker. If it acquired merely an equitable interest (such as a charge), the client will generally win, on the basis that her interest was prior in time. However, if the collateral taker acquired a legal interest (such as a legal mortgage) the collateral taker will generally win. This is on the basis that the collateral taker is equity's darling.

5 *Dearle v Hall* (1828) 3 Russ 1, [1824–34] All ER Rep 28. Where the collateral assets comprise securities held in global custody, the well advised collateral taker will give immediate written notice of its interest to the global custodian.

6 Registration of Security Interests: Company Charges and Property other than Land, Consultation paper No 164, 2002. A system of notice filing is proposed and, very broadly speaking, priority would be determined by the time of filing (rather than the time of creation of the security interest); however, purchase-money interests (where the collateral asset was purchased with money advanced by the collateral taker) would have priority over previously filed security interests.

Security interests

4.19 The above sensitivities apply to any type of collateral structure. Additionally, the following sensitivities should be considered where the interest of the collateral taker consists of a security interest (as opposed to an outright collateral transfer).

PERFECTION

4.20 It is a general principle of commercial law that security interests require to be perfected before they are enforceable against third parties such as unsecured creditors of the collateral giver. 'Perfected' for this purpose does not mean 'made perfect', because even a perfected security interest may be defective, for example because it is weaker in priority than another perfected security interest. In this context, 'perfected' means potentially[1] enforceable against third parties. Perfection requirements often involve an act of publicity such as notarisation of the security agreement, or physical delivery of the collateral assets[2]. Perfection requirements vary from jurisdiction to jurisdiction and in relation to the types of security interest and/or underlying asset. At one extreme, an English law floating charge may be perfected merely by the execution of a valid agreement and identification of the pool of assets to which it relates. In contrast, civil law security interests may require notarisation of the security agreement and the inclusion of special forms of wording. In the case of financial collateral assets, it is necessary carefully to consider the type of account entries that are required to perfect a security interest.

Within the EU and in relation to financial collateral, the position will be simplified by the implementation of the Financial Collateral Directive, as discussed below.

1 Subject to priorities and any registration requirements.

2 The legal theory behind perfection is that, because property rights bind third parties, they should not become enforceable unless they are visible to third parties.

REGISTRATION

4.21 In the case of security interests created by a company incorporated in England and Wales, certain types of security interest are registrable[1]. Unless particulars of registrable charges so created are delivered to the Registrar of Companies within 21 days of the date of creation of the charge, the charge will be void as against the liquidator, administrator or any creditor of the company. In the international financial markets, two types of registrable charge regularly fall to be considered. These are floating charges (over any type of asset) and fixed charges over book debts[2]. Considerable legal effort is exerted in seeking so to structure collateral arrangements that such registrable charges are not created, in order to avoid the administrative burden and publicity involved in registration.

Sweeping reforms are proposed by the Law Commission[3]. In place of the above arrangements, a simplified electronic notice filing system is proposed, under which priority is generally determined by the time of filing. However, where the secured creditor advanced the purchase price of the collateral assets, their security interest (a 'purchase-money security interest') will take priority over an already filed non-purchase money security interest[4]. The 21-day time limit would not apply, and failure to file would not avoid the security, but would potentially result in loss of priority. It is proposed that all charges should be registrable unless excluded[5]. Exclusions are proposed for registered security interests over shares, and those involving delivery of certificates[6]. While certain 'quasi-security' arrangements (such as retention of title clauses and hire purchase agreements) would be registrable, it is proposed that repos should be excluded[7]. Interestingly, it is proposed to extend the regime to unincorporated businesses[8]. Global custodians will need to consider whether certain of their trustee and managed fund clients may be required to register the security interests they give to the global custodian.

1 Under s 395 et seq of the Companies Act 1985. Equivalent provisions for overseas companies having an established place of business in the England and Wales are contained in s 409 et seq.

2 The law relating to fixed charges over book debts has recently been clarified by *Agnew v IRC* [2001] UKPC 28, [2001] 2 AC 710, [2001] 3 WLR 454.

3 *Registration of Security Interests: Company Charges and Property other than Land*, Consultation paper No 164, 2002.

4 See paras 12.36. Depending on whether and how these proposals are implemented, this may be of particular assistance to prime brokers and custodians funding their client's purchases.

5 Paragraph 12.55.

6 Paragraph 12.59. The reference to certificates is somewhat anachronistic. The contemporary functional equivalent to the delivery of share certificates to support a security interest is crediting interests in the shares to a separate blocked account in the books of CREST (escrow balance), the custodian or other intermediary. However, this is not currently proposed to be excluded, and nor is any security interest over bonds. Exemptions are proposed for charges over bank accounts where the chargee takes control of the account; a similar approach for securities accounts may be desirable.

7 Paragraph 12.85. Express exclusion for collateral taken under outright transfers in relation to securities loans and swaps may also be desirable.

8 Paragraph 12.92.

RIGHT OF USE

4.22 It was indicated above that the essential feature of a security interest, which distinguishes it from an outright collateral transfer, is that the collateral giver retains a residual property right in the collateral assets, known as the equity of redemption[1]. The equity of redemption entitles the collateral giver to the return of the original collateral assets upon the discharge of the secured obligation. Because the collateral giver retains a property right in the collateral assets, the collateral taker is in general not free to dispose of them in the absence of collateral giver default, but must hold the original collateral assets available for return upon the discharge of the secured obligation[2]. While certain techniques have been developed with a view to reconciling a right of use with the equity of redemption, they are rarely both legally robust and commercially appropriate in the international financial markets, and it is difficult to obtain clean legal opinions in relation to them.

This creates a real tension in practice, for the following reason. It was indicated above (in the discussion of outright collateral transfers) that institutional collateral takers are under commercial pressure to use the assets they receive from collateral givers to collateralise their own obligations to third parties. It was also indicated that in such cases, the appropriate arrangement is for the assets to be received under an outright collateral transfer, which confers such a right of use. However, there are cases in which a collateral taker, who requires a right of use, is unable to take collateral under an outright transfer, and must receive it under a security interest. As discussed below, these include cases where the insolvency jurisdiction of the counterparty does not permit insolvency set off[3], and where recharacterisation risk is present[4]. Such cases should be carefully considered on a case by case basis. As discussed below, in wholesale transactions within the EU relating to financial collateral, a right of use will be conferred by the implementation of the Financial Collateral Directive. This will serve to erode the legal difference between outright collateral transfers and security interests, following the US model.

1 It can be of considerable importance for taxation purposes that the giver of collateral should retain the ability to enjoy an asset as the 'owner' of that asset (see, for example, *J Sainsbury plc v O'Connor* [1991] STC 318). If beneficial ownership were to pass to a collateral taker, the collateral giver could be treated as having disposed of the property and would realise a taxable gain or a loss for taxation purposes. Furthermore, in the context of withholding tax, an exemption from withholding tax could (depending on the terms of the exemption) cease to apply unless the collateral giver were to remain beneficially entitled to interest payments. Finally, if beneficial ownership were to pass, a charge to *ad valorem* stamp duty/SDRT could arise. (See also para **10.33**.)

2 The general rule is that a contractual provision which is incompatible with the equity of redemption may not be effectively included in the collateral contract. 'The principle invoked by the Plaintiff is summed up in the epigrammatic formula "once a mortgage always a mortgage". Whenever a transaction is in reality one of mortgage, equity regards the mortgaged property as security only for money, and will permit of no attempt to clog, fetter, or impede the borrower's right to redeem and to rescue what was, and still remains, in equity his own': *Marquess of Northampton v Pollock* (1890) 45 Ch D 190 at 215, per Bowen LJ. For a fuller discussion of this area of law, see Benjamin *Interests in Securities* (2000, OUP), ch 5, section C.

3 However, as discussed in Chapter 5, within the EU the Insolvency Regulation and the Banking Winding Up Directive protect insolvency set off which is permitted by the law governing the claim of the insolvent, even where the law of the insolvency jurisdiction does not permit it.

4 As discussed below, the Financial Collateral Directive provides protection against recharacterisation risk in wholesale transactions within the EU.

Outright collateral transfers

4.23 The previous section considered certain legal sensitivities potentially associated with security interests. This section will consider key legal sensitivities potentially associated with outright collateral transfers.

INSOLVENCY SET OFF AND NETTING

4.24 As indicated above, a security interest confers a property right in the collateral assets on the collateral taker. This protects the collateral taker in the insolvency of the collateral giver in the following way. Only assets belonging to the insolvent are available to the insolvency official to make available to general creditors. Because the collateral assets are impressed with the property rights of the collateral taker, they are not available to the insolvency official until the collateral taker has been paid off, and these rights are discharged. Thus, a perfected and enforceable security interest is protected from the collateral giver's insolvency under the most basic principle of insolvency law, namely the principle that third party assets are not available to general creditors.

In contrast, an outright collateral transfer protects the collateral taker in the insolvency of the collateral giver through insolvency set off, as indicated above. Under English law, insolvency set off of mutual debits and credits is mandatory[1]. However, it is crucial to note that the circumstances in which mandatory insolvency set off operates are strictly controlled[2]. In certain systems of law, insolvency set off is available only in narrowly defined circumstances, which may not include standard financial collateral arrangements. For these reasons, it is important to establish that the default arrangements of a proposed outright collateral transfer would be recognised under the system of law that would govern the insolvency of the counterparty. If it may not be, outright collateral transfer is not appropriate, and a security interest should be considered. Protection is provided by each of the Financial Collateral Directive[3], the Insolvency Regulation[4] and the Banking Winding Up Directive[5].

Many collateralised transactions are entered into (together with large numbers of like transactions) under the terms of master agreements. Such master agreements contain close out netting provisions. Close out netting is a procedure which takes place upon the default of either party, as a preliminary to set off. Very broadly speaking, close out netting may involve four stages:

(1) All outstanding transactions are accelerated so as to be 'closed'[6] immediately (ie the collateralised exposure becomes repayable, and equivalent collateral redeliverable, immediately).
(2) All non-cash obligations are converted into debts (so that the obligation to redeliver equivalent collateral is converted into an obligation to pay its current market price).
(3) All debts in a currency other than the contractually specified base currency are converted into base currency at an agreed rate of exchange.
(4) All debts are aggregated.

At this stage, the parties should each owe the other a single debt. As mutual debits and credits, these are candidates for insolvency set off.

Certain jurisdictions restrict the availability of close out netting. As a precondition to insolvency set off, it is important for the collateral taker to ensure that close out netting is available under the insolvency law of the collateral giver. Protection is provided by the Financial Collateral Directive and the Banking Winding Up Directive[7] (but unfortunately not the Insolvency Regulation)[8].

1 Under Insolvency Rules 1986, r 4.90.
2 Rule 4.90 requires, inter alia, that debits and credits should be mutual (ie owed by each party in the same capacity) in order to be set off. This raises potential sensitivities in relation to agency and trust transactions.
3 See below.

4 As discussed in Chapter 5, The Insolvency Regulation provides that, in general, the law of the forum will determine the availability of insolvency set off. However, even where the law of the forum does not permit set off, creditors may nevertheless set off their claims against the claims of the insolvent where the law governing the latter claims set off.

5 As with the Insolvency Regulation, the law of the forum will determine the availability of insolvency set off, but even where this does not permit set off, creditors may nevertheless set off their claims against the claims of the insolvent where the law governing the latter claims permits set off. See Chapter 5.

6 In *Drexel Burnham Lambert International v Mohamed El Nasr* [1986] 1 Lloyd's Rep 356 at 359, Staughton J refers to '. . . the process described as closing – or by those with a fondness for the unnecessary adverb, closing out.'

7 Article 25.

8 Discussed below.

RECHARACTERISATION RISK

4.25 If the availability of insolvency set off is the first major precondition for robust outright collateral transfers, the second is the absence of recharacterisation risk. In general terms, recharacterisation risk is the risk that the courts may reject the characterisation that the parties have given to a transaction, for example by declaring that a purported property license is a lease, or that a purported fixed charge is a floating charge. Recharacterisation is generally based on the principle[1] that the courts look to the substance and not the form of a transaction. In relation to purported outright collateral transfers, the sensitivity is that the courts may declare the transaction to be a security interest. This is potentially undesirable for a number of reasons, including the danger that a security interest may be avoidable for want of registration[2].

English law is slow to recharacterise outright collateral transfers, and in general will only do so if the transaction is a sham, or contains provisions which are legally inconsistent with outright transfer[3]. Provided industry standard documentation is used in accordance with its terms, recharacterisation risk is likely to be absent, and standard form opinions to this effect have been prepared by leading trade associations. However, a number of commercially important jurisdictions would recharacterise purported outright collateral transfers. It is important to address recharacterisation risk, not only under the governing law of the agreement, but also under the insolvency jurisdiction of the counterparty as well as, ideally, under the law of the jurisdiction where the collateral assets are located[4].

1 Derived from the law of equity.

2 For a note of other disadvantages of such recharacterisation, see J Benjamin 'Recharacterisation and Conflict of Laws', in *Butterworths Journal of International Banking and Financial Law*, December 1997.

3 See *Welsh Development Agency v Export Finance Co Ltd* [1992] BCLC 148.

4 Admittedly, this last step is not customary, except where very large values are involved. As discussed in Chapter 5, the Banking Winding Up Directive provides that repurchase agreements (which rely on outright transfer) are governed solely by their contractual governing law: art 26. However, it is not clear that this will address recharacterisation risk, as the latter is not purely a matter of contractual construction, but relates to the proprietary effect of a contract. Further protection is provided in EU wholesale transactions by the Financial Collateral Directive, as discussed below.

For collateral comprising securities held in custody

4.26 This section will consider sensitivities that arise where the custody portfolio is used as collateral, looking in turn at points that may arise in all cases; at those that arise when the collateral taker is a custodian; and at those that arise when the collateral taker is a prime broker.

In all structures – intermediation and lex situs

4.27 As discussed in Chapter 1, global custody involves intermediation, in the sense that one or more custodian, sub-custodian, depositary or other intermediary stands between the client and the issuer of underlying securities. An interesting legal question is posed by the such intermediation. As indicated in Chapter 5, it is a general principle of private international law that property rights (including those enjoyed by collateral takers) are determined by the law of the place where the assets in question are legally located, or *lex situs*. Where, for example, interests in bonds are held by a London global custodian for its client, through (in turn) Euroclear (in Belgium) and a local depositary (in Italy), the question arises whether the client's assets are located in London, Belgium or Italy. Where the client seeks to deliver those assets as collateral to a bank, the bank has to determine the location of the assets as a precondition of establishing (if it has taken a security interest) that its interest is perfected and (if it has taken an outright collateral transfer) arguably, that recharacterisation risk is absent.

As discussed in Chapter 5, the better view is that such assets are located in the jurisdiction of the account to which they are credited, ie England in the case of assets credited to an account maintained by a London custodian. This approach simplifies tremendously the legal and operational aspects of cross-border financial collateral, and a number of law reform initiatives (considered in Chapter 5) are being developed in order to ensure that it applies. However, until that process of law reform is complete, cross-border collateral arrangements must be considered on a case by case basis.

In favour of global custodian

4.28 In addition to the issues discussed above, the following sensitivities should be considered where the global custodian seeks to use its client's custody assets as collateral for the global custodian's exposures to the client. Some types of client present legal sensitivities related to their institutional nature. For example, local authorities are restricted from creating charges to s 47(7) of the Local Government and Housing Act 1989, and there is a debate as to whether charges created by trustees over trust assets should be registered against the trustee or the beneficial owner[1]. However, such issues are beyond the scope of this discussion.

1 However, see Law Commission Consultation Paper No 164.

CLIENT'S FREEDOM TO DEAL

4.29 One of the major services performed by the global custodian for its clients is to settle its client's transactions, including of course the delivery of assets out of the custody portfolio when the client or its agent so instructs. At an operational level, the custodian's systems may provide for 'straight through processing', as discussed in Chapter 8, whereby client instructions are implemented automatically, without human intervention. At a commercial level, the client may expect all such transactions to be promptly settled, and will be unwilling for the global custodian to restrict its asset management strategy in any way. However, there may be good commercial and legal reasons for the custodian to restrict the automatic settlement of all client instructions[1].

1 See Chapter 8 for a more developed discussion.

CREDIT LIMITS

4.30 The following is a commercial rather than a legal point. A global custodian's credit policy may require that uncollateralised exposures to the client above a certain limit should be assessed by senior staff before they are incurred. The commercial effect of settling a transaction may be very significantly to reduce the value of the collateral relative to the exposure (either because it depletes the portfolio, or because it increases the exposure). Prior credit assessment will not be possible if implementation of settlement instructions is automatic. This may be an argument for limiting the circumstances in which client instructions are implemented 'straight through'.

FLOATING CHARGE

4.31 As discussed above, it is the hallmark of a floating charge that the collateral giver is free to remove assets from the collateral pool without the consent of the collateral taker. The legal risk therefore arises that the collateral interest of the global custodian is a floating charge, notwithstanding the terminology used in the relevant documentation, unless the client is willing to make the settlement of transactions that deplete the collateral pool subject to the consent of the global custodian. In practice, most custodians do not seek to impose such terms. However, because of the disadvantages associated with floating charges[1], custodians have negotiated appropriate settlement restrictions where very major credit exposures are involved[2].

1 These include registrability, low priority and potential insolvency avoidance. See J Benjamin *Interests in Securities* (2000, OUP), p 103 for further detail.

2 Arguably, since the decision in *Agnew v IRC* [2001] UKPC 28, [2001] 2 AC 710, [2001] 3 WLR 454, it would be necessary also to restrict the client's freedom to withdraw proceeds of sale from custody cash accounts in order to avoid the danger of recharacterisation as a floating charge.

NOT LIEN

4.32 Traditional custody documentation often describes the interest of the custodian as a lien. However, this does not remove the very real risk that such an interest will be recharacterised by the courts as a floating charge, because the courts look to the substance and not the form of transactions. In most cases the substance of the transaction will not suggest a lien. The first reason for this is that, broadly speaking, a contractual lien is a possession-based security interest, and cannot relate to intangible assets such as those generally making up the custody portfolio. Second, standard drafting grants the custodian a power of sale on the default of the client. A contractual lien confers a right to retain possession, but not a right of sale[1]. A security interest over intangibles which confers a right of sale on the collateral taker and a right of withdrawal on the collateral giver is (in the authors' view) likely to be characterised as a floating charge.

1 A banker's lien confers a right of sale. However, the custodian's lien is not a banker's lien (even if the custodian happens to be a bank) because it holds the assets as custodian, and not as a banker (eg for the purpose of presenting instruments for payment): *Brandao v Barnett*, per Lord Campbell, cited in Palmer *Bailment (*2nd edn, Sweet & Maxwell), p 879.

The case of *Trident International Ltd v Barlow* [1999] 2 BCLC 506 held a purported lien with a contractual power of sale could take effect in accordance with its terms. However, it is submitted that the case does not assist here, as it related to tangible goods, so that the security interest with a power of sale could take effect as a pledge. Pledges are not registrable as they involve dispossession of the collateral giver, which is visible to third parties; the chief purpose of registration is rendering security interests registrable. On this basis, the principle in that case would not apply where the collateral assets are intangible. The authors are grateful to Mark Evans of Travers Smith Braithwaite for this point.

In favour of prime broker

4.33 The economic basis for the low rates of interest charged by the prime broker to its hedge fund clients is the prime broker's ability to use the client assets for its own account. Thus, as indicated above, the prime broker is permitted to remove assets from the client's account (for example, in order to deliver them to a third party under a repo transaction), subject to a contractual obligation to return equivalent assets to the client's account. Because the client assets also serve as collateral for the prime broker's exposure to its client, the following points arise.

RIGHT OF USE

4.34 Characteristically, the prime broker's collateral interest in the client assets arises under a security interest. In some cases, it is provided in the terms and conditions of business that, should the prime broker elect to remove assets from the client account, this security interest will be automatically converted into an outright collateral transfer. Under English law (and prior to the implementation, or outside the scope, of the Financial Collateral Directive) such provision may by contractually invalid under the rules discussed above which protect the equity of redemption. The implications for the collateral interest of the prime broker must be assessed[1]. Also, on the prime broker's insolvency, the hedge fund client may be exposed. This is because the value of its assets held by the prime broker may exceed the value of its borrowings from the prime broker by a significant margin[2]. It may be unable to recover this margin from the insolvent prime broker if the assets have been delivered out to a third party collateral taker. This raises the prospect of the third party collateral taker facing a tracing action from the hedge fund client. However, such an action may be unlikely to succeed where the third party is a good faith purchaser of the legal interest in the disputed securities, for value and without notice of the client's equity of redemption[3].

1 It might be argued that there can be no continuing security interest, because the removal of the original assets from the prime broker's hands extinguishes the original security interest. Further, the receipt by the prime broker of equivalent collateral at a time after the delivery of original collateral may raise priority problems, and insolvency displacement risk. However, the Financial Collateral Directive provides protection against the latter, as discussed below.
2 Unfortunately, the reverse proved to be the case in the default of LTCM.
3 Under the rule in *Pilcher v Rawlins* (1872) 7 Ch App 259 discussed above.

FLOATING CHARGE

4.35 The collateral pool held by the prime broker is likely to change from time to time, for two reasons. First, the hedge fund client will continue to manage the portfolio in the normal course, disposing of old assets and acquiring new assets. As discussed above, an unfettered right on the part of the client to remove assets from the collateral pool may cause collateral interest to be recharacterised as a floating charge. Therefore the prime broker may wish to reserve the right to decline to settle instructions that deplete the collateral pool. Second, the prime broker will from time to time remove securities from the pool for its own use, replacing them with a contractual redelivery obligation, and in due course returning equivalent securities. However, this latter point should not raise recharacterisation risk, as the hallmark of a floating charge is the collateral *giver*'s freedom to deal in the assets, and the prime broker is the collateral *taker*.

The Financial Collateral Directive[1]

4.36 In the last decade, significant industry and public sector effort has been devoted to addressing legal risk in the use of financial assets as collateral, and this has led to a number of collateral related law reform initiatives. This section will consider the Financial Collateral Directive ('the Directive'). Other key initiatives concerned primarily with insolvency and the conflict of laws, but highly relevant to collateral, are discussed in Chapter 5.

1 2002/47/EC, OJ L168, 27 June 2002, pp 43–50. See D Turing 'The EU Collateral Directive' (2002) 5 JIBFL 187.

Progress

4.37 In its 1999 Financial Services Action Plan[1], the European Commission emphasised the importance of addressing legal risk in cross-border financial collateral arrangements[2], and identified the introduction of the Directive as a 'priority 1' action[3]. The Directive is due to be implemented in member states by the end of 2003.

1 *Financial Services: Implementing the Framework for Financial Markets: Action Plan*, Communication of the Commission, Com (1999) 232, 11 May 1999.
2 'Work on the implementation of the Settlement . . . Finality Directive shows the importance of common rules for collateral pledged to payment and securities systems. Priority should be given to further progress in the field of collateral beyond this field. The mutual acceptance and enforceability of cross-border collateral is indispensable for the stability of the EU financial system and for a cost-effective and integrated securities settlement structure. At present, these conditions are not fulfilled: there is a higher risk of invalidation of cross-border collateral arrangements and uncertainty as regards enforceability should the collateral provider become insolvent. If such difficulties are not resolved, cross-border securities transactions will be subject to higher costs and risks' (p 8).
3 In relation to priority 1 actions the Commission indicates 'There is broad consensus that these actions call for immediate attention. These measure are crucial to realisation of the full benefits of the euro and to ensuring the competitiveness of the Union's financial services sector and industry whilst safeguarding consumer interests' (p 21).

Overview

4.38 The Directive complements the Settlement Finality Directive[1] and the insolvency related directives discussed in Chapter 5. It addresses the legal risk associated with financial collateral, particularly that associated with the differing provisions of national insolvency laws within the EU[2]. The Directive seeks to facilitate the use of cash and securities collateral[3] in the wholesale financial markets[4] through a number of measures. These inter alia disapply certain provisions of insolvency law. Their overall effect is to protect the position of the collateral taker. The recitals state the objective of establishing '[a] Community regime . . . for the provision of securities and cash as collateral under both security interest and title transfer structures including repurchase agreements (repos). This will contribute to the integration and cost-efficiency of the financial markets as well as to the stability of the financial system in the Community . . .'[5] The Directive is thus intended to facilitate the implementation of the common monetary policy[6].

The Directive seeks to achieve these aims by removing formal requirements[7]; providing insolvency protection for collateral arrangements, close out netting, margining and substitution[8]; confirming that the law applicable to questions of property rights and enforcement is the law of the place where the account to which they are credited is maintained[9]; facilitating enforcement[10]; permitting the use of collateral by the collateral taker[11]; and addressing recharacterisation risk for outright collateral transfers[12]. These provisions are considered in turn below.

1 See Chapter 8.
2 See European Parliament *Recommendation for Second Reading*, 24 April 2002, p 6.
3 Article 1(4)(a). Member states may exclude collateral consisting of the shares of the collateral giver and comparable arrangements: art 1(4)(b). Such assets are excludable as they are directly linked to the means of production of the collateral provider.
4 Retail transactions are excluded by the criteria set out in art 1(2), discussed below.
5 Recital 3.
6 Recital 12. See also *Communication from the Commission to the European Parliament*, March 2002, SEC (2002) 278 final, p 2: 'The proposed directive seeks to resolve the main problems affecting cross-border use of collateral in wholesale financial markets. It therefore promotes integration of the European financial market and secures the full benefits of the single currency.'
7 Article 3.
8 Articles 7 and 8.
9 Article 9.
10 Article 4.
11 Article 5.
12 Article 6.

Removing formal requirements

4.39 Article 3 removes the requirement for formalities (such as execution of a deed, notarisation, advertisement etc)[1] for the creation, validity, perfection, enforceability or admissibility in evidence of collateral arrangements[2]. However, in order to address fraud risk[3], the Directive does require in effect that the collateral taker should have possession or control of the collateral assets[4]. Moreover, the Directive applies only to financial collateral once it has been provided and if that provision can be evidenced in writing or in a legally equivalent manner[5]. Such evidencing must (broadly) identify the collateral assets; identification of the relevant account is sufficient for this purpose[6]. On this basis, where interests in securities[7] are delivered as collateral, no formalities beyond book entry transfers are required[8]. It might be argued that the Directive, once implemented, removes the need to register fixed charges over book debts under the Companies Act 1985; in this connection, it will be interesting to see how the Directive is implemented in the UK[9].

1 Article 4 of the original Proposal gave a non-exhaustive list of such formalities; this now appears in Recital 10.
2 Article 3(1).
3 See Recital 10.
4 Article 2(2).
5 Articles 1(5) and 3(2). 'In this respect it should be noted that the common position aims at providing a balance between market efficiency, which is the reason behind the exclusion of formal acts, and the safety of the parties to the arrangement and third parties, thereby avoiding inter alia the risk of fraud': *Statement of the Council's Reasons*, 5 March 2002, 5530/3/02 REV 3 ADD 1, p 8. An example of evidencing which is legally equivalent to writing is the taping of telephone conversations: ibid, p 6.
6 Article 1(5). See, however, *Statement of the Council's Reasons*, 5 March 2002, 5530/3/02 REV 3 ADD 1, p 6: 'The financial collateral arrangement must be evidenced in writing or in any other legally enforceable manner provided for by the law applicable to the financial collateral arrangement, eg taped telephone conversations.'
7 'For the purposes of this Directive, acts required under the law of a Member State as conditions for transferring or creating a security interest on financial instruments other than book entry securities, such as an endorsement in the case of instruments to order, or recording on the issuer's register in the case of registered instruments, are not considered as formal acts': *Statement of the Council's Reasons*, 5 March 2002, 5530/3/02 REV 3 ADD 1, p 8.
8 The text of the Directive suggests that either crediting the assets to the account of the collateral taker,

or to a special account of the collateral giver (where they are not subject to the collateral giver's control, such as escrow accounts in CREST), will be sufficient: see art 2(2). However, the text of implementing legislation should be carefully examined to determine whether this remains the position once the Directive is implemented.

9 See also Law Commission consultation paper 164.

Insolvency protection

4.40 Article 7 provides for the recognition of close out netting provisions, ensuring that they can take effect in accordance with their terms, notwithstanding the winding-up or reorganisation of either party[1] or interveners[2], and without formalities[3].

Article 8 protects collateral arrangements[4] from insolvency displacement on the basis of zero hour rules[5]; hardening periods[6]; and (broadly) where the relevant insolvency event having taken place on the same day as the collateral arrangement, collateralised obligation or collateral delivery, where the collateral taker did not have actual or constructive notice of it[7]. Margining or mark to market and substitution provisions are protected from displacement on the basis of hardening periods, zero hour rules[8] and the absence of new money[9]. However, by virtue of art 8(4), these provisions are '. . . without prejudice to existing ex-post judiciary safeguards, which remain necessary in the case of ill-faith and commercially unreasonable transactions.'[10]

1 Article 7(1)(a).
2 Article 7(1)(b). This provides that close out netting provisions will take effect in accordance with their terms notwithstanding (inter alia) any purported assignment. While helpful to collateral takers, this may be unhelpful to some securitisations, which may rely on silent assignments.
3 Other than those agreed by the parties, such as notice: art 7(2).
4 Improving on the drafting of the original Proposal, art 8 serves to protect both the collateral contract and the delivery of assets pursuant to it.
5 Article 8(1)(a).
6 Article 8(1)(b).
7 Article 8(2).
8 Article 8(3)(i).
9 Article 8(3)(ii).
10 See also *Communication from the Commission to the European Parliament*, March 2002, SEC (2002)278 final, p 4. See also *Statement of the Council's Reasons*, 5 March 2002, 5530/3/02 REV 3 ADD 1, p 12, and Recital 16: '. . . this article does not prejudice the possibility of questioning the financial collateral arrangement and the provision of financial collateral as part of the initial provision, top-up or substitution of financial collateral, under national law for *other* reasons [than the timing of the provision of the original, top-up or substitute collateral], for example where this has been done intentionally to the detriment of the other creditors (this covers inter alia actions based on fraud or similar avoidance rules which may apply in a prescribed period).'

Enforcement

4.41 Article 4 provides for the collateral taker, upon the default of the collateral giver[1], to realise securities collateral by sale, appropriation[2] or set off[3] and to realise cash collateral by set off[4].

1 Note that the enforcement provisions in the Directive are not reciprocal, even through the standard close out netting provisions in outright collateral transfer arrangements are reciprocal, ie apply equally to collateral giver and collateral taker.
2 Appropriation is only possible if it has been agreed to by the parties, and valuation has been agreed upon: art 4(2). Member states not permitting appropriation on the date on which the Directive comes into force are not obliged to permit it pursuant to the Directive: art 4(3).
3 Article 4(1)(a).

4 Article 4(1)(b). Interestingly, the different drafting for cash and securities collateral suggests that the Directive favours *Re Charge Card Services Ltd* [1987] 1 Ch 150, [1986] 3 WLR 697, [1986] 3 All ER 289 over *Re BCCI (No 8)* [1995] Ch 46, [1994] 3 WLR 911, [1994] 3 All ER 565. See the discussion on charge backs in J Benjamin *Interests in Securities* (2000, OUP), pp 109, 110.

Right of use[1]

4.42 Article 5 in effect protects provisions in collateral agreements conferring a right of use, even where the collateral assets have been provided under a security interest[2]. Where the collateral taker exercises this right of use, it incurs a contractual obligation (broadly) to replace the original assets with equivalent assets[3], which upon default is set off against the collateralised obligation[4]. The collateral taker's interest in such redelivered assets is protected generally[5], and from priority and insolvency displacement problems that might otherwise arise due to their not having formed part of the original collateral delivery[6].

1 These provisions do not alter the position that the right of use involves a credit exposure for the collateral giver, as discussed earlier.
2 Article 5(1). It improves on the drafting of the original Proposal (art 6), which discussed the right of use but did not confer it.
3 Article 5(2). Alternatively, the collateral arrangements may provide for automatic set off (even in the absence of default): art 5(2), second para.
4 Article 5(5).
5 The drafting of art 5(4) appears obscure to the authors. However, the above interpretation accords with the comments in *Statement of the Council's Reasons*, 5 March 2002, 5530/3/02 REV 3 ADD 1, p 10. The *Communication from the Commission to the European Parliament* March 2002 SEC (2002) 278 final, pp 7, 8 comments that 'The new paragraph 4 in Article 5 in the Common Position makes it clear that the use of collateral does not invalidate the collateral arrangement vis-à-vis third parties for the reason that the collateral is not in the possession or under the control of the collateral [taker] as required in Articles 1(5) and 2(2).'
6 Article 5(3). Equivalent collateral is treated as subject to the same security interest as the original collateral, and provided at the same time.

Recharacterisation risk

4.43 Article 6 requires member states to ensure that outright collateral transfer arrangements can take effect in accordance with their terms[1], subject to default close out netting[2]. This serves to address the risk that such arrangements might be recharacterised as security interests.

1 Article 6(1). This is an improvement on the drafting of the equivalent provision in the original Proposal (art 7), which in effect provided that such arrangements *would* take effect in accordance with their terms, thus appearing to prevent recharacterisation even where the arrangement was a sham, or contains provisions which are inconsistent with outright transfer. By providing that such arrangements *can* take effect in accordance with their terms, art 6 of the Directive is compatible with existing English case law, which recognises transfer of title *provided* contractual provisions reflect the genuine intention of parties and nothing in the arrangement is inconsistent with outright transfer.
2 Article 6(2).

Criteria[1]

4.44 In order to benefit from the Directive, each of the parties must be[2]:

- a public authority[3];
- a public bank, ie a central bank, the ECB, the BIS, a multilateral development bank, the IMF or the EIB[4];

- a financial institution subject to prudential supervision[5];
- an infrastructure service provider, ie a CCP, settlement agent or clearing house[6];
- trustees acting for bondholders or for any of the above[7]; or
- a counterparty (other than a natural person)[8] to any of the above[9].

The last criterion (counterparty to any of the above) was not included in the original Proposals. This raised concerns that many economically important collateral arrangements were excluded, including the collateralisation of securities lending from pension funds[10] and collateralised swaps with special purpose vehicles in structured finance arrangements. However, the inclusion of the counterparty criterion significantly extends the scope of the Directive, in effect requiring only one institutional party, whereas the original Proposal required two.

1 The policy reasoning behind the threshold criteria may have been as follows. The proposals significantly enhance the position of collateral takers relative to unsecured creditors, and in this respect represent an erosion of the pari passu principle. They could therefore not be justified if their application were general, and in particular should not apply to retail arrangements. However, between major financial institutions, the systemic benefits of addressing legal risk in collateralisation may outweigh the policy objections to eroding the pari passu principle.
2 Article 1(2). The original Proposal included a threshold criterion of a capital base of €100 million or gross assets of €1000 million (art 2.4(c)); this does not appear in the Directive.
3 Article 1(2)(a).
4 Article 1(2)(b).
5 Article 1(2)(c). Unlike the original Proposal, the Directive gives a non-exhaustive list of financial institutions subject to prudential supervision including (i) credit institutions, (ii) investment firms, (iii) financial institutions, (iv) insurance undertakings, (v) UCITS and (vi) UCITS' management companies.
6 Article 12(2)(c).
7 Article 1(2)(d).
8 Many fund and SPV structures are constituted as trusts and partnerships. These appear to be included.
9 Article 1(2)(e). Member states may opt out of this provision: art 1(3).
10 It is not clear that a pension fund is subject to prudential regulation for the purposes of the threshold criteria.

Floating charges

4.45 As discussed above, the collateral interest of the global custodian over the client's portfolio will in many cases be characterisable as a floating charge, because of the client's freedom to remove assets from the portfolio. While a range of opinion has been expressed on the point, the authors would argue that the Directive does not apply to floating charges. Article 2(2) in effect requires dispossession, or the transfer of control of the collateral to the collateral taker[1]. Because the defining characteristic of a floating charge is that the collateral taker retains some measure of control over the collateral assets, as discussed above, it would be prudent to assume that art 2(2) serves to exclude floating charges from the Directive.

1 'References in this Directive to financial collateral being "provided", or to the "provision" of financial collateral, are to the financial collateral being delivered, transferred, held, registered or otherwise designated so as to be in the possession or under the control of the collateral taker or of a person acting on the collateral taker's behalf.' The words 'or otherwise designated' do not remove the requirement for the collateral taker to have possession or control, but are subject to that requirement.

Policy issues

4.46 The original proposal for the Directive was controversial, as it enhanced the position of the collateral taker at the expense of that of the collateral giver and its general creditors. Some commentators have argued that it represented the assertion of Anglo-Saxon (and particularly New York) legal concepts and business practices that are in many respects at odds with continental European law and practice[1]. There are indications that the drafting of the final form of the Directive has sought in some measure to respond to such concerns[2].

1 In particular, the proposal to confer a right of use on the collateral taker reflects the provisions of art 9 of the US Uniform Commercial Code, but cuts across established principles of some systems of continental civil law, which protect the residual rights of the collateral giver in the collateral assets.

2 In relation to the right of use, Recital 19 provides that 'This reuse however should be without prejudice to national legislation about separation of assets and unfair treatment of creditors.' This tends to suggest that member states may require that the equity of redemption be protected by the segregation of collateral, so that it is not available for use by the collateral taker. However, this theme is not picked up in the body of the Directive. In the UK, the FSA client asset rules in effect relieve collateral takers of the usual duty to segregate collateral where there is a right of use: see r 9.4.3.

The original proposal provided that enforcement must be subject to any national legal requirements for commercial reasonableness in collateral realisation or valuation (art 5(4)). In the final form of the Directive, this provision is extended to include also commercial reasonableness in the calculation of collateralised obligations, and applies not only to enforcement, but also to the right of use, and the recognition of outright transfer arrangements and close out netting (art 4(6)). See also Recital 17.

Further, in relation to the types of collateral asset covered by the Directive, in art 1(4) 'Subparagraph (b) has been introduced to make sure that Member States may exclude from scope certain financial collateral which, although it might fall under the definition of financial instruments, is directly linked to the means of production of the collateral provider' (*Statement of the Council's Reasons*, 5 March 2002, 5530/3/02 REV 3 ADD 1, p 5).

Chapter 5*

Cross-border questions

5.1

> 'The expanding volume of cross-border securities transactions in recent years can be attributed to several factors. In a global context, these factors include technological advancement, the growth in size of financial markets as international capital movements have been liberalised and as financial deregulation has resulted in a wider range of financial products and services. In an EU-specific context, cross-border securities transactions have been further stimulated by the introduction of the euro . . .'[1]

The greater part of the legal complexity associated with global securities investment and collateral arrangements relates to their cross-border nature. Market participants need to know which system of law will determine a number of important legal questions, including the following:

- Will the client assets be at risk in the sub-custodian's insolvency?
- Does the collateral taker have a good interest in the collateral securities?

The treatment of these questions in cross-border situations will be considered at paras **5.14–5.18** and **5.19–5.32** respectively. Paragraphs **5.2–5.13** will provide a very brief introduction to the branch of law governing cross-border questions, known as the conflict of laws. The focus of the following discussion is the English conflict of laws rules.

The conflict of laws is a complex area, and important conflict of laws questions are far from settled. The discussion in this chapter is highly simplified and generalised. It is intended as an elementary introduction only, which suggests an initial approach to cross-border questions; for more precise analysis, readers are referred to the excellent textbooks which are available, and in particular to *Dicey and Morris*[2].

* The authors are grateful to Dr Eva Micheler, London School of Economics, for kindly reviewing this chapter. Any errors are their own.

1 The Giovannini Group *Cross-Border Clearing and Settlement Arrangements in the European Union*, Brussels, November 2001, p 7.

2 L Collins (ed) *Dicey and Morris on the Conflict of Laws* (2000, 13th edn, Sweet & Maxwell).

The conflict of laws

5.2 The areas of law that are important to global securities investment and collateral arrangements (including the law of property and insolvency law) differ from country to country[1]. For example, French insolvency law is fundamentally different from New York insolvency law. Financial arrangements may span countries whose systems of law provide different answers to key legal questions. Where the answer to a legal question depends upon which of several potentially relevant systems of law applies, it is clearly important to identify the applicable law. This is the role of conflict of laws rules.

Conflict of laws rules, also known as private international law, form part of the law of each country. Thus, where an English court hears a matter involving cross-border questions, it applies the English conflict of laws rules.

1 Or, to be precise, from jurisdiction to jurisdiction. 'Jurisdiction' in this context means law system, eg France, England and Wales, and New York. 'Jurisdiction' also means the power of a court to hear cases. Because of this dual meaning and in order to avoid confusion in the discussion of the jurisdiction of the courts below, the term 'country' is used to indicate 'law system'. Of course, 'country' is an inexact equivalent of 'law system': eg New York is the latter but not the former.

Jurisdiction

Overview

5.3 Where a cross-border matter requires litigation, the first issue to be determined is which court or courts have jurisdiction to hear it. The courts of a number of different countries may potentially have jurisdiction. Because their treatment of the questions in issue may differ, choice of forum[1] is often decisively important. This is a complex area of law, and jurisdiction clauses in global custody and collateral agreements should always be professionally drafted.

The rules of jurisdiction differ depending on whether or not the matter relates to insolvency.

1 That is, the choice of which country's courts will hear the matter.

Jurisdiction – non-insolvency

5.4 In non-insolvency matters, the position is currently somewhat fragmented.

(1) Where the defendant is domiciled in an EU member state other than Denmark, the position is now governed by the Brussels Regulation[1].
(2) Where the defendant is domiciled in Denmark, the position is governed by the Brussels Convention[2].
(3) Where the defendant is domiciled in EFTA[3] the position is governed by the Lugano Convention[4].
(4) Broadly, if the defendant is domiciled elsewhere, the rules of common law jurisdiction apply.

The rules under the Brussels and Lugano Conventions are broadly similar (although not identical with) those under the more recent Brussels Regulation. For the sake of simplicity, only the Brussels Regulation (1) and the common law rules (4) will be discussed below.

1 Council Regulation (EC) No 44/2001 on Jurisdiction and the Recognition and Enforcement of Judgments in Civil and Commercial Matters. This came into force (except in relation to Denmark: see art 1(3)) on 1 March 2002.
2 The Brussels Convention on Jurisdiction and the Enforcement of Judgements, as implemented in the UK by the Civil Jurisdiction and Judgments Act 1982.
3 The European Free Trade Area. However, Liechtenstein is excluded, and Poland is included.

4 The Lugano Convention on Jurisdiction and the Enforcement of Judgments, as implemented in the UK by the Civil Jurisdiction and Judgements Act 1982.

BRUSSELS REGULATION [1]

5.5 The Regulation generally applies to civil and commercial matters[2] (but not insolvency-related matters or arbitration)[3]. The rules determining jurisdiction under the Regulation are primarily based on the domicile of the defendant[4]. The general rule is that a defendant shall be sued in the member state where it is domiciled[5], and may be sued in another member state only in accordance with special rules of jurisdiction[6]. Different rules (designed to protect the weaker party)[7] apply in matters relating to insurance[8]; consumer contracts[9]; and individual contracts of employment[10]. In proceedings concerning any rem rights in immovable property[11], exclusive jurisdiction is conferred on the contracting state where the property is situated[12]. However, there is no such general provision for moveable property. The Regulation generally gives support to exclusive jurisdiction clauses[13].

1 For a general discussion, see W Kennett 'The Brussels I Regulation' (2001) ICLQ 725.
2 Article 1.
3 Article 1(2)(b) and (d).
4 A company or other legal person or association is domiciled where it has its statutory seat, or central administration, or principal place of business: art 60(1). In the UK, 'statutory seat' means registered office or, if none, place of incorporation or, if none, place under the law of which formation took place: see art 60(2).
5 Article 2(1).
6 Article 3(1).
7 See Recital 13.
8 Section 3.
9 Section 4. Provision in art 16 that a consumer may sue the contractual counterparty in either the counterparty's or its own domicile were resisted by those seeking to promote E-Commerce in the EU.
10 Section 5.
11 Whereas, in the domestic law of property, a distinction is made between real (ie land related) and personal property, in private international law the distinction is between immovable and movable property.
12 Article 22(1). Other cases where the Regulation confers exclusive jurisdiction include (broadly) proceedings concerning the constitution of companies; entries in public registers; patents, trademarks and designs; and the enforcement of judgments: art 22.
13 Article 23. In many cases, UK global custodians and collateral takers provide for the English courts to have non-exclusive jurisdiction, so that they have the option (but are not obliged) to litigate any dispute locally.

COMMON LAW REGIME[1]

5.6 The common law rules of jurisdiction apply where the European regime is inapplicable. Whereas the European regime discussed above is based on *domicile*, the common law regime discussed below is based on *presence*[2]. An English court has jurisdiction if the defendant is present (at the time of service of process, even fleetingly) in England, or submits to the jurisdiction of the court[3]. It would seem that this is the case even where the action relates to movable property which is situated in another country[4].

The circumstances in which process may be served on a defendant abroad are set out in the Civil Procedure Rules[5].

The English court may lose or, as a matter of discretion, decline jurisdiction which it prima facie has in accordance with certain rules[6].

1 A broadly similar picture emerges under the proposed Hague Convention on International Jurisdiction and Foreign Judgments in Civil and Commercial Matters. See Summary of the Outcome of the Discussion in commission II of the First part of the Diplomatic Conference 6–20 June 2001,

Interim Text Prepared by the Permanent Bureau and the Co-reporters, at www.hcch.net/e/workprog/judgm.html.

The Convention provides for the general enforceability of exclusive jurisdiction clauses (art 4). It contains no express provision relating to disputes concerning rights in rem in personal property (although there has been a proposal to prohibit the assertion of jurisdiction on the grounds of the presence in the jurisdiction of property belonging to the defendant, except where the dispute is directly related to that property (art 18(2)). However, there is no consensus on this issue (see para **5.24**, n 6)). Proposed art 12(1) provides (broadly) that in proceedings concerning rights in rem in immovable property, the court of the contracting state where the property is situated has exclusive jurisdiction. 'A general view very soon emerged to the effect that it must be possible for all actions relating to immovable property rights (challenging the title of property, for example) to be brought before the court of the place where the immovable property is situated. This is in fact a universally recognised jurisdiction . . .': Synthesis of the Work of the Special Commission of June 1997 on International Jurisdiction and the Effects of Foreign Judgments in Civil and Commercial Matters, drawn up by Catherine Kassedjian, November 1997, para 35. Insolvency proceedings are excluded from the scope of the Convention: art 2(e).

2 The rules of jurisdiction are in effect based on the ability to serve process; a claimant can serve as of right if a defendant is in England (even fleetingly); a claimant can only serve out of the jurisdiction with the permission of the court, which will only be granted if the case falls within one of those listed in the Civil Procedure Rules.

3 A well-drafted English jurisdiction clause (appointing an English process agent) will bring a defendant within the jurisdiction of the English court.

4 However, as indicated below, the practical value of a court order obtained in such an action may depend on its enforceability against the foreign assets.

5 Part 6 III (Special Provisions about Service Out of the Jurisdiction). The Civil Procedure Rules are available on www.ldc.gov.uk/civil/procrules_fin/. See also L Collins (ed) *Dicey and Morris on the Conflict of Laws* (2000, 13th edn, Sweet & Maxwell), para 8-049–052.

6 Including the following:

- The rule of sovereign immunity (codified in the State Immunity Act 1978, implementing the European Convention of State Immunity 1972) provides that a foreign state is generally immune from the jurisdiction of the English courts, subject to important exceptions (including an exception in relation to commercial transactions: see s 3(1) of the Act, according with the earlier common law rule reflected in *Trendtex v Central Bank of Nigeria* [1977] QB 529, [1977] 2 WLR 356, [1977] 1 All ER 881, CA).
- In accordance with the doctrine of *forum non conveniens* the English courts may inter alia stay or strike out an action when this is necessary to prevent injustice. This doctrine is based on the view that some other forum is more appropriate, and may be invoked to prevent forum shopping. See *Spiliada Maritime Corpn v Cansulex* [1987] AC 460, [1986] 3 WLR 972, [1986] 3 All ER 843; *Re Harrods (Buenos Aires) Ltd* [1992] Ch 72, [1991] 3 WLR 397, [1991] 4 All ER 334.
- The related doctrine of *lis alibi pendens* applies when simultaneous actions are pending in different contracting states involving the same parties and the same or related matters. In the case of simultaneous actions in England and (broadly) EC or EFTA countries, the Conventions require proceedings in the second jurisdiction to be stayed, and jurisdiction to be declined, in certain circumstances. A broad commonsense approach should be taken to determining whether two matters are 'related' for this purpose: see *Sarrio v Kuwait Investment Authority* [1999] 1 AC 32 at 41 per Lord Saville.
- The English court also has no jurisdiction in matters such as those concerning the validity of entries in public registers maintained in a contracting state other than the UK, where the Conventions confer exclusive jurisdiction on the court of that other contracting state.

Jurisdiction – insolvency[1]

5.7 Different rules of jurisdiction apply in insolvency. Clearly, these will be relevant in the insolvency of a UK sub-custodian. Also, in practice, legal disputes concerning collateral arrangements are most likely to arise in the context of insolvency[2]. (However, as discussed below, legal actions in which collateral arrangements are tested may or may not form part of insolvency proceedings.)

In the theory of the private international law of insolvency, two conflicting sets of principles determine the varying approaches of different courts to insolvency jurisdiction. Under the principles of universality and unity, one set of insolvency proceedings governs the insolvent's assets worldwide[3]. Under the principles of plurality and territoriality, each forum deals with assets located within its territory[4].

5.7 Cross-border questions

1 The rules of insolvency jurisdiction (and choice of law) are complex, and the following general comments are intended to be indicative only. For more detail, see Fletcher *Insolvency in Private International Law* (1999, Clarendon Press) and P Smart *Cross-Border Insolvency* (1998, 2nd edn, Butterworths).
2 This is because (broadly speaking) the purpose of collateral is to protect the collateral taker from the insolvency of the collateral giver by removing it from the ranks of unsecured creditors. Thus, it is in the insolvency of the collateral giver that the collateral taker is most interested in enforcing its rights in relation to the collateral (by legal action if necessary). Because effective collateralisation depletes the pool of assets available to general creditors, the insolvency official of the collateral giver may have an interest (and indeed a legal duty) to challenge the legal effectiveness of collateral arrangements. For these reasons, insolvency provides the richest source of collateral-related litigation.
3 See Recital 16 of the Winding Up Directive (2001/24).
4 In practice, a compromise between the two is usually reached.

EUROPEAN INSOLVENCY REGULATION

5.8 Within the EU, the position is governed by the European Insolvency Regulation[1]. The Regulation confers international insolvency jurisdiction on the courts of the member state within the territory in which the centre of a debtor's main interests is situated ('main proceedings'). In the case of a company or other legal person, its registered office is presumed to be its centre of main interests[2]. Recital 13 provides that the centre of main interests 'should correspond to the place where the debtor conducts the administration of his interests on a regular basis and is therefore ascertainable by third parties.' This should probably be taken to refer to management and not to the location of assets.

In addition, the courts of another member state where the debtor has an establishment[3] may open insolvency proceedings ('local proceedings'). Such local proceedings are restricted to assets of the debtor situated in that member state[4].

1 Council Regulation (EC) No 1346/2000 of 29 May 2000 on insolvency proceedings came into force on 31 May 2002 (except in Denmark – see Recital 33).
2 Article 3(1).
3 Article 2(h): '"establishment" shall mean any place of operations where the debtor carries out a non-transitory economic activity with human means and goods.' In the absence of local operations, the presence in the jurisdiction of local creditors and assets is insufficient.
4 Article 3(2). See also art 27.

RECOGNITION OF PROCEEDINGS

5.9 Main or local proceedings will be automatically recognised in all other member states[1]. If main proceedings have already been opened, local proceedings will proceed as secondary insolvency proceedings[2]. Main proceedings take automatic effect in all member states, provided local proceedings have not been opened[3]. Local proceedings are effective to restrict creditors' rights only in relation to local assets, or with the consent of creditors[4]. Provided no other insolvency proceedings have been opened, the liquidator in the main proceedings may exercise his powers in, and remove assets from, another member state. However, this is subject to third party rights in rem (including collateral interests) and reservation of title arrangements[5]. Judgments relating to either the main or local proceedings are automatically recognised in other member states, and must be enforced by them[6].

The Regulation applies to collective insolvency proceedings which entail the partial or total divestment of a debtor and the appointment of a liquidator[7]. Under UK law, this includes administration and members' voluntary winding up, but does not include administrative receivership[8].

1 Article 16(1).
2 Article 16(2). Article 33 provides a procedure whereby the liquidator in the main proceedings may request the stay of secondary proceedings.

3 Article 17(1).
4 Article 17(2).
5 Articles 18(1), 5 and 7. Of course reservation of title arrangements involve third party rights in rem. The better view is that art 5 (together with art 2(g)) does not create a new rule of conflict of laws whereby rights in rem in receivables are governed by lex situs as opposed to governing law. See art 95 of the Virgos Report. Clearly, this is a key concern in securitisations and related structures.
6 Article 25. A member state may refuse to recognise proceedings or enforce judgments relating to it on grounds of public policy: art 26.
7 Article 1(1).
8 The types of proceedings covered by the Regulation are listed in Annex A. See art 2(a).

EUROPEAN WINDING UP DIRECTIVE

5.10 As discussed in Chapter 4, the Regulation does not in general apply to insolvency proceedings concerning financial institutions[1]. In the reorganisation or winding up of credit institutions[2], the position will be governed by the European Winding Up Directive[3], which is due to be implemented in May 2004[4]. Under the Winding Up Directive, as also discussed in Chapter 4, authorities of the home member state where the credit institution is authorised are responsible for its reorganisation[5] and winding up[6], including that of offices in other member states.

1 Article 1(2): 'This Regulation shall not apply to insolvency proceedings concerning insurance undertakings, credit institutions, investment undertakings which provide services involving the holding of funds or securities for third parties, or to collective investment undertakings.' Pure reinsurance companies seem to be covered, however.
2 Under art 1(1) the Directive applies to EU credit institutions having their head office and branches in different member states. Certain of its provisions also apply to non-EU credit institutions having their head office outside the EU, but branches in at least two member states: art1(2).
3 Directive 2001/24/EC of 4 April 2001 on the reorganisation and winding up of credit institutions.
4 Article 34(1).
5 Article 3(1).
6 Article 9(1).

JURISDICTION OF ENGLISH COURTS

5.11 The English courts' jurisdiction to wind up a company depends on whether the company is English registered and, if it is not, whether there is a sufficient connection with England and Wales. The English courts have discretionary jurisdiction to wind up any company registered in England[1]. An unregistered company is a company not registered under the Companies Acts[2]. The English courts have jurisdiction to wind up an unregistered company if, broadly, the company has ceased business, is unable to pay its debts, or if it is just and equitable to do so[3]. In practice the English courts take a liberal approach to this provision, and may assume jurisdiction to wind up a foreign company if either the company at the time a petition is presented has assets in England, or at any time has carried on business in England either directly or through an agent, and in both cases where there is a reasonable possibility of benefit accruing to English creditors[4].

In principle, English insolvency relates to the assets of the insolvent irrespective of where they are located[5]. However, in practice, this universal approach may be limited by pragmatic difficulties of enforcement. The co-operation of foreign courts is required for enforcement of any order against foreign assets, and where insolvency proceedings are taken out in other countries, the English courts will in general seek to co-operate. The English courts do not necessarily limit their own jurisdiction over English assets of foreign companies in accordance with the same universal approach[6].

1 Insolvency Act 1986, s 117.
2 Insolvency Act 1986, s 220. 'Company' for this purpose is widely defined.

3 Insolvency Act 1986, s 221.
4 In practice it may also be necessary to show that there are no home state proceedings or that the home state liquidator agrees to the institution of an English liquidator, or alternatively that the foreign proceedings are prejudicial to English creditors. See the discussion of the relevant case law in Fletcher *Insolvency in Private International Law* (1999, Clarendon Press), pp 127–39.
5 Insolvency Act 1986, s 144.
6 As indicated above, the English courts may assume jurisdiction over the liquidation of a foreign company in certain circumstances. Where a court does so, its jurisdiction is not limited to an English branch of the company or its English assets, but in principle may extend to the whole of the company (although, if there is also a home-state proceeding an English court is likely to order that the English liquidation be ancillary, ie territorial.) Contrast this 'universal approach' to the 'ring fence' approach of Germany (where it is understood that local proceedings for a foreign company are confined to the local branch and local assets) and the 'no local proceedings' approach of Belgium (where it is understood that no local proceedings are held for a foreign company, but where there is recognition of home state liquidation).

Choice of law

5.12 Where an English court has assumed jurisdiction to hear a case, it is then necessary to determine which system of law will apply to each cross-border question it considers. An English court will apply foreign law to cross-border questions, where the English rules of private international law so require[1]. The court will hear evidence on the provisions of foreign law from expert witnesses such as foreign law academics or practitioners[2]. Of course, a single case may involve a number of different cross-border questions, and a different system of law may apply to each of these.

In general, the methodology of the English courts to choice of law questions involves a two stage process as follows[3]. First, each cross-border question is placed into a private international law category. English law as the law of the forum determines categorisation. Thus, where a custodian wrongly delivers client securities to a third party as collateral for the custodian's own borrowings, the English courts may categorise the ensuing dispute between the defrauded client and the third party as a matter of priorities.

Second, the courts refer to the rules of private international law to identify the factor linking questions within the relevant category to a particular system of law. For example, the connecting factor for priorities disputes[4] is the law of the place where the disputed assets are legally located, or lex situs[5].

In insolvency proceedings, courts will generally apply local insolvency law[6]. Within the EU, under the Insolvency Regulation, main proceedings[7] and local proceedings[8] are generally governed by the law of the forum[9]. For credit institutions, under the Winding Up Directive reorganisation[10] and winding up proceedings[11], they are generally governed by the law of the home member state (ie the member state where the credit institution is authorised). However, there are important exceptions to this general rule. The English courts may apply foreign law at the request of certain foreign courts[12]. Within the EU, both the Insolvency Regulation and the Winding Up Directive create special rules in relation to the availability of set off[13]; and post insolvency dispositions of (under the Insolvency Regulation) registered securities and (under the Winding Up Directive) book entry instruments[14]. The Insolvency Regulation creates special rules in relation to rights of and obligations to payment systems, settlement systems and financial markets[15]. The Winding Up Directive creates special rules in relation to property rights in registered or book entry instruments[16]; netting agreements[17]; repurchase agreements[18]; and transactions carried out on regulated markets[19].

1 In commercial matters, foreign law means foreign domestic law, and not foreign private international law. The problem of 'renvoi' arises when a reference to foreign law is taken to mean foreign private international law, which in turn refers the matter to a third jurisdiction (or indeed back to England, creating a hall of mirrors). See L Collins (ed) *Dicey and Morris on the Conflict of Laws* (2000, 13th edn, Sweet & Maxwell), vol I, p 66, para 4-005. Renvoi has long enchanted academics. It originated in nineteenth-century cases concerning the formal validity of wills. It is excluded by the Rome Convention on the Law Applicable to Contractual Obligations (art 15). English case law provides some argument that renvoi is inapplicable to commercial matters: see *Macmillan Inc v Bishopsgate Investment Trust plc (No 3)* [1995] 3 All ER 747 at 766, 777, per Millet J.

2 Foreign law must be proved by the parties as a question of fact. See L Collins (ed) *Dicey and Morris on the Conflict of Laws* (2000, 13th edn, Sweet & Maxwell), vol I, p 221, para 9-002. See also *Baker v Archer-Shee* [1927] AC 844 at 874, HL, per Lord Blanesburgh.

3 'Both parties accept that, at common law, the identification of the appropriate law may be viewed as involving a three-stage process: (1) characterisation of the relevant issue; (2) selection of the rule of conflict of laws which lays down a connecting factor for that issue; and (3) identification of the system of law which is tied by that connecting factor to that issue: see *Macmillan Inc v Bishopsgate Investment Trust plc (No 3)* [1996] 1 WLR 387 at 391–2 per Staughton LJ. The process falls to be undertaken in a broad internationalist spirit in accordance with the principles of conflict of laws of the forum, here England': *Raiffeisen Zentralbank Österreich AG v Five Star Trading LLC* [2001] EWCA Civ 68, [2001] QB 825 at 840 per Mance LJ.

4 Of the above type, ie between defrauded clients and third party good faith purchasers.

5 *Macmillan v Bishopsgate Investment Trust plc (No 3)* [1995] 1 WLR 978 at 989. Another example is that the formal validity of a marriage is determined by the place where it is celebrated.

6 See Fletcher *Insolvency in Private International Law* (1999, Clarendon Press), p 152.

7 Article 4(1).

8 Articles 4(1) and 28.

9 Although the Regulation does not apply in the UK to the extent it is irreconcilable with insolvency law obligations arising from arrangements with the Commonwealth: art 44(3)(b). This ties in with s 426 of the Insolvency Act 1986.

10 Article 3(2).

11 Article 10(1).

12 Under Insolvency Act 1986, s 426

13 See the discussion of set off below.

14 See the discussion in Chapter 4.

15 See Chapter 8.

16 See Chapter 4.

17 Under art 25 these are governed solely by the contractual governing law.

18 Under art 26 these are governed solely by the contractual governing law. However, it is not clear whether this addresses recharacterisation risk, in relation to which the Financial Collateral Directive may assist. See Chapter 4.

19 Under art 27 these are governed solely by the contractual governing law. See Chapter 8.

Enforcement

5.13 The well advised custody client and collateral taker will consider, not only jurisdiction and choice of law, but also the practicalities of enforcement. It will identify the courts that are in a position to deliver the disputed assets, or alternatively to withhold them. This will often be the courts in the country where the assets are located. When assessing the legal robustness of custody or collateral arrangements, the opinion of lawyers in the country where the assets are located is therefore crucial[1].

1 This is the case whether those courts are being asked to enforce their own order, or the order of a foreign court. A large body of law has been developed to determine the circumstances in which courts will recognise and enforce foreign judgments. Where, for example, judgment is obtained in England concerning assets held abroad, local recognition and enforcement of that judgment remains a key issue, and the enforcement of competing local or foreign judgments against the assets cannot be excluded.

Sub-custodian insolvency issues[1]

5.14 As discussed in Chapter 1, the global custodian is unlikely to have branches in each country in which its clients wish to hold assets, and in practice relies on a network of sub-custodians. These sub-custodians may be companies in the same group as the global custodian or independent institutions. However, in each case they are separate legal entities, appointed by the global custodian to hold client assets on its behalf under the terms of a sub-custody agreement. Clearly, both the global custodian and its clients will be concerned to ensure that, in the event of a sub-custodian's insolvency, the assets will not be at risk[2]. This is sometimes referred to as establishing an 'insolvency ring fence'. Chapter 3 discussed the position under English law. It explained that the traditional method of establishing an insolvency ring fence for custody assets is under a bailment, but that in the electronic environment an insolvency ring fence is established under a trust.

1 See Chapter 7 for a note of the regulatory requirements relating to sub-custodian risk.
2 To be more accurate, the concern is to establish that the client assets will not be available to the creditors of the sub-custodian, in its insolvency or otherwise. For example, an unpaid creditor of a solvent sub-custodian may obtain judgment against it, and seek to enforce this against the client assets. However, in practice, insolvency is the chief concern.

Trust and bailment

5.15 The trust is an Anglo-Saxon concept, and not generally recognised as part of the domestic law of civil law countries[1].

The concept of bailment may not be available under civil law in cases where client assets are held on an unallocated basis. In countries where neither trust nor bailment is available, an alternative basis for an insolvency ring fence must be established. For this reason, the major international settlements systems have legislative backing that provides for an insolvency ring-fence[2].

1 The full equitable trust as recognised in common law systems does not form part of the domestic law of civil law jurisdictions, and in the past the perception arose that the trust was alien to civil law, involving as it does the separation of legal and beneficial ownership. 'Is [the trust] not rooted in the duality between law and equity, ie in the separation in English history of two jurisdictions, namely equity in the Court of Chancery, and law in the common law courts, which finds no parallel in continental legal history?': Hayton, Kortmann and Verhagen (eds) *Principles of European Trust Law* (1999, Kluwer), p 3. However, 'The truth is rather different. The elements of the law of trusts are and always have been present in the Roman-based systems and are to be found in the library of the Roman law itself. The question is only as to the extent to which those foundations are used and built upon' (ibid). 'It is also evident that ends achieved by the trust in the common law have also been achieved by other civil law jurisdictions by way of functionally equivalent, but doctrinally different institutions' (ibid, p 4).

However, an English law trust may be recognised if a country is bound by the Hague Trusts Convention. The Convention was implemented in the UK by the Recognition of Trusts Act 1987. It has also been implemented by Italy, the Netherlands, [Luxembourg], Australia, Malta, Canada (except for Ontario and Quebec), Hong Kong, Bermuda, Jersey, Guernsey, Isle of Man, Gibraltar, British Virgin Islands, and the Turks and Caicos islands. 'The Convention *does not* introduce the trust concept into the domestic law of countries lacking the concept ("non-trust countries") . . . The Convention *does* make non-trust countries, like trust countries, recognise trusts of property as a matter of private international law (subject to significant safeguards)': J Glasson *International Trust Laws* (1992, Penguin), cl 5 and 6.

The Convention provides as follows: 'Such recognition shall imply, as a minimum, that the trust property constitutes a separate fund . . . In so far as the law applicable to a trust requires or provides, such recognition shall imply, in particular –

(a) that personal creditors of the trustee shall have no recourse against the trust assets;

(b) that the trust assets shall not form part of the trustee's estate upon his insolvency or bankruptcy . . .' (art 11).

2 In the case of Euroclear, the Royal Decree No 62 of 10 November 1967, and in the case of Clearstream, the Grand Ducal Decree of 17 February 1971 (as amended). See also the Luxembourg Fiduciary Contracts law of 18 July 1983.

In New York, art 8 of the Uniform Commercial Code creates an insolvency ring fence in favour of purchasers of interests in securities (known as securities entitlements) held by financial intermediaries on an unallocated basis: art 8-313(1)(d)(ii) and (iii), and 8-313(2). Of course, New York is not a civil law jurisdiction.

Risks of sub-custodian insolvency

5.16 It is crucial to appreciate that terms of the sub-custody agreement providing for an insolvency ring-fence will not necessarily be reliable. This is because, when a foreign sub-custodian becomes insolvent, the mandatory provisions of applicable insolvency law will determine the fate of the disputed assets. Where these conflict with contractual provisions, the latter will generally be disregarded[1].

In assessing the risk of sub-custodian insolvency, it is necessary to consider, first, which courts are likely to assert jurisdiction over the insolvent sub-custodian and, second, which system of insolvency law those courts are likely to apply. In the light of the rules discussed at paras **5.2–5.13**, where the sub-custodian is an EU bank, with effect from 2004, the law of the member state where it is authorised should be considered. Outside the EU, it should be very broadly assumed that the courts of the country of incorporation will take jurisdiction. In addition, where the sub-custodian operates through a branch in a second country, the courts of that country may also assert jurisdiction, particularly where local assets are available to meet the claims of local creditors.

1 Under English law, see *British Eagle International Airlines Ltd v Compagnie Nationale Air France* [1975] 1 WLR 758, [1975] 2 All ER 390; *National Westminster Bank Ltd v Halesowen Presswork and Assemblies Ltd* [1972] AC 785, [1972] 2 WLR 455, [1972] 1 All ER 641, HL; *Ex p Mackay* (1873) 8 Ch App 643.

Local ring-fence opinions

5.17 As indicated at paras **5.2–5.13**, courts having insolvency jurisdiction often apply their local law to insolvency questions. For this reason, global custodians seek the opinions of lawyers practising in the sub-custodian's country, to the effect that the client assets are protected by an insolvency ring-fence under local law ('local ring-fence opinions')[1].

The risk may arise that client assets are not ring-fenced where special structures are introduced in order to hide the identity of investors and thereby to avoid aspects of the regime of the issuer country. For example, securities may be placed in 'street names', ie the names of local brokers, in order to escape local restrictions on foreign holdings of securities in a number of far eastern countries. Also, intermediaries may be introduced in countries having a double taxation treaty with the issuer country. In each case, it would appear to the authorities in the issuer country that the intermediary is the beneficial owner. The legality and effect of such arrangements should be carefully considered. Moreover, in the insolvency of the intermediary, the beneficial owner or the global custodian acting on its behalf will probably require the co-operation of the courts in the issuer country to recover the assets. In the circumstances, the local courts may be unsympathetic to their claims.

1 Standard opinions obtained pursuant to Rule 17f-5 of the US Investment Companies Act 1940 include answers to the following question: 'If the Bank becomes insolvent, are there (in addition to the period necessary for the liquidator on insolvency to sort out the affairs and assets of the bank) restrictions under the laws of England on the ability of the client or the client's customers to recover securities or cash assets held directly by the Bank?'

Other risks

5.18 Of course, an insolvency ring-fence will only be effective to protect assets which remain in the hands of the insolvent sub-custodian. It addresses the risk of insolvency, but not the further risk that assets may be missing from the sub-custodian's client holding. Such a shortfall may arise for a wide range of reasons[1], including sub-custodian negligence and fraud. The pressures faced by a sub-custodian shortly before insolvency may sometimes make negligence and fraud more likely[2]. In practice, therefore, in addition to obtaining local ring-fence opinions, global custodians and their clients require regular due diligence to be undertaken to establish that the sub-custodian's systems and procedures are adequate, and that the global custodian's and the sub-custodian's accounts are regularly reconciled[3].

1 Where contractual settlement (discussed in Chapter 4) is offered in relation to securities, it is important to ensure that the custodian is not in effect using the securities of one client to lend to another client who has suffered a delay in settlement. If this is the case, this may be an additional source of shortfalls in the client securities accounts.
2 London Business School *Custodianship and the Protection of Client Property*, July 1994. This study of the London markets has shown that losses of client securities in the hands of intermediaries have not been caused by fraud alone (presumably because a fraudulent but solvent intermediary would be compelled to return the missing assets), but by the combination of fraud and insolvency (p 3).
3 See Chapter 7 for a discussion of regulatory requirements.

Cross-border collateral issues

Overview

5.19 Chapter 4 discussed the importance of securities in financial collateral arrangements. Such collateral arrangements often operate cross-border. Indeed, a bank in one country may take collateral from a debtor in a second country, consisting of securities issued from a third country, and held through an intermediary in a fourth. This raises a number of interesting conflict of laws questions.

Conflict of laws analysis of collateral arrangements

5.20 Chapter 4 provides a detailed discussion of the use of the custody portfolio as collateral. As discussed there, the essential achievement of successful collateral arrangements is to confer on the collateral taker property rights in the collateral assets, thereby addressing the risk of the collateral giver's default. The greater part of this section therefore considers the conflict of laws analysis of property rights. However, the collateral taker must address a number of other issues, including the following. It must address issues of power (or capacity)[1] and authority[2] (under the law of the collateral giver's constitution)[3]. It must establish that the collateral arrangement is entered into with essential[4] validity (under the governing law of the contract)[5] and formal validity[6] (under either the governing law or the law of the place where it was concluded)[7], and also that is has been duly executed (generally under the law of the collateral giver's constitution). The collateral giver may be subject to registration requirements[8] and regulatory requirements[9] (under the law of incorporation or of any branch through which it operates), and these must be satisfied.

As indicated in Chapter 4, the acquisition of property rights in the collateral assets breaks down into several issues. The collateral assets in question must generally be identified in a process known as attachment[10]; property rights must generally be rendered enforceable against third parties by a process known as perfection[11]; and where more than one property interest is perfected in the same assets, the priorities between them must be determined[12]. Arguably, because they relate to property rights, all these issues are determined by the law of the place where the assets are located, or lex situs[13].

As a practical matter, the collateral taker must identify the steps required to enforce its interest and remit the proceeds[14] (generally under lex situs)[15]. Finally, the collateral taker must assess the risk that, after enforcement, its collateral interest might be displaced if the collateral giver is affected by insolvency[16] (under the insolvency law of the country of incorporation or any branch)[17], or if the collateral assets beneficially belonged to clients of the collateral taker, and were delivered in breach of duty[18] (arguably, under lex situs)[19].

1 That is, that the constitution of the collateral giver, being an institution, permits such business.
2 That is, that the individual who executed the agreement on behalf of the collateral giver had authority to bind the collateral giver.
3 *Carl Zeiss Stifftung v Rayner & Keeler (No 2)* [1967] 1 AC 853 at 972E and 919G.
4 That is, that nothing in its essential nature invalidates it, such as (under English law) the absence of consideration.
5 Article 8 of the Rome Convention 1980.
6 That is, that any formal requirements are satisfied, such as the agreement being in writing, in the form of a deed, signed or notarised.
7 Article 9 of the Rome Convention.
8 For example, for companies incorporated in England and Wales, the registration requirements of s 395 and the following sections of the Companies Act 1985. See the Law Commission's proposals for reform, discussed in Chapter 4.
9 That is, regulatory requirements affecting its business.
10 Although English law recognises floating charges, which do not attach to particular assets, but relate to a changing class of assets; see Chapter 4. Attachment in this sense should not be confused with attachment in the sense of enforcement against assets.
11 Perfection often involves a process of publicity, eg registration or notarisation.
12 That is, it must be determined which interest will be met first: this is crucial where the value of the assets is insufficient to meet all the interests in full.
13 The choice of law rules for priorities disputes are discussed by Millett J in *Macmillan v Bishopsgate Investment Trust plc (No 3)* [1996] 1 WLR 387 at 758. He indicates that, where a fiduciary wrongly disposes of client assets to a third party, in a priorities dispute between the client and the third party, lex situs applies. In contrast, where a priorities dispute arises due to successive dealings in the same asset, Millett J argued that the law of the forum applies, ie English law in the English courts. However, the case law on this latter point is complex. Some cases support the lex fori rule (for example, *Bankers Trust International Ltd v Todd Shipyards Corpn, The Halcyon Isle* [1981] AC 221 at 230–1). Others suggest governing law of the contract constituting the disputed asset (for example, *Republica de Guatemala v Nunez* [1927] 1 KB 669, and others lex situs (for example, *Re Queensland Mercantile and Agency Co* [1891] 1 Ch 536.
14 That is, it must ascertain whether there are any exchange controls in place.
15 Because, as a practical matter, enforcement by exercising a power of sale and remittance of proceeds of sale take place in and from the jurisdiction where the assets are located. (Of course, legal location (lex situs) and geographical location do not always coincide.)
16 Under preference rules or other rules of insolvency displacement.
17 Or, within the EU, under the detailed rules of jurisdiction and choice of law discussed in Chapter 4.
18 The risk for the collateral taker here is that the defrauded beneficial owners will bring an action for the return of their assets.
19 See *Macmillan v Bishopsgate Investment Trust plc (No 3)* [1996] 1 WLR 387.

Property rights

5.21 The fundamental premise on which collateralisation relies is that the collateral taker is not merely a creditor with personal rights against the insolvent debtor, but also enjoys property rights in the collateral assets. This enables it to jump the queue of unsecured creditors in insolvency by removing the collateral assets from the insolvent's estate, and applying them to satisfy its claims. In cross-border arrangements, therefore, it is crucial to establish that the collateral taker's property rights will stand up under the relevant system or systems of law, and hence the intense commercial interest in these conflict of laws issues.

Property rights in intangible assets

5.22 The collateral taker's rights are proprietary, notwithstanding that the assets in question are intangible assets such as registered securities. As indicated in Chapter 1, this proposition has to be considered both as against the issuer and as against the insolvent collateral giver.

It might be objected that an intangible asset is merely an obligation (in the case of debt securities, broadly the right to be paid by the issuer). Obligations or claims are personal and not proprietary by nature and (it might be argued) cannot therefore be subject to property rights. Thus, *as against the issuer*, the holder of unsecured debt securities has only personal rights, which may become valueless in the issuer's insolvency.

However, as several (common law) commentators have pointed out, obligations may be subject to property rights *as against third parties* such as collateral givers. If the collateral giver becomes insolvent, but the issuer remains solvent, the lender who took debt securities as collateral expects to be paid, because, *as against the collateral taker* its rights in relation to the securities are proprietary.

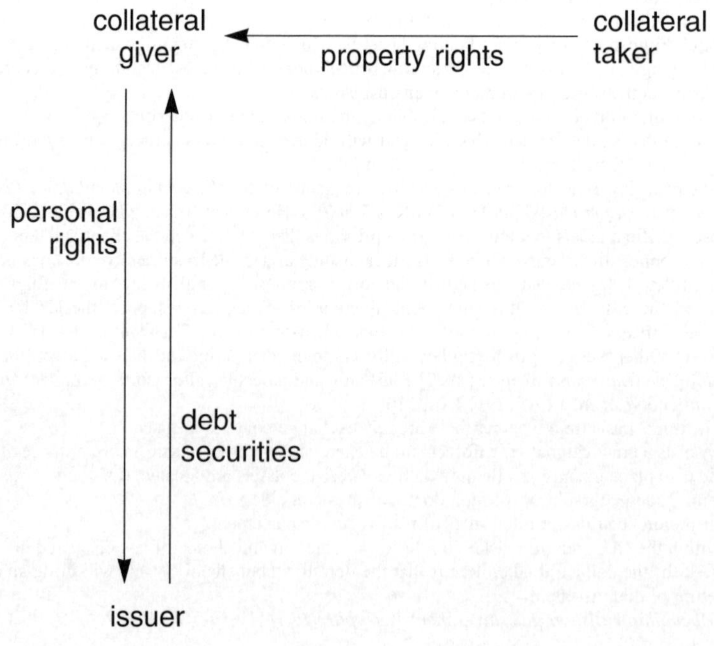

Jurisdiction

5.23 Legal proceedings that test the validity of collateral arrangements may originate in different ways. The collateral taker may seek to enforce its interest by suing the collateral giver (whether directly or through its insolvency official). Alternatively, the insolvency official may itself commence the hearing by seeking directions from the court as part of the insolvency proceedings. Although the procedural conflict of laws analysis of these many alternatives differ, it will be argued that the result is the same.

As discussed above, proceedings commenced by the collateral taker may often be brought in the country where the assets are located, because of the practicalities of enforcement. Insolvency proceedings may be most likely to take place in the country of incorporation of the insolvent collateral giver, although they may be brought in a branch country, or even a third country where there are significant local assets. Within the EU, see the detailed rules discussed in Chapter 4.

Choice of law – the lex situs rule

5.24 In non-insolvency proceedings, the general rule is that property rights are determined in accordance with lex situs or the law of the place where the assets in question are located[1]. The courts will therefore apply lex situs to determine whether the collateral taker enjoys property rights in the collateral assets, which are effective to protect its interest in the insolvency of the collateral giver.

The same approach should also be adopted in insolvency proceedings. It was indicated above that, as a general rule, insolvency proceedings are governed by the law of the country in which they are conducted. However, this general rule relates to the substantive law of insolvency (including such matters as insolvency displacement). The impact of insolvency law on collateral arrangements is subject to an important principle concerning the recognition of pre-existing property rights. Property rights arising under foreign law prior to the onset of insolvency should be recognised in insolvency proceedings[2], providing of course that the transactions giving rise to such rights are not avoidable under preference rules or other mandatory provisions of insolvency law[3]. If such mandatory provisions are satisfied, the courts governing the insolvency of the collateral taker should respect the interest of the collateral taker, provided such interest amounted to a property interest under lex situs[4], prior to the onset of insolvency. However, the risk may remain that the insolvency courts of certain countries outside the scope of the EU measures would be tempted to disregard legal principle, and refuse to recognise foreign law property rights that would not have been recognised under domestic law, if this would serve to increase the assets available to local creditors[5]. It is therefore customary for collateral takers to assess their property rights under the law of the insolvency country, as well as lex situs[6].

Within the EU, the impact of the Insolvency Regulation on the lex situs rule must be assessed. Article 5(1) provides that the opening of insolvency proceedings shall not affect the rights in rem[7] of creditors or third parties in respect of assets belonging to the debtor and situated in a third party state. This must be read together with art 2(g), which provides broadly that for this purpose publicly registered assets are situated in the member state under the authority of which the register is kept, and that claims are situated in the member state where the obligor has the centre of his main interests. In the case of a company, this is presumed to be the place of its registered office[8]. These rules equate broadly but not exactly[9] to the rules of English law for determining the situs of such assets. However, it does not appear that the

Regulation is intended to alter the lex situs rule. The provisions of art 5(1) merely serve to limit the impact of insolvency proceedings for pre-existing property rights; they do not provide for such rights to be acquired.

1 *Cammell v Sewell* (1858) 3 H & N 617: 'If personal property is disposed of in a manner binding according to the law of the country where it is, that disposition is binding everywhere' per Pollock CB at 624. The Rome Convention on the Law Applicable to Contractual Obligations (implemented by the Contracts (Applicable Law) Act 1990, does not apply to property rights: see p 10 of the *Guiliano and Lagarde Report on the Rome Convention.*

2 See art 5 of the European Insolvency Regulation (1346/2000): 'The opening of insolvency proceedings shall not affect the rights in rem of creditors or third parties in respect of tangible or intangible, movable or immovable assets – both specific assets and collections of indefinite assets as a whole which change from time to time – belonging to the debtor which are situated within the territory of another Member State at the time of the opening of the proceedings.' Article 21 of the Winding Up Directive (2001/24), which will apply to credit institutions from May 2004, is in like terms.

3 See art 5(4) of the Insolvency Regulation and art 21(4) of the Winding Up Directive.

4 See Recital 25 and art 5 of the Insolvency Regulation, and art 21 of the Winding Up Directive.

5 It is understood that provision is proposed to be included in the Hague Convention discussed below to prevent such action by insolvency courts.

6 As a practical matter, if the assets are located in country A, which recognises the interest of the collateral taker, but the insolvency jurisdiction is country B, which does not, the collateral taker may seek to enforce its interest in A (assuming it is able to ignore any penalties B may seek to impose).

7 This term was deliberately left undefined: see para 100 of M Virgos and E Schmit *Report on the Convention on Insolvency Proceedings* (1996) ('Virgos Report').

8 Article 3(1).

9 For example, under arts 2(g) and 3(1), bank debts payable at a particular branch would be treated as located at the member state in which the bank has its registered office. This contrasts with the position under English law, whereby such a bank debt would be located with the relevant branch: *Martin v Nadel* [1906] 2 KB 26 at 31.

Applicability to intangibles

5.25 The lex situs rule undoubtedly applies to land[1] and to chattels[2]. There has been a debate as to whether the rule applies also to intangible assets[3]. One school of thought has argued that, because intangibles are creatures of contract, their transfer is determined by the governing law of the contracts that constitute them[4]. However, on the basis outlined earlier that intangibles may be subject to property rights as against third parties, it is argued that lex situs remains the correct connecting factor[5], and this is now supported by case law[6]. The situs of intangibles is generally the place where they are in the ordinary course enforceable[7] so that, for example, a simple debt is located with the debtor[8].

The traditional rules for determining property rights in securities might be very broadly summarised as follows[9]. Registered shares are located with the register[10], which usually[11] coincides with the place of incorporation, and bearer securities, as tangible assets, are located with the instrument constituting them from time to time[12]. The challenge is how to adapt these traditional rules in an electronic environment.

They need to be adapted for two reasons. First, paper instruments have receded in favour of electronic databases. Second, these databases have proliferated through the use of intermediaries. As discussed in Chapter 1, it is customary for investors to hold their securities through custodians and other intermediaries which participate in wholesale electronic delivery systems. In cross-border investment arrangements, several intermediaries are likely to stand between the investor or collateral taker and the issuer of the underlying assets. Each intermediary maintains its own database as a record of its clients' entitlements. If an investor's holding in securities generates credit entries in the accounts of three intermediaries, each standing between it and the issuer, and if each intermediary is located in a different country, the question then arises, where are the investor's assets located?

1 *Norris v Chambers* (1861) 29 Beav 246.
2 *Inglis v Usherwood* (1801) 1 East 515.
3 This debate has of course become very important with the development of the weightless economy, in which the more significant part of economic activity relates to intangibles.
4 See P J Rogerson 'The Situs of Debts in the conflict of Laws – Illogical, Unnecessary and Misleading' [1990] CLJ 441.
5 This choice of connecting factor is supported by *Re Maudslay* [1900] 1 Ch 602; *New York Life Insurance Co v Public Trustee* [1924] 2 Ch 101 and *Jabbour v Custodian* [1954] 1 All ER 145.
6 *Macmillan v Bishopsgate (No 3)* [1996] 1 WLR 387 at 404, 405, per Staughton LJ; at 410, 411, 412, per Auld LJ; at 423, 424 per Auldous LJ. For a contrary view in the context of an assignment of an insurance assignment, however, see *Raiffeisen Zentralbank Österreich AG v Five Star Trading LLC* [2001] EWCA Civ 68, [2001] QB 825.
7 *Alloway v Phillips* [1980] 1 WLR 888 at 894, per Waller LJ; *Re Russian Bank for Foreign Trade* [1934] 1 Ch 720 at 767, per Maugham J.
8 See, for example, *Kwok Chi Leung Karl v Comr Estate Duty* [1988] 1 WLR 1035 at 1040, per Lord Oliver, and *Comr of Stamps v Hope* [1891] AC 476 at 481, per Lord Field.
9 This is a complex area of law. For a more detailed discussion, see Potok (ed) *Cross Border Collateral: Legal Risk and the Conflict of Laws* (2002, Butterworths), ch 10.
10 *Macmillan v Bishopsgate (No 3)* [1996] 1 WLR 387 at 411, per Auld LJ. However, different views were also expressed in this complex judgment. See also art 2(g), second indent, of the Insolvency Regulation.
11 But not always. See *Brassard v Smith* [1925] AC 371 at 376, per Lord Dunedin.
12 *Alcock v Smith* [1892] 1 Ch 238.

PRIMA[1]

5.26 It is argued that, under the existing principles of English private international law, the assets are located with the intermediary with whom the investor has a direct relationship and against whom she has a directly enforceable claim. This conclusion follows from a number of points. First, intangibles are legally located where they are in the normal course enforceable[2], and a client's interests in securities are normally enforceable against the custodian which maintains a securities account in the client's name. Second, it was argued in Chapter 3 that the custody client's interest is an unallocated[3] interest arising under a trust: existing case law indicates that such interests are legally located with the trustee (ie in this case, the custodian)[4]. Third, this approach is helpful in simplifying the legal analysis of cross-border collateral arrangements, because it enables the collateral taker to refer to a single system of law (that of the intermediary's country) as lex situs[5]. Where the collateral asset consists of a portfolio comprising interests in securities issued from a number of underlying countries, this approach avoids the need to refer to each of them[6].

These arguments are now reflected in *Dicey and Morris*[7]. The approach broadly accords with the US rules for of securities entitlements, which under the UCC are generally located with the intermediary providing services directly to the client[8].

Internationally, this approach has gained widespread acceptance under the term 'Place of the Relevant Intermediary Account' or 'PRIMA'. PRIMA is being adopted in a range of legislative measures discussed below and the authors would argue that this development is wholly welcome. However, PRIMA is not universally accepted, and a measure of legal risk will remain as long as the courts of countries which do not accept PRIMA may assume jurisdiction[9].

1 Richard Potok of Potok & Co takes credit for promoting this concept and also this happy acronym. See, inter alia, *Cross Border Collateral: Legal Risk and the Conflict of Laws* (2002, Butterworths). The first edition of this book (and an earlier article by Benjamin ('Custody – An English Law Analysis' (1994 0 9 JIBFL 121, 188) used the term 'Intermediary Jurisdiction Approach' in place of PRIMA. For an early advocation of PRIMA (although not by that name) see Randall Guynn in *Modernising Securities Ownership, Transfer and Pledging Laws* (1996, IBA).
2 See L Collins (ed) *Dicey and Morris on the Conflict of Laws* (2000, 13th edn, Sweet & Maxwell), para 24-043.

3 As discussed in Chapter 3, it is customary for the holdings of different clients to be commingled in the hands of custodians and other intermediaries, and this serves to break the direct property link between the investor and the underlying issuer.

4 See, for example, *Lord Sudeley v A-G* [1897] AC 11; *Baker v Archer-Shee* [1927] AC 844; and *Marshall v Kerr* [1995] 1 AC 148, [1994] 3 WLR 299, [1994] 3 All ER 106. See also *Re Cigala's Settlement Trusts* (1878) 7 Ch D 351; *A-G v Johnson* [1907] 2 KB 885; *Favorke v Steinkopf* [1922] 1 Ch 174; and *Stamp Duty Comr (Queensland) v Hugh Duncan Livingston* [1965] AC 694, [1964] 3 WLR 963, [1964] 3 All ER 692. A different rule applies to allocated trust interests: see *A-G for Hong Kong v Reid* [1994] 1 AC 324, [1993] 3 WLR 1143, [1994] 1 All ER 1.

5 Commercial convenience is an important factor shaping the rules of private international law.

6 The authors are grateful to Lee Mitchell for raising the following interesting question relating to priorities. Where interests in securities are held for a client through a chain of intermediaries, if each of the client and the intermediaries grants a security interest, which takes priority? The position is understood to be as follows. If an underlying intermediary gives a security interest over client assets for its own borrowings *with the consent of its client*, this interest in general takes priority over a security interest granted by the client. This is on the basis that the client's asset derives from the asset held by the intermediary, and is therefore subject to any encumbrances on the latter.

If the above happens *without the consent of the client, ie in breach of duty*, the above proposition would be subject to the rules of equitable tracing and following. Thus (broadly) the collateral taker from the intermediary could only take the security interest in priority if it could show that it was the good faith purchaser of the legal estate for value without notice of the breach of duty. Importantly, it would not be in this position if its interest was a charge (ie equitable only). However, this is a complex area of law, on which the authors are not aware of any direct authority.

7 L Collins (ed) *Dicey and Morris on the Conflict of Laws* (2000, 13th edn, Sweet & Maxwell), Vol II, 986, para 24-064.

8 Article 8.110. 'Because [the client's] property is "located" at Custodian, it is clear, as a matter of general principle, that the only proper subject of legal process by [the client's] creditors would be Custodian': S J Rogers *Policy Perspectives on Revised UCC, Article 8*, UCLA Law Rev, June 1996, 431 at 1457.

9 In such countries, local courts may be less likely to decline jurisdiction in matters affecting locally issued securities. For this reason, the forum of a dispute is a key issue. Indeed, once an action concerning foreign securities has been commenced in the country of the issuer, the English courts may be most unlikely to entertain an action on the same issue.

A measure of pragmatism is called for. Collateral takers will often have to tolerate some measure of legal risk, and should focus upon practical issues relating to enforcement. Control of the assets is of primary importance. Will the intermediary settlement system or custodian co-operate in enforcing the collateral interest sufficiently rapidly, so that challenge at issuer level may come too late? Does the settlement system have more than one depositary in the relevant jurisdiction, so that a third party claiming the assets would be unable to identify and therefore attach the assets through the local courts? Finally, and subject to the need to avoid illegality, does the collateral taker have any assets of its own in the issuer jurisdiction against which adverse claims or penalties might be enforced?

Settlement Finality Directive

5.27 The Settlement Finality Directive is discussed in detail in Chapter 4. Article 9(2) supports PRIMA in relation to collateral delivered through designated settlement systems[1]. Unfortunately, in the initial implementation of the Directive in the UK under the Financial Markets and Insolvency (Settlement Finality) Regulations 1999[2], art 9(2) is interpreted narrowly[3]. It does not benefit, for example, collateral provided by one commercial participant to another. However, in 2001 the Treasury published a consultation document[4] in which it proposed to widen the interpretation of art 9(2). Under these proposals, PRIMA would appear to benefit all securities collateral arrangements where 'a register, account or centralised deposit system legally records the entitlement of the collateral taker'[5]. Thus, the class of collateral takers to which PRIMA applies is not limited, and nor is PRIMA restricted to designated settlement systems.

1 It provides as follows.

'Where securities (including rights in securities) are provided as collateral security to participants and/or central banks of the Member States or the future European central bank . . . and their right (or that of any nominee, agent or third party acting on their behalf) with respect to the securities is legally recorded on a register, account or centralised deposit system located in a Member State, the determination of the rights of such entities as holders of collateral security in relation to those securities shall be governed by the law of that Member State.'

2 SI 1999/2979.

3 In reg 23. 'Both "collateral securities" and "participant" are defined terms in regulation 2. As a result of these definitions, regulation 23 as originally drafted implements article 9(2) of the EU Settlement Finality Directive in a "narrow" sense, with the result that, broadly, a collateral taker is covered only if it is (i) a central bank, (ii) the European Central Bank or (iii) a regulated financial institution or public authority acting as a central counterparty, settlement agent, clearing house or provider of liquidity to an EU settlement system designated under the EU Settlement Finality Directive': see Potok (ed) *Cross Border Collateral: Legal Risk and the Conflict of Laws* (2002, Butterworths), ch 10, para 10.9.

4 HM Treasury *Domestic and International Initiatives Concerning Conflict of Law Issues Relating to Securities: Consultation Document*, July 2001.

5 Proposed amended reg 23.

Other EU measures

5.28 Provisions supporting PRIMA are also contained in the Insolvency Regulation[1], the Winding Up Directive[2], and the Financial Collateral Directive[3].

1 Article 14.

2 Articles 24 and 31.

3 Proposal for a directive on financial collateral arrangements, published by the Commission on 27 March 2001, art 10. See the discussion of the proposed Financial Collateral Directive in Chapter 4.

Proposed Hague Convention on Indirectly Held Securities[1]

5.29 The Hague Conference on Private International Law has been undertaking a project on securities held with an intermediary, and has developed a draft multilateral *Convention on the Law Applicable to Proprietary Rights in Indirectly Held Securities.*

A preliminary draft of the Convention was adopted by the Special Commission in January 2002[2], and it is hoped that the convention will be adopted in a plenary session of the Conference in late 2002 or early 2003. Whereas the PRIMA provisions in the SFD relate only to collateral arrangements, the Hague Convention extends to all dealings in intermediated securities, whether by way of collateral or otherwise[3]. This is welcome, as a fragmented approach depending on the purpose of the transfer is conceptually and practically unsatisfactory.

The primary choice of law rule in the Convention is contained in art 4. In an interesting departure from the EU measures discussed above[4], rules for determining applicable law are influenced by the agreement of the parties, and do not simply follow the place where the account is maintained[5]. (The difficulties of agreeing objective rules for the latter in an electronic environment were extensively debated during the drafting of the Convention[6].)

1 For a detailed background discussion, see Christophe Bernasconi *The Law Applicable to Dispositions of Securities Held through Indirect Holding Systems*, Hague Conference on Private International Law, to the working group of January 2001 on securities collateral (Bernasconi Report).

2 References in this discussion are to the most recent draft available at the time of writing, ie that of June 2002.

3 See art 2.

4 And perhaps reflecting a US commitment to party autonomy.

5 Two options are available in art 4. In option A, the applicable law is that agreed to be applicable by the account holder and the relevant intermediary. In option B, it is that so agreed to be the law of the state in which the securities account is maintained, subject to account-related criteria set out in option B.

6 See option B of art 4, and art 6.

Conceptual issues

5.30 Although it is gaining widespread commercial support, PRIMA has its critics and much of this criticism is conceptual. Critics have argued that the root of title of the securities in relation to which investors and collateral takers have property interests, and therefore the location of their assets, is with the underlying paper (in the case of bearer instruments) or with the underlying issuer register (in the case of registered securities). This is called the 'look through' approach[1]. Market participants have generally resisted the look through approach for pragmatic reasons. As indicated above, where the collateral portfolio comprises interests in securities issued from 20 underlying countries, the look through approach would involve the expense and administrative burden of 20 legal opinions (some of which may be unfavourable)[2].

Of course, it is not a sufficient answer to the look through approach to state that it is inconvenient[3]. It is necessary also to develop the substantive law analysis on which PRIMA rests[4]. The investor or collateral taker holds its interest through one or more intermediary. The investor's asset is not at risk in the insolvency of the intermediary and therefore economically, and also for balance sheet, taxation and regulatory purposes the asset is indistinguishable from the underlying securities. However, as was argued in Chapter 3, it is legally distinct. The commingling of the assets of different clients in the hands of the intermediary prevents the claims of any client from attaching to particular underlying securities, so that the client's rights are not allocated, but in the nature of co-ownership. Moreover, in the normal course the client has no direct rights of enforcement except through the intermediary. Thus, such intermediation is a form of legal repackaging, and the client's assets consist of indirect co-ownership rights, which the authors have called interests in securities, and which the UCC terms securities entitlements. Common lawyers have long been familiar with structures like the unit trust, where investors hold units conferring indirect co-ownership rights in an underlying portfolio. We intuitively distinguish the unit from the underlying assets to which they are legally and economically related. With the intermediation that computerisation has brought to the financial markets, it is argued that this old common law conception now has a new use, as it simplifies the cross-border aspects of property rights in the electronic securities markets[5].

1 On the basis that it involves 'looking', from the point of view of the investor or collateral taker, 'through' the intermediaries to the underlying issuer.
2 The difficulty is compounded where actively traded, so that the issuer jurisdictions involved change from time to time.
3 Although it is part of an answer. The reason regularly given for the lex situs rule in early judgments is the importance of enabling purchasers conveniently to establish title. See, for example, *Cammell v Sewell* (1860) 5 H & N 728 at 1374, per Crompton J. More recently, see *Winkworth v Christie* [1980] 1 Ch 496 at 512, per Slade J.
4 This was the purpose of J Benjamin *Interests in Securities* (2000, OUP).
5 See J Benjamin *Interests in Securities* (2000, OUP) for a fuller discussion.

Interests in securities and cash

5.31 PRIMA has been advocated in relation to interests in securities. Of course, global custody clients also hold multi-currency cash balances, and may wish to deliver these to third parties as collateral. However, the analysis here is different. In the case of interests in securities, the clients enjoy property rights in relation to the underlying securities, and hence the debate as to whether PRIMA or look through is the correct approach. In the case of cash balances, the client does not enjoy property rights in any underlying foreign currency balance[1], but is merely a debtor of the global custodian[2]. As a bank debt, the client's assets are located with the global custodian[3], and no question of the look through approach arises.

1 Because of the structure of the international banking settlement system, currency is generally held in the country in which it is legal tender. See the discussion of Eurodollars by Terrence Prime in *International Bonds and Certificates of Deposit* (1990, Butterworths) pp 4, 5. Thus, where a London global custodian (being a UK bank) maintains a credit balance of US$10,000 for a custody client, it will not of course keep a large pile of dollar bills in its vaults in London to match that credit balance. The asset of the global custodian corresponding to the credit balance will be a further credit balance of, say US$1,000,000 in favour of the global custodian in the books of its correspondent bank in New York. Where US dollar income or proceeds of sale of custody securities are paid to the global custodian on behalf of clients, they are likely to be credited directly to the account of the New York correspondent bank. This account in New York may be said to constitute dollars, and that in favour of the custody client in the books of the London global custodian may be said to constitute Eurodollars. Because of the use of correspondent banks, it might be thought that the global custodian is holding the client's non-sterling cash overseas. However, this is not the case. The asset of the client is not the dollars in New York, but the Eurodollars in London. Thus the client's asset comprises a debt owed by the global custodian to pay $10,000. The debt of the New York correspondent bank to pay US$1,000,000 is owed, not to the client, but to the global custodian, and the client enjoys no rights in it.

2 See Chapter 3 for a discussion of this principle.

3 Or, if the sums credited to the account are payable at a particular branch of the global custodian, at that branch: *Martin v Nadel* [1906] 2 KB 26 at 31.

Set off

5.32 Rights of set off are widely relied on by banks and other financial institutions to manage their credit exposures to clients. As discussed in Chapter 4, outright collateral transfer arrangements depend for their effectiveness on the availability of insolvency set off. It is therefore crucial for the collateral taker to confirm that set off would be available in the insolvency of the collateral giver[1]. Both The European Insolvency Regulation and the Winding Up Directive provide that, in general, the law of the main insolvency forum will determine the availability of insolvency set off[2]. However, even where the law of the forum does not permit set off, creditors may nevertheless set off their claims against the claims of the insolvent where the law governing the latter claims set off[3]. (This is subject to the normal rules against preferences etc[4].)

1 In the case of *Bank of Credit and Commerce International SA (No 10)* [1997] Ch 213, [1997] 2 WLR 172, [1996] 4 All ER 796, the English courts applied English insolvency set off in ancillary proceedings, even through insolvency set off was not available under Luxembourg law which governed the main proceedings. This decision has been widely criticised. See Fletcher *Insolvency in Private International Law* (1999, Clarendon Press), p 366, n 4. See also Fletcher 'International Insolvency: Recent Cases' (1997) JBL 471.

2 Article 4(2)(d) of the Insolvency Regulation and art 10(2)(c) of the Winding Up Directive.

3 Article 6(1) of the Insolvency Regulation and art 23(1) of the Winding Up Directive. This in effect permits the parties contractually to choose the insolvency laws that will apply to set off. Thus, under the Winding Up Directive, in Greek law insolvency proceedings against a Greek bank, and English bank could set off an English law overdrawn account against an account in credit, even if Greek insolvency law did not permit such set off.

4 Article 6(2) of the Insolvency Regulation and art 23(2) of the Winding Up Directive.

Thus for example in the Greek insolvency of a company which owed a debt governed by English law to X, art 6 permits X to set off that debt pursuant to English law insolvency set off rules, notwithstanding that such insolvency set off would not be permitted by Greek insolvency law. This allows financial institutions by contract to avoid the impact of debtor-friendly jurisdictions' restrictions on insolvency set off. In the light of these provisions, financial institutions may wish to review the governing law clauses of the financial agreements which rely on insolvency set off to ensure they take advantage where appropriate of these provisions. However, it is important to note that art 6(1) relates to the governing law of the claim which it is sought to set off, and not the governing law of any master agreement or netting agreement, if different.

Conversely, in English law insolvency proceedings, insolvency set off would not be disturbed by the insolvent's claim being governed by Greek law, because art 6(1) is drafted in permissive and not mandatory terms, so that the position remains governed by art 4(2)(d). See Recital 26 and para 109 of the Vigos Report.

Unlike the Winding Up Directive, the Insolvency Regulation does not make similar provisions for netting. Therefore these appear not to be protected in debtor friendly jurisdictions.

Chapter 6*

The global custodian's duties

6.1 The global custodian owes legal duties arising from a number of different sources. This chapter will consider duties at civil law. Duties under the regulatory regime established under the Financial Services and Markets Act 2000 will be considered in Chapter 7. The question of criminal liability is beyond the scope of this book.

* The authors are grateful to Professor David Hayton, of King's College London, for kindly reviewing this chapter. Any errors are their own.

Overview

6.2 Operational failures in the holding, settlement and administration of a portfolio of securities can cause significant losses to clients. Where such losses occur, global custodians may choose to make them good irrespective of legal liability, in order to preserve the client relationship. However, losses may be so great that liability would have severe consequences for the global custodian, so that the question of legal liability arises. Very broadly speaking, the custodian will not be liable unless client losses have been caused[1] by the custodian's breach of duty[2]. Duty is the measure of potential liability. Control of levels of legal duty is therefore a part of risk management for the global custodian.

The chief method of controlling levels of duty is the inclusion in the global custody contract of duty defining clauses and limitation of liability clauses. The global custody contract should contain an exhaustive list of the services that will be provided, and as much operational detail as possible should be included[3]. Also, the level of care to be taken by the global custodian in providing these services should be specified. These duty defining clauses define the extent of the contractual duties of the global custodian to the client. While duty defining clauses specify what the client is entitled to expect, limitation clauses serve to limit its recourse if it is disappointed.

The emphasis of the following sections is on the duties and liabilities of the global custodian associated with its trustee status. In relation to contractual and tortious duties and liabilities, there is only a very brief discussion of some of the fundamental principles.

1 The question of causation is extremely complex, particularly in the electronic securities markets, where a loss may be overdetermined (ie attributable to more than one cause). See the discussion of intervening cause in the context of breach of contract in P Birks (ed) *English Private Law* (2000,

Oxford University Press), Vol II, 18.43. See also the interesting discussion of causation in the context of tortious liability in *Bristol and West Building Society v Mothew* [1998] Ch 1, [1997] 2 WLR 436, [1996] 4 All ER 698. A detailed discussion of legal causation is beyond the scope of this chapter.

2 Breach of duty is a necessary but not sufficient condition for the client to establish liability for contractual, tortious, equitable or fiduciary liability. As discussed below (except in the case of breach of fiduciary duty), it may also be necessary to satisfy requirements of causation and remoteness of damage.

3 It is customary to specify detailed provisions in a service level agreement or service annex, which is incorporated by reference in the global custody agreement.

Limitation clauses

Generally

6.3 Limitation of liability is arguably the chief commercial benefit for the global custodian of putting a global custody contract in place[1]. These clauses are highly effective in protecting the global custodian from liability where it has been in breach of its duties to the client.

However, their use is subject to a number of restrictions. Statutory restrictions are discussed below in this section. In addition, special restrictions apply to clauses which seek to limit liability for breach of trustee's duties; these are discussed below in paras **6.10–6.20**. Further, UK regulated custodians are not permitted to seek to exclude liability for breach of a regulatory duty[2].

Any limitation clause will be restrictively construed by the court and any doubt or ambiguity resolved against the global custodian seeking to rely on it[3]. It is advisable to draw clients' attention to limitation clauses prior to the execution of the custody agreement, but there is no need to suggest that clients should take independent legal advice on such clauses[4].

It is customary for global custodians operating in London to accept liability for their ordinary negligence and wilful default. As discussed in Chapter 7, UK regulated global custodians are required to accept liability for their own negligence. However, other global custodians (particularly those based in the US) may seek to exclude liability for ordinary negligence and only accept liability for gross negligence. The legal meaning of these terms is discussed below.

1 Conversely, the practice of offering undocumented global custodian services exposes the global custodian to the risk of unmodified general law duties, implying commercially unacceptable levels of potential liability.

Of course, UK regulated custodians are required to put in place client documentation as discussed in Chapter 7. Also, where trustees appoint a custodian under Trustee Act 2000, s 17 (discussed below), the appointment must be in or evidenced in writing: s 17(3).

2 See the FSA Conduct of Business Sourcebook, Rule 2.5.3.

3 *Photo Production Ltd v Securicor Ltd* [1980] AC 827, [1980] 2 WLR 283, [1980] 1 All ER 556; *Midland Bank Trust Co (Jersey) Ltd v Federated Pension Services* [1995] JLR 352 at 391; *Wight v Olswang* (1999) 1 ITELR 783, CA.

4 This is important on the basis that the global custodian is a trustee (see Chapter 3). See David Hayton 'The Irreducible Core of Trusteeship' [1996] JTCP, p 3: '. . . there needs to be full frank disclosure . . . so that a fully informed consent can be given, because a fiduciary relationship exists even before the trust instrument is finally executed'. See *Bogg v Raper* (1998) 1 ITELR 267, CA.

Negligence and gross negligence

6.4 The difference between negligence and gross negligence is discussed in *Midland Bank Trust Company (Jersey) Ltd v Federated Pension Services*[1]. In this case, the trustee's conduct 'was not mere negligence consisting of a departure from the normal standards of conduct of a paid professional trustee, but a serious, unusual and marked departure from that standard which amounted to "gross negligence".'[2] However, gross negligence does not connote bad faith[3]. The difference between negligence and gross negligence is not fundamental in English law[4].

1 [1995] JLR 352.
2 [1995] JLR 352.
3 It is different from recklessness, as pointed out by the Court of Appeal in *Armitage v Nurse* [1998] Ch 241 at 252 per Millett LJ.
4 'It would be very surprising if our law drew the line between liability for ordinary negligence and liability for gross negligence. In this respect English law differs from civil law systems, for it has always drawn a sharp distinction between negligence, however gross, on the one hand and fraud, bad faith and wilful misconduct on the other. The doctrine of the common law is that : "Gross negligence may be evidence of mala fides, but is not the same thing". (See *Goodman v Harvey* (1836) 4 Ad & El 870 at 876, All ER 1011 at 1013 per Lord Denman CJ.) But while we regard the difference between fraud on the one hand and mere negligence, however gross, on the other as a difference in kind, we regard the difference between negligence and gross negligence as merely one of degree. English lawyers have always had a healthy disrespect for the latter distinctions. In *Hinton v Dibbin* (1842) 2 QB 646, 114 ER 253 Lord Denman CJ doubted whether any intelligible distinction exists; while in *Grill v General Iron Screw Collier Co* (1866) 35 LJCP 321 at 330 Willes J famously observed that gross negligence is ordinary negligence with a vituperative epithet. But civilian systems draw the line in a different place. The doctrine is *culpa lata dolo aequiparetur*; and although the maxim itself is not Roman the principle is classical. There is no room for the maxim in the common law; it is not mentioned in Broom *Selection of Legal Maxims Classified and Illustrated* (10th edn, 1939)': *Armitage v Nurse* [1998] Ch 241 at 254 per Millett LJ. However, the court did not have cited to it bailment cases revealing that gross negligence is required before gratuitous bailees (as opposed to bailees for reward) can be liable. See the Trust Law Committee Consultative Paper on Trustee Exemption Clauses on www.kcl.ac.uk/depsta/law/tlc.

Wilful default

6.5 The meaning of the term 'wilful default' has been the subject of much judicial and scholarly discussion[1]. In the context of a limitation clause, wilful default probably means deliberate or reckless breach of duty[2], which (as indicated below) may not be excluded at general law.

1 Much of this discussion has been in the context of Trustee Act 1925, s 30(1); this has been repealed by the Trustee Act 2000
2 '. . . the expression "wilful default" is used in the cases in two senses. A trustee is said to be accountable on the footing of wilful default when he is accountable not only for money which he had in fact received but also for money which he could with reasonable diligence have received. It is sufficient that the trustee has been guilty of a want of ordinary prudence (see eg *Re Chapman, Cocks v Chapman* [1896] 2 Ch 763). In the context of a trustee exclusion clause, however, such as s 30 of the Trustee Act 1925, it means a deliberate breach of trust (*Re Vickery, Vickery v Stephens* [1931] 1 Ch 572, [1931] All ER Rep 562). The decision has been criticised, but it is in line with earlier authority (see *Lewis v Great Western Rly Co* (1877) 3 QBD 195; *Re Trusts of Leeds City Brewery Ltd's Debenture Stock Trust Deed, Leeds City Brewery Ltd v Platts* [1925] Ch 532n and *Re City Equitable Fire Insurance Co Ltd* [1925] Ch 407, [1924] All ER Rep 485). Nothing less than conscious and wilful misconduct is sufficient' : *Armitage v Nurse* [1998] Ch 241 at 252, per Millett LJ.

Statutory restrictions

Unfair Contract Terms Act 1977 ('UCTA')

6.6 In accordance with s 3 of UCTA, exclusion clauses relating to liability of businesses for breach of contract contained in one party's written standard terms of business are subject to a test of reasonableness.

An exemption may be available as follows. Paragraph 1 of Sch 1 to the Act provides that:

> '. . . sections 2 to 4 of this Act do not extend to . . . any contract so far as it relates to the creation or transfer of securities or of any right or interest of securities.'

This exclusion was designed primarily to assist brokers and not custodians. It does not clearly exempt the terms of the global custody agreement, as of course this relates to the holding and administration of securities as well as their transfer. However, this exemption may protect the settlement side of the global custody service[1].

To the extent that the exemption is not available, the custodian's limitation clauses are subject to a statutory reasonableness test[2]. It might be argued that this test is satisfied in cases where terms in question are in market standard form.

1 The view that UCTA applies to a limitation clause in some circumstances and not others may be supported by the case of *Micklefield v SAC Technology* [1990] 1 WLR 1002, [1991] 1 All ER 275, [1990] IRLR 218. In this case the court emphasised that the exception applies to 'any contract *insofar as* it relates to the creation or transfer of securities' (at 281).

2 Section 2(2). This is defined in s 11 as the requirement 'that the term shall have been a fair and reasonable one to be included having regard to the circumstances which were, or ought reasonably to have been, known to or in the contemplation of the parties when the contract was made.'

Unfair Terms in Consumer Contracts Regulations 1999[1]

6.7 These regulations apply (in addition to UCTA) to terms which have not been individually negotiated, in contracts for the supply of goods or services by businesses to consumers. For this purpose, a consumer is a natural person (ie not a company or, probably, in a partnership or unincorporated association) who is acting for purposes which are 'outside his business'. Thus, terms in standard form global custody contracts with high net worth individuals who are not involved in investment business may be prima facie caught.

The regulations impose requirements of fairness and plain English.

1 SI 1999/2083 (amended by SI 2001/1186, Unfair Terms in Consumer Contracts (Amendment) Regulations 2001). These implement the EC Directive on Unfair Terms in Consumer Contracts (93/13/EEC).

Contractual duties[1]

6.8

> 'The general aim of damages for breach of contract is to put the claimant into as good a position as if the contract had been performed.'[2]

In other words, the approach is prospective (in contrast with the retrospective approach for assessing tortious damages: see below).

> '. . . [A] defendant will not be liable for loss suffered by the claimant that is too remote from the breach of contract.'[3]

This may be a significant restriction in the context of securities market operations, where a default may produce complex chains of consequential defaults (see the discussion of systemic risk in Chapter 8).

> '. . . [A] claimant must take all reasonable steps to minimise its loss so that it cannot recover for any loss which it could reasonably have avoided but has failed to avoid.'[4]

Under the Contracts (Rights of Third Parties) Act 1999 a person who is not a party to a contract (a 'third party') may enforce a term of the contract if either the contract expressly so provides or the term purports to confer a benefit on the third party[5] (unless, in the latter case, on a proper construction of the contract it appears that the parties did not intend the term to be enforceable by the third party[6]). Global custodians may consider it prudent expressly to exclude the right of third party beneficial owners in their own right to enforce the terms of the contract with a fund.

1 See generally A G Guest (ed) *Chitty on Contracts* (1994, 27th edn, Sweet & Maxwell).
2 P Birks (ed) *English Private Law* (2000, Oxford University Press), Vol II, 18.19.
3 P Birks (ed) *English Private Law* (2000, Oxford University Press), Vol II, 18.31. 'Where two parties have made a contract which one of them has broken, the damages which the other party ought to receive in respect of such breach of contract, should be such as may fairly and reasonably be considered, either arising naturally, ie according to the usual course of things from such breach of contract itself, or such as may reasonably be supposed to have been in the contemplation of both parties, at the time they made the contract as the probable result of the breach of it': *Hadley v Baxendale* (1854) 9 Exch 341 at 354, per Alderson B.
4 P Birks (ed) *English Private Law* (2000, Oxford University Press), Vol II, 18.45.
5 Contracts (Rights of Third Parties) Act 1999, s 1(1).
6 Contracts (Rights of Third Parties) Act 1999, s 1(2).

Tortious duty of care[1]

6.9

> 'The boundaries of liability for negligence are drawn by the three principle elements of the tort, a duty of care, breach of that duty, and damage caused by that breach.'[2]

The measure of damages for negligence or other torts is the award which is necessary to put the plaintiff back into the position it would have been in had the tort never occurred (ie it is retrospective)[3]. As with contractual liability, the claimant is under a duty to mitigate losses, and tortious liability does not extend to damages which are too remote. Further, there are limits to the ability to recover damages for pure economic loss in negligence[4].

Contractual and tortious liability can be concurrent[5]. However, the courts are reluctant to find tortious liability where the parties' relationship is contractual[6].

The relationship between negligence and breach of a fiduciary's duty of care is discussed by Lord Browne-Wilkinson in *Henderson v Merrett*[7]: 'A fiduciary's liability in negligence is derived from equitable duties of care. The two heads of liability cannot be claimed as alternatives, for the tortious and equitable duties of care are in essence the same. In either case, a contractual relationship between the parties determines the extent and nature of the duty of care'[8].

1 See generally W Rogers *Winfield and Jolowicz on Tort* (2002, 16th edn, Sweet & Maxwell).
2 P Birks (ed) *English Private Law* (2000, Oxford University Press), Vol II, 14.25.
3 See *Livingstone v Rawyards Coal Co* (1880) 5 App Cas 25 at 39 per Lord Blackburn:

> 'The basic principle for the measure of damages in tort . . . is that there should be *restitutio in integrum*. Apart from the special cases we have considered, where any injury is to be compensated by damages, in settling the sum of money to be given for reparation of damages you should as nearly as possible get at that sum of money which will put the party who has been injured, or who has suffered, in the same position as he would have been in if he had not sustained the wrong for which he is now getting his compensation or reparation'.

4 See *Hedley Byrne v Heller* [1964] AC 465, [1963] 3 WLR 101, [1963] 2 All ER 575. A huge literature has been written on this topic.

5 See *Henderson v Merrett* [1995] 2 AC 145, [1994] 3 WLR 761, [1994] 3 All ER 506 and *White v Jones* [1995] 2 AC 207, [1995] 2 WLR 187, [1995] 1 All ER 691 at 730.

6 *Tai Hing Cotton Mill Ltd v Liu Chong Hing Bank Ltd* [1986] AC 80 at 956, per Lord Scarman:

'Their Lordships do not believe that there is anything to the advantage of the law's development in searching for a liability in tort where the parties are in a contractual relationship. This is particularly so in a commercial relationship . . . their Lordships believe it to be correct in principle and necessary for the avoidance of confusion in the law to adhere to the contractual analysis: on principle because it is a relationship in which the parties have, subject to a few exceptions, the right to determine their obligations to each other, and for the avoidance of confusion because different consequences do follow according to whether liability arises from contract or tort, eg in the limitation of action . . . Their Lordships do not, therefore, embark on an investigation whether in the relationship of banker and customer it is possible to identify tort as well as contract as a source of the obligations owed by the one to the other. Their Lordships do not, however, accept that the parties' mutual obligations in tort can be any greater than those to be found expressly or by necessary implication in their contract.'

7 [1995] 2 AC 145 at 205.

8 [1995] 2 AC 145 at 206.

Trustee's duties

6.10 The traditional legal characterisation of the custodian of securities is as bailee of the client[1]. However, Chapter 3 argued that the global custodian is not a bailee but a trustee.

The courts are likely to seek to take a commercial approach to the application of trust law to the global custodian, particularly where non-private clients are involved[2]. However, the principle remains that a custodian incurs liability to the client where it is in breach of trust and this breach results in loss to the client. The measure of this liability is to make good such loss[3]. Remote or unforeseeable damages are arguably not excluded[4], and the plaintiff is not obliged to mitigate its losses[5], but there must be some causal connection between the breach of duty and the loss to establish liability[6]. Liability is subject to contractual or statutory relieving provisions.

Statutory relief is in theory available under s 61 of the Trustee Act 1925, where the custodian has acted honestly and reasonably and ought fairly to be excused[7]. However, it is considered unlikely that such relief would be granted to a professional trustee such as a global custodian[8].

The duties of the global custodian as trustee will be considered in two parts, namely the trustee's duty of care, and fiduciary duties.

1 The bailee's duty of care at common law is as follows. 'A bailee for reward must take reasonable care of any articles in his possession: *British Road Service Ltd v Arthur v Crutchley Ltd* [1986] 1 Lloyd's Rep 271, [1968] 1 All ER 811. The degree of precaution must be gauged according to the value of the goods, their disposability and portability, their vulnerability to theft, and to such other factors as the overall risk to them and the prevalence of crime in the vicinity. In the case of a bank the duty is to take such care as a reasonably prudent banker would take, in like circumstances, of the property of his clients': Palmer *Liability of Bankers as Custodians of Client Property* (1979), pp 9, 10.

2 *Target Holdings Ltd v Redferns* [1996] AC 421 at 435, per Lord Browne-Wilkinson:

'But in my judgment it is important, if the trust is not to be rendered commercially useless, to distinguish between the basic principles of trust law and those specialist rules developed in relation to traditional trusts which are applicable only to such trusts and the rationale of which has no application to trusts of quite a different kind.'

3 This is essentially akin to the position at common law. See *Target Holdings v Redferns* [1996] AC 421 at 432, per Lord Browne-Wilkinson:

'At common law there are two principles fundamental to the award of damages. First, that the defendant's wrongful act must cause the damage complained of. Second, that the plaintiff is to be put "in the same position as he would have been in if he had not sustained the wrong for which he is now getting his compensation or reparation" . . . Although, as will appear, in many ways equity approaches liability for making good a breach of trust from a different starting point, in my judgment those two principles are applicable as much in equity as at common law.'

4 See the discussion of *Bristol and West Building Society v Mothew* [1998] Ch 1, [1997] 2 WLR 436, [1996] 4 All ER 698 below.

5 See *Target Holdings v Redferns* [1996] AC 421 at 799, quoting from the judgment of Hoffmann LJ in *Bishopsgate Investment Management Ltd (in liquidation) v Maxwell (No 2)* [1994] 1 All ER 261: '. . . it is sound law that a plaintiff is not required to engage in hazardous litigation in order to mitigate his loss.'

6 See *Target Holdings v Redferns* [1996] AC 421 at 434, per Lord Browne-Wilkinson:

'Even if the immediate cause of the loss is the dishonesty or failure of a third party, the trustee is liable to make good that loss to the trust estate if, but for the breach, such loss would not have occurred . . . Thus the common law rules of remoteness of damages and causation do not apply. However, there does have to be some causal connection between the breach of trust and the loss to the trust estate for which compensation is recoverable, viz the fact that the loss would not have occurred but for the breach.'

In *Target* the issue was breach of an equitable duty of care and not breach of core fiduciary duty. This latter issue is considered in the following cases.

The insistence on some causal connection alters the earlier rule that loss flowing from non-disclosure by a fiduciary attracts strict liability (*Brickenden v London Loan & Savings Co* [1934] 3 DLR 465 at 469). However, in respect of active misrepresentations, liability remains strict: *Bristol and West Building Society v Mothew* [1998] Ch 1, [1997] 2 WLR 436, [1996] 4 All ER 698.

7 '61. If it appears to the court that a trustee, whether appointed by the court or otherwise, is or may be personally liable for any breach of trust, whether the transaction alleged to be a breach of trust occurred before or after the commencement of this Act, but has acted honestly and reasonably, and ought fairly to be excused for the breach of trust and for omitting to obtain the directions from the court in the matter in which he committed such breach, then the courts may relieve him either wholly or partly from personal liability for the same.'

Similar provisions in relation to company directors are contained in s 727 of the Companies Act 1985 (directors etc).

8 'Although there is no doubt about the court's jurisdiction to grant relief under section 61 to a trustee who is remunerated, there appears from the cases to be a marked reluctance to do so': Law Commission Report *Fiduciary Duties and Regulatory Rules*, December 1995, p 95.

The 23rd Report of the Law Reform Committee looked at the whole question of the powers and duties of trustees and considered the issue of whether it was desirable to incorporate the distinction between professional and voluntary trustees into statute. It concluded that this was not necessary, stating that s 61 was an adequate statutory provision to allow this difference to be recognised. The courts would be far more likely to give relief to a voluntary trustee under s 61 than to a professional trustee.

Trustee's duty of care

6.11 The trustee's duty of care is as follows.

Trustee Act 2000

6.12 The Trustee Act 2000 provides[1] for a statutory duty of care, which applies in certain circumstances[2], including the exercise and review of investment powers[3], and the appointment and review of agents, nominees and custodians (including sub-custodians)[4]. The statutory duty of care may be expressly excluded[5]. Where it applies, the trustee must –

'. . . exercise such care and skill as is reasonable in the circumstances, having regard in particular –

(a) to any special knowledge or experience that he has or holds himself out as having, and

(b) if he acts as trustee in the course of a business or profession, to any special knowledge or experience that it is reasonable to expect of a person acting in the course of that kind of business or profession.'[6]

1 TA 2000, s 1.
2 These are specified in Sch 1. See TA 2000, s 2
3 TA 2000, Sch 1, para 1. A global custodian is unlikely to have general powers of investment, but may have specific powers of investment, for example under cash management or securities lending arrangements.
4 TA 2000, Sch 1, para 3.
5 TA 2000, Sch 1, para 7.
6 TA 2000, s 1(1).

Case law

6.13 Where the statutory duty of care does not apply, the duty of care of the trustee is defined by case law in broadly similar terms[1].

The rule in *Re Waterman's Will Trusts*[2] provides that the trustee holding itself out as possessing special skills and which is paid for its services must observe a higher standard of diligence and knowledge than an unpaid trustee; and will be expected to exercise a greater degree of care. This rule was expanded in the case of *Bartlett v Barclays Bank*[3] in which Brightman J set the test as 'the special skill and care which [the professional trustee] professes to have'[4].

1 They are similar in the case of professional trustees. The general law test for a non-professional trustee is the level of care with which an ordinary prudent man of business would conduct his own affairs: *Speight v Gaunt* (1883) 9 App Cas 1 at 19 per Lord Blackburn:

> '. . . as a general rule the trustee sufficiently discharges his duty if he takes in the managing of trust affairs all those precautions which an ordinary prudent man of business would take in managing similar affairs of his own.'

2 [1952] 2 All ER 1054 at 1055 per Harman J:

> 'I do not forget that a professional trustee is expected to exercise a higher standard of diligence and knowledge than an unpaid trustee and that a bank which advertises itself largely in the public press as taking charge of administrations is under a special duty.'

3 [1980] Ch 515.
4 [1980] Ch 515 at 534.

Limitation clauses

6.14 Limitation clauses are highly effective in limiting the liability of trustees for breach of their duty of care[1]. Old authority indicates that liability for gross negligence and wilful default[2] is inexcludable. However, it is now clear that a properly drafted exemption clause may relieve a fiduciary from liability for loss caused by his own gross negligence, provided the exclusion is clearly brought to the attention of the client[3]. Such a clause cannot relieve liability for actual fraud, ie dishonesty[4].

> 'In my judgment cl 15 exempts the trustee from liability for loss or damage to the trust property no matter how indolent, imprudent, lacking in diligence, negligent or wilful he may have been, so long as he has not acted dishonestly.'[5]

Dishonesty for this purpose does not necessarily involve personal gain[6]. There is an irreducible core of fiduciary obligation, but it relates to honesty and does not involve any level of care[7].

> 'The duty to act in good faith (ie honestly and consciously) in respect of any trust matter cannot, of course, be excluded. To do so would make a nonsense of the trust relationship as an obligation of confidence.'[8]

Also, limitation clauses are effective retrospectively but not prospectively, as –

> '. . . a trustee who relied on the presence of a trustee exemption clause to justify what he proposed to do would thereby lose its protection: he would be acting recklessly in the proper sense of the term.'[9]

1 See the unreported High Court judgment of Harman J in *Galmerrow Securities Ltd v National Westminster Bank* [2002] WTLR 125, in which a trust deed is considered which contained relieving provisions limiting trustee liability to losses resulting from its fraud and negligence:

> 'However high a standard of skill and care is imposed by the general law, and I would wish to impose the highest standard on Trustee departments of major clearing banks, the duty has still to be defined by reference to the actual trust deed in the case before the Court. In *Bartlett*'s case (supra) no terms like those in the Trust Deed constituting the 22nd PAUT existed.' (p 35).

This view is endorsed by the Law Commission in its Report No 236, December 1995, Cm 3049, *Fiduciary Duties and Regulatory Rules*, p 11:

> 'We stated in the consultation paper that a fiduciary could not exclude liability for fraud, deliberate breach of duty and, possibly, gross negligence. Beyond that, our provisional view was that, in general, no restriction operated as a matter of fiduciary law to prevent a fiduciary from contracting out of or modifying his fiduciary duties, particularly where no prior fiduciary relationship existed and the contract sought to define the duties of the parties.'

2 In the case of *Pass v Dundas* (1880) 43 LT 665 Bacon VC held that the effect of the decision in *Wilkins v Hogg* (1861) 66 ER 346 was that an appropriate exemption clause 'does protect a trustee from loss that may have been sustained in the course of administering the trust estate, unless you can impute to him gross negligence or personal misconduct.'

3 In *Midland Bank Trust (Jersey) Ltd v Federated Pension Services* [1995] JLR 352 the Jersey Court of Appeal held that liability for gross negligence may be excluded unless prohibited by statute.

In *Walker v Stones* [2001] QB 902, the same line of reasoning was followed, it being accepted that the exclusion clause could effectively restrict liability to cases of 'wilful fraud or dishonesty', although it was stated that the 'test of honesty may vary from case to case, depending on, among other things, the role and calling of the trustee' (per Slade LJ at 939). (In *Walker*, it was considered that a solicitor-trustee would be dishonest even if it met the subjective test in *Armitage v Nurse* [1998] Ch 241 in that it honestly believed that it was acting in the interests of the beneficiaries, if 'by any objective standard, no reasonable solicitor-trustee could have thought that what he did or agreed to do was for the benefit of the beneficiaries' (per Slade LJ at 939). This is clearly important in the context of a professional custodian where a limitation clause may successfully exclude liability for gross negligence, but under the high level of care expected of a custodian, a decision of a custodian may be regarded as dishonest and therefore incurring liability for fraud if it is a decision which in the context would not be expected from a 'reasonable' professional custodian. See also *Twinsectra v Yardley* [2002] UKHL 12, [2002] 2 AC 164, [2002] 2 WLR 802, in which the test of dishonesty for the purpose of dishonest assistance was held to have a mixed subjective and objective element.

4 See *Armitage v Nurse* [1998] Ch 241. In this judgment Millett LJ considered a limitation clause in the following terms: 'No Trustee shall be liable for any loss or damage which may happen to [the beneficiary's] fund or any part thereof or the income thereof at any time or from any cause whatsoever unless such loss or damage shall be caused by his own actual fraud . . .' He held that 'In my judgment, therefore, cl 15 is apt to exclude liability for breach of trust in the absence of a dishonest intention on the part of the trustee whose conduct is impugned' (at 250).

5 *Armitage v Nurse* [1998] Ch 241 at 251.

6 *Armitage v Nurse* [1998] Ch 241 at 710:

> 'It is the duty of a trustee to manage the trust property and deal with it in the interests of the beneficiaries. If he acts in a way which he does not honestly believe is in their interests then he is acting dishonestly. It does not matter whether he stands or thinks he stands to gain personally from his actions. A trustee who acts with the intention of benefiting persons who are not the objects of the trust is not the less dishonest because he does not intend to benefit himself.'

7 *Armitage v Nurse* [1998] Ch 241 at 712:

> 'I accept . . . that there is an irreducible core of obligations owed by the trustee to the beneficiaries and enforceable by them which is fundamental to the concept of a trust. If the beneficiaries have no rights enforceable against the trustees there are no trusts. But I do not accept the further submission that these core obligations include the duties of skill or care, prudence and diligence. The duty of the trustees to perform the trusts honestly and in good faith for the benefit of the beneficiaries is the minimum necessary to give substance to the trusts, but in my opinion it is sufficient.'

8 David Hayton 'The Irreducible Core Content of Trusteeship' [1996] JTCP, p 3.

9 *Armitage v Nurse* [1998] Ch 241 at 254, per Millett LJ.

Fiduciary duty[1]

6.15

'To describe some one as a fiduciary, without more, is meaningless.'[2]

There may be considerable tactical advantages to the claimant in establishing breach of fiduciary duty. Unlike breach of contract and negligence, breach of fiduciary duty may provide the basis of a proprietary claim (and therefore be effective against an insolvent defendant); it is not subject to common law rules of causation and remoteness[3]; and the plaintiff is not obliged to mitigate its losses by litigation[4]. However, for this purpose, breach of fiduciary duty is narrowly[5] defined to connote disloyalty or infidelity[6]. It should not be confused with the wider category of breach of trust[7], or with breach of the trustee's duty of care[8]. Liability for the latter two is (arguably) subject to rules on causation and remoteness[9].

1 The acknowledged expert on fiduciary duty is P D Finn. See *Fiduciary Obligations* (1977, Law Book Co, Sydney) (described by Millett LJ as his 'classic work' in *Bristol and West Building Society v Mothew* [1998] Ch 1 at 18) and T G Youdan (ed) *The Fiduciary Principle, Equity, Fiduciaries and Trusts* (1989, Carswell).

The interrelation of fiduciary duties and regulatory rules has been much discussed in recent years. Debate has been stimulated by a May 1992 Law Commission Consultative Paper, *Fiduciary Duties and Regulatory Rules* and a subsequent report having the same title and published in December 1995 (Cm 3049). Dr Black explains that the tension between fiduciary duty and regulatory rules provided one of the original motives for the Financial Services Act 1986 (the predecessor of the Financial Services and Markets Act 2000): see Julia Black *Rules and Regulators* (1997, Clarendon Press).

2 *Re Goldcorp Exchange Ltd (in receivership)* [1995] 1 AC 74 at 98, per Lord Mustill.

3 See *Bristol and West Building Society v Mothew* [1998] Ch 1 at 8 per Millett LJ:

> 'It was common ground below that no damages would be recoverable at common law for breach of contract or tort unless the society could show that it would not have proceeded with the transaction if it had been informed of the facts. The society, however, submitted that the position was different in equity. It alleged that the defendant had committed a breach of trust or fiduciary duty, and submitted that common law principles of causation and remoteness of damage have no application in such a case so that it was not necessary for the society to show that it would not have proceeded with the transaction if it had been informed of the facts.'

4 See *Bishopsgate Investment Management Ltd (in liquidation) v Maxwell (No 2)* [1994] 1 All ER 261, quoted in *Target Holdings v Redferns* [1996] AC 421 at 440.

5 See *Bristol and West Building Society v Mothew* [1998] Ch 1 at 16 per Millett LJ:

> 'The expression "fiduciary duty" is properly confined to those duties which are peculiar to fiduciaries . . . it is obvious that not every breach of duty by a fiduciary is a breach of fiduciary duty.'

6 See *Bristol and West Building Society v Mothew* [1998] Ch 1 at 18 per Millett LJ:

> 'Breach of fiduciary obligation, therefore, connotes disloyalty or infidelity. Mere incompetence is not enough. A servant who loyally does his incompetent best for his master is not unfaithful and is not guilty of breach of fiduciary duty.'

The no profit and no conflict rules are proscriptive, as opposed to the trustee's duty of care, and specific trust duties, which are prescriptive.

7 See *Armitage v Nurse* [1998] Ch 241 at 251, per Millett LJ:

> 'Breaches of trust are of many different kinds. A breach of trust may be deliberate or inadvertent; it may consist of an actual misappropriation or misapplication of the trust property or merely of an investment or other dealing which is outside the trustee's powers; it may consist of a failure to carry out a positive obligation of the trustees or merely of a want of skill and care on their part in the management of the trust property;'

8 See *Bristol and West Building Society v Mothew* [1998] Ch 1 at 16 per Millett LJ:

> '. . . there can be no justification for treating an unconscious failure as demonstrating want of fidelity . . . It is similarly inappropriate to apply the expression to the obligation of a trustee or other fiduciary to use proper skill and care in the discharge of his duties.'

9 See *Bristol and West Building Society v Mothew* [1998] Ch 1 at 17 per Millett LJ:

> 'Equitable compensation for breach of the duty of skill and care resembles common law damages in that it is awarded by way of compensation to the plaintiff for his loss. These is no reason in

principle why the common law rules of causation, remoteness of damage and measure of damage should not be applied by analogy in such a case. It should not be confused with equitable compensation for breach of fiduciary duty . . .'

The nature of fiduciary duty

6.16 While fiduciary duty is a very uncertain area of law, it is possible to make the following generalisations. Fiduciary relationships are relationships of special trust, so that the fiduciary is required to put the client's interests above her own interests[1]: 'The "fiduciary" standard for its part enjoins one party to act in the interests of another – to act selflessly and with undivided loyalty'[2]. The significance of fiduciary status here is that fiduciaries owe special implied[3] duties to their beneficiaries[4]. Fiduciary duties are summarised in four basic rules:

- the no conflict rule,
- the no profit rule,
- the undivided loyalty rule, and
- the duty of confidentiality[5].

Beyond these rules (which are derived from the general duty to act in the interests of the beneficiary) fiduciary status does not prescribe positive duties. Thus, the particular services that a global custodian must render are determined by its agreement with its client, and not by implied fiduciary status. Fiduciary status does not determine the content of the relationship between the parties; rather it is (in essence) merely a judicial remedy for want of loyalty where loyalty is owed[6].

1 See *Bristol and West Building Society v Mothew* [1998] Ch 1 at 18 per Millett LJ:

> 'A fiduciary is someone who has undertaken to act for or on behalf of another in a particular matter in circumstances which give rise to a relationship of trust or confidence. The distinguishing obligation of a fiduciary is the obligation of loyalty. The principal is entitled to the single-minded loyalty of his fiduciary. This core liability has several facets. A fiduciary must act in good faith; he must not make a profit out of his trust; he must not place himself in a position where his duty and his interest may conflict; he may not act for his own benefit or the benefit of a third person without the informed consent of his principal. This is not intended to be an exhaustive list, but it is sufficient to indicate the nature of fiduciary obligations. They are the defining characteristics of the fiduciary.'

Law Commission Report, pp 1, 11:

> 'Broadly speaking, a fiduciary relationship is one in which a person undertakes to act on behalf of or for the benefit of another, often as an intermediary with a discretion or power which affects the interests of the other who depends on the fiduciary for information and advice . . . in determining whether a relationship was fiduciary, and if so, the extent of the fiduciary duties, a court would look at the substance of a relationship and not merely its description in the contract.'

2 P D Finn *The Fiduciary Principle, Equity, Fiduciaries and Trusts* (1989, Youdan (ed), Carswell), p 4.

3 Arguably, fiduciary duties are imposed and not implied. See the discussion of tortious duties in *Tai Hing Cotton Mill Ltd v Liu Chong Hing Bank Ltd* [1986] AC 80, per Lord Scarman at 104:

> '. . . the test of implication is necessity . . . Implication is the way in which necessary incidents come to the recognised in the absence of express agreement in a contractual relationship. Imposition is apt to describe a duty arising in tort, but inept to describe the necessary incident arising from a contractual relationship.'

4 More generally, in certain common law jurisdictions including England, '. . . to designate someone a fiduciary is to expose that person to the full rigour of equity both in method [for example, in reversal of the onus of proof, in presumptions of wrongdoing and in disregard of notions such as causation, foreseeability and remoteness] and in remedy [from avoidance through damages and the account of profits to the constructive trust] . . .' P D Finn *The Fiduciary Principle*, p 2.

Arguably, it would be more correct to refer to these as *imposed* duties rather than *implied* duties. See *Tai Hing Cotton Mill Ltd v Liu Chong Hing Bank Ltd* [1986] AC 80, in which Lord Scarman discusses (at 104) non-contractual (tortious) duties; the same analysis may apply to fiduciary duties.

5 Law Commission Report, pp 1, 2:

'The exact scope of the fiduciary's obligations and the consequences of breach vary according to the particular circumstances but the duties may conveniently be summarised in the following basic rules:

(i) *The "no conflict" rule* A fiduciary must not place himself in a position where his own interest conflicts with that of his customer, the beneficiary. There must be a "real sensible possibility of conflict";

(ii) *The "no profit" rule* A fiduciary must not profit from his position at the expense of his customer, the beneficiary;

(iii) *The "undivided loyalty" rule* A fiduciary owes undivided loyalty to his customer, the beneficiary, not to place himself in a position where his duty towards one customer conflicts with a duty that he owes to another customer. A consequence of this is that a fiduciary must make available to a customer all the information that is relevant to the customer's affairs;

(iv) *The "duty of confidentiality"* A fiduciary must only use information obtained in confidence from his customer, the beneficiary, for the benefit of the customer and must not use it for his own advantage, or for the benefit of any other person.'

These are default rules that can be ousted by contractual provision, or provision in the trust deed. See *Kelly v Cooper Associates* [1993] AC 205.

6 See P D Finn *The Fiduciary Principle, Equity, Fiduciaries and Trusts* (1989, Youdan (ed), Carswell), p 28.

The global custodian as fiduciary

6.17 The argument that a global custodian is not a fiduciary is considered to be untenable. Because of its safekeeping role, the custodian is either a trustee or (in the rare cases where client assets comprise physical securities in the hands of the custodian) a bailee[1]. A trustee is always a fiduciary[2]. Whether or not a bailee is a fiduciary will depend on all the circumstances and the terms of the bailment[3]. However, because the custodian role actively combines safekeeping with administration and settlement on behalf of the client, it would be prudent to assume that the global custodian is a fiduciary[4].

1 See Chapter 3.

2 Law Commission Consultation Paper, pp 27, 28:

'. . . it is possible to divide fiduciaries into two categories, status-based fiduciaries and fact-based fiduciaries . . . [The latter] include people who, by virtue of their involvement in certain relationships are considered, without further inquiry, to be fiduciaries. Such relationships include those between trustee-beneficiary, solicitor-client, agent-principal, director-company, and partner-partner.'

3 *Re Andrabell Ltd (in liquidation), Airborne Accessories Ltd* [1984] 3 All ER 407 per Peter Gibson J.

4 *Reading v A-G* [1949] 2 KB 232, [1949] 2 All ER 68:

'. . . a "fiduciary relation" exists . . . wherever the plaintiff entrusts to the defendant property . . . and relies on the defendant to deal with such property for the benefit of the plaintiff or for purposes authorised by him, and not otherwise . . .'

Thus, the argument that the global custodian is a fiduciary is strengthened in cases where, for example, the global custodian operates a discretionary securities lending programme on the client's behalf.

See also *Re Brooke Bond & Co Ltd's Trust Deed* [1963] Ch 357, [1963] 2 WLR 320, [1963] 1 All ER 454 , in which a custodian trustee is held to be subject to the fiduciary 'no profit' rule. See also P D Finn *The Fiduciary Principle, Equity, Fiduciaries and Trusts* (1989, Youdan (ed), Carswell), p 35:

'In many instances property is a subject of a legal relationship with one party having custodial or other rights in or to that property. To the extent that party has limited or indeed no rights to its beneficial use and enjoyment, that person's position is incipiently fiduciary.'

In a writ issued on 5 June 1992 by MGN Pension Trustees Limited against Bank of America National Trust and Savings Association and Crédit Suisse, the trustees of the Maxwell pension fund sued Bank of America as custodians of the pension fund assets, asserting that they should not have settled instructions from the managers whereby the pension fund assets were lost. The writ asserted that Bank of America was a fiduciary:

'In the premises, and by reason of the [custody] Agreement and by reason of its position as custodian of assets of the [pension fund], BA owed fiduciary duties to the Trustee and the [pension fund]' (p 25).

Limitation clauses[1]

6.18 There is longstanding authority that the terms of a fiduciary's appointment may limit its duties[2]. Moreover, the position of the global custodian seeking to rely on contractual limitation of their fiduciary duties was enormously strengthened by the case of *Kelly v Cooper Associates*[3]. In this case it was stated[4] that a fiduciary relationship arising in the context of a contractual deal should not alter the nature of the deal. Lord Browne-Wilkinson quoted[5] an earlier case[6] as follows:

> 'That contractual and fiduciary relationships may co-exist between the same parties has never been doubted. Indeed, the existence of a basic contractual relationship has in many situations provided a foundation for the erection of a fiduciary relationship. In these situations, it is the contractual foundation which is all important because it is the contract that regulates the basic rights and liabilities of the parties. The fiduciary relationship, if it is to exist at all, must accommodate itself to the terms of the contract so that it is consistent with, and conforms to them. The fiduciary relationship cannot be superimposed upon the contract in such a way as to alter the operation which the contract was intended to have according to its true construction.'

The Law Commission discusses *Kelly* in the following terms:

> 'It confirmed that where a fiduciary relationship arises out of a contract, a clearly worded duty defining or exclusion clause will circumscribe the extent of the fiduciary duties owed to the other party.'[7]

The report summarises the conditions that must be satisfied before the principle in *Kelly* may be relied upon[8] and draws attention to its limits[9].

This approach was endorsed in the case of *Clark Boyce v Mouat*[10]. 'A fiduciary duty . . . cannot be prayed in aid to enlarge the scope of contractual duties.'[11] There is much judicial authority to the effect that implied fiduciary duty cannot distort a commercial contractual relationship[12]. However, while fiduciary duties must conform with the contract, they are not entirely subsumed within it, for '. . . the essence of a fiduciary relationship is that it creates obligations of a different character from those deriving from the contract itself.'[13]

It is also clear from case law that fiduciaries have a core minimum duty of loyalty that cannot be excluded by any relieving provisions[14].

It is customary for global custodians (and indeed fund managers, brokers and other financial institutions who may be characterised as fiduciaries) to include in their contracts provisions designed to modify implied fiduciary. These permit conflicts of interest to arise (both between the client and the global custodian and between the client and other clients of the global custodian); disclose profits that the global custodian may derive from the relationship with the client and permit the global custodian to retain them; and relax the implied duty of confidentiality by permitting the global custodian to disclose client information to associates or other third parties.

1 Limitation clauses cannot remove the fiduciary status of the global custodian; however, they are effective to modify its fiduciary duties, subject to the core fiduciary duty of loyalty as discussed below.
2 See *Wilkins v Hogg* (1861) 66 ER 346.
3 [1993] AC 205. This was a Privy Council decision, on appeal from the Court of Appeal of Bermuda. The case concerned the practices of an estate agent and its failure to notify one vendor client that it also acted for a vendor of an adjoining property.
4 Obiter, by Lord Browne-Wilkinson.
5 [1993] AC 205 at 215.

6 Mason J in the case of *Hospital Products International Pty Ltd v United States Surgical Corpn* (1984) 156 CLR 41.
7 Law Commission Report 1995, p 4.
8 Law Commission Report 1995, pp 85, 86:

'*Kelly* will provide a solution where the following conditions are satisfied. First, the duty defining and exclusion clause must clearly cover the transaction in question: it will have to do so unambiguously since it will be subject to the *contra proferentum* rule of interpretation. Secondly, in those situations where the relationship between the firm and client has altered over time, this altered relationship will also have to be caught by the clause. And thirdly, it must be the substance of the relationship between the client and the firm that is covered by the clause and not what the parties call it. If these three conditions are satisfied, then *Kelly* provides a way of solving the problems that arise from any mismatch between fiduciary rules, regulatory rules and market structure.'

9 Law Commission Report 1995, p 24 in relation to conflicts of interest:

'However, there are three situations of conflict in which, despite *Kelly*, it will be necessary either to make appropriate provision in the contract or obtain the informed consent of the customer in order to avoid breaching a fiduciary duty. The first is where the firm is acting for two customers in the same transaction. The second is where there is a conflict between the firm's own interest and the duty which it owes to a customer and that conflict is more acute than that which arose in *Kelly* . . . The conflict would be more acute if, for example, (i) a firm has a direct beneficial interest in a transaction with a customer, such as where it sells its own property to a customer . . . The third situation is where there has been "iniquity".'

10 [1994] 1 AC 428, [1993] 3 WLR 1021, [1993] 4 All ER 268. This was another Privy Council decision, on appeal from the Court of Appeal of New Zealand. The case concerned a claim against a solicitor; the plaintiff mortgaged her house to secure a loan to her son, and the solicitor acted for both of them.
11 Per Lord Jauncey of Tullichettle, at 437.
12 In addition to the judgments in *Kelly* and *Clarke Boyce* see, for example, *Target Holdings Ltd v Redferns* [1996] AC 421, [1995] 3 WLR 352, [1995] 3 All ER 785.
13 *Re Goldcorp Exchange Ltd* [1995] 1 AC 74 at 98. See also *Henderson v Merrett* [1995] 2 AC 145 at 206 per Lord Browne-Wilkinson.
14 *Wilkins v Hogg* (1861) 66 ER 346 at 348.

Conflicts of interest

6.19 As briefly indicated above, the fiduciary must avoid two types of potential conflict of interest. First, it must not allow its own interests to conflict with those of its customer ('the no conflicts rule')[1]. Second, it must not allow its duties to one customer to conflict with its duties to another customer ('the undivided loyalty rule')[2].

Many of the global custodians in London are multi-function financial institutions, whose divisions may include fund management, brokerage and corporate finance. Therefore, conflicts of interest routinely arise, and must be managed by the informed consent of the client[3].

As discussed in Chapter 4, an important and growing function of custody securities is collateral. For reasons of administrative convenience[4] custodians are often asked to act in two capacities, both as custodian for their clients and as collateral trustee for their client's secured creditors[5]. The arrangement may be documented by one tri-party contract[6]. Clearly, acting for the parties on both sides of a collateral arrangement involves such a conflict. Very careful drafting is required to manage this conflict. Indeed, where the custodian has any discretionary powers in relation to the management or enforcement of collateral on behalf of the collateral taker, its position may be untenable.

Where a trustee appoints a custodian under s 17 of the Trustee Act 2000, it is not permitted to allow the custodian to restrict its liability or act in circumstances capable of giving rise to a conflict of interest, unless it is reasonably necessary to do so[7]. As such terms are standard in global custody contracts[8], and no major global custodian is likely to be willing to act without them, trustee clients are likely to find that their inclusion is reasonably necessary for the purposes of the Trustee Act.

1 *Bray v Ford* [1896] AC 44.
2 See *Bristol and West Building Society v Mothew* [1998] Ch 1 at 18, 19 per Millett LJ:

> 'A fiduciary who acts for two principals with potentially conflicting interests without the informed consent of both is in breach of the obligation of undivided loyalty; he puts himself in a position where his duty to one principal *may* conflict with his duty to the other': see *Clark Boyce v Mouat* [1993] 3 WLR 1021, [1994] 1 AC 428, [1993] 4 All ER 268, and the cases there cited. This is sometimes described as "the double employment rule". Breach of the rule automatically constitutes a breach of fiduciary duty.'

And at 19 per Millett LJ:

> 'Even if a fiduciary is properly acting for two principals with potentially conflicting interests he must act in good faith in the interests of each and must not act with the intention of furthering the interests of one principal to the prejudice of those of the other . . . I shall call this "the duty of good faith". But it goes further than this. He must not allow the performance of his obligations to one principal to be influenced by his relationship with the other. He must serve each as faithfully and loyally as if he were his only principal. Conduct which is in breach of this duty need not be dishonest but it must be intentional. An unconscious omission which happens to benefit one principal at the expense of the other does not constitute a breach of fiduciary duty, though it may constitute a breach of the duty of skill and care . . . Finally, the fiduciary must take care not to find himself in a position where there is an *actual* conflict of duty so that he cannot fulfil his obligations to one principal without failing in his obligations to the other: see *Moody v Cox* [1917] 2 Ch 71, [1916–17] All ER Rep 548 and *Commonwealth Bank of Australia v Smith* (1991) 102 ALR 453. If he does, he may have no alternative but to cease to act for at least one and preferably both. That fact that he cannot fulfil his obligations to one principal without being in breach of his obligations to the other will not absolve him from liability. I shall call this "the actual conflict rule".'

3 An ad hoc Chinese Wall may not be effective in addressing a conflict of interest. See *Prince Jefri Bolkiah v KPMG* [1999] 2 AC 222, [1999] 2 WLR 215, [1999] 1 All ER 517.
4 And because the transfer of securities can involve delay, expense and tax.
5 In other words, the client both places its securities with the custodian, and charges them to the creditor, and the creditor appoints the custodian to act on its behalf in relation to the administration and enforcement of the charge.
6 To which the client, the secured creditor and the custodian are parties.
7 TA 2000, s 20(2), (3). The same restriction is placed by these subsections on terms permitting the sub-custodian to appoint a substitute.
8 Where the global custodian is a multi-function financial institution, conflicts of interest will regularly arise.

Secret profits

6.20 It was indicated above that, as a fiduciary, the global custodian is generally not permitted to profit from its position at the expense of the client[1]. An aspect of the rule is that in general the global custodian can retain no profits indirectly derived from its service to the client. While this rule can be modified by the informed consent of the client, any 'secret profits'[2] must be accounted for to the client[3].

Competitive pressure has reduced custodian fees to minimal levels, and the profits associated with global custody are no longer fee-based, but derived from the 'cross selling' of the financial services which the bank custodian is able to offer. The global custodian may undertake discretionary securities lending of the clients' portfolios, and provide foreign exchange and derivative services, retaining significant profits in each case. These profits are not always expressly disclosed.

Many custodians take a middle course, and include provision in the global custody contract giving general advance disclosures relating to cross selling and associated profits. In its report[4] the Law Commission argues that *Kelly v Cooper Associates* [1993] AC 205, [1992] 3 WLR 936 permits firms to rely on advance disclosures[5].

However, some clients who are trustees may fear that general advance consent may involve them in breach of trust to their beneficiaries[6]. Further, a note of caution is sounded by the case of *Glynwill Investments NV v Thomson McKinnon Futures Ltd*[7], where a foreign exchange dealer was held liable for breach of fiduciary duty, and was not able to rely on contractual provision which did not accord with the commercial realities of its client business[8].

The prudent approach would be to assume that profits from cross selling may only be retained if expressly detailed in the global custody agreement.

1 Prior to the Trustee Act 2000, the custodian could not be remunerated unless fees were expressly agreed with the client. Today, in the absence of express provision (s 29(5)) the custodian is entitled to receive reasonable remuneration for its services (s 29(1) and (3)). Also, the custodian is entitled to be reimbursed expenses properly incurred by it (s 31(1)) and may remunerate and reimburse the expenses of agents, nominees and [sub]-custodians (s 32).

2 That is, profits to which the client has not informedly consented.

3 See *Re Brooke Bond Trust Deed* [1963] Ch 357, [1963] 2 WLR 320, [1963] 1 All ER 454. See the *Myners Report on Institutional Investment* (2001), which calls for greater transparency in charges to institutional investors.

4 December 1995.

5 Law Commission Report (1995), p 47:

> 'We now believe that a sufficiently precise general advanced disclosure made in a contract will be effective provided that the contract clearly delimits the fiduciary duties owed to the customer and displaces the obligation to make full disclosure of all material facts, and the customer has not been misled as to the nature of the relationship between the parties.'

6 See Hayton 'Developing the Law of Trusts for the Twenty-First Century' (1990) 106 LQR 87 at 89.

7 (13 February 1992, unreported), Tuckey QC.

8 Law Commission Report (1995) , pp 29, 30:

> 'This case also considered the extent to which the contract can determine the scope of fiduciary duties. The defendant firm was a foreign exchange dealer. It acted for the plaintiff in currency transaction, charging a commission and also, in some cases, taking a mark-up on the price at which it had bought in the market. It did not disclose the mark-up to the plaintiff. The plaintiff contended that the defendant was acting as its agent and was therefore liable to account for the mark-up. The defendant claimed that it was acting, as the contract between it and the plaintiff specified, as principal. However, the deputy judge concluded that in the light of the other evidence, including the agreement of commission and the market order method used by the plaintiffs, the trading relationship was one of principal and agent. The plaintiff was therefore entitled to recover the amount of the mark-up from the defendant.'

Liability for third parties[1]

6.21 The global custodian is at the centre of a communications and service network. When losses occur to a client's portfolio, they will often be attributable, not to the global custodian itself, but to a third party. For this reason, global custody contracts often seek to exclude liability for the defaults of third parties, including brokers[2]. This section will consider two topical issues, namely the liability of the global custodian in respect of sub-custodian default, and fraudulent instructions from managers.

1 See the discussion of outsourcing in Chapter 7.

2 Exclusion of liability for the defaults of brokers may be unnecessary: as brokers are not appointed or supervised by the global custodian, it is unlikely that the global custodian owes any general duty to the client in respect of the actions of brokers.

Liability for sub-custodians

6.22 One of the most commercially sensitive issues facing the global custodian is the extent to which it should stand behind its sub-custodians.

Some clients mistakenly believe that the law imposes strict liability upon custodians for the defaults of their delegates, but this is far from true. Where the sub-custodian is a nominee or close associate of the global custodian, it may be unrealistic for the global custodian to expect to escape liability. However, for independent sub-custodians, liability is much more limited.

Technically, the legal position depends upon whether the sub-custodian was appointed under s 17 of the Trustee Act 2000 or under an express term of the global custody agreement[1]. In the former case, the global custodian is obliged to comply with the statutory duty of care[2] when entering into the sub-custody arrangements[3]. Also, it must keep the sub-custody arrangements under review[4] and (broadly) where appropriate, exercise their powers of intervention[5], again complying with the statutory duty of care. Provided it complies with these requirements, the global custodian is not liable for any act or default of the sub-custodian.

Where the sub-custodian is not appointed under s 17 of the Trustee Act, it is possible that a similar position arises under case law, so that provided a global custodian exercises reasonable care in the appointment and supervision of its global custodial network, it should escape liability for their defaults[6]. On this basis, to avoid liability under this section for third party losses, the global custodian must show ordinary prudence in the appointment and supervision of its global custodial network.

Global custodians should take care in the initial choice of the members of their network, and in reviewing that choice from time to time. Criteria should include all matters affecting the safety of client assets, including local custodial and administrative arrangements and staff controls. These should be considered in the light of local law and market practice. In particular, the global custodian should consider the impact of local insolvency law on its ability to recover client assets in the event of the third party's insolvency[7].

It should be noted that since there is now a statutory power to appoint agents, custodians and nominees in the Trustee Act 2000, the omission of the power of delegation from a custody agreement will no longer result in a custodian incurring strict liability for its delegates because it made the delegation in breach of trust[8].

Global custodians sometimes take indemnities from sub-custodians. However, the usefulness of any such indemnity might be limited for the following reasons. The major risk associated with sub-custodians may be their credit risk; their insolvency would clearly affect the value of an indemnity issued by them. Moreover, if the global custodian's exposure is due to its breach of duty, an indemnity in respect of it may be unenforceable, as discussed below.

1 Of course, global custody agreements should always include such an express power to appoint sub-custodians. If a global custodian wished to bring its power of appointment under s 17, and so benefit from the exclusion of liability in s 23(1) discussed below, it could provide in the global custody agreement that the power of appointment arises pursuant to Trustee Act 2000, s 17.

2 That is, as discussed above, to exercise the care and skill which is reasonable in the circumstances (having regard to any special knowledge or experience that the custodian has or holds himself out as having, and, if acting as a trustee in the course of a business or profession, any special knowledge or experience that it is reasonable to expect of a person acting in the course of that kind of business or profession). As indicated earlier, the duty of care may be expressly disapplied: TA 2000, Sch 1, para 7.

3 TA 2000, s 23(1)

4 TA 2000, s 22(1)(a).

5 TA 2000, s 22(1)(b). Of course, the Act does not compel the global custodian to exercise powers of intervention which it does not have under the terms of the sub-custody agreement.

6 This was the position under Trustee Act 1925, s 30(1), now repealed; it reflected the earlier equitable position prior to codification in its legislative predecessors.

7 See Chapter 7 for a note of the regulatory requirements.

8 TA 2000, s 17. This in effect disapplies the general rule of English law that *delegatus non potest delegare*, which would otherwise mean that the custodian must act personally, on the basis that the client is deemed to have chosen the custodian personally to carry out its duties, without delegation or sub-delegation, unless expressly permitted to delegate by the custody agreement.

Fraudulent instructions

6.23 An important potential exposure to the custodian is the arrangement, customary in pensions business, where instructions come not from the client, but from a fund manager[1].

Following the Maxwell scandal, the pension trustees sued Bank America as custodian for implementing the manager's instructions to make the free deliveries that led to the loss of the pension assets. Bank America settled the claim. It was not disputed that the instructions were technically valid[2]. The basis for the claim was that the custodian's suspicions should have been raised and, as a fiduciary, it should have reviewed the instructions and enquired into the circumstances surrounding them. This claim raises the suggestion that the custodian's duties may extend to oversight of the manager, or even co-management[3]. As the claim was settled out of court, these issues have not been judicially clarified.

The suggestion that the custodian is obliged to vet manager's instructions is worrying for the custodian. First, it is contractually obliged to implement instructions, so that any obligation to decline to implement certain instructions might put it in breach of contract[4]. Second, in view of the high level of automation that is increasingly customary in settlement operations[5], any duty to review or subjectively appraise particular instructions may be impractical to discharge. In any case, the staff involved in settlement may be trained for administrative duties, and not in a position to exercise judgments as to the propriety of instructions.

There are strong arguments that the custodian is not under a general duty to review manager's instructions[6]. The case of *Galmerrow Securities Ltd v National Westminster Bank plc*[7] considered the position of the trustee of an unauthorised[8] unit trust scheme. Mr Justice Harman noted that the trust deed conferred exclusive power of and responsibility for management on the managers: 'Plainly these terms are inconsistent with NatWest as Trustee exercising a general supervision over the choice of property.'[9] On this basis, the trustee was held not to be liable for losses attributable to bad management[10].

Contractual provisions should be included in the global custody agreement confirming the ability to assume that technically valid instructions are in order[11] and that there is no duty of oversight of the manager. However, it would be prudent for global custodians to assume there may be some risk that they may not escape liability for acting on evidently fraudulent instructions, and for this reason may consider implementing controls that alert them to free deliveries or possibly unusually large transfers[12]. Timely transaction reports to clients may also reduce risk.

1 For the position relating to the liability of custodian trustees (as opposed to managing trustees) see The Public Trustee Act 1906, s 4(2).

2 Although it may be argued that fraudulent instructions cannot be valid instructions under a custody contract.

3 The writ alleged that a number of terms were implied into the custody agreement, including the following (p 27):

> '(5) that BA would immediately inform the Trustees and if necessary each of the directors thereof of any instructions that it received in relation to the funds, which might involve risks to the assets under their management or alter the nature of their rights and duties and/or their performance thereof or which were abnormal, suspicious or otherwise out of the ordinary.
>
> (6) that BA would not deal with the funds and securities that it held in any way which put them at risk or allowed them to be stolen or used for improper purposes or lost to the MGPS . . .'

4 As delayed settlement may put the manager into default and also prevent it from taking advantage of investment opportunities, damages may be significant.

5 See the discussion of straight through processing in Chapter 8.

6 Although it can be liable for dishonest assistance in breach of fiduciary duty: *Royal Brunei Airlines v Tan* [1995] 2 AC 378, [1995] 3 WLR 64, [1995] 3 All ER 97; *Twinsectra v Yardley* [2002] UKHL 12, [2002] 2 AC 164, [2002] 2 WLR 802, [2002] 2 All ER 377.

7 [2002] WTLR 125.
8 Of course, the trustee of an authorised unit trust scheme has regulatory monitoring functions; see rule 7.9.1 of the FSA Handbook.
9 *Galmerrow Securities Ltd v National Westminster Bank* [2002] WTLR 125.
10 The Goode Report also provides some support for this position. During September 1993 the Pension Law Review Committee, chaired by Professor Roy Goode, published its report on pension law reform. There is a section discussing the custody of pension assets and the desirability of using a custodian independent of the sponsor and the manager. The report concludes as follows:

> '. . . whilst recognising the value of custodianship services, we do not consider that it would be right to require trustees . . . to place pension funds assets with independent custodians' (p 369).

Part of the basis for this conclusion is –

> '. . . the fact that the custodian exercises ministerial rather than managerial functions and has no duty to investigate the propriety of instructions given to it, which appear to be in order, unless it has specifically undertaken a monitoring function' (p 367).

> 'The custodian will wish to see the provisions of the trust deed relating to the trustees' investment powers. When dealing with a fund manager the custodian should also verify the authority given to the fund manager, and, where that authority does not come direct from the trustees as a whole but from individual trustees or from a third party, the source of their power to confer that authority. But when these steps have been taken, the custodian is free to act on its instructions in the absence of circumstances putting it on enquiry that something may be amiss' (p 368).

> 'The use of custodians may well give the semblance of protection without the reality' (p 369).

11 It should be provided that the custodian is entitled to act in accordance with instructions unless it has actual knowledge that the instructions are fraudulent or in breach of the instructor's duties.
12 Because the contractual provision may not be wholly enforceable, care should be taken to ensure that 'partial invalidity' boilerplate is also included (ie provision that, if any part of the agreement is invalid, the remainder will remain in effect).

Nexus

6.24 Where a custody client suffers loss due to the default of a sub-custodian, its ability to recover damages for breach of duty at civil law will often depend on its ability to demonstrate that it is in a direct relationship with the defendant[1]. Of course, such relationships can be established between the client and the global custodian. However, unless the global custodian was in breach of its duty of care in appointing or supervising the sub-custodian, fault does not arise at this level. There may be fault at sub-custodian level, but no liability, because there was no relationship on which to establish duty owed to the client[2]. In an intermediated service such as global custody, the client has no direct nexus with the sub-delegates responsible for losses: therefore duty and fault may be unlikely to coincide in the same person, and the client is more exposed than in a service where there is no sub-delegation.

1 Because, under English law, fiduciary duties only arise where there is a relationship of special trust, and negligence can only be established where duties of care are owed. However, as discussed above, the Contracts (Rights of Third Parties) Act 1999 permits third parties to enforce contractual rights in certain circumstances.
2 Any agency between the global custodian and sub-custodians is usually avoided, in order to prevent a direct contractual relationship between the third parties and the global custody clients, which might in turn undermine the commercial position of the global custodian.

Particular clauses

6.25 Certain additional exclusions are customary in global custody agreements. Precisely what is included depends on the concerns and negotiating strengths of the parties. The following are important examples[1].

1 Other specific limitations that are commonly included in global custody contracts include receipt of invalid or forged securities; reversals of credits to an account; delays while the custodian seeks clarification of ambiguous instructions; and the investment risks of assets held by the custodian.

Force majeure

6.26 The global custodian's ability to discharge its duties may be particularly vulnerable to computer failure. Force majeure clauses (excusing performance where it is rendered impossible or impracticable) are very important[1]. However, they can be no substitute for practical measures such as disaster recovery systems and insurance. Following the events of 11 September 2001, new industry attention has focused on disaster recovery, and in particular the importance of a geographical spread of data processing back-up systems. Global custodians are also placing new emphasis on clarifying the adequacy of their clients' back-up systems[2].

1 See generally A G Guest (ed) *Chitty on Contracts* (1994, 27th edn, Sweet & Maxwell), para 14-126 et seq.
2 J Brown 'Recovery Wakes up to Extreme Risk' (November 2001) *Euromoney* 82 at 84–5.

Consequential damages

6.27 In view of the judgment in *Target Holdings Ltd v Redferns*[1] it is important for global custodians contractually to exclude liability for consequential damages; such provision must, however, be brought clearly to the attention of clients.

1 [1996] AC 421 at 434, per Lord Browne-Wilkinson:

> '. . . the common law rules of remoteness of damages and causation do not apply . . . The plaintiff's actual loss as a consequence of the breach is to be assessed with the full benefit of hindsight. Foreseeability is not a concern in assessing compensation . . .'

Erroneous instructions

6.28 It is common practice among global custodians to provide in the global custody agreement that customers must examine the periodic statements provided by the global custodian, and notify it of any error within a stated period, and further that in the absence of such notification the customer may not challenge the statement. In a banking context, such provision was held to be ineffective in *Tai Hing Cotton Mill Ltd v Liu Chong Hing Bank Ltd*[1] because it was not sufficiently clear and unambiguous to bring home to the customer the burden of examining the statements and the consequences of its failing to so do[2]. It is likely that many such clauses that are included in standard global custody agreements would fail the test in *Tai Hing*[3].

1 [1986] AC 80, [1985] 3 WLR 317, [1985] 2 All ER 947. Tai Hing was a Hong Kong textile manufacturer. It was defrauded by its clerk, which inter alia forged the managing director's signature on cheques drawn on the company's banks. The cheques were paid and the sums debited from the company's accounts. The banks' terms of business provided that its bank periodic account statements would be deemed to be confirmed by the company if no errors were notified to the bank within a stated period. However, the company's internal control systems were inadequate, the clerk was almost unsupervised and the fraud was not discovered for many years. The company sought a declaration in the Hong Kong High Court that the sums had been wrongly debited. It was held that the company was estopped by its implied representation (by its silence) that the accounts were correct, and that the banks had relied on this to their detriment. An appeal to the Hong Kong Court of Appeal was dismissed on the basis that the company was estopped by its negligence from disputing the correctness of the statements. On appeal to the Privy Council, judgment was given for

the company. If a bank wished to oblige the customer to examine bank statements and to estop the customer from challenging those statements after a certain period, the effect of this must be very clearly brought to the customer's attention. At general law, the duty of the customer in relation to forged cheques was only to refrain from drawing a cheque in such a manner as may facilitate fraud or forgery (and not to take care in the operation of its business as a whole), and to inform the bank as soon as it became aware of any fraud or forgery.

2 *Tai Hing Cotton Mill Ltd v Liu Chong Hing Bank Ltd* [1986] AC 80 at 985 per Lord Scarman:

> 'If banks wish to impose on their customers an express obligation to examine their monthly statements and to make those statements, in the absence of query, unchallengeable by the customer after expiry of a time limit, the burden of the obligation and of the sanction imposed must be brought home to the customer. In their Lordships' view the provisions which they have set out above do not meet this undoubtedly rigorous test . . . Clear and unambiguous provision is needed if the banks are to introduce into the contract a binding obligation on the customer who does not query his bank statement to accept the statement as accurately setting out the debit items in the accounts.'

3 The three different provisions which were treated as failing the test were as follows: 'A monthly statement for each account will be sent by the Bank to the depositor by post or messenger and the balance shown therein may be deemed to be correct by the Bank if the depositor does not notify the Bank in writing of any error therein within ten days after the sending of such statement . . .' (at 957). 'The Bank's statement of my/our account will be confirmed by me/us without delay. In the case of absence of such confirmation within a fortnight, the bank may take the said statement as approved by me/us' (at 957). 'A statement of the customer's account will be rendered once a month. Customers are desired: (1) to examine all entries in the statement of account and to report at once to the bank any error found therein. (2) to return the confirmation slip duly signed. In the absence of any objection to the statement within seven days after its receipt by the customer, the account shall be deemed to have been confirmed' (at 958).

The impact of the Unfair Contract Terms Act 1977 should also be considered.

Information

6.29 The global custody service may involve the global custodian in receiving information provided by third parties and forwarding it to the client[1]. Clearly, errors and omissions in the information may cause loss to the client. It is important to establish whether or not the global custodian will be liable for such losses. This of course turns on whether or not the duties of the global custodian include examining such information. In the absence of express provision, the global custody contract may be construed as including such a duty within the general duty of care. Therefore, where the global custodian will not in practice examine third party information, this should be made clear by stating that no such service will be provided, and that no liability will be accepted[2].

1 See the discussion of corporate actions below.

2 Such clear provision is preferable to a bare limitation of liability. In other words, the point should be addressed both in the duty defining and in the limitation of liability provisions of the global custody contract.

Indemnities for breach of duty

6.30 Where a manager wishes the global custodian to act in breach of its duties to its client (for example by appointing a sub-custodian in a jurisdiction where it cannot prudently do so) the manager may offer the global custodian an indemnity in respect of the global custodian's exposure for that breach. The global custodian should treat this with caution, as such an indemnity may be unenforceable[1].

1 See A G Guest (ed) *Chitty on Contracts* (1994, 27th edn, Sweet & Maxwell), para, 17-167.

Corporate actions

6.31 In the light of the preceding discussion of the nature of a custodian's duties it may be useful to consider a particular example of a situation where a custodian may be required to take action in relation to the assets it holds. As indicated in Chapter 3, unless a custodian is holding physical assets (eg bearer securities), a custodian is most likely to be regarded as a trustee by English law. As a trustee, the custodian has the legal title to the securities but holds the entire beneficial interest for the benefit of the custody client[1]. This means that in principle any matter affecting the securities, whether rights arising in connection with the securities, or benefits accruing to a holder of the securities[2], must be passed on by the custodian to the client, so that the client is effectively in the same position as if it were the direct holder of the securities. While this is the basic position, it will be subject to the express terms of the custody contract[3].

1 Subject to the terms of the custody agreement, such as rights of set off or lien, whether phrased as such or in the form of permission to deduct fees or expenses from cash held for the custody client.

2 In theory, the liabilities relating to the relevant assets should also be passed on; however, technically any liabilities under relevant securities would be the liability of the holder of such securities but would be passed to the underlying client of the holder as a result of the holder claiming under the indemnity in its agreement with the client (or pursuant to Trustee Act 2000, s 31 which (broadly) entitles a trustee to reimbursement of expenses properly incurred by him).

3 However, to the extent relevant attributes of the ownership of the securities are not dealt with in the contract, the general law will apply. It is for this reason that the content of a custody contract is of great importance to both custodian and client, and in particular in relation to corporate actions.

What do we mean by 'corporate action'?

6.32 In its widest sense, 'corporate action' is the term used to refer to any event involving the issuer of the securities arising in relation to securities, where such event has an affect on, or requires action by, the holder of the securities. The custodian must determine how the impact of such events can be passed to the client. For convenience, we may regard corporate actions as falling into three main categories:

(1) 'mandatory' events, where the event occurs without intervention from the holder of the securities, and the holder of securities has no choice as to what happens, but is required to accept the relevant resulting asset (such events would include a decision by a company to make a stock-split by replacing each share of a particular class with a number of shares of reduced nominal value);

(2) 'discretionary' events, where the event occurs and a holder of securities has an option whether to take action in connection with such event, for example to exercise voting rights or to participate in a rights issue; and

(3) 'voluntary' events, where the event is triggered if the holder of the securities exercises a right available to it at its option, for example the exercise of rights to requisition an extraordinary meeting[1] or other rights which may be granted to shareholders of that specific class[2].

1 Under Companies Act 1985, s 368 a requisition to convene an extraordinary general meeting may be made by holders of not less than one tenth of the paid up shares carrying voting rights.

2 Other examples may be a 'right' or 'benefit' which does not arise from the nature of the asset itself, but results from the actions of third parties: for example, a class action proposed by third parties who invite other shareholders to participate.

Generally

6.33 Unless the custodian has specifically agreed with the custody client that it will not assist with the exercise of the relevant rights, or has limited its duties in such areas to the matters set out in the agreement, the custodian would arguably be obliged to take steps to enable the relevant rights to be exercised by or on behalf of the client, since the custodian would otherwise be depriving the client of part of the benefits held on trust for the client and would be in breach of trust.

A custody agreement would normally contain provisions relating to the processing of 'mandatory' corporate actions, because in practice neither the custodian nor the client has any choice whether such events occur. Such provisions would, in broad terms, deal with the passing on by the custodian to the client of benefits requiring no positive actions by the holder of the securities[1]. Where there are 'discretionary' corporate actions, decisions need to be taken by the holder of the securities, and therefore in such cases the custodian would normally agree to seek instructions from the client. It is usual to include specific provisions relating to the exercise of voting rights, whether by simply agreeing that voting rights will not be exercised, or setting out detailed procedures whereby the custodian will pass to the client company notices of issues to be voted upon, the client will instruct the custodian regarding the manner in which votes should be exercised, and the custodian will arrange the exercise of proxy votes in accordance with such instructions. In general, provisions relating to other types of 'discretionary' or 'voluntary' corporate actions are either not included (which is unwise given the residual fiduciary obligations of the custodian which would then apply as discussed above), or are drafted without specific detail because of the difficulty of predicting, and creating exhaustive provisions dealing with, all possible corporate action events.

1 This would include the receipt and remittance of dividends or non-cash distributions, although such matters are usually covered separately rather than included in provisions respecting corporate actions.

Issues for the client

6.34 The custody client's attitude to corporate actions may vary, depending on the underlying reasons for holding the relevant securities. For example, the custody client may not be concerned to exercise voting rights[1], although in principle would probably wish to ensure that rights issues offered on favourable terms were accepted. In contrast, a custody client may regard as a high priority the ability to attend and vote at meetings[2]. A blanket refusal by the custodian to deal with any corporate action events would potentially mean the loss of a significant part of the value of the holding of the securities for the client in the same way as a blanket refusal to pass on any benefits in the form of income arising on assets held (and would in practice be unusual). The level of corporate action service provided by the custodian will depend on which issues are important to the client and of course the question of what steps the custodian is able to take in practice.

If a client is concerned to have the facility to decide in each case whether to exercise rights or take up opportunities, whether or not it is in a position to do so will depend on the ability of the custodian to forward in good time all information received from the relevant company (or other relevant sources). Whether the client requires that all information of any description relating to the assets held is forwarded, or is just concerned about notification of voting rights or rights issues, timing will be a key issue. For example, if the custodian is delayed in passing to the client information regarding the existence of an issue on which the client may wish to vote, or a rights issue which the client may wish to accept, there may be very little time for the client to come to a decision regarding its preferred course of action, and there is a risk that by the time instructions are given to the custodian by the client, the deadline for exercising the relevant rights will have passed. A custodian may be able to offer systems specifically designed to facilitate communication in relation to these types of issue, but the custody client will need to consider whether this in practice provides the service required. (Such systems may range from dedicated electronic communication services between custodian and client to provision for straight-through-processing, where client instructions which are to be forwarded by the custodian can simply be sent via the custodian's systems to the relevant destination).

In principle, where a client is concerned to receive the benefit of any rights or opportunities arising in connection with its assets, ideally the custody agreement should set out clearly what steps the custodian would take in each envisaged situation. However, in practice, because of the problem of covering all possible scenarios, it is more likely that the relevant agreement would deal with the main issues of concern in detail, and attempt to cover any other eventualities with appropriate general wording. The challenge would of course be to provide a general approach which satisfied the client that there was a mechanism for passing on all benefits, but which was not too vague to be helpful or too onerous for a custodian to accept.

1 It should be noted that the Myners Report ('Institutional Investment in the United Kingdom: A Review', prepared by Paul Myners, published 4 March 2001) included the observation that fund managers do not make enough effort to exercise rights arising from shares and should intervene more actively where this would increase the value of the shares. Depending on the way in which the Myners Report is acted upon, this could prompt more focus on 'discretionary' and 'voluntary' corporate actions, resulting in fund managers becoming more demanding of custodians in this respect. However, other views have been expressed in the wake of the Myners Report. For example, the Association of British Insurers has expressed the concern that legislation requiring particular action by shareholders and pension fund trustees is likely to increase efforts to narrow the particular situations where action would be required, in order to restrict the exposure to liability, rather than causing the relevant parties to focus on involvement in the companies in which shares are held (See ABI News Release, 7 May 2002).

2 Whether a client can be permitted to attend at shareholder or bondholder meetings will depend on whether the custodian is willing to appoint the client as its representative (whether a proxy or otherwise) or to transfer the relevant securities into the name of the client for the purposes of the relevant meeting.

Issues for the custodian

6.35 The main issue for the custodian is to determine the types of corporate actions where it is prepared to provide assistance. Accordingly it will need to decide what limitations of the scope of its services are appropriate in the custody contract so that the client is clear what services are being provided. It is also important to consider how the custodian can best carry out the agreed functions, taking into account matters such as the timing issues when forwarding information and receiving instructions.

If a corporate action is not processed properly, and the contractual documentation does not cover the circumstances in which this happened (for example, specifically limiting or excluding liability if there is a delay in transmitting information), the potential loss to the client may be large. This means there is the risk of large claims by the client against the custodian. The consequences for the client of being unable to exercise voting rights or accept a rights issue may be considerable. There may also be added complexity in valuing the client's claim, since it may be unclear what the consequences would have been if the relevant voting rights had been exercised, or it may be difficult to value the securities which the client had wanted to subscribe for in the rights issue. It may not be possible to compensate the client directly (by replacing the assets) if there is illiquidity in the relevant securities following the corporate action so that it is not possible to obtain such securities in the open market. If the amount of damages due is then calculated, the normal contractual measure of damages is to put the client in the position it would have been in had the contract been performed. However, here, it is difficult to define the extent of the loss, because the market price of the securities might have been different if the client had exercised the relevant rights. Because of the different types of corporate action and the potentially broad range of events causing problems, this is a complicated matter to cover comprehensively in documentation and it is likely that there will be areas where the liability of the parties and values involved can only be determined with difficulty. It is at least helpful if a custodian includes in its custody terms clear contractual terms defining the extent of liabilities, for example setting a cap on liability of the market value of the securities as at the date of the breach of duty.

There is the further question of how a failure to arrange for the exercise of rights in relation to 'discretionary' or 'voluntary' corporate actions would be treated in the context of the general level of liability accepted by the custodian. While most custodians would accept liability for their own negligence (or possibly gross negligence: see discussion in paras **6.3–6.4** and **6.14**), it may be debatable, depending on the terms of the contract, the facts of the matter, or market practice generally, whether the events which have occurred involve negligence on the part of the custodian or not.

As discussed above, while the timing of instructions is a major concern for the client, it is also an issue for the custodian. Where information is to be passed from the custodian to the client, instructions given by the client to the custodian, and then action taken by the custodian, there are various stages at which the transmission of information may be delayed, lost or corrupted. The custodian will need to ensure that it has made clear to the client the nature of the service being offered, and also what the limits of the service being offered are, making, as necessary, appropriate disclosures and disclaimers in the agreement with the client.

In theory a custodian might wish to try to circumvent the timing issues for seeking instructions by simply agreeing to deal with the corporate actions on behalf of the client without the need to seek instructions. In order to do so, the custodian would need authority from the client to exercise its discretion in the exercise of rights arising in relation to the securities held for the client. However, this is undesirable for a number of reasons. In principle, it is preferable for the client if the client takes this type of decision itself, rather than delegating it to an entity with less in-depth knowledge of the client's business and investment strategy. From the custodian's perspective, such a service could be seen as an investment management function, thus importing additional regulatory considerations. In addition, as a fiduciary the custodian would in principle be under a high level of care when making decisions regarding the exercise of the corporate actions and would therefore be exposed to a further risk of claims for breach of fiduciary duty from the client if the client were to dispute the decisions made.

Chapter 7

Regulatory duties

7.1 In order to give a better idea of the regulatory context in which a custodian operates in the UK, this section gives an overview of the UK regulatory requirements affecting custody and deposit taking in the UK at the time of writing, with a particular focus on rules applicable to the holding of securities. Starting first with a short summary of the regulatory structure up to 30 November 2001, this section will then turn to the arrangements under the Financial Services and Markets 2000.

Financial Services Act 1986/Banking Act 1987[1]

Regulation of custody

7.2 Custody has not always been a regulated form of business, but following an amendment to the Financial Services Act 1986[2], with effect from 1 June 1997 custody became one of the specified forms of investment business[3], although the term 'custody' was not itself used in the operative wording of the Act (despite the relevant heading of 'Custody of Investments').

As discussed in Chapter 1 the term 'custody' itself may be interpreted as meaning a range of activities, from the simple holding of a safe-deposit box, to the provision of a global securities handling and settlement service in numerous different jurisdictions, together with cash management, stocklending and other services. Consequently, for the purposes of the Act it was necessary to clarify the particular area of activity concerned. The text of the relevant section referred to 'safeguarding and administering or arranging for the safeguarding and administering of assets belonging to another', or offering or agreeing to do so. It is important to note the conjunctive way in which this is worded, because the provision of either one of the elements of safeguarding (for example just providing a safe-deposit box) or administering (for example, giving instructions in relation to assets held by a third party) on its own would not constitute investment business. Both elements had to be conducted together, and conducted in relation to the same investments[4].

As a result of this amendment to the Act, any custodian operating in the UK had to ensure that it complied with the requirements of the Act if its activities involved it in providing the services caught by the relevant provisions of the Act and, if no relevant exemption[5] applied, non-authorised custodians had to become authorised persons. Custodians with existing authorisation in respect of other investment business had to ensure that their scope of business as authorised persons was wide enough to cover this area of activity. In practice, most custodians fell into the latter category.

1 Both Acts repealed by SI 2001/3649, arts 3(1)(c) and (d) respectively, with effect from 1 December 2001.
2 The Financial Services Act 1986 (Extension of Scope of Act) Order 1996, made 25 November 1996, arts 1 and 2 in force 6 January 1997, remainder in force 1 June 1997.
3 Financial Services Act 1986, Sch 1, para 13A.
4 A useful discussion of the regulators' approach to the meaning of 'safeguarding' and 'administration' was set out in the Guidance Release produced by the Securities and Investments Board Limited ('SIB', now the Financial Services Authority, the 'FSA') in June 1997 (SIB Guidance Release 5/97), although the list of functions set out in this Guidance is not exhaustive (see further discussion in the context of FSMA below where this Guidance is still relevant).
5 For example, the Bank of England was an exempted person, as were any entities fulfilling the SIB requirements in order to be a recognised investment exchange or recognised clearing house.

Cash holdings

7.3 In relation to the holding of cash, under the Banking Act 1987 an entity was required to be an approved deposit-taking institution in order to conduct the business of taking deposits[1] in the UK. Since custody services normally also include a cash element (for example, receipt of income arising in respect of securities held, or the proceeds of sale of securities), custodians who were not banks would arrange that such cash was held in an appropriate bank account. Such account might be the client's own bank account in respect of which the custodian had authority to make deposits and withdrawals, or a bank account in the name of the custodian maintained either in accordance with the relevant client money rules[2] or subject to an opt out from such rules.

1 Banking Act 1987, s 5(1) (essentially the same wording as in the Regulated Activities Order: see para **7.9**, n 3).
2 The Financial Services (Client Money) Regulations 1991, as amended, made by SIB, applied to IMRO members, but for SFA members the relevant client money rules were those set out in the SFA Rules (Rule 4-50 to 4-73) plus certain designated parts of the 1991 Regulations (Part 3 (Default Regulators) and Regulation 4.01 (Duty to pay interest)).

Authorised persons

7.4 One of the most usual ways of becoming an authorised person for the purposes of the Financial Services Act 1986 was to become a member of a self regulatory organisation (an 'SRO') such as the Securities and Futures Authority Limited (the 'SFA') or the Investment Management Regulatory Organisation Limited ('IMRO'). A custodian which was a member of IMRO or the SFA would have to comply with the rules of such authorities in relation to custody[1]. It was also necessary to remember that the general Principles[2] laid down by the Securities and Investments Board ('SIB') (now the Financial Services Authority) applied to all SFA and IMRO members.

1 In summary, such rules contained requirements regarding how bearer and registered instruments were to be held, segregation of assets, appointment of sub-custodians, terms of agreements with clients, and reconciliation and record keeping.
2 Requiring general standards of good behaviour, such as 'high standards of integrity and fair dealing', acting with 'due skill, care and diligence' and 'high standards of market conduct', as well as providing to and seeking from customers relevant information, avoiding conflicts of interest, arranging 'proper protection' for client assets controlled or held by the firm, maintaining 'adequate financial resources', organising internal affairs 'in a responsible manner' and dealing with the regulators 'in an open and co-operative manner'.

Approaches of IMRO and SFA

7.5 It is worth noting that the approach adopted by IMRO and the SFA was not always the same. The SIB 'standards for the Custody of Customers' Investments' (Guidance Release 3/96, August 1996) were intended to indicate the scope of the custody rules to be formulated by both IMRO and the SFA in order to cover this new area of investment business under the Financial Services Act 1986, but were interpreted by IMRO and the SFA in somewhat different ways in various respects[1].

1 For example, SIB Standard 1.4: 'The SIB looks to SROs and RPBs to prohibit an authorised firm from disclaiming responsibility for losses of investments due to fraud, wilful default or negligence arising from its or its nominees' activities.' This resulted in the IMRO requirements that custodian terms should include wording stating 'the extent to which the firm accepts liability for any loss of Customer Investments' and 'the arrangements for recording and separately identifying registrable Customer Investments and, where the registered holder is the Firms' Own Nominee, that the Firm will be responsible for the acts and omissions of that person'. In the SFA rules, the corresponding wording requires a custodian to 'notify the customer in writing of the obligations which the firm will have to the customer in relation to . . . the extent of the firms' liability in the event of default of an eligible custodian, except that a firm must accept the same level of responsibility to its customers for any nominee company controlled by the firm or by its affiliated company as for itself and may not disclaim responsibility for losses arising directly from the fraud, wilful default or negligence of the firm.'

Collateral

7.6 One particular example is that SFA had specific rules about holding collateral (see SFA Rule 4-13) although IMRO did not. It is important to consider this in the light of the current FSA regulatory requirements[1]. In the SFA Rules 'collateral' was defined as 'an investment falling within paragraphs 1 to 6 of Schedule 1 to the [Financial Services] Act [1986][2] or a commodity warrant which has been paid for in full by a customer and which is held or controlled by the firm, other than by way of safe custody, under the terms of a deposit, pledge, charge or other security arrangement.'

The SFA rules required that certain of the custody rules (relating to written terms, statements and reconciliation) should apply to the holding of collateral, as well as certain specific additional provisions regarding how collateral should be recorded and held. As a result, for SFA regulated entities, custody regulations could also apply where such entities held collateral, even if such entities would not normally be involved in the business of carrying out the functions of a custodian. This is important because the situations in which collateral is held may vary.

For example, C may hold A's assets, over which A has granted a security interest to B. C knows that it holds for A, and A is C's client for custody purposes, even if, as is likely in a security arrangement, there are restrictions on C implementing certain instructions from A (such as transferring the assets to third parties) until the secured obligation is fulfilled. Such an arrangement is similar to a normal custody relationship, and C was required to be authorised to provide custody services, and comply with relevant custody regulatory requirements. In contrast, C may hold assets provided by A as collateral for obligations owed by A to C. In this case, if the collateral was provided by way of outright transfer (eg under a stock loan or repo[3]), C holds the collateral assets for its own account, not as custodian, and was not providing the regulatable service of safeguarding and administering the assets of another in relation to those assets.

A further possibility is the situation where C holds assets provided by A as collateral for obligations owned by A to C, but C only has a security interest over the collateral assets held, not outright title. In this case, C may have been holding as custodian subject to relevant regulatory rules regarding holding collateral. However, based on the SIB Guidance paper of June 1997[4], it was also arguable that where the delivery by A was made to C by way of security (whether or not there is a pre-existing custody relationship), C held the assets for his own reasons, and the deal between the parties was not that C was safeguarding and administering assets for A.

However, even under the old regulatory regime, this required careful thought, because to a regulator the facts would look very similar to a situation which *is* subject to regulatory rules in relation to the holding of collateral. As noted above, SFA defined collateral for the purposes of application of the collateral rules as, broadly, investments held 'other than by way of safe custody', and on such basis it was arguable that even if the Guidance paper analysis assisted an unauthorised entity, so that such entity could argue it was not providing a service which required authorisation under the Financial Services Act 1986, the safer approach for a holder of the assets over which security was granted where such holder was an SFA regulated entity, was to hold such assets in accordance with the SFA collateral rules. The position is clearer under FSMA, as discussed below.

1 See paras **7.35–7.38**.
2 Broadly, shares, debt instruments, government securities, warrants, certificates representing any of the foregoing (eg depositary receipts) and units in a fund.
3 See Chapter 4
4 See para **7.2**, n 5. 'Paragraph 49 of the Treasury Consultation document indicated that the Treasury were of the view that the holding of investments as security for a loan would not constitute custody business. Whilst the SIB can conceive of circumstances where the lender might be carrying on custody business in respect of these assets (for example, if he arranges for a third party to safeguard and administer them), it agrees with the Treasury that, in general, a firm which holds securities as collateral or takes a legal charge over them as a means of providing the firm with security for a loan will not be carrying on custody business. In such cases the lender looks after the assets for his own reason as he usually becomes the contingent beneficial owner of the security, leaving legal ownership of the security unchanged' (SIB Guidance Release 5/97, para 33). (It must be admitted that the last seven words of this passage do not add to the clarity of the whole, and it is unclear what circumstances they are intended to cover.)

Financial Services and Markets Act 2000

7.7 The Financial Services and Markets Act 2000 ('FSMA') came fully into force at midnight on 30 November 2001 and, inter alia, replaced the regulatory regime under the Financial Services Act 1986 and the Banking Act 1987. The basic structure of FSMA is much the same as in the Financial Services Act 1986, namely that a person cannot carry on a 'regulated activity' in the UK, or purport to do so, unless they are an 'authorised person' or an 'exempt person'[1]. However, the regulated activities in question are not limited to the old investment business activities as under the Financial Services Act 1986, but cover both functions formerly regulated as investment business and also a wide range of other activities too, including deposit-taking business[2]. Most of the detail of whether a particular activity is regulated under FSMA is contained in subsidiary legislation rather than in FSMA itself[3].

1 FSMA 2000, s 19(1)
2 FSMA also covers insurance business (including in the context of Lloyds) and the activities of building societies and friendly societies.
3 For example, The Financial Services and Markets Act 2000 (Regulated Activities) Order 2001 (SI 2001/544), as amended, discussed below.

Financial Services Authority

7.8 Under the new regulatory structure set up under FSMA, the sole regulatory body is the Financial Services Authority (the 'FSA')[1]. All relevant entities conducting regulated activities therefore have to become authorised by the FSA (unless falling within a relevant exemption), and must comply with the FSA Rules set out in the FSA Handbook. The Handbook consists of various sections (known as sourcebooks or manuals), different parts of which will apply to the relevant regulated entities, depending on the type of activities carried out by such entities in the UK. Certain sections apply to all regulated entities, such as the High Level Standards, and others have specific application, such as the Interim Prudential Sourcebook for Banks. At the time of writing the Handbook comprises:

- High Level Standards (Principles for Business, Senior Management Arrangements, Systems and Controls, Threshold Conditions, Statements of Principle and Code of Practice for Approved Persons, The Fit and Proper Test for Approved Persons, and General Provisions).
- Business Standards (Interim Prudential Sourcebook for, respectively, Banks, Building Societies, Friendly Societies, Insurers, and Investment Businesses, Conduct of Business, Market Conduct (including Code of Market Conduct, Price stabilising rules and Inter-professional conduct), Training and Competence, and Money Laundering).
- Regulatory Processes (Authorisation, Supervision, Enforcement and Decision making).
- Redress (Dispute resolution: Complaints, Compensation, and Complaints against the FSA).
- Specialist Sourcebooks (Collective Investment Schemes, Credit Unions, Professional firms, Lloyd's and Recognised Investment Exchanges and Recognised Clearing Houses).
- Special Guides (Energy Market Participants, Oil Market Participants, The Service Company Regime, and Small Friendly Societies).
- Glossary.
- Guidance Notes.
- Forms.

1 In some senses, this is not a new entity. The SIB existed under the earlier regime, but it changed its name, and now has much wider powers under FSMA including replacing the functions of entities such as IMRO and the SFA. The FSA took over the control of the SFA and IMRO, and such entities legally ceased to exist on 1 December 2001.

Regulated activities

7.9 An activity will be a regulated activity for the purposes of FSMA if it is 'an activity of a specified kind', is carried on by way of business, and either 'relates to an investment of a specified kind' or is an activity specified as regulated in relation to 'property of any kind'[1]. In order to determine whether an activity falls within the category of regulated activity, it is necessary to look at the relevant subsidiary legislation which determines the meaning of the various aspects of a regulated activity, namely the Financial Services and Markets Act 2000 (Regulated Activities) Order 2001[2], as amended (the 'Regulated Activities Order'), and the Financial Services and Markets Act 2000 (Carrying on Regulated Activities by Way of Business) Order 2001[3]. The activities specified in the Regulated Activities Order include accepting deposits[4], effecting and carrying out contracts of insurance, dealing in investments as principal or agent, arranging deals in investments, managing investments, establishing or operating a collective investment scheme, advising on investments, activities relating to Lloyd's syndicates, providing funeral plan contracts and entering into regulated mortgage contracts, as well as safeguarding and administering investments. The term 'investment' is not defined, but the types of investment which are relevant for the purposes of the Regulated Activities Order are listed in arts 74 to 89 of that Order (although not all types are relevant for each specified activity.)

Pursuant to the Financial Services and Markets Act 2000 (Carrying on Regulated Activities by Way of Business) Order 2001, a person carries on the specified activity of accepting deposits 'by way of business' if he holds himself out as accepting deposits on a day to day basis, and the deposits are not 'accepted only on particular occasions'. In relation to the specified activities of dealing in investments as principal or agent, arranging deals (subject to certain exceptions[5]), managing investments, safeguarding and administering investments, sending dematerialised instructions, establishing or operating a collective investment scheme, establishing or operating a stakeholder pension scheme, advising on investments, or agreeing to provide any of these services, a person is not to be regarded as carrying on such activities by way of business 'unless he carries on the business of engaging in one or more such activities'. It should be noted that in this case it is not required that the person performing a particular specified activity should be engaging in *that* particular activity by way of business, nor is it necessary that the relevant activity which is engaged in by way of business should be carried out in the UK.

1 FSMA 2000, s 22.
2 SI 2001/544.
3 SI 2001/1177.
4 Subject to certain exemptions, in the Regulated Activities Order 'deposit' means 'a sum of money . . . paid on terms (a) under which it will be repaid, with or without interest or premium, and either on demand or at a time or in circumstances agreed by or on behalf of the person making the payment and the person receiving it; and (b) which are not referable to the provision of property (other than currency) or services or the giving of security' (art 5(2)).
5 Broadly, in relation to Lloyds' syndicate capacity and syndicate membership.

Specified activities

7.10 As in the Financial Services Act 1986, the form of regulated activity which is informally called custody involves carrying out both safeguarding of assets belonging to another, and administration of such assets. Therefore carrying out only safeguarding or only administration will not of itself be subject to regulation. It is also a specified activity to arrange for such services to be provided, or to agree to do so. However, the action of *offering* to provide safeguarding and administering services is no longer itself an activity attracting regulation. (This is probably uncontentious in that it was never clear how relevant regulation would apply to the 'offering' on its own, other than by requiring any such offers to be made subject to the relevant rules regarding the issuance of investment advertisements or the making of unsolicited calls.)

Meaning of 'safeguarding' and 'administration'

7.11 The guidance regarding the meaning of 'safeguarding' and 'administration' as set out in the Guidance Release produced by the Securities and Investments Board

Limited ('SIB', now the Financial Services Authority, the 'FSA') in June 1997[1] is still helpful to indicate the probable interpretation of such words. For example, 'administration' is said to include 'any one or more of . . . (a) maintaining accounts with clearing houses; (b) settling transactions in investments; (c) operating through depositories or sub-custodians in the United Kingdom or elsewhere; (d) operating nominee accounts, including pooled accounts, which identify each customer's assets in a ledger; (e) cash processing associated with customers' assets; (f) collecting and dealing with dividends and other income associated with the assets; (g) carrying out corporate actions such as proxy voting (including exercising rights conferred by an investment on behalf of the beneficial owner).' It is also worth noting that the Regulated Activities Order itself (like the Financial Services Act 1986 previously) specifies certain actions which would *not* be regarded as administration, namely providing information on the number or value of assets held, converting currency, or receiving documents in relation to assets held simply in order to forward such documents as instructed. However, this should be considered carefully in view of the fact that, as noted, the 1997 Guidance Release indicates that, for example, 'cash processing' or 'collecting and dealing with dividends' would be regarded as administration. In principle, it is difficult to see how an entity could hold assets and provide a currency conversion service, without also being regarded as providing a service involving 'cash processing' or 'collecting and dealing with dividends'. In practice, therefore, careful consideration would have to be given to any argument that either safeguarding, or administration, was being provided, but not both.

1 Guidance Release 5/97 'Custody of Investments under the Financial Services Act 1986'.

Nominees

7.12 In this context, consider also the position of a nominee. Usually, this would be little more than a shelf company with the bare minimum of assets and officials in order to be properly constituted as a company, but nevertheless providing a separate legal entity in whose name registrable assets may be registered, where a custodian wishes to provide added protection to its clients by registering registrable securities in a name separate from that of the custodian. Although the nominee is not a substantial entity, it is legally holding the assets on behalf of another (normally the custodian, which in turn holds for the client). As a result, if it provides such service in the UK, the nominee would be regarded as both safeguarding and administering (since it both holds legal title and would legally be the entity responsible for receiving and forwarding dividends). Consequently, such a nominee must be authorised for regulatory purposes. Because such authorisation requirement could be quite onerous for an insubstantial entity, the Regulated Activities Order (as also the Financial Services Act 1986 previously) provides an exception from the authorisation requirement which could apply to the nominee. This exception applies where a third party regulated for the provision of custody in the UK[1] accepts the same responsibility for the activity of the nominee[2] as it does for itself.

1 Authorised under the Financial Services Act 1986 or operating under the passport arrangements available under the ISD (the Investment Services Directive, which is the Council Directive of 10 May 1993 on investment services in the securities field (No 93/22/EEC) or the BCD (formerly the Second Banking Co-ordination Directive, which is the Second Council Directive on the co-ordination of laws, regulations and administrative provisions relating to the taking up and pursuit of the business of credit institutions and amending directive 77/780/EEC (Directive No. 89/646/EEC), but now repealed and replaced by the Council Directive of 20 March 2000 relating to the taking up and pursuit of the business of credit institutions (No 2000/12/EC).

2 Or other entity. The exception is not restricted to nominees, but this is the most likely situation in which it would apply, as a custodian would not normally wish to accept liability for a third party with functions other than limited nominee functions.

Relevant rules

7.13 The relevant rules in relation to the conduct of custody business are now set out in the FSA Conduct of Business sourcebook which fall within the Business Standards section of the FSA Handbook (the 'Conduct of Business Rules' or 'CoB'). The Conduct of Business Rules contain separate sections on custody, client money and collateral in the section entitled Client Assets (chapter 9), as well as general provisions regarding the content of agreements between persons authorised by the FSA and their clients (chapter 4, which applies generally as well as to custodians).

General principles

7.14 As under the old Financial Services Act 1986 regime, there are still general principles which apply directly to all persons regulated by the FSA, and these will affect the way in which a custodian provides its services. The FSA can impose sanctions if a firm is in breach of such Principles. The FSA Principles are part of the High Level Standards and are very similar to the old SIB Principles, with the exception of the addition of a requirement to 'pay due regard to the interests of customers and treat them fairly'. Arguably this new Principle goes beyond the idea of avoiding conflicts between the interests of clients, and introduces a general idea of consideration of what is appropriate or suitable for customers, as well as the need to avoid preferential treatment of one client in contrast with other clients.

Protection of client assets

7.15 The FSA Principle of particular relevance to custodians is the Principle concerning client assets[1]. Under the old SIB Principles, the general requirement was to arrange 'proper' protection for client assets over which a regulated firm has control, whether by segregation and identification or otherwise 'in accordance with the responsibility it has accepted'. Under the new FSA Principle, a firm is required to arrange 'adequate protection' where it is responsible for client assets. Despite the change in wording, it seems likely that both the old and new Principle are aimed at similar circumstances, namely where an entity regulated by the FSA is holding client assets as custodian, or is arranging for a third party to hold the client's assets, or has authority to give instructions to the client's custodian.

1 Principle 10.

General provisions

7.16 In addition to the particular Conduct of Business Rules and the Principles which relate to custody, a custodian will also need to bear in mind the 'General Provisions' which apply to all sections of business regulated by the FSA, as well as the other areas of the Handbook which apply to specific aspects of business operations, such as senior management responsibilities or money laundering controls.

Custody services

7.17 Looking at custody services in particular, on balance, the FSA Rules relating specifically to custody activities[1] are substantially the same as the old SFA custody rules[2], although there are certain small changes which may in some cases raise issues for custodians. While it would be tedious to analyse such changes at length, it is worth considering some examples.

1 See Conduct of Business Rules, ch 9, section 9.1, 9.2 (9.3 and 9.5 concern client money, and 9.4 concerns collateral, discussed further below).

2 In particular, it is useful to note that the regulator still does not require custodians to accept a particular level of liability for delegates (other than nominees), although as before requires an 'appropriate risk assessment' of sub-custodians (CoB 9.1.43R) and in guidance indicates that ongoing monitoring of subcustodians is expected (see CoB 9.145G). See further discussion of custodians' liability for delegates in Chapter 6.

Custodians

7.18 The word 'custodian' is used in the FSA Rules instead of 'eligible custodian' which is the equivalent term used in the SFA Rules, and the way in which these terms are defined is different. This is important when considering the range of entities to which a regulated custodian may delegate the holding of assets, and is therefore worth a closer look.

Under the SFA Rules, the rules relating to custody applied regardless of whether the custody client was a market counterparty[1], a non-private customer[2] or a private customer[3], although with certain differences in the manner of application, for example additional warnings were required to be given to private customers, and certain written consents were required from private customers. If a client was a non-private customer, the categories of 'eligible custodian' included 'any person whom the firm reasonably believes to be a person whose business includes the provision of investment custodial services'. Also, in relation to any type of client, there was the possibility of obtaining specific approval from the SFA for a custodian not covered by one of the other categories.

1 Market counterparty (cf FSA definition at para **7.27**, n 2) meant a person dealing with the SFA member as principal or as agent for an unidentified principal in the course of investment business of the same description as that in the course of which the SFA member acted, or a person treated as a market counterparty in accordance with the SFA Rules.

2 Non-private customer (cf FSA definition of intermediate customer at para **7.29**, n 1) meant a person who had elected to be treated as a non-private customer in accordance with the SFA Rules, or for the purposes of the Common Unsolicited Calls Regulations (Regulations issued by SIB pursuant to powers under the FSA 1986, s 56, Sch 11, para 20, in effect from 1 January 1992 (reg 20(4)) and 1 September 1991 for the rest) a person who was not a private customer, or for all other purposes, a customer who is not a private customer. (The difference between a 'person' and a 'customer' was, broadly, that a customer was someone to whom an SFA member provided investment services (including a potential customer), whereas a person includes any person whether or not a customer.).

3 Private customer (cf FSA definition at para **7.29**, n 2) meant a customer who is an individual and who is not acting in the course of carrying on investment business, or unless he is reasonably believed to be an ordinary business investor, a customer who is a small business investor and who is not acting in the course of carrying on investment business.

Ordinary business investor meant a customer who is reasonably believed to be a government, local authority or public authority within the meaning of Sch 1 to the Act, or a company, partnership or unincorporated association which satisfies (or which has satisfied at any time during the previous two years) any of the following size requirements: (i) that it is a body corporate which has more than 20 members (or is the subsidiary of a company which has more than 20 members) and it (or any of its holding companies or subsidiaries) has a called up share capital or net assets of £500,000 or more; (ii) that it is a body corporate and it (or any of its holding companies or subsidiaries) has a called up share capital or net assets of £5 million or more; or (iii) if it is not a body corporate, it has net assets of £5 million or more; or a trustee of a trust which satisfies either of the following size requirements: (i) that the aggregate value of the cash and investments which form part of the trust's assets (before deducting the amount of its liabilities) is £10 million or more; or (ii) that the aggregate value has been £10 million or more at any time during the previous two years; or any authorised person, listed money market institution, overseas person or passported institution which is not already within one of the above categories; or other than for the purposes of the Common Unsolicited Calls Regulations, in relation to a transaction in an investment and subject to the SFA Rules, a company or partnership which carries on a main business which is not investment business and which enters into that transaction as an integral part of that main business.

Small business investor meant a company, partnership or unincorporated association, or a trustee acting for a trust, where the company, partnership, association or trust is not of a size within the categories for an ordinary business investor and is not otherwise an ordinary business investor.

FSA and SFA Rules compared

7.19 In the FSA Rules, as with the SFA Rules, the particular compliance rules for custody apply to all categories of client, subject to additional protections for private customers. However, the former SFA approach to 'eligible custodians' is not continued by the FSA. Under the FSA Rules the same requirements for a 'custodian' (the term replacing the SFA term 'eligible custodian' and referring, broadly, to a custodian appointed by a regulated entity) apply, regardless of the type of client involved. In principle, a custodian must fall within one of the specified categories[1], but if it is 'not feasible' to use such a custodian, *and* there are 'reasonable grounds to show that a person outside the United Kingdom, whose business includes the provision of custodial services, is able to provide such services which are appropriate to the client and in the client's best interest to use', that person may constitute a custodian for FSA purposes[2]. This will be relevant where a person authorised by the FSA is appointing a custodian, whether as its delegate to act as sub-custodian, or when arranging custody to be provided to its client.

1 In the FSA Glossary, subject to the exception discussed above, a 'custodian' must be: (a) an approved bank, (b) an approved depositary, (c) a member of a recognised investment exchange or designated investment exchange, (d) a firm whose permitted activities include safeguarding and administering investments, or (e) a regulated clearing firm.

2 FSA Glossary, definition of 'custodian'.

FSA and IMRO Rules compared

7.20 It is important to bear in mind that this exception only applies where the custodian to be appointed is outside the UK, and due consideration has been given to such custodian's business profile, and to whether such custodian is 'appropriate' for the relevant client, and whether it is in the client's best interests to appoint such person. In practice, this will require detailed knowledge of the business of both the non-UK custodian concerned, and the client, in order to be able to make the decision required by these provisions. As a result of this change, the possible range of custodians which may be appointed by a person regulated by the FSA is more restricted than under the SFA Rules[1]. This may also be contrasted with the approach under the old IMRO rules regarding custody, where there was an additional more generic category of 'eligible custodian' which could assist IMRO members whose appointed custodians or sub-custodians did not otherwise fall within a relevant category. This generic category under the IMRO Rules was in fact narrower than the SFA example discussed above, although, unlike the SFA term, it applied regardless of the category of client concerned. The relevant entity had to have a head office outside the UK, and not only did the IMRO member need to be satisfied that such entity was regulated by a regulatory body in the jurisdiction where it carried out the custody services or was subject to independent review by appropriately qualified auditors, but also the IMRO member had to be satisfied that such entity provided investment custodial services. The IMRO term was therefore somewhat closer to the approach used by the FSA than the SFA term, but nevertheless contained fewer conditions to be fulfilled than are required by the relevant FSA rules. Consequently, for entities formerly regulated by either SFA or IMRO, the new term presents a narrowing of the category of entities which may be used as custodians or sub-custodians.

1 The FSA transitional provisions are only of limited help here, since after 30 June 2002 all custodians must fall within the new FSA definition.

Notification of terms

7.21 In relation to the required content of custody terms which are to be notified to the client, the basic requirement set out in the FSA Rules[1] is to notify the client of 'appropriate' terms. It is stated in addition that such terms should include the items listed in the Rules[2] 'where applicable'. This may be contrasted with the SFA requirement to 'notify the customer in writing of the obligations which the firm will have to the customer in relation to' the listed items[3], and the IMRO requirement to 'include some provisions about' the relevant items (those listed in the relevant IMRO rules[4]) in the customer agreement or terms of business.

The reference to the inclusion of terms which are 'applicable' is helpful, because not all the terms may be relevant in all cases, and therefore there is scope for arguing that certain terms may be omitted as inapplicable.

1 FSA Conduct of Business Rule 9.1.49.
2 CoB Rule 9.1.49(1)–(10).
3 SFA Rule 4-109(1)(a)–(f) .
4 IMRO Rules, ch II, Appendix 2.4(1)(a), Pt II, para 13(a), (b)(i)–(ix) and (c).

'Appropriate' terms

7.22 Because of the general obligation to include terms which are 'appropriate', there is now the possibility that a custodian could be criticised or disciplined if the agreement contains all terms which seem reasonable to it, and those which are described in the relevant FSA Rule, but the regulator nevertheless considers that certain additional terms would have been 'appropriate' but were not included[1].

In practice, unless there are particular reasons why to do so would cause difficulties, it seems likely that most custodians would prefer to include provisions dealing with each of the specific points listed in the relevant FSA Rule, on the basis that these points are generally matters which relate to how the custodian provides its services and should as a matter of good practice be considered anyway. In addition, it is probably easier to follow the list rather than to argue later that such points were inapplicable. If there were particular areas of the custody terms recommended by the FSA which in the context of a particular matter were considered by a custodian to cause problems, and there was any doubt as to the view which would be taken by the FSA, the prudent approach would of course be to discuss the matter with the FSA in advance of finalising the relevant agreement.

1 This may in practice be fairly unlikely, since there seems no reason to suppose that a custodian would wish to enter into terms which it did not think were appropriate, but there is nonetheless a potential (if slight) risk that after the event, if there were to be a dispute, it would be open to the regulator to conclude that on the facts the terms were not 'appropriate'.

Stock lending

7.23 The section of the Conduct of Business Rules relating to custody also includes a section concerning stock lending (9.1.74R–9.1.84G). This is in fact not a requirement which is new to entities previously regulated by the SFA ,since the terms of these provisions are effectively the same as the terms set out in an SFA Board Notice 471[1]. The IMRO Rules also contained certain requirements in relation to securities lending of client assets, but such requirements were less detailed (see IMRO Rules, ch II, section 5.1(8)). The FSA provisions, broadly, require the consent of the client and appropriate terms for stock lending undertaken for or with the client, and certain additional requirements regarding assets lent from a pooled holding of assets, and stock lending services provided to private clients. As with the SFA approach, these provisions do not apply where the firm's client is a market counterparty, and are largely aimed at protecting the position of private customers, or customers generally where lending is being made from a pooled account. It is important to note that such rules are relevant not just where the custodian and its client have clearly agreed to enter into a securities lending relationship. Such a relationship would also arise where the parties are in practice entering into arrangements which achieve the same result. The most obvious example of this is what is known as contractual settlement, where a custodian holding assets or cash for a client agrees to credit the client's securities account or cash account with the relevant securities or cash on the date such assets are due to be received by the client, whether or not such assets are actually received[2]. In relation to cash, this arrangement is in effect allowing the client to borrow the relevant cash from the custodian by making credit available to such circumstances. Similarly, where securities are made available, a loan of securities by the custodian to the client is taking place, presumably to be reversed once the relevant securities are received by the custodian for the account of the client. The question to be asked in relation to the loan of securities is where the securities for the loan are provided from, since they may be the custodian's own securities, or may be provided from the pooled securities of the relevant type held by the custodian for other clients. If the second scenario is true, the custodian must ensure that the other clients entitled to such assets have been notified of the arrangement (or if private customers have given prior written consent) (FSA CoB Rule 9.1.73), and also comply with the FSA securities lending requirements.

1 SFA Board Notice 471 'For Firms Which Arrange or Engage in Lending of Investments on behalf of Customers', dated 15 April 1998 (confirming SFA Board Notice 459, subject to amendment).
2 See also Chapter 4 for a discussion of contractual settlement. The contractual settlement of securities is less common than that of cash.

Maintenance of records

7.24 The FSA Rules contain specific rules relating to the situation where a regulated firm does not *hold* assets, but is authorised to control the use of the assets under a suitable mandate from the client. These provisions essentially focus on the maintenance of adequate records, and are similar to the equivalent provisions in the SFA Rules except for the addition of a specific requirement to safeguard any documents of the client held by the regulated firm in connection with the mandate.

Client money[1]

7.25 The new FSA rules respecting client money have a similar approach to the earlier client money rules[2]. The essence of the protection for clients under the FSA's client money rules[3] is that client money will be held by the regulated entity in an account with an approved bank[4] and that such money will be held by the regulated entity on trust[5]. The client money account must also be segregated from money belonging to the firm, in that the client money account can only be used to hold client money (apart from certain exceptions)[6]. This means that the client money is protected in the insolvency of the regulated entity, although the client is still exposed to the credit risk of the approved bank.

The client money rules specify the terms of the trust on which the cash is held. Broadly, the firm holds the client money for the client (but subject to payment of proper costs if the firm becomes insolvent), and thereafter for the firm itself (which is useful where for example a firm has had to put in its own money to keep account open). In addition, the bank holding the client money for the firm will be required to acknowledge that the money is held by the firm as trustee, and that the bank will have no right to set off against the client money any amounts owed by the firm in respect of any other accounts maintained with that bank.

1 See the discussion of custody cash accounts in Chapter 3.
2 See para **7.3**, n 2.
3 Conduct of Business Rules, ch 9.3 (Client money) and ch 9.5 (Client money distribution).
4 '(In relation to a bank account opened by a *firm*): (a) if the account is opened at a branch in the *United Kingdom*: (i) the Bank of England; or (ii) the central bank of a member state of the *OECD*; or (iii) a *bank*; or (iv) a *building society* which offers, unrestrictedly, banking services; or (v) a bank which is supervised by the central bank or other banking regulator of a member state of the *OECD* ; or (b) if the account is opened elsewhere: (i) a bank in (a); or (ii) a *credit institution* established in an *EEA State* other than the *United Kingdom* and duly authorised by the relevant *Home State regulator* [broadly, the FSA or the relevant authority identified in the relevant treaty or European Directive]; or (iii) a bank which is regulated in the Isle of Man or the Channel Islands; or (c) a bank supervised by the South African Reserve Bank; or (d) any other bank that: (i) is subject to regulation by a national banking regulator; (ii) is required to provide audited accounts; (iii) has minimum net assets of £5 million (or its equivalent in any other currency at the relevant time) and has a surplus revenue over expenditure for the last two financial years; and (iv) has an annual audit report which is not materially qualified' (FSA Glossary).
5 As explained in Chapter 3, cash on deposit with a bank constitutes a debt owned by the bank of the depositor. Thus, the trust asset is the debt owed by the bank to the firm, which the firm in turn holds as trustee for clients.
6 Such as a minimum amount necessary to keep the account open, or a payment comprising amounts due to both the firm and its client which is required to be paid into the client account in the first instance, but while in such account will be treated as client money.

Application of rules

7.26 The client money rules apply where a regulated firm receives money from a client, or holds money on behalf of a client, in the course of or in connection with designated investment business (broadly, the activities specified in the Regulated Activities Order, subject to certain exceptions).

Disapplication of rules

7.27 As with the earlier client money rules, the FSA client money rules state that they do not apply if the firm holding or receiving client money is an approved bank and holds the money 'in an account with itself'[1]. Many custodians are approved banks and will therefore take advantage of this provision, but it is important to note that this disapplication only applies where the money is an account with, and therefore where the client takes the credit risk of, the approved bank. If the custodian opens a bank account in the name of the client with a third party[2] such that the client takes the credit risk of such third party itself, it is clear that the relevant cash is not held in an account with the custodian itself: therefore, despite the fact that the custodian is an approved bank, the disapplication will not apply and the custodian will be subject to the client money rules in relation to such cash.

1 CoB 9.3.3R.
2 For example, a correspondent bank, or perhaps in circumstances where the local law in the jurisdiction where a sub-custodian is appointed requires that a cash account is maintained in the name of the ultimate client.

Examples of holdings

7.28 This can perhaps be most easily understood by considering three possible scenarios for the manner in which cash may be 'held' by a custodian which is a bank.

(A) Client cash is held by the custodian bank 'in an account with itself', such that the account record on the books of the custodian bank shows the debt owed by the bank to the client from time to time, and the account record is marked up or down accordingly when cash is received or paid out by the custodian bank's correspondent banks or sub-custodians. The debt owed by the custodian bank to the client is separate from, although it corresponds to the amounts of, the debts owed to the custodian from time to time by the correspondent banks and sub-custodians. If a correspondent bank or sub-custodian becomes insolvent and cannot in practice make payment to the custodian, the custodian is still subject to its debt obligation to its client. In effect, the custodian bank does not delegate the holding of cash in the same way that it delegates the holding of securities, because the 'holding' of cash is in reality the creation of a debt to the client. The client bears the credit risk of the custodian but not that of the correspondent banks or sub-custodians.

(B) The custodian holds cash received from the sale of, or income paid in respect of, client assets in a cash account with a third party bank (for example, a sub-custodian which is a bank). The cash account is in the name of the custodian and the custodian will maintain a corresponding cash account in its own books in the name of the client. However, the custodian has agreed with the client that in the event of the insolvency or other failure to pay by the third party bank, the custodian's obligation to pay the client is conditional upon the custodian being paid in turn by the third party bank, so that the credit risk of the third party bank is upon the client rather than the custodian.

(C) The custodian bank, on behalf of its client, opens a cash account with a third party bank in the name of the client, and the third party bank owes the amount recorded in such account to the client rather than to the custodian. The custodian does not itself hold that cash or owe it to the client, although it will probably have authorisation from the client to operate that account. In relation to the cash in this account, the client bears the credit risk of the third party bank but not the credit risk of the custodian.

Scenario	**Entity maintaining bank account**	**Bank account in name of**	**Client bears credit risk of custodian bank**	**Client keeps credit risk of third party bank**	**CMRs apply to custodian bank**
A	Custodian bank	Client	✓	×	×
B	Third party bank	Custodian	✓	✓	Arguably
C	Third party bank	Client	×	✓	×

In scenario (C), the client money rules do not apply at all because the cash is held by the third party not by the custodian, whereas in scenario (A) the client's cash is held by the custodian subject to what is arguably a normal banking relationship (although the client money rules are disapplied to the extent that the approved bank exemption applies, as discussed above). Scenario (B) is more difficult because the client has a cash account with the custodian, but it is difficult to view the cash in the third party account as held by the custodian in an account with itself, because the client is bearing the credit risk of the third party bank as well as the credit risk of the custodian. Consequently, it is arguable that in this case the custodian should be complying with the client money rules in relation to the cash held with the third party bank. In this context, it is important for a custodian bank to consider carefully the terms agreed with clients regarding the holding of cash because, if there is any lack of clarity regarding the proposed arrangements, a custodian may risk being in the position of needing to comply with the client money rules but may not be aware of this.

Opting out

7.29 An entity regulated by the FSA can, where the client is a market counterparty[1] or intermediate customer[2], opt out of the client money rules. However, it cannot opt out in relation to a private customer[3]. Again, this is the same approach as that in the earlier client money rules.

1 '(1) (except in *COB* 3 [FSA Conduct of Business Rules relating to financial promotions]) a *client* who is: (a) a properly constituted government (including a quasi-governmental body or a government agency) of any country or territory; (b) a central bank or other national monetary authority of any country or territory; (c) a supranational whose members are either countries or central banks or national monetary authorities; (d) a State investment body, or a body charged with, or intervening in, the management of the public debt; (e) another *firm*, or an *overseas financial services institution* [broadly, an institution authorised to provide financial services by a regulatory body other than the FSA], except in relation to *designated investment business* , and related *ancillary activities* , conducted with or for that *firm* or institution, when that *firm* or institution is an *intermediate customer* in accordance with *COB* 4.1.7R (Classification of another firm or an overseas financial services institution); (f) any *associate* of a *firm* (except an *OPS firm* [broadly, a firm providing services in connection with an occupational pension scheme]), or of an *overseas financial services institution*, if the *firm* or institution consents; (g) a *client* when he is classified as a *market counterparty* in accordance with *COB* 4.1.12R (Large intermediate customer classified as a market counterparty); but excluding: (A) a *collective investment scheme*; and (B) (except for the purposes of *DISP* [FSA Rules regarding dispute resolution and complaints]) a *client*, who would otherwise be a *market counterparty*, when he is classified as a *private customer* in accordance with *COB* 4.1.14R (Client classified as private customer). (2) (in *COB* 3) a *person* in (1) and a *person* who would be such a *person* if he were a *client*' (FSA Glossary).

2 '(1) (except in *COB* 3 [FSA Conduct of Business Rules relating to financial promotions]) a *client* who is not a *market counterparty* and who is: (a) a local authority or public authority; (b) a *body corporate* whose *shares* have been *listed* or *admitted to trading* on any *EEA* exchange; (c) a *body corporate* whose *shares* have been *listed* or *admitted to trading* on the primary board of any *IOSCO* member country official exchange; (d) a *body corporate* (including a *limited liability partnership*) which has (or any of whose *holding companies* or *subsidiaries* has) (or has had at any time during the previous two years) called up share capital or net assets of at least £5 million (or its equivalent in any other currency at the relevant time); (e) a *special purpose vehicle*; (f) a *partnership* or unincorporated association which has (or has had at any time during the previous two years) net assets of at least £5 million (or its equivalent in any other currency at the relevant time) and calculated in the case of a limited *partnership* without deducting loans owing to any of the *partners*; (g) a trustee of a trust (other than an *occupational pension scheme*, *SSAS* [a small self-administered occupational pension scheme] or *stakeholder pension scheme*) which has (or has had at any time during the previous two years) assets of at least £10 million (or its equivalent in any other currency at the relevant time) calculated by aggregating the value of the cash and *designated investments* forming part of the trust's assets, but before deducting its liabilities; (h) a trustee of an *occupational pension scheme*, *SSAS* or *stakeholder pension scheme* where the trust has (or has had at any time during the previous two

years): (i) at least 50 members; and (ii) assets under management of at least £10 million (or its equivalent in any other currency at the relevant time); (i) another *firm*, or an *overseas financial services institution*, when, in relation to *designated investment business* , or related *ancillary activities*, conducted with or for that *firm* or institution, that *firm* or institution is an *intermediate customer* in accordance with *COB* 4.1.7R (Classification of another firm or an overseas financial services institution); (j) an *unregulated collective investment scheme*; (k) a *client* when he is classified as an *intermediate customer* in accordance with *COB* 4.1.9R (Expert private customer classified as intermediate customer); but excluding: (i) a *regulated collective investment scheme*; and (ii) a *client* who would otherwise be an *intermediate customer*, when he is classified in accordance with: (A) *COB* 4.1.12R (Large intermediate customer classified as market counterparty); or (B) (except for the purposes of *DISP*) *COB* 4.1.14R (Client classified as private customer). (2) (in *COB* 3) a *person* in (1) or a *person* who would be such a *person* if he were a *client*' (FSA Glossary).

3 '(1) (except in COB 3) a *client* who is not a *market counterparty* or an *intermediate customer*, including: (a) an individual who is not a *firm*; (b) an overseas individual who is not an *overseas financial services institution*; (c) a *regulated collective investment scheme*; (d) (except for the purposes of *DISP*) a *client* when he is classified as a *private customer* in accordance with *COB* 4.1.14R (Client classified as a private customer); but excluding a *client*, who would otherwise be a *private customer*, when he is classified as an *intermediate customer* in accordance with *COB* 4.1.9R (Expert private customer classified as an intermediate customer). (2) (in *COB* 3) a *person* in (1) or a *person* who would be such a *person* if he were a *client*' (FSA Glossary).

Trustee firms

7.30 Only specific parts of the client money rules apply to a trustee firm (a firm which is acting as a trustee or personal representative but not a trustee for an occupational person scheme). This of course assumes that a trustee is conducting investment business subject to the FSA regulatory requirements, rather than operating under an applicable exemption available in the Regulated Activities Order[1]. A trustee firm is required by the FSA rules to hold client money primarily on the terms of the relevant trust deed but, subject to such terms, holds subject to the limited client money rules specified to be applicable to a trustee[2]. This will of course depend on whether the trustee is holding the relevant cash on trust[3].

1 See para **7.40**.
2 CoB 9.3.34R.
3 See discussion in Chapter 3 regarding the status of the custodian as trustee in relation to the holding of securities but not (usually) cash.

Use of a non-approved bank

7.31 Although generally client money should be held in a client bank account with an approved bank, the FSA Rules will in certain limited circumstances allow a regulated entity (but not a trustee firm) to use a bank which is not an approved bank[1]. Broadly, the relevant circumstances are that:

- the client money in question arises from (or is to be used for) settlement or income distribution outside the UK;
- local law or market practice means it is not possible to hold the money with an approved bank;
- the money must be held with the relevant bank no longer than necessary;
- the firm must notify its client (and obtain prior written consent from a private customer) that the money will not be held with an approved bank, that the legal/regulatory regime applying to the bank may be different from the UK regime, that the money may be treated differently if the bank becomes insolvent, and (if relevant) that the bank will not agree that it has no right of set off in respect of the money; and
- the money must be held by the bank in a designated bank account.

Although the use of banks which are not approved banks is thus heavily restricted, this provision does at least provide a mechanism enabling a custodian to make alternative arrangements where, as a result of the particular jurisdiction in which assets are being held, no approved bank is available or local law requires the use of a particular bank which is not an approved bank.

1 CoB 9.3.74R.

Prior written notice

7.32 Even where an FSA firm is using an approved bank for the holding of client money, if the client account is maintained outside the UK, then as under the previous client money rules, the firm must give prior written notice that this is the case, that the legal and regulatory regime applicable to the bank may be different, that upon the insolvency of the bank the client money may be treated differently from how it would be treated in the UK, and (if relevant) that the bank has not agreed that it has no right of set off over the client money[1].

1 CoB 9.3.90.

Unclaimed funds

7.33 While the FSA client money rules are in general not very different from the client money rules under the previous regulatory regime, the new provision which allows firm to cease to treat unclaimed money as client money may be of particular interest to custodians[1].

As a practical matter, it is not uncommon for custodians holding assets for clients to find that there are funds in the client account which for some reason have over time not been claimed by clients and where it is now not possible to trace the clients entitled to such funds[2]. Since this is client money, the custodian remains subject to all relevant requirements under the FSA rules, including the obligation to provide statements to the client, although in practice it will be unable to do so if the relevant client cannot be identified. Similarly, the custodian will be unable to terminate the arrangement with the client if it does not know to whom a termination notice should be given. Unless the arrangement is terminated, then in principle the firm must continue to hold the client money in accordance with the client money rules, since it is unable to vary the terms on which it holds such money (because it cannot agree this with an unidentified client)[3].

1 CoB 9.3.137G, CoB 9.3.138R, CoB 9.3.139E and CoB 9.3.140G.
2 See further discussion regarding unclaimed securities as well as cash at para **7.48**.
3 It is risky for the custodian simply decide to treat the client money as its own money, because the unidentified client still has a claim to the relevant amount, and therefore any such step by the custodian could leave the custodian open to claims for unjust enrichment, conversion or in extreme cases theft.

'Reasonable steps'

7.34 The FSA client money rules[1] have introduced a new provision which is intended to allow a firm to cease to treat money as client money where it has not been claimed, but only if the firm 'can demonstrate that it has taken reasonable steps to trace the client concerned and to return the balance'. The 'reasonable steps' required might, for example, include advertising in appropriate publications, such as the London Gazette. However, the FSA specifies particular steps which it considers should be included in the reasonable steps taken by a firm to trace a client. These steps consist of:

(a) having a written agreement with the client that after six years in which there has been no movement on the client money balance, it may cease to be treated as client money;
(b) checking that there has been no movement on the client's balance in the last six years;
(c) writing to the client at the last known address warning that money will cease to be treated as client money and giving 28 days to claim;
(d) keeping records of all balances ceasing to be treated as client money; and
(e) giving an undertaking to make good any valid claim to released balances (such undertaking to be legally enforceable by persons with a valid claim).

These steps are not stated to be *requirements* of the FSA in a binding FSA Rule, but the evidential provisions in this section state that failure to perform any of the specified steps may be regarded by the FSA as indicating that a firm has not taken reasonable steps as required.

As may be seen, in practice these specified steps are quite onerous because, if the relevant cash is unclaimed and it is unclear to whom it belongs, it will be difficult to enter into the written agreement mentioned in (a) or to write to the client as mentioned in (c). While the equivalent result to (c) could probably be achieved by suitable advertisements, it is likely that the need for written agreement can only be satisfied if standard client terms include such a provision, and it is clear that, even if the particular client cannot be identified, such client must have become a client of the custodian by becoming party to an agreement incorporating such a provision. It will depend on the facts whether it is possible to achieve this result, but in future custodians may need to consider including such a provision in standard client agreements. In addition, a custodian entity may not wish to create legally enforceable undertakings in favour of unknown third parties as suggested by the guidance term described in (e) above, and may consider that the burden of maintaining client money procedures in relation to unclaimed client money does not outweigh the burden created by this type of undertaking. Nevertheless, if the main concern for a custodian is to end unnecessary compliance with the client money rules, this new Rule does at least provide a basis for discussion with the FSA[2].

1 CoB 9.3.138R.
2 There is no equivalent regulatory provision regarding unclaimed assets, the situation regarding which is considered further at para **7.48**.

Collateral

Under the SFA Rules

7.35 As discussed above, the SFA had specific rules which applied to the holding of collateral, namely assets held or controlled 'other than by way of safe custody'. Under the SFA Rules, in relation to collateral, it was necessary to comply not only with certain of the standard custody rules (regarding terms to be notified to client, reconciliation, content of statements and despatch of statements), but also with specific additional obligations, including requirements respecting safeguarding, separate identification from assets of the firm, and written consent (or notification if not a private customer) from customer if the firm intended to use the collateral to collateralise the firm's own obligations, obligations of other persons, or to deposit with, or charge the collateral to, a third party.

Under the FSA Rules

7.36 Under the FSA Rules there is a somewhat different approach. The collateral section[1] only applies if a firm holds assets 'in connection with an arrangement to secure the obligations of a client in the course of, or in connection with, its designated investment business'. The terms of this section state that if the firm has a right to use the collateral asset[2], or can treat the collateral 'as if' all legal title and associated rights are transferred to the firm, then subject to an obligation to return equivalent assets, the only requirement is to maintain 'adequate records' to enable the firm to meet its further obligations, including delivery obligations. This is arguably a somewhat strange approach, given that the only rules applying to 'collateral' under this section are designed to apply to assets which are not collateral in the sense of being subject to a security interest, since they are transferred outright to the firm (for example as in the case of collateral provided in an English law repo or stock loan)[3]. Since the firm receives full title to the relevant assets and is not holding on behalf of the client, the firm is entitled to do what it likes with its own assets, and would as a matter of practice maintain records of its contractual obligations to return securities. It is difficult to see what these requirements add to the relevant rules relating to stock lending discussed earlier. In principle, the main impact of this section is the clarification of the way in which FSA regulated entities must comply with the custody and client money rules in relation to assets received by such entity by way of security where a security interest (but not outright title) is granted to such entity.

1 Conduct of Business Rules, ch 9, section 9.4.
2 See Chapter 4 for a discussion of collateral takers' rights to use collateral assets.
3 As discussed in Chapter 4, the Financial Collateral Directive will however permit a right of use of collateral provided under a security interest.

Compliance

7.37 If the firm has *only* a security interest over assets held by it (with no right of use), it *must* comply with custody rules or client money rules, as applicable. This seems logical because in principle, if a firm has a security interest in the assets, rather than full legal and beneficial title, the remainder of the interest in the assets (the equity of redemption, as discussed in Chapter 4) must remain with the person granting the security interest, and therefore that part of the interest in the assets is held by the custodian and should arguably be held subject to the protections set out in the custody rules or client money rules (depending on the nature of the assets held).

Extension of Rules

7.38 Where then does this leave the old argument outlined at para **7.6**, that a delivery of assets by way of security is not subject to custody regulation? In principle, if an entity is not an authorised person regulated by the FSA, and the only reason that such entity could be regarded as requiring authorisation by the FSA is because it receives assets over which it takes security, it would still be possible to argue that the entity taking the security interest is *not* providing custody. As noted above, it would be extremely important in such case (a) to maintain appropriate records of such arrangement, in order (b) for the entity to avoid any indication that it regarded the assets as held in custody, and (c) ideally to clear such approach with the regulatory authority in advance[1]. In contrast, if the entity taking security is regulated by the FSA[2], it is subject to the FSA Rules. CoB 9.4.3R is clear that a firm with a security interest must hold the assets subject to the relevant FSA Rules.

Consequently, CoB 9.4.3R results in the FSA custody rules applying, even though CoB 9.1.1R is only stated to apply to the activity which is the regulated activity of safeguarding and administration and, as discussed above, holding assets by way of security may technically not fall within the scope of such activity. Nevertheless, this may be seen as an example of a situation where the rules applicable to an authorised person extend to activities which are not necessarily activities for which authorisation would be necessary.

1 This is particularly important where the question of whether or not the entity is providing custody determines whether or not the entity should be authorised for the purposes of FSMA. If the FSA took the view that holding assets as security would in the relevant case constitute a regulated activity, the entity could face criminal penalties for carrying on a regulated activity in breach of FSMA. When receiving assets by way of security, the holder has a security interest but does not have full title to the assets; the assets are held subject to the chargeors' interest. The holder must therefore keep the assets safe but cannot use the assets for its own purpose. The manner of holding is difficult, because the chargee does not have legal title in the same sense that a custodian does, but has a title more akin to that of a mortgagee. In principle, therefore, the assets received by way of security should probably be recorded in a separate house account, and clearly designated and blocked to avoid any transfer or use of such assets until either enforcement of the security interest or transfer back to the chargeor. In this context, see also Chapter 4.

2 As would be the case with most custodian entities in practice.

Control and custodians

7.39 Another area which may be of potential concern for custodians is the section of FSMA (Pt XII, ss 178–192) itself which requires notification to the FSA by any person in advance of taking steps to acquire control over a UK authorised person, to add to the ways in which it controls a UK authorised person, or to increase existing control over an authorised person. The FSA has three months in which to consider such notification, and it is an offence for a person to carry out the proposed action within the three months if the FSA has not granted approval (s 191).

A person will acquire control of the purposes of this part of FSMA when it obtains 10 per cent or more of the shares in an authorised person[1], or is able to exercise 'significant influence' over the management of such person as a result of his shareholding (or voting power) in such person[2], or holds 10 per cent or more of the shares in a parent company of the authorised person[3], or is able to exercise 'significant influence' over the management of the parent as a result of a shareholding (or voting power) in the parent[4], or is entitled to exercise or control 10 per cent or more of the voting power in the authorised person or its parent[5]. Similar provisions apply regarding the increase (or reduction) of control in an authorised person.

The issue here is that there is no mention of any distinction between the person who is the ultimate beneficial owner of, for example, shares, or the person holding such shares for another, such as a custodian. In principle, therefore, this provision requires a custodian to give due notice to the FSA in respect of an acquisition of shares, as well as the custodian's client, and even if the custodian's client is not caught because its shareholding is not of a sufficient size, the custodian may well be caught as a result of holding the same type of shares for other clients. This may be a particular problem for custodians in a volatile market where many clients are wishing to acquire the same stock, and in theory means that the custodian cannot agree to accept delivery of the relevant stock into the name of the custodian or its delegate unless the time limit imposed by the FSA has been followed. This could be a significant delay on business. There is provision[6] for the Treasury to provide exemptions from these sections, but at present the exemptions only relate to building societies and friendly societies[7].

1 FSMA 2000, s 179(2)(a).
2 FSMA 2000, s 179(2)(b), (f).
3 FSMA 2000, s 179(2)(c).
4 FSMA 2000, s 179(2)(d), (h).
5 FSMA 2000, s 179(2)(e), (g).
6 FSMA 2000, s 192.
7 See The Financial Services and Markets Act 2000 (Controllers) (Exemption) Order 2001 (SI 2001/2638) and The Financial Services and Markets Act 2000 (Controllers) (Exemption) (No 2) Order 2001 (SI 2001/3338).

Trustees and custody

7.40 We have discussed earlier (see Chapter 3) the idea that as a matter of English law it is probably most realistic to regard a custodian as a trustee, and in the above sections of this Chapter 7 have considered some of the regulatory requirements which apply to custodians as a result of FSMA and certain sections of the FSA Handbook. However, in the context of identifying activities which may constitute regulated activities (see para **7.9**), it is interesting to note that the Regulated Activities Order provides certain exemptions for trustees[1]. As a result, if a person which is a trustee carries out an activity specified in the Order and would otherwise need to be authorised by the FSA to carry on such activity in the UK, it may avoid the need for authorisation if it carries out the activity within the parameters of the relevant exemption. In relation to custody specifically, a person will not be regarded as performing the relevant activity[2] if it is done when 'acting as trustee or personal representative' *unless* 'he holds himself out as providing a service comprising' the relevant activity, or 'is remunerated for what he does in addition to any remuneration he receives as trustee or personal representative'.

On the basis that a custodian is a form of trustee, there is a certain amount of debate as to how the regulated activity of custody and the trustee exemption interrelate. At one extreme, it could be argued that apart from the case where a custodian is clearly a bailee of physical assets, a custodian will invariably be a trustee and fall within the trustee exemption and would therefore not need to become authorised for custody activities alone. At the other end of the spectrum, there is the argument that the exemptions in art 66 are essentially aimed at activities carried out ancillary to trustee functions, that the holding of assets is a core function of a trustee and so can never be ancillary, and that therefore a trustee which holds assets is always required to be authorised. While there is perhaps no clear answer to this, both these extreme arguments would seem to make something of a nonsense of the legislation. One way of approaching this is to go back to the analysis of a custodian as a particular type of trustee which has by agreement restricted its functions and liabilities. On this basis, the requirement of authorisation and regulatory compliance may be regarded as additional client protection which is advisable where the 'trustee' is in fact a custodian, whereas such additional protection is in principle not necessary where the trustee is subject to all usual trust obligations. Clearly, such analysis is not perfect, given that trustees in certain structures would aim to clarify and restrict the scope of their functions to the extent appropriate, but it does at least draw some form of distinction between a service described as a custody service and a service described as a trustee service. This is consistent with the requirements of the exemption that there should be no holding out of the provision of custody services separately, or separate remuneration for custody services. After all, if a client thinks that they are paying for a custody service, or has appointed the relevant entity because it has made claims about the nature of its custody services, it does not seem unreasonable to require the service provider to comply with the usual requirements that apply to custodians. It is useful to note that art 66(7) states that 'a person is not to be regarded as receiving additional remuneration merely because his remuneration is calculated by reference to time spent'. In principle, therefore, a trustee is not prevented from charging for the time spent on aspects of the trustee function which in practice relate to safeguarding and administering assets, but, in contrast, it would be difficult to argue that the trustee was not 'receiving additional remuneration' if, for example, the agreed terms allocated the trustee a separate fee for separate aspects of the services provided, including custody as a separate function.

As we have suggested in the discussion above, for the purposes of the trustee exemption, the position where custody services are involved is perhaps not as clear as it might be[3]. It is a particular concern for entities wishing to rely on the trustee exemption as a reason why authorisation is not required, and in such cases great care should be taken to weigh up all the factors involved including the risks, since the consequences of conducting without authorisation an activity where authorisation is required are potentially significant.

1 Article 66 specifically (although art 67 may also assist, together with certain other general exemptions).
2 Article 40(1) '... both (a) the safeguarding of assets belonging to another, and (b) the administration of those assets, or arranging for one or more other persons to carry on that activity'.
3 There remains the question of whether an entity providing a custody service would need to be authorised if effectively selling the service as a trustee service rather than custody. It seems likely that the regulatory authorities would have little sympathy for an entity clearly trying to escape the regulatory regime by disguising its service, but it is conceivable that there could be situations where the answer is less clear cut.

Customer classification

7.41 As may be seen from the categories of customer referred to above[1], broadly the categories for classification of customer have not changed greatly under the new regulatory regime under FSMA. However, it is important to note that strictly, under the new FSA categories, a regulated collective investment scheme[2] must be treated as a private customer[3]. In recognition of the fact that this may cause difficulties for firms with existing clients of this description, the FSA has published a form of waiver[4] to the effect that a firm can comply with classification requirements of its former regulator. However, such waiver only applies to a firm if such firm sends the FSA written consent in the specified form (although a formal waiver application is not required), and such waiver only applies until 31 March 2003 or, if earlier, the date an amendment or revocation of the relevant rules comes into force.

1 See para **7.17**, n 2; para **7.18**, nn 1 and 2; para **7.27**, n 2; para **7.29**, nn 1 and 2.
2 An authorised unit trust for the purposes of FSMA, a body incorporated under schemes recognised under the Open-Ended Investment Companies Regulations 2001 (SI 2001/1228) or an overseas scheme recognised in the UK pursuant to FSMA.
3 See CoB 4.1.7R(4).
4 Handbook Release dated 4 May 2002.

Outsourcing

SYSC

7.42 An additional potential area of concern for custodians arises not from the CoB Rules but from certain other parts of the Handbook, namely the section of the High Level Standards relating to 'Senior Management Arrangements, Systems and

Controls' ('SYSC') and the proposals for the Integrated Prudential Sourcebook (which will apply to all entities regulated by the FSA in replacement of the individual Interim Prudential Sourcebooks: see description at para **7.8**). The FSA Consultation Paper 142 produced in July 2002[1] entitled 'Operational risk systems and controls' ('CP142') contains draft wording for the guidance which is to form part of SYSC and the Integrated Prudential Sourcebook. Even though the provisions are intended to have the status of guidance, rather than rules or evidential provisions, it is important for regulated entities to consider carefully the terms of such guidance as an indication of what the FSA would expect the firm to do in the relevant circumstances. The creation of new wording regarding this area also indicates the FSA's growing awareness of, and concern in relation to, the particular matters covered.

The underlying rules which impose regulatory requirements on FSA members in this context, and in connection with which the guidance is provided, are set out in SYSC. In particular, a firm is required to 'take reasonable care to establish and maintain such systems and controls as are appropriate to its business' and to 'take reasonable care to establish and maintain effective systems and controls for compliance with applicable requirements and standards under the regulatory system and for countering the risk that the firm might be used to further financial crime'[2]. There is also the obligation under Principle 3 of the FSA's Principles to 'take reasonable care to organise and control its affairs responsibly and effectively, with adequate risk management systems.'

1 Consultation period ends 31 October 2002.
2 SYSC 3.1.1 and 3.2.6.

CP142

7.43 As the name of CP142 suggests, the guidance covers, broadly, the steps and controls which the FSA would expect of a regulated firm in order to safeguard against problems arising from human resources, internal procedures and technology systems. In principle, the intention appears to be to keep the scope of the guidance as wide as possible, encouraging firms to look at any aspects of their operations which may have an impact on 'the solvency and business operations of the firm, threatening the regulatory objectives of market confidence and consumer protection', or which may 'lead to the unfair treatment of the firm's customers or the mishandling of client assets, threatening the regulatory objectives of market confidence and consumer protection' or which may 'threaten the financial crime regulatory objective by making the firm more susceptive to fraud or money laundering'[1]. The draft guidance contains particular sections focusing on people, systems, external events, outsourcing and insurance, indicating the procedures expected of FSA members in such contexts, and assisting with interpretation of the SYSC rules which, as may be seen, are drafted in wide terms. However, the FSA will expect a firm to approach the rules and guidance with regard to its own particular circumstances: hence it is not the case that a firm can necessarily conclude with certainty that compliance with the rules will be achieved by following the guidance[2]. It is not surprising that the relevant rules and guidance in this context are in such wide terms, given that the aim is to regulate all aspects of 'operational risk', a term which itself has a potentially broad scope, but this does not make the task of compliance with the relevant regulations any easier[3]. A related concern in this area is the Basle proposal of capital weighting for operational risk[4]. Given that 'operational risk' is a concept which is rather more difficult to pin down than, for example, counterparty risk, because it covers a range of factors, it is important that careful consideration is given to the proposed regulation in order to avoid both an approach which is unnecessarily onerous and that is so wide that it is unworkable.

1 Draft guidance 3A.1.2, CP142.
2 'A firm should assess the appropriateness of any particular item of guidance in the light of the scale, nature and complexity of its activities as well as its obligations as set out in Principle 3 to organise and control its affairs responsibly and effectively' (Draft guidance 3A.1.4, CP142).
3 'Operational risk is a concept that can have a different application for different firms' (Draft guidance 3A.3.1, CP142).
4 See para **7.56**.

Regulation

7.44 This increased focus on operational risk is an issue for all regulated entities including custodians, but the aspect which may be of particular interest to persons using or providing custody services is the regulation of outsourcing.

Regulatory obligations already exist in relation to outsourcing, eg the requirement in the FSA Supervision sourcebook for a firm to notify the FSA when entering into (or significantly changing) a 'material outsourcing' and to enable the FSA to obtain information about a 'material outsourcing'[1]. There is also at present the outsourcing section of the Interim Prudential Sourcebook for Banks, but this will change once the Integrated Prudential Sourcebook replaces it, as the comparable outsourcing provisions will appear in SYSC in the form of guidance rather than as rules in the Prudential Sourcebook.

The outsourcing guidance appears in section 3A.7 of the draft[2] and applies to any outsourcing, not just a material outsourcing, although it is noted that 'Particular care should be taken to manage material outsourcing arrangements'[3]. In principle, therefore, such guidance should be taken into account by a person appointing a custodian, sub-custodian, agent or other delegate to provide services which would otherwise be carried out by that person itself. The FSA defines 'outsourcing' to mean 'the use of a person to provide customised services to a firm other than: (a) a member of the firm's governing body acting in his capacity as such; or (b) an individual employed by a firm under a contract of service.' It could therefore be argued that use of a custodian or sub-custodian is a standard service provided on standard terms rather than a 'customised service'[4] and hence not an outsourcing for these purposes. Nevertheless it remains a point to bear in mind, because depending on the context and terms of the delegation, the arrangement could be considered an outsourcing or material outsourcing and therefore the relevant issues cannot be simply assumed to be inapplicable[5].

In practice, the outsourcing guidance may not be particularly onerous, given that it is intended to reflect what the FSA understands to be good business practice, but it is of course another aspect of the regulatory regime to bear in mind as a possible issue when appointing delegates.

From the opposite perspective, custodians and other service providers will also need to bear in mind the regulatory context when providing services to FSA members if the custody service or any ancillary services[6] are of a nature or extent such that delegation could be regarded as an outsourcing or material outsourcing. In such cases, the entity outsourcing the services will undoubtedly be concerned to impose as many controls on the delegates as it can in order to protect its regulatory position.

1 Supervision sourcebook, 15.3.1.R and 15.3.8G(1)(e), and section 2.3.
2 CP142.
3 Section 3A.7.3, draft guidance, CP142.
4 This term is not defined.

5 Contrast with the Interim Prudential Sourcebook for Banks, Outsourcing section, where it is stated specifically that 'The purchase of a standardised service . . . and the provision of custody arrangements fall outside the definition of material outsourcing', and the earlier draft wording for the Integrated Prudential Sourcebook (CP97, published June 2001) where in the section relating to outsourcing it was stated that 'The provision of custody services does not constitute material outsourcing'.

6 For example 'middle office' functions such as trade matching, allocation and reporting which may be delegated by fund managers to custodians along with custody business.

Related issues

Clients' right of action

7.45 Having considered the nature of the regulatory obligations which apply to the provision of custody services for clients, it may also be useful to consider whether breach of such obligations will give rise to a direct claim by the client against the custodian. This is in addition to any claim for breach of contract, in tort, or for breach of fiduciary duty, as discussed in Chapter 6.

The regulated entity may be subject to fines or other disciplinary action by the FSA if it breaches applicable requirements under FSMA such as the CoB rules. However, there are essentially two situations where the FSA requirements may give rise to claims by the custodian's client.

Breach of FSA rules

7.46 Under FSMA, s 150 a 'private person'[1] is entitled to bring a claim against a member of the FSA for breach of FSA rules. This is treated as a claim for breach of statutory duty and is therefore subject to any defences which the FSA member would have for such a claim.

1 See The Financial Services and Markets Act 2000 (Rights of Action) Regulations 2001, reg 3:

'(1) In these Regulations, "private person" means –

(a) any individual, unless he suffers the loss in question in the course of carrying on –

(i) any regulated activity; or

(iii) any activity which would be a regulated activity apart from any exclusion made by article 72 of the Regulated Activities Order (overseas persons); and

(b) any person who is not an individual, unless he suffers the loss in question in the course of carrying on business of any kind; but does not include a government, a local authority (in the United Kingdom or elsewhere) or an international organisation.

(2) For the purposes of paragraph (1)(a), an individual who suffers loss in the course of effecting or carrying out contracts of insurance (within the meaning of article 10 of the Regulated Activities Order) written at Lloyds' is not to be taken to suffer loss in the course of carrying on a regulated activity.'

Breach of regulatory requirements

7.47 A client will have a claim against the custodian under the terms of the custody agreement (and therefore subject to any relevant limitations in such agreement) for breach of regulatory requirements if the regulatory requirements have been incorporated into the agreement as contractual terms. While it seems unlikely in normal circumstances that a custodian would wish to agree to this, case law[1] has shown that there may be a risk of inadvertently incorporating terms by reference when intending to make references for other purposes: therefore care should be taken when drafting cross-references to the terms of regulatory requirements (or other relevant wording, eg standard settlement system or stock exchange rules). There is of course the argument that a custodian intending to comply with its regulatory obligations should have no difficulty in stating in its agreement that it will do so, but it is not necessarily the case that a custodian would wish to give a person who is not a private person for the purposes of FSMA a direct right of claim which it would not otherwise have.

1 *Chigi v CS First Boston Ltd* [1997] All ER (D) 121 (QBD, Commercial Court) In this case, the wording causing particular problems was the following: 'All transactions in Securities shall be subject to the rules and customs of the exchange or market and/or any clearing house through which the transactions are executed (if any), the rules and regulations of the Securities and Investments Board, The Securities and Futures Authority Limited and the Bank of England so far as they are applicable and to applicable law so that: (a) if there is any conflict between: (i) these Terms and Conditions and (ii) any such rules, customs and applicable law, the latter shall prevail.' The client argued that this wording made the transactions subject to the London Code of Conduct (being applicable regulations of the Bank of England) which prevailed over the brokers' standard terms and conditions. The broker argued that the wording 'was intended to ensure that if there was any conflict between the general terms of business and any regulatory provision' it would 'be entitled to comply with that regulatory provision.' The judge concluded that notwithstanding the intended limited effect of this wording, 'it did not naturally read in that way' and therefore it was correct that 'the transactions were made subject to the applicable regulations of The Bank of England, namely the London Code of Conduct' and as a result 'although no claim based upon a paragraph of the London Code gives rise to any statutory duty' the broker was nonetheless 'under the duties imposed by that code as a matter of contract.'

Unclaimed assets

7.48 As noted above in the context of unclaimed money, the issue of unclaimed assets can be a considerable problem for custodians[1]. In such cases, the custodian is required by the regulatory regime to provide all appropriate protections for the client securities or cash but, because the client is unknown, may simply be unable to comply with certain requirements, such as reviewing the client classification for the client or providing regular statements to the client. Similarly, unless the custodian has always used the same form of custody terms, it may be impossible to identify what contractual terms are in place between the custodian and the unknown clients and the custodian cannot amend or replace such terms since it cannot obtain the agreement of the client to do so. Are any methods of resolution open to the custodian, apart from the limited assistance which may be available under the Client Money Rules (see paras **7.33–7.34**)? In practice, the situation is very difficult because there is no principle of law which extinguishes rights to unclaimed securities or cash, merely because such assets are unclaimed; therefore any attempt by a custodian to simply treat the assets as its own assets would risk the possibility of a claimant appearing at a later date and claiming for breach of contract (assuming it is a former client), conversion or unjust enrichment or, in extreme circumstances, alleging theft has occurred. In such a case, the custodian would also be in breach of trust and in breach of its regulatory obligations under the CoB rules not to combine client assets with its own assets. While there might be circumstances in which a custodian could become comfortable with the risks of treating the assets as its own, eg after examining the effect of any relevant limitation periods and making provisions for possible claims, it seems unlikely that the regulators would be happy with this approach. Also, it is crucial to avoid any question of dishonesty, by giving clients adequate details of the proposed action. In practice, the best way to be relieved of the unwanted burden of unclaimed client assets is probably to go through the process of paying into court[2].

1 A possible source of unclaimed assets may be administrative error. Assets may be 'unclaimed' for a variety of reasons and through no fault of the custodian, for example late delivery of cash or non-cash distributions to the custodian in respect of assets which were held by the custodian for a client but

are no longer. If the delivery identifies the assets to which they relate, the custodian should be able to determine which former client is entitled to the assets, but if the relevant person declines responsibility for the assets, the custodian is left with the assets. Similarly, confusion might arise if a client sells securities, then a late distribution is made, but neither client nor purchaser claim the distribution.

2 Under the Trustee Act 1925.

International regulatory developments

7.49 It is of course also important to consider the international regulatory context in which a custodian is providing services. This section considers international regulatory developments relating to the post trade infrastructure. The importance of custodians, settlement systems and central counterparties to the financial markets has received considerable industry and public sector attention, and a number of initiatives are proposed in relation to their regulation[1].

1 Note also that a collaboration project between the Committee of European Securities Regulators (CESR) and the European System of Central Banks (ESCB) in relation to securities clearing and settlement was announced in October 2001, with a view to developing standards for the post trade infrastructure.

Investment services regulation

7.50 Internationally, there have been a number of calls for the effective regulation of post-trade infrastructure service providers[1]. In 2001 the Lamfalussy Securities Markets Report[2] included among its recommendations consideration of whether a regulatory framework is needed for clearing and settlement[3]. The regulatory debate in the EU has been stimulated by the Commission's 2000 Consultation Document on proposed amendments to the Investment Services Directive ('ISD') ('the ISD Consultation Document')[4], which was followed in 2002 by a second consultation[5].

1 Recommendation 18: 'Regulation and oversight. Securities settlement systems should be subject to regulation and oversight. The responsibilities and objectives of the securities regulator and the central bank with respect to the SSSs should be clearly defined, and their roles and major policies should be publicly disclosed. They should have the ability and the resources to perform their responsibilities, including assessment and promoting implementation of these recommendations. They should co-operate with each other and with other relevant authorities' (CPSS/IOSCO Recommendations for Securities Settlement Systems, 2002).

2 *Final Report of the Committee of Wise Men on the Regulation of European Securities Markets*, Brussels, 15 February 2001 ('Lamfalussy Securities Market Report').

3 Lamfalussy Securities Market Report, p 16.

4 European Commission, Internal Market Directorate General *Overview of Proposed Adjustments to the Investment Services Directive*, available on http://europa.eu.int/comm/internal_market/en/finances/mobil/isd.htm ('the ISD Consultation Document').

5 *Revision of Investment Services Directive; Second Consultation; Overview Paper*, March 2002.

Access rights

7.51 A number of bodies have raised the concern that restricted access to clearing and settlement services creates possible competitive distortions[1], and the need for a regulatory response is widely felt. In the ISD Consultation Document the Commission indicates that it proposes to give market participants and regulated markets rights of direct and cross border access to clearing and settlement systems[2].

'Market participants should not be constrained in making investment decisions by the location of counterparty, securities or infrastructure. There should be generalised access . . . to all necessary systems. A first step in achieving this objective is envisaged in the proposed revision of the Investment Services Directive, which provides for the possibility of choice of systems for post-trade activity. The parallel application of competition policy can be used to reinforce these measures.'[3]

The proposed amendments to the ISD will permit market participants to use partner country clearing/central counterparty facilities for off market positions; permit market participants to use the non-default settlement system of choice to which links exist; and permit regulated markets cross-border rights of access to recognised central counterparties, subject to regulatory approvals[4]. However, rights of access will not be unlimited[5].

The commercial implications of this are very interesting, as it precludes any strategic element in market access to clearing[6]. Thus, the revised ISD will seek to ensure that 'access to post trading facilities should not be made conditional on execution of trades on the affiliated trading platform'[7]. However, access rights are conditional on suitable commercial, technical and prudential criteria; and links to CCSs are subject to veto by the regulators of the markets in question[8].

1 For example, the Giovannini Report identifies restricted access to cross-border settlement, requiring the need for market participants to use multiple settlement systems, as a major barrier to cross-border business. The European Securities Foundation submission on the proposal to upgrade the ISD discusses the lack of real competition in the clearing sector. The CPSS/IOSCO Recommendations provide, in recommendation 14, that 'CSDs and central counterparties should have objective and publicly disclosed criteria for participation that permit fair and open access.' It goes on to comment (p 22) that 'Discrimination against competitors and others providing comparable services is only acceptable if clearly justifiable on risk grounds.'

2 ISD Consultation Document, p 34:

'. . . it is proposed to supplement the existing remote access rights for market participants (under article 15(1)) to partner country clearing and settlement systems with the following additional options for market participants and regulated markets:

(1) possibility for market participants to use central clearing counterparty to novate and/or net "off-market" positions;
(2) possibility for market participant to request that a position be settled in a settlement system provided that the central counterparty has satisfactory direct or indirect links to the settlement system;
(3) possibility for a "regulated market" to route some or all confirmed trades to central clearing counterparty in another Member State, subject to approval of the competent authority responsible for oversight of the market.'

3 Communication from the Commission *Clearing and settlement in the European Union; Main policy issues and future challenges*, May 2002, p 3.

4 See the Commission's Second Consultation, pp 27, 28.

5 *Clearing and settlement in the European Union; Main policy issues and future challenges*, May 2002, p 14:

'Neither the existing ISD, nor the plans for its revision contain truly comprehensive rights of access and choice. They address some of the restrictions facing participants on location of settlement, but do not offer a corresponding right for central counterparties and central securities depositories to become members of other clearing and settlement systems.'

6 The Commission comments in ISD Consultation Document, p 35:

'The proposed measures do not call into question existing ownership or management arrangements for regulated markets/trading platforms, central counterparties/clearing houses or settlement systems. However, the provisions seek to ensure that joint or linked ownership of regulated markets and central clearing counterparties does not impinge on any decision by the operator of central clearing counterparty to make access available to unaffiliated "regulated markets". Article 38 (annex 3) seeks to enshrine the principle that the operator of the central clearing counterparty should decide to make its facilities available to other "regulated markets" on technical or commercial grounds, and should not seek to restrict access so as to maximise trading on any affiliated "regulated market".'

7 ISD Consultation Document, p 35:

'The decision of the central counterparty or clearing house should be made on objective commercial, technical and prudential grounds and should not be influenced by considerations relating to competitive implications for any affiliated "regulated market" (art 38, annex 3).'

8 ISD Consultation Document, p 36.

No passport

7.52

'At present there is no agreed common regulatory status for central counterparties, settlement systems and custodians in the EU.'[1]

Existing EU legislative provisions are contained in the Investment Services Directive, the Capital Adequacy Directive, the solvency ration provisions of the Banking Coordination Directive; relevant provisions are also contained in Settlement Finality Directive and the Financial Collateral Directive[2], and have the disadvantage of being institutionally and not functionally defined[3]. This raises particular concerns for service providers who are neither securities firms nor banks:

'Custody is a non-core service under the ISD, such that investment firms (and banks) with a passport to provide core services can also provide custody on a cross-border basis. Custody services have been widely interpreted to include settlement of securities across account at the custodian. This therefore amounts to a passport for banks/investment firm licensed custodians to provide settlement across the EU. No corresponding right exists for those CSDs that are neither banks nor investment firms. However, as custodians expand the range of their activities, the boundary between the services provided by custodians and those of settlement systems is becoming less clear, such that the members of these systems could be seen as competitors to the systems themselves for certain services, for example asset servicing. The consultation on the ISD has highlighted this regulatory imbalance and has led to calls for a clear legal framework covering the activities of clearing and settlement.'[4]

The Commission does not currently propose to bring the provision of post trade infrastructure services within the scope of the ISD[5], but will leave the regulation of such services as a national matter. This means that harmonised European prudential and other standards will not at this stage be imposed, and the European passport (permitting cross-border business on the basis of home state regulation) will not be available:

'. . . [T]he ISD should not become the legal instrument for common regulation of clearing and settlement systems . . .'[6]

However, a joint working group of central banks and securities regulators, the ECB/CESR Joint Working Group, is seeking to develop standards in relation to the post trade infrastructure:

'The implementation of these standards should go a long way to reducing the concerns of regulators about use of systems in other member States. However, common standards may prove to be insufficient . . . If this were the case, some high-level principles (eg defining relevant functions, authorising providers and governing their ongoing supervision) could be enshrined in law at EU level.'[7]

1 Communication from the Commission, p 15.

2 Details of this regime are given in Annex I to *Clearing and settlement in the European Union; Main policy issues and future challenges.*

3 See *Clearing and settlement in the European Union; Main policy issues and future challenges*, p 8.
4 *Clearing and settlement in the European Union; Main policy issues and future challenges*, p 13. See also the Commission's Second Consultation, p 28:

> 'There is a need for a comprehensive reconsideration of the regulatory and competitive treatment of the increasingly related activities of custodianship (open to banks/investment firms) and traditional forms of settlement activity (CSDs).'

5 This is on the basis that:

> 'Central clearing counterparties and securities settlement embody functions and risks which are very distinct from the regulatory concerns at the heart of the ISD. In view of the distinct risk-profile of these entities, and the absence of sufficiently developed consensus on common prudential standards for these clearing and settlement systems, DG MARKT proposes not to regulate these activities directly through the ISD' (ISD Consultation document, p 34).

6 EU Consultation document, p 35. However, the ESF argues that some member states may use the lack of a passport as a protectionist means of blocking remote services, by arguing that they fall within the scope of the existing restrictions. Therefore, ESF argues clearing should be excepted from the scope of those restrictions (and their equivalent under the Second Banking Directive) and further that a system of mutual recognition of existing national authorisations should be introduced. (See ESF Submission on Communication on Upgrading the ISD, March 2000, available on www.eurosf.com, pp 2, 3, 4.)
7 Communication from the Commission, pp 3, 4.

Prudential regulation

7.53 Another important area is the prudential regulatory, or capital adequacy treatment of custody, clearing and settlement. Debate focuses on two issues in particular, namely the treatment of exposures of market participants to clearing houses[1], and the question of operational risk.

1 See Lamfalussy Securities Market Report's examination of systemic risk, including the consideration of 'the prudential implications of one central counterparty' (p 16).

Basel proposals

7.54 The original standards for the prudential regulation of internationally active banks were set in the 1988 Basel Accord. In 2001 the Basel Committee of Banking Supervision published proposals for a new capital accord. A number of important elements are unchanged from the 1986 Accord[1]. However, the new accord ('The New Capital Accord') offers a more flexible and risk sensitive framework[2]. In particular, it introduces a more flexible measure of credit risk, and weighting for operational risk.

1 'The new framework maintains both the current definition of capital and the minimum requirement of 8 per cent of capital to risk-weighted assets.' Tier 2 capital remains limited to 100 per cent of Tier 1 capital. Also, the measure of market risk is unchanged.
2 Secretariat of the Basel Committee on Banking Supervision, Bank for International Settlements *The New Basel Capital Accord: an explanatory note*, Basel, January 2001, p 1:

> 'Building on [the 1988 Accord], the new framework intends to improve safety and soundness in the financial system by placing more emphasis on banks' own internal control and management, the supervisory review process, and market discipline.'

The New Accord rests on three pillars. In addition to imposing minimum capital requirements (the first pillar), the Accord introduces the supervisory review process (the second pillar), which 'requires supervisors to ensure that each bank has sound internal processes in place to assess the adequacy of its capital based on a thorough evaluation of its risks' (Explanatory note, p 5). Market discipline forms the third pillar, which 'aims to bolster market discipline through enchanted disclosure by banks' (Explanatory note, p 5).

Credit risk

7.55 'The 1988 Accord provided essentially only one option for measuring the appropriate capital of internationally active banks. The best way to measure, manage and mitigate risks, however, differs from bank to bank.'[1] For this reason, the 1998 amendment '. . . allowed banks for the first time to use their own systems to measure their market risks.'[2] Thus, credit risk may be measured on a standardised approach (which is akin to, but more sensitive than, the approach under the 1988 Accord), or alternatively on an Internal Rating Based ('IRB') Approach[3]. Commentators (including, notably, the ESF) have called for preferential treatment for recognised clearing houses, in view of the special risk management framework in which they operate[4].

1 Explanatory note, p 2.
2 Explanatory note, p 2.
3 Two IRB approaches are permitted, namely foundation and advanced: Explanatory note, p 2.
4 See ESF Submission to Basel on the New Capital Accord, pp 4, 5. Under the Basel and EU existing capital regime, claims on clearing houses (including claims for the return of margin) are risk weighted. Thus, under the Capital Adequacy Directive, claims on recognised clearing houses may be treated like claims on banks, and attract a 20 per cent capital hit (art 2(9)).

Operational risk[1]

7.56 A 1996 amendment to the 1988 Accord introduced a separate market risk component to the minimum capital requirement. The New Accord goes on to introduce operational risk. Three alternatives are currently proposed for the measurement of operational risk requirement, of varying levels of sophistication. The first is the basis indicator requirement (which is a fixed percentage of gross income)[2]. The second and third are the standardised approach and the internal measurement approach: for these, measurement of risk differentiates between different business lines[3].

These proposals have attracted considerable debate:

> 'In the clearing and settlement industry, the requirement for capital in respect of operational risk will be most affected by high impact, low frequency events such as a mainframe computer breakdown.'[4]

Moreover:

> 'Insurance typically covers low-frequency, high-severity events rather than capital. Historically, banks have relied on insurance to cover such events. Why should banks pay insurance premiums if they cannot benefit from this investment through reduced capital charge?'[5]

1 For further information, see The BIS Operational Risk Background Paper available on www.bis.org/publ/bcbsca.htm.
2 However, Euroclear comments that 'There is no proven link between operational risk/losses and gross income.' See *Comments from Euroclear to the Basel Committee on Banking supervision on the New Basel Capital Accord, 31 May 2001*, p 11.
3 As Clearstream International states in its comments on the New Accord, the cruder measures are likely to result in a higher capital hit, so that it and like institutions are likely to adopt the internal measurement approach. Under this approach, '. . . a bank has to categorise its activities into a number of business lines. For each of these, the regulator/supervisor specifies an exposure indicator (EI) which is a proxy for the size (or amount of risk) of each business lines' operational risk exposure' (p 4). Clearstream refers to the business lines specified for the Internal Measurement Approach and comments that:

> 'The definitions of these business lines are . . . very loose: for example, they categorise "Clearing and Settlement" together with "Payment and Collections" . . . Clearstream International is of the

opinion that its settlement operations – which are highly automated and require minimal manual processing – differ substantially from that of the settlement department of a trading bank, for example' (Comments, p 4).

4 Comments of Clearstream International to the Basel Committee on Banking Supervision on the New Basel Capital Accord, p 5.

5 Euroclear Comments, p 15. Clearstream calls for:

> '. . . acknowledgment of the legal frameworks protecting Clearstream International. Contractual agreements with clients and providers as well as the national legal framework can impact significantly the level of operational losses. This type of risk mitigation technique has not been discussed in the Operational Risk framework and it is still unclear whether it should be taken into account when computing the Capital charge' (Comments, p 5).

EU capital framework

7.57 The EU capital framework is based on the existing Basel Accord. However, unlike Basel, it is statutory, and also extends beyond internationally active banks to small banks and investment firms[1]. The EU Financial Services Action Plan of 1999 identified reform of the EU capital framework as a priority action, and the Commission's second[2] consultation document on regulatory capital[3] proposes amendments broadly tracking those proposed by Basel, to be implemented by the same deadline of 2004. In relation to operational risk, it should be noted in this context that the EU takes an equally cautious approach to that taken by Basel to operational risk mitigation techniques, including insurance[4].

1 European Commission Internal Market DG *Commission Services' Second Consultative Document on Review of Regulatory Capital for Credit Institutions and Investment Firms* (MARKT/1000/01), p 5:

> 'There are two distinguishing features of the capital regime in the EU: first it is a legislative framework and second it applies to the entire banking industry and to investment firms irrespective of their size. A common regulatory capital framework was introduced by the Capital Adequacy Directive which stated that it was desirable to achieve equality in the treatment of credit institutions and investment firms as these institutions engaged in direct competition with one another within the common financial market [Capital Adequacy Directive 93/6/EEC]'.

2 The first consultation was made in November 1999, prior to the publication of the Basel proposals for the New Capital Accord.

3 European Commission Internal Market DG *Commission Services' Second Consultative Document on Review of Regulatory Capital for Credit Institutions and Investment Firms* (MARKT/1000/01).

4 See European Commission Internal Market DG *Commission Services' Second Consultative Document on Review of Regulatory Capital for Credit Institutions and Investment Firms* (MARKT/1000/01), p 43.

Impact on clearing and settlement

7.58 Most global custodians, and the ICSDs, Clearstream and Euroclear, are banks and fall under the scope of the New Basel Accord, but many national settlement systems are non-banks and accordingly outside its scope[1].

While global custodians and ICSDs offer services to their clients which involve them in credit exposures, the chief impact of the New Basel Accord on their main business of settlement and securities administration involves operational risk and not credit risk. The proposed introduction of a capital weighting for operational risk is clearly the key feature of the new regime, and its key implication for global custodians, settlement systems and other service providers in the post trading infrastructure.

1 For this reason, Euroclear has called for the Accord to be extended to all national systems. See *Comments from Euroclear to the Basel Committee on Banking supervision on the New Basel Capital Accord*, 31 May 2001, p 9.

Chapter 8*

Overview of post-trade infrastructure

8.1 This chapter considers the clearing and settlement functions that constitute the post-trading infrastructure of the securities markets. This area is currently attracting considerable attention from the securities industry and the public sector. Inefficiencies in the post-trading infrastructure have been identified as a significant source of risk and cost. A number of important initiatives are currently devoted to the reform of clearing and settlement, with a view to achieving operational efficiencies and managing risk. The need for such reforms is urgent because the volumes of domestic and cross-border securities transactions are expected to increase greatly in the years ahead. Although many reforming initiatives relate to the wider financial markets, including the markets in cash and derivatives transactions, the focus of this chapter will be the clearing and settlement of securities transactions in the European markets.

* The authors are grateful to Mark Harding, partner, Clifford Chance for kindly reviewing this chapter. Any errors are their own.

Background

8.2 This section will briefly consider the background to the reform of the post-trading infrastructure. The following sections will consider in turn: risk management issues; the process of consolidation; and underlying legal principles.

Overview

8.3 Chapter 1 briefly explained the differences between trading, settlement and clearing. After a trade for the purchase or sale of securities has taken place, the next step is to ensure that the terms of the trade are agreed. This is achieved by a process called confirmation[1]. After this, the parties to the trade (or their agents) must arrange for the securities to be delivered from the seller to the buyer (or their agents). They must also arrange for the purchase price to be paid by the buyer to the seller (or their agents). This process of delivery, with associated payments, is called settlement. Although settlement is becoming quicker, in many markets a number of business days still elapse between trading and settlement ('the settlement interval'). As discussed below, a number of risks arise for the parties during the settlement interval. Clearing is a process which takes place in order to manage such risks.

1 The existence of a separate operational stage to establish agreement upon the terms of a contract may perplex legal theorists who regard a contract as expressing the agreement of the parties. See The Giovannini Group *Cross Border Clearing and Settlement in the European Union*, 2001 ('Giovannini Report'), p 5:

> 'OTC transactions are typically confirmed directly between the buyer and seller by electronic means, by telefax, or by specialised messaging service. Some trading systems provide automatic confirmation, while other securities exchanges or clearing agents produce confirmations based on data submitted by counterparties.'

For a discussion of confirmation, see also CPSS/IOSCO Joint Talk Force on Securities Settlement Systems *Recommendations for Securities Settlement Systems* ('CPSS/IOSCO Recommendations') 2001, pp 9, 38. An alternative to confirmation and affirmation is automatic execution matching: see DTCC *T+1 White Paper*, 2002, p 13.

Nature of settlement

8.4 Although in practice a trade is cleared before it is settled, it is conceptually easier to consider the nature of settlement before considering the nature of clearing.

Delivery and payment

8.5 As indicated above, settlement involves the delivery of securities (or, to be more accurate, legal rights in relation to them) from A to B. Delivery usually takes place against payment from B to A[1]. However, some deliveries are 'free', ie made without a corresponding payment. Examples would be the delivery of securities collateral against a loan of securities, and a delivery made pursuant to a margin call[2].

1 This would be the case in a purchase of securities, or a collateralised loan.
2 As discussed in Chapter 4, a margin call is a call for additional collateral to be delivered to eliminate a collateral shortfall pursuant to marking to market arrangements.

Book entry transfer

8.6 Chapter 2 briefly discussed the transition from paper based settlement to electronic book entry transfer. Historically, settlement involved the movement of pieces of paper. Bearer securities were transferred by the delivery of paper instruments; registered securities were transferred by the delivery of paper certificates and transfer forms, followed by reregistration; and payment was made by cheque. Paper-based settlement is risky, expensive, error-prone and slow. With rising transaction volumes, paper-based settlement was unable to keep pace with trading volumes. In the 1970s (in the US) and the 1980s (in the UK), the securities markets experienced what has become known as 'the paper crunch', as backlogs of unsettled trades threatened the integrity of the securities markets.

The answer to the paper crunch was electronic settlement, involving a technique called book entry transfer. This involves the use of an electronic settlement system, in which market participants (or their agents) maintain accounts which record their entitlements to securities and cash. When participant A wishes to settle a sale of securities to participant B, A and B give matching instructions to the settlement system. In response to these instructions[1], the settlement system debits the securities account of A and credits that of B. At the same time, it debits the cash account of B and credits that of A. Thus, delivery and payment are made promptly and synchronously.

In a 1989 the Group of Thirty ('G30')[2] published its report *Clearance and Settlement Systems in the World's Securities Markets* ('the 1989 G30 Report'). This tremendously influential report put the need for book entry transfer beyond doubt. It identified two models of book entry transfer, namely immobilisation and dematerialisation.

As explained in Chapter 2, immobilisation involves the use of a depositary, which is electronically linked to a settlement system. Paper instruments and/or certificates are held by the depositary on behalf of a settlement system or its participants. The entitlements of participants in respect of the securities are recorded in electronic securities accounts maintained by the settlement system, and transferred by debiting and crediting those accounts. Thus, with immobilisation, paper securities exist, but they do not move in the course of settlement. In contrast, with dematerialisation, securities are issued in electronic form, 'straight onto the screen'. The terms of issue of dematerialised securities provide that such securities will be constituted by the electronic records of the settlement system. In the historic transition from paper-based to electronic practice in the securities markets, immobilisation often serves as a transitional phase prior to dematerialisation.

The 1989 G30 Report's call for book entry transfer has been widely heeded. 'In 1989, depositories and book entry settlement were used in only a minority of markets. Today, almost all markets use such systems.'[3] Important international electronic settlement systems[4] include, (in New York) the DTC[5]; (in Brussels) Euroclear and (in Luxembourg) Clearstream. The UK settlement system is CREST[6].

1 Provided that sufficient assets are available in the parties' accounts.
2 'The Group of Thirty, established in 1978, is a private, nonprofit, international body composed of very senior representatives of the private and public sectors and academia. It aims to deepen understanding of international economic and financial issues . . .' See the G30 website at www.group30.org
3 1995 G30/ISSA Recommendations, p 10. Indeed, in some jurisdictions book entry transfer is not merely available, but mandatory.
4 Referred to in the industry as international central securities depositories, or 'ICSDs'.
5 The Depository Trust Company of New York. Both DTC and National Securities Clearing Corporation (NSCC) are operating subsidiaries of The Depository Trust & Clearing Corporation (DTCC).
6 See Chapter 9.

Nature of clearing

8.7 The term 'clearing' is used in different senses. In its narrower sense, the term is used to mean the calculation of the mutual post-trade obligations of market participants, usually on a net basis[1]. In its wider sense (which will be used in this discussion) the term 'clearing' involves the management of post-trading, pre-settlement credit exposures, to ensure that trades are settled in accordance with market rules, even if a buyer or seller becomes insolvent prior to settlement.

1 See The Giovannini Report, p 5.

Central counterparty

8.8 Clearing generally involves the use of a well capitalised financial institution known as a central counterparty ('CCP'). In the markets in which a CCP provides a clearing service, it becomes a party to every trade, acting as buyer to market participant sellers, and seller to market participant buyers[1]. In respect of unsettled trades, market participants therefore bear the credit risk of the CCP, and not that of each other. 'A CCP thus provides a standard credit risk to replace the variable, bilateral risk that firms take on each other in a decentralised market.'[2]

1 In many cases this is contractually achieved by novation, ie by replacing an original contract between two market participants with two new contracts, one between the CCP as seller and the market participant buyer, and one between the CCP as buyer and the market participant seller. In other cases (eg where the London Clearing House ('LCH') clears UK equities and OTC swap and repo trades) there is no market participant to market participant contract, and each trade is originally entered into with the CCP.

2 DTCC *Central Counterparties: Development, Cooperation and Consolidation*, October 2000 ('DTCC White CCP Paper'), p 16.

Netting

8.9 Another important clearing function is netting. Since each market participant has only one counterparty to its trades (the CCP) it can net its daily purchases and sales in like securities. Such netting '. . . is an especially effective tool for reducing risks vis-à-vis active market participants, who often buy and sell the same security for settlement on the same date.'[1] Netting is widely identified as the key benefit offered by the use of a CCP.

Netting can operate at two different levels[2]. First, trade or obligation netting may take effect contractually, so as to reduce the unsettled contractual obligations of the CCP to each market participant from gross to net. This significantly reduces the credit risk of the market participant to the CCP, and therefore related margin and regulatory capital requirement applicable to the market participant for its cleared trades, as discussed below.

Second, even where contractual netting is not available, as an operational matter settlement netting[3] permits settlement instructions to be given on a net and not gross basis, very significantly reducing the volume of settlements. Reduced settlement volumes in turn reduce costs and liquidity pressures.

1 CPSS/IOSCO Recommendations, p 11.

2 See CPSS/IOSCO Recommendations, p 39.

3 Which is offered by The London Clearing House for its equity trades, even though contractual netting is not offered, at least initially.

Challenges

8.10 There is a widespread perception among market participants, industry bodies and regulatory authorities that the post trade infrastructure of the securities markets faces a number of new challenges.

The central challenge is an anticipated surge in the volume of securities trades[1]. Volumes are expected to increase beyond the capacity of the existing infrastructure, creating an urgent need for reform. For this reason, settlement netting in particular has been identified by the European Securities Forum ('ESF')[2] as a crucial development[3].

A further challenge is an increase in the proportion of cross-border trades. Where the buyer, the seller and/or the assets are located in different jurisdictions, clearing and settlement must often be provided on a cross-border basis. As discussed below, this involves special risks both operationally (due to variations in systems, procedures and operating hours) and legally (due to the conflict of laws issues). The issue of cross-border trades is intended to be the focus of the new G30 Report (see para **8.35**).

These developments coincide with rising levels of commercial and regulatory risk awareness. Competitive pressures within the securities industry, together with a growing perception of the importance of a robust infrastructure, have generated a high level of commitment to meet these challenges. A series of important studies and reports have and continue to generate new benchmarks, industry reforms and regulatory initiatives devoted to improving the post-trade infrastructure. Certain of the key studies and benchmarks are briefly considered below.

1 See DTCC *T+1 White Paper*, p 2.
2 See ESF Submission to the Basel Committee on Banking Supervision, The New Basel Capital Accord, 2001 ('ESF Submission on Basel'):

> 'The European Securities Forum (ESF) is an organisation established by the major users of Europe's clearing and settlement infrastructure. ESF was established in response to rationalisation initiatives within the industry, to act as a neutral and objective facilitator of a rapid progression towards a powerful, efficient European capital market infrastructure. For more information on ESF and its activities, see our website at http://www.eurosf.com/ ' (p 1).

3 See the ESF Submission to DG MARKT in Response to the European Communication on Upgrading the Investment Services Directive 2000 ('ESF Submission on ISD'), p 10.

Risk management

8.11 This section will consider the key risks in the post trade infrastructure; the basic risk management techniques that have been developed in relation to them; together with the leading studies and reports on such risks and their management.

Key risks in post-trade infrastructure

8.12 The securities industry has developed a sophisticated risk analysis in relation to the post-trade infrastructure. The following brief discussion involves a simplification of these risks, in order to provide a clear basis for the legal analysis developed in this chapter. Industry attention has focused on the following types of risk to which participants in the securities markets are exposed after trading and prior to the completion of settlement[1].

1 The Giovannini Report also identifies cash deposit risk, custody risk and foreign exchange risk: see p 18.

Credit risk – principal risk

8.13 If a party to a securities trade delivers assets by way of settlement prior to receiving corresponding assets from the counterparty, it faces the risk that the counterparty will default without discharging its settlement obligations. This raises a form of credit risk known as principal risk, 'that is, the risk that the seller of a security could deliver but not receive payment or that the buyer could make payment but not receive delivery'[1]. In the foreign exchange markets, principal risk was so vividly illustrated by the 1974 failure of Bank Herstatt that it is often called 'Herstatt risk'[2]. The technique for addressing principal risk is the synchronisation of settlement of both sides of the transaction. In the securities markets, this is called delivery versus payment, or DVP[3]. While conceptually simple, the achievement of true DVP is a complex and difficult matter for operational and legal reasons, as discussed later in this chapter.

1 CPSS/IOSCO Recommendations, p 41.
2 The bank became insolvent after having received payment under a foreign exchange transaction, but before making payment under the same transaction. The consequent disruption threatened the operation of wholesale dollar deliveries. See the discussion in BIS *Settlement Risk in Foreign Exchange Transaction*, 1996.

3 The concept of DVP is derived from that of payment versus payment (PVP), which was developed in the foreign exchange markets to address Herstatt risk.

Credit risk – replacement cost risk

8.14 A second type of credit risk known as replacement cost risk is best illustrated by example. Suppose that on day 1 A agrees to sell to B 1,000 XYZ shares for £100,000. On day 2, this trade remains unsettled, and the market price of 1,000 XYZ shares has fallen to £50,000. If the trade is settled on day 3, A will make a profit, and such settlement will involve a corresponding loss for B. A's trade is said to be 'in the money' and B's trade 'out of the money'. If B defaults prior to settlement, A will lose the profit associated with the trade. On any day, the extent of A's potential loss is measured by the price A would need to pay to a third party in the market to induce them to enter into a like transaction on that day, so as to replace the defaulted transaction with B. For this reason, A's risk is called replacement cost risk, '. . . that is, the risk of loss of unrealised gains on unsettled contracts with the defaulting participant.'[1] Because replacement cost risk arises prior to the settlement of the transaction, it is present even in a DVP environment.

Replacement cost risk is addressed by two techniques. Firstly, ensuring that settlement occurs as early as possible after a trade serves to reduce the interval of time during which replacement cost risk arises. This explains the pressure to achieve shorter settlement cycles[2]. Secondly, even during short settlement cycles, the risk of counterparty default is reduced by the use of central counterparties, as discussed later in this chapter.

1 CPSS/IOSCO Recommendations, p 41.
2 The benefit of shorter settlement cycles is also analysed as addressing market risk. See DTCC *T+1 White Paper*, p 24.

Liquidity risk

8.15 The precise nature of liquidity is a matter of extensive debate[1]. However, one may state in general terms that a liquid securities market is one in which securities may be bought and sold without delay at a fair price. Illiquidity arises when market participants wishing to deal are unable promptly to find counterparties willing to deal with them at a fair price. Illiquidity may arise because markets are underdeveloped or fragmented. Illiquidity may also arise because of operational problems, where failure promptly to process existing trades delays the implementation of future trades. Failure of market confidence may also cause illiquidity, where participants withdraw from trading due to fears concerning the credit of market counterparties[2].

A number of techniques which are desirable in themselves also serve to improve liquidity, including infrastructure consolidation and the effective management of credit and operational risks. In addition, securities lending is a technique which serves directly to address illiquidity[3]. Because of the potential seriousness of liquidity problems[4], many settlement systems offer automatic securities lending facilities.

1 See the discussion in Ruben Lee *What is an Exchange? The Automation, Management, and Regulation of the Financial Markets* (1998, Oxford University Press), p 283:

> 'Other characteristics of a market have also been associated with liquidity by the SEC, including immediacy, depth, and continuity . . . The SEC has expressly avoided equating liquidity with trading volume, stating that the two are not equivalent.'

2 A very vivid illustration of this is provided by the near failure of Long Term Capital Management in September 1998.
3 Controversially, short selling serves the same purpose.

4 See CPSS/IOSCO Recommendations, p 42:

> 'Liquidity problems have the potential to create systemic problems, particularly if they occur at a time when securities prices are changing rapidly and failures to meet obligations when due are more likely to create concerns about solvency.'

Operational risk – generally

8.16 Operational risk is defined in the proposed new Basel Capital Accord[1] as 'the risk of direct or indirect loss resulting from inadequate or failed internal processes, people or systems or from external events'. This is interpreted to include 'legal risk'[2]. Operational risk is particularly important in the post-trading infrastructure. 'As clearing and settlement systems become increasingly dependent on information technology systems, the reliability of these systems is a key element in operational risk.'[3] Both the automation[4] and the consolidation[5] of clearing and settlement serve potentially to increase operational risk. In recent years it has attracted new levels of industry and regulatory attention. Importantly, the new Basel Capital Accord introduces a capital weighting for operational risk, as discussed below.

1 Basel Committee on Banking Supervision, Bank for International Settlements *Consultative Document, The New Basel Capital Accord*, Basel, January 2001. Compare the definition in the CPSS/IOSCO Recommendations:

> 'Operational risk is the risk that deficiencies in information systems or internal controls, human errors or management failures will result in unexpected losses' (p 18).

2 *Consultative Document, The New Basel Capital Accord*, p 94.
3 CPSS/IOSCO Recommendations, p 18.
4 See CPSS/IOSCO Recommendations, p 18.
5 See Hills et al 'Central Counterparty Clearing Houses and Financial Stability' (June 1999) *Bank of England Financial Stability Review* 124 at 131–2.

Operational risk – legal risk[1]

8.17 Legal risk might be defined as the risk that the legal effect of a transaction or arrangement differs from that intended by one or more of the parties to it. As discussed below, the operation of the post-trade infrastructure relies importantly on a number of legal techniques. Some measure of legal risk may be a fact of financial life. However, several factors raise the level of legal risk currently associated with the post-trade infrastructure to an unhelpful level. These include, in particular, the cross-border nature of the infrastructure; the relative novelty of some aspects of the automation of securities administration; and (in some jurisdictions) policy concerns relating to the protection of general creditors in insolvency. A number of key legal risk issues are discussed later in this chapter, together with law reform initiatives designed to address them.

1 The IBA has recently established a working party on legal risk, chaired by Hugh Pigott.

Systemic risk

8.18 'Systemic risk is the risk that the inability of one institution to meets its obligations when due will cause other institutions to fail to meet their obligations when due.'[1] Both clearing systems[2] and settlement systems[3] are potential sources of systemic risk, and they may transmit systemic risk to payment systems to which they are linked[4]. A further factor is the consolidation of the financial markets[5]. 'Increased integration of securities markets entails more interconnection between financial intermediaries on a cross-border basis, increasing their exposure to common shocks.'[6]

1 CPSS/IOSCO Recommendations, p 42.
2 As discussed later in this chapter, clearing serves to concentrate risk in CCPs. This may have the effect of reducing risk overall if the clearing house is financially stable, but of increasing it if it is not. See CPSS/IOSCO Recommendations, p 11.
3 See CPSS/IOSCO Recommendations, p 42.
4 See DTCC *T+1 White Paper*, p 1 and CPSS/IOSCO Recommendations.
5 Communication of the Commission *Financial Services: Implementing the Framework for Financial Markets: Action Plan*, COM (1999) 232, 11 May 1999 ('The Financial Services Action Plan'), p 13:

> 'The heightened tempo of consolidation in the industry, and the intensification of links between financial markets because of the euro call for careful consideration of structures for containing and supervising institutional and systemic risk.'

6 *Final Report of The Committee of Wise Men on The Regulation of European Securities Markets*, Brussels, 15 February 2001 ('the Lamfalussy Securities Markets Report'), p 17.

Risk in cross-border trades

8.19 A cross-border trade is one where the seller, the buyer and/or the assets are located in different jurisdictions[1]. In practice, the types of risk discussed above may be particularly acute in relation to the clearing and settlement of cross-border trades, for operational reasons[2]. Also, the conflict of laws may introduce legal risk, as discussed below.

1 Further, agents through which the parties act and/or intermediaries through which the assets are held may be in different jurisdictions.
2 See CPSS/IOSCO Recommendations, pp 45, 46 and The Giovannini Report, p 10: '. . . cross-border clearing and settlement almost always involves intermediaries in the transaction chain, implying a significantly greater degree of complexity in the process.' This report identifies nine separate steps in the instruction flow for processing a cross border equity transaction, involving 11 intermediaries and 14 instructions between parties: see pp 12 and 15.

Basic risk management techniques

8.20 The following discussion deals with the key techniques that have been developed to manage risk in the post-trade securities infrastructure.

DVP

8.21 As discussed above, principal risk is addressed by DVP[1]. However, DVP does not address several important risks, including replacement cost risk[2] and custody risk[3]. In assessing DVP within any system, it is important to consider the model of DVP; the quality of delivery and payment; and also the question of finality.

1 See CPSS/IOSCO Recommendations, p 14.
2 See below.
3 CPSS/IOSCO Recommendations, p 14:

> 'DVP eliminates principal risk between direct participants in an SSS. However, settlement arrangements are typically tiered, with only a subset of market participants and intermediaries having direct access to the SSS. Achievement of DVP for direct participants in the SSS does not eliminate principal risk exposures between direct participants and their customers.'

For a discussion of managing the risk of custodian insolvency, see Chapter 3.

MODELS

8.22 In its important 1992 study of DVP[1], the Bank for International Settlements ('BIS') identifies three models. The key to understanding the different models is to distinguish between (on the one hand) the operational debiting and crediting of cash and securities accounts within the settlement system (which happens throughout the business day) and (on the other hand) the legal transfer of assets pursuant to such book entries. Model 1 DVP is the ideal. Here, the book entries have the immediate effect of achieving delivery and payment, so that both cash and securities are transferred on a gross basis throughout the business day (real time gross settlement and payment). The least desirable is model 3, in which both payment and delivery is deferred until the end of the business day, and made on a net basis (end of day net settlement and payment). Model 2 involves real time gross settlement but end of day net payment[2].

Risks associated with end of day net settlement and payment have been discussed in detail, both in the BIS DVP Report and elsewhere[3]. However, the benefits of settlement netting in reducing volumes to manageable levels are also widely acknowledged, and '. . . it is important to ensure that credit risk reductions should not be at the expense of operational performance.'[4] The CPSS/IOSCO Recommendations do not call for model 1 DVP in all cases, but only where necessary to reduce risks[5]. As an alternative to real time gross settlement, the G30/ISSA recommendations call for legally robust netting[6].

1 Bank for International Settlements *Delivery Versus Payment in Securities Settlement Systems*, Basel, 1992.
2 Until recently, CREST operated on a model 2 basis. See Chapter 9.
3 See CPSS/IOSCO Recommendations, p 14.
4 1995 G30/ISSA Recommendations, p 21.
5 See Recommendation 8.
6 1995 G30/ISSA Recommendations, Recommendation 4.

QUALITIES

8.23 In assessing the quality of DVP, one must also consider the nature of the assets which are transferred synchronously. In relation to securities, the best quality of delivery is immediate legal title. In simple terms, this generally involves ensuring that the securities accounts of the settlement system determine legal title to the settled assets. 'If a CSD is also the registrar, it can eliminate any delay between settlement and registration.'[1] In CREST, the delivery event which is synchronised with the payment event was until recently the transfer of equitable interest in securities, with legal title following within two hours. However, this was upgraded to immediate legal title in November 2001, as discussed in Chapter 9.

In securities settlement (and indeed in the financial markets generally) payment is made by crediting a cash account[2]. The quality of payment depends on the credit standing of the bank which maintains this account. 'The settlement of the cash leg of the transactions can be effected through transfers on the books of a central bank, a CSD organised as a limited purpose bank, or one or more commercial banks.'[3] The best quality of payment is in central bank money, and a number of European settlement systems have introduced, or propose to introduce it[4]. However, '[u]se of the central bank of issue as the single settlement bank may not . . . always be practicable.'[5] There may also be arguments that it is not desirable. Securities settlement can involve very significant credit exposures, and it is not clear that these should be automatically borne by central banks. The use of commercial bank money in securities settlement would leave central banks with the regulatory choice of whether or not to bear the credit exposures associated with securities settlement, by acting as lender of last resort to a commercial settlement bank in financial difficulties. It is interesting to note that The CPSS/IOSCO Recommendations do not call for the use of central bank money in all cases, but rather for credit and liquidity risk to be effectively managed[6].

1 CPSS/IOSCO Recommendations, p 14.
2 The bank may be the settlement system itself, as in the case of Euroclear and Clearstream, or a third party bank to which the settlement system is linked, as with CREST.

3 CPSS/IOSCO Recommendations, p 17:

'When multiple settlement banks are involved, any resulting interbank obligations between these commercial settlement banks are settled through an interbank payment system, typically a central bank payment system.'

4 In the UK, a modified form of access to central bank money is available, as discussed in Chapter 9.

5 CPSS/IOSCO Recommendations, p 17.

6 See Recommendation 10.

FINALITY

8.24

> 'Whichever [model] of DVP is taken, what is essential is that the technical, legal and contractual framework ensures that each transfer of securities is final if and only if the corresponding transfer of funds is final.'[1]

It must be established as an operational matter that the transfer cannot be revoked by the party making payment or delivery, or by the operator of the settlement system[2]. Ideally it should also be established as a legal matter that a transfer cannot be reversed by the courts. Most systems of law provide for certain transfers to be reversible in certain circumstances if the transferor is affected by insolvency at the time of the transfer or shortly thereafter, and also in the case of fraud. As discussed below, certain legislative provisions address insolvency displacement, particularly in relation to key infrastructure systems[3]. However, to the authors' knowledge, no existing or proposed initiative addresses fraud risk[4].

1 CPSS/IOSCO Recommendations, p 14.

2 See CPSS/IOSCO Recommendations, p 39.

3 Although the benefit of Financial Collateral Directive is not limited to major systems, as discussed in Chapter 4.

4 The concept of negotiability was developed in the medieval period to provide for finality of delivery to the holder in due course (broadly, the good faith purchaser of a negotiable instrument) even where a transferor acts fraudulently. However, as discussed in Chapter 2, intangible interests in securities recorded electronically do not benefit from negotiable status.

Shorter settlement cycles

8.25 As discussed above, one simple technique for addressing replacement cost risk is the introduction of shorter settlement cycles[1]. Batch settlement, in which all trades during a settlement account period remain unsettled until a specified date, has been widely rejected in favour of rolling settlement, in which settlement occurs on every business day, a fixed number of days after each trade. The length of the settlement interval is customarily indicated by the number of business days between trade date ('T') and settlement, so that 'T+3' indicates settlement on the third business day after trade date. Like the 1989 G30 Report[2], the CPSS/IOSCO Recommendations call for T+3 as standard[3]. 'However, T+3 is often no longer regarded as best practice. In many markets, government securities already settle on T+1 or even T+0, and some equity markets are currently considering a T+1 settlement cycle'[4], although at the time of writing T+1 is not a short-term prospect in the US equity markets. Also, there is a call for unified settlement cycles for all instrument types. 'The variation in settlement periods between the international deposit and lending markets, corporate debt, government debt, equity securities and traded derivatives is inefficient and costly.'[5]

1 See CPSS/IOSCO Recommendations, p 10 and FIBV Clearing and Settlement Best Practices Report 1999, p 5. However, unduly short settlement cycles may increase settlement failures. See *Joint work of the European System of Central Banks and the Committee of European Securities Regulators in the field of clearing and settlement, a call for contributions from interested parties*, March 2002, p 4.

2 Recommendation 7.
3 Recommendation 3.
4 CPSS/IOSCO Recommendations, p 10.
5 See also the European Securities Forum *Contribution on the Joint CESR/ECB Consultation on Clearing and Settlement*, 2002, ESF comment on consultation question 2.7:

> 'There are benefits to ensuring that the settlement cycles of different securities are harmonised given the increasing frequency of complex trades.'

T+1

8.26 T+1 settlement has been set as the target for the developed international securities markets[1]. This is undoubtedly a considerable challenge[2], particularly in relation to cross-border trades[3], which will require very considerable operational improvements in the post trade infrastructure. In July 2000 the Depository Trust & Clearing Corporation ('DTCC') published *The T+1 White Paper*[4], which '... details DTCC's best thinking on the changes that we as an industry – and our depository and clearing subsidiaries – need to make to provide for straight-through processing and, ultimately, T+1 settlement.'[5]

1 See 1995 G30/ISSA Recommendations, p 22.
2 See CPSS/IOSCO Recommendations, p 10 and DTCC *T+1 White Paper*, p 2.
3 CPSS/IOSCO Recommendations, p 10.
4 http://www.dtcc.com/whitepapers/tplus1body.html
5 *T+1 White Paper*, p 1.

STP

8.27 An important operational development which has been identified as a precondition of T+1 settlement is straight through processing, or STP. STP involves the automation of the post-trade processing of securities[1] transactions, so as to avoid the re-entry of trade data by the different parties involved[2]. The need for STP is clear in the light of the levels of manual intervention[3], repetition[4], fragmentation[5], redundancy[6], error[7] and delay[8] currently involved in post-trade processing. To be simplistic, there are two problems with the pre-STP environment, namely multiple operational stages, and data re-entry. First, as the initial 2001 Giovannini Report on Cross-Border Clearing and Settlement Arrangements in the European Union clearly illustrated, transaction processing involves multiple intermediaries and operational stages. This report identifies nine separate steps in the instruction flow for processing a cross-border equity transaction, involving 11 intermediaries and 14 instructions between parties. The heavily intermediated nature of the contemporary securities, cash and derivatives markets arises for a number of reasons, including restrictions on direct access to large value delivery systems, and the development of cross-border links. In the managed funds industry, the chain of intermediaries is lengthened further by the involvement of brokers and fund managers, and here the potential benefits of STP are particularly clear. For example, a broker may communicate its bids and offers to a fund manager by fax, and an agreement for a block trade between the broker and fund manager may be concluded by telephone. Then the fund manager may make a telephone call to the broker indicating how the block trade is to be allocated among its various clients. Trade confirmation may well be automated, but regulatory trade reporting may not be. The broker may then send a telex or SWIFT message to the lead custodian giving settlement instructions. If settlement involves a sub-custodian, the global custodian may send a fax to it in respect of the same trade. Finally the global custodian or sub-custodian will need to instruct that system. A separate intervention is required to progress each stage, and a delay in any of these stages serves to delay the transaction as a whole. A related point is that each stage requires the intermediary not only to act, but also to input trade data. As every industry commentator will tell you, and as no computer scientist will be surprised to learn, the chief cause of delay in transaction processing is erroneous data entry. Without STP, the same trade details are recorded again and again, sometimes incorrectly. The impact of the current lack of automation '. . . is exacerbated by global economic, demographic and financial trends such as the increase in cross-border investing, an increase in the complexity of investment strategies, public pension reform, and the ageing of the world population.'[9] STP is needed, not merely to deliver shorter settlement cycles, but also to accommodate rapidly growing trade volumes[10].

In the international securities markets, two leading models of STP have emerged. Many commentators have argued that this is one too many. These are The Global Straight Through Processing Association (GSTPA) and Omgeo. GSTPA is an association of broker dealers, fund managers and global custodians. It was formed in 1998 to promote STP in cross-border trades. It has appointed Axion4gstp, a consortium including Swift and SIS-SeggaIntersettle, to build its STP system, which is called the Transaction Flow Monitor, or TFM. In the US, the competitor Omgeo was formed in 2001. Omgeo is a joint venture between Thompsons Financial ESG and the DTCC. Omgeo's STP system is called Central Trade Manager or CTM. Some commentators anticipate that GSTPA will attract predominantly cross-border business, while Omgeo will attract predominantly US business.

It is understood that both initiatives currently relate to post-trade, pre-settlement transaction processing. Thus the proposed systems will not be exchanges or settlement systems, and will involve neither the formation of contracts nor the delivery of cash or securities. Ultimately, however, there is no doubt that the industry will move to the straight through processing of all stages of securities trades.

Both models are designed to permit T+l by automating the progress of a transaction from one operational stage to the next. Thus, provided the conditions for progressing the transaction are present, they will automatically proceed. Intervention will be required, not to progress the transaction, but to halt its progress.

The need for data re-entry will be avoided by the use of a central record, to which all parties involved in the transaction will have access, and which will be updated as the transaction progresses.

The GSTPA model of STP is designed to assist global custodians in a number of ways, notably by offering better access to information through earlier involvement in the post-trade processing cycle, thus permitting cost savings and enhanced customer services[11]. Global custodians may act as 'concentrators', channelling business from smaller managers and brokers to central marketing utilities, including GSTPA and Omgeo.

However, STP is not without cost. Its development involves a significant investment, and it may benefit the larger players more than smaller institutions. Trades which will be processed straight through, without the possibility of manual intervention, will include bad trades, ie those which are input in error or unlawful. 'As settlement cycles shorten, the room for error and subsequent correction diminishes . . .'[12]

1 Similar initiatives are taking place in the cash and derivatives markets.
2 See CPSS/IOSCO Recommendations, p 10.
3 See GSTPA Services – An Executive Summary, www.gstpa.org, p 1.
4 DTCC *T+1 White Paper*, p 11:

> 'Today, institutional trades are primed for settlement through a series of sequential and repetitive steps, using process developed when the volume of trades was far lower than it is today and settlement occurred on T+5.'

See also p 14.

5 See GSTPA Services – An Executive Summary, p 3. See also DTCC *T+1 White Paper*, p 14.
6 See DTCC *T+1 White Paper*, p 13.
7 See DTCC *T+1 White Paper*, p 14.
8 See DTCC *T+1 White Paper*, p 14.
9 GSTPA Services – An Executive Summary, p 1.
10 Although trade volumes declined in 2001.
11 New service opportunities include pro-active liquidity management, benchmarking, facilitated auditing and reporting, and information management generally. Shorter timeframes will generate new needs for securities lending.
12 DTCC *CCP White Paper*, p 9. For a discussion of the possible legal implication of the straight through processing of unlawful trades, see J Benjamin *Interests in Securities* (2000, Oxford University Press), pp 242–4.

Central counterparty

8.28 A further technique for managing replacement cost risk is the use of a central counterparty ('CCP'). The role of the CCP was discussed briefly above. The CCP serves to '. . . redistribute credit and market risk to those that are best able to bear them.'[1]

This section will consider those aspects of the role of the CCP that are most relevant to the reform of the post trade infrastructure.

1 The DTCC *CCP White Paper*, p 2.

Collateralisation

8.29 In order to manage the risks that it assumes, it is customary for the CCP to take collateral from the market participants to which it provides clearing services. Collateral comprises a range of financial assets and is actively marked to market[1]. Demand for high quality financial collateral assets exceeds supply. As discussed below, a major factor in the drive towards consolidation of the European post-trading infrastructure is the need to achieve netting efficiencies in the collateralisation of clearing exposures, so that collateral surpluses in certain markets can offset collateral shortfalls in others.

1 See Hills et al 'Central Counterparty Clearing Houses and Financial Stability' (June 1999) *Bank of England Financial Stability Review* 124 at 127. Marking to market is discussed in Chapter 4.

Default provisions

8.30 Even when a market participant member firm fails, the CCP settles that firm's trades as central counterparty. In order to manage the potential cost of such settlements without prejudicing the CCP's own solvency, detailed default provisions are put in place. These concern '. . . what happens when a market participant is unable to meet a margin call and defaults, leaving the central counterparty with uncollateralised losses. It will usually attempt to crystallise the loss immediately by closing out the defaulting member's proprietary positions and closing out or transferring any customer positions to other market participants. Central counterparties can then have various ways of allocating losses.'[1] While different CCPs have different approaches, the order of recourse of the DTCC is outlined by it as follows:

'– margin cover of the defaulting member;
– any additional default/participant fund[2] contributions of the defaulting member (this and the preceding source of funds are used to ensure that defaulting members bear a significant cost first, protecting other members);
– excess assets held by the defaulting member at other CCPs linked through cross-guarantee arrangements;

- other members' participant fund contributions and the CCP's assessment rights (mutualising the risk);
- insurance cover (laying off the risk);
- reserves of the CCP; and
- capital of the CCP (as a final line of defence before there are assessments against remaining members, with the risk that losses become systemic and require the intervention of the authorities)'[3].

It is important to note that some of the default techniques relied on by CCPs may not accord with the general principles of insolvency law, for example because they may involve multi-lateral netting, or post-insolvency dispositions. Legal support may therefore be required, through special legislative protections. It is crucial to establish that such support is effective to permit the default provisions to withstand participant insolvency[4]. In cross-border arrangements, where more than one system of insolvency law is involved, this may involve a considerable challenge, as discussed below. Within the EU, a number of measures serve to protect default provisions from the general principles of insolvency law, as discussed briefly below and in Chapter 5.

1 Hills et al 'Central Counterparty Clearing Houses and Financial Stability' (June 1999) *Bank of England Financial Stability Review* 124 at 127.
2 See also CPSS/IOSCO Recommendations, p 12.
3 The DTCC *CCP White Paper*, pp 5, 6.
4 See ESF *EuroCCP; ESF's blueprint for a Single Pan-European Central Counterparty*, 2000, ('ESF Blueprint'), pp 15, 16.

Benefits of clearing for market participants

8.31 Clearing offers important benefits to market participants[1]. These are, primarily, the reduction and standardisation of counterparty credit exposures[2]; related collateral and regulatory capital efficiencies[3]; and operational efficiencies[4]. Netting assists liquidity, both in normal market conditions and during market disturbances[5]. Additionally, the use of a central counterparty may offer post-trade anonymity[6]. The unrivalled access enjoyed by a CCP to market data is an important regulatory tool[7] in the management of macro risks (as well as a commercial sensitivity)[8].

However, because of the costs involved, 'Not all markets are necessarily suitable for central counterparty clearing.'[9] Moreover, the use of a CCP may introduce moral hazard. A series of financial crises historically associated with clearing houses are discussed by the Bank of England[10]. 'Previous failures (though rare) provide some cautionary tales.'[11]

1 Although these may vary from market to market. See Hills et al 'Central Counterparty Clearing Houses and Financial Stability' (June 1999) *Bank of England Financial Stability Review* 124 at 125.
2 See Hills et al, p 126.
3 With trade netting, these are calculated in relation to net and not gross credit exposures.
4 With settlement netting, the volume of settlements is reduced. Margin deliveries may also benefit from netting.
5 See Hills et al, p 130.
6 See Hills et al, pp 125, 126.
7 Hills et al, p 133.
8 See DTCC *CCP White Paper*, p 9.
9 See Hills et al, p 124.
10 In Hills et al, p 129.
11 Hills et al, p 133.

The development of clearing

8.32 In Europe, a number of clearing systems offer services in a range of markets[1]. While clearing in the US is relatively integrated, a number of distinct systems still operate[2]. In the development of clearing, two trends in particular are apparent.

1 See the discussions in the DTCC *T+1 White paper*, p 7 and The Giovannini Report, pp 21–30. The DTCC *CCP White Paper*, p 7:

> 'A group of the larger market participants in Europe have recently banded together to form the European Securities Forum (ESF), which, amongst several initiatives in trading, clearing, settlement and custody, is making the case for creating a single CCP supporting equity markets in Europe.'

2 See The DTCC *CCP White Paper*, p 6.

DERIVATIVES TO CASH SECURITIES

8.33 Clearing originated in the derivatives markets, where the need to manage post-trade, pre-settlement risk was perceived early due to the long settlement periods associated with derivatives. More recently, with greater emphasis on risk management and capital efficiency, clearing is being introduced into the cash securities markets.

MARKET SPECIFIC TO MULTI-MARKET AND REMOTE CLEARING

8.34 'Until very recently, most CCPs have confined their operations to supporting a single market in a single country.'[1] This arrangement is described as a 'vertical silo'. However, the ESF explains that, in the US, the case for moving away from this model became clear in the 1960s and 70s[2]. More recently, the multi-market model of clearing has developed across the financial sector, so that '. . . the CCP can, for example, use the correlations between, say, derivatives and equities to offset exposures . . .'[3] Multi-market clearing is often associated with the provisions of cross-border clearing services, known as remote clearing[4]. However, the 'horizontal' model is not universally accepted.

1 The DTCC *CCP White Paper*, p 4.
2 See ESF Blueprint, pp 3, 4.
3 The DTCC *CCP White Paper*, p 8. See also Hills et al 'Central Counterparty Clearing Houses and Financial Stability' (June 1999) *Bank of England Financial Stability Review* 124 at 125:

> 'Where a clearing house acts as central counterparty to several markets which are subject to identical or highly correlated risks, the benefit of exposure netting may extend to market risk. This creates the possibility of margin offsets where firms are long in one market and short in another (for instance, margin against a long position in a bond futures contract might be offset against margin against a matching short position in repo).'

4 See ESF Submission on ISD, p 2.

Leading studies and reports

8.35 As indicated above, a series of important studies and reports address risk and propose reform in the post-trading infrastructure. The 1989 G30 Report broke new ground with nine recommendations relating respectively to:

- trade comparison;
- trade confirmation/affirmation;
- central securities depositories;
- trade netting;
- DVP;

- same day funds;
- T+3 settlement;
- securities lending; and
- common message standards.

'[T]he 1989 G30 recommendations remain the only standards that have achieved widespread support and official endorsement.'[1] However, the G30 1989 report is now out of date[2], and must be read together with subsequent works that built on its seminal insights. The 1992 report of the BIS on DVP, discussed above, importantly refined the industry's understanding of delivery versus payment. Its different DVP models are widely cited although, as indicated above, model 1 DVP is not universally accepted as a standard. In 1995 ISSA reviewed the 1989 G30 Report, and produced the nine *1995 G30/ISSA Recommendations*, which updated the original recommendations in the light of market changes. Also in 1995 the BIS produced a report on *Cross-Border Securities Settlement*, which contained important insights including the problem of 'the leap of faith': market participants or their agents are routinely required to give instructions for the transfer of securities or cash before confirmation that corresponding value will be received on the due date.

In 1997, the BIS and IOSCO published a *Disclosure Framework for Securities Settlement Systems* in order to facilitate the assessment of risk management in key settlement systems. This is a standard form questionnaire, to which settlement systems have published answers[3]. In 1998, ECSDA[4] published standards with which a European national settlement system must comply in order to participate in a series of bilateral settlement links. The initial purpose of this is to facilitate the cross-border delivery of collateral to central banks providing Euro liquidity through TARGET[5].

In 2000, ISSA published eight revised recommendations. The following year the CPSS-IOSCO Joint Talk Force on Securities Settlement Systems published 18 recommendations[6] (the CPSS/IOSCO Recommendations[7]) which set best practice standards for settlement. It identifies in 18 headline recommendations both the minimum requirements and best practice for securities settlement systems. The CPSS/IOSCO Recommendations relate to legal risk (recommendation 1, on the legal framework); pre-settlement risk (recommendations 2–5, on trade confirmations, settlement cycles, central counterparties and securities lending respectively); settlement risk (recommendations 6–10 on central securities depositories (CSDs), DVP, timing of settlement finality, CSD risk controls to address participant defaults, and cash settlement of assets respectively); operational risk (recommendation 11 on operational reliability); custody risk (recommendation 12 on protection of customers' securities); and other issues (recommendations 13–18 on governance, access, efficiency, communication procedures and standards, transparency and regulation and oversight respectively). In October 2000, the DTCC published *Central Counterparties: Development, Cooperation and Consolidation*, October 2000 ('DTCC *White CCP Paper*').

In 2001 The Giovannini Group[8] published its first report on *Cross-Border Clearing and Settlement Arrangements in the European Union* ('The Giovannini Report'), identifying the sources of inefficiency that currently exist. A second report is proposed for 2002[9]. In 2002, the European Commission issued its consultative *Communication on clearing and settlement in the European Union; Main policy issues and future challenges*[10], in which it sets out Commission policy. It identifies the twin objectives in achieving an integrated post-trade infrastructure by removing barriers to finalising individual cross-border transactions, and removing competitive distortions in the EU post-trading environment[11]. Options on which it seeks responses include the development of a harmonised EU regulatory environment for clearing and settlement entities[12]. The European System of Central banks (ESCB) and the Committee of European Securities Regulators (CESR) have established a joint working group on clearing and settlement[13], with a view to adopting common European standards[14]. At the time of writing, G30 is undertaking a major project on clearing and settlement, reviewing the current state of the post-trade infrastructure worldwide; analysing existing standards and principles with a view to proposing new ones; and considering governance and ownership issues. Its report, which will highlight cross-border issues particularly, is awaited with considerable interest[15].

1 DTCC *T+1 White Paper*, p 1.
2 See DTCC *T+1 White Paper*, p 1.
3 Some more informative than others.
4 The European Central Securities Depository Association.
5 See Standards for the use of EU securities settlement systems in ESCB credit operations, 1998.
6 *Recommendations for Securities Settlement Systems*. See also *Joint work of the European System of Central Banks and the Committee of European Securities Regulators in the field of clearing and Settlement, a call for contributions from interested parties* March 2002, p 2:

> 'It was recognised from the outset that the CPSS/IOSCO recommendations represent an obvious starting point for any work to be undertaken on the issue of setting standards for securities clearing and settlement.'

7 Available on www.bis.org and www.iosco.org
8 'The Giovannini Group was formed in 1996 to advise the Commission on issues relating to EU financial integration and the efficiency of euro-denominated financial markets' (Giovannini Report, p 1).
9 'A second report – to be published in 2002 – will be more forward looking and will attempt to assess the prospects for the EU clearing and settlement architecture, with a particular emphasis on public policy aspects' (Giovannini Report, Foreword).
10 COM(2002)257.
11 European Commission *Communication on clearing and settlement in the European Union; Main policy issues and future challenges*, p 9.
12 See the discussion in Chapter 7.
13 See *A call for contributions from Interested parties*, March 2002. Their work may be the basis for European legislation: see p 2.
14 'Common standards will contribute to creating a level playing-field for the providers of securities clearing and settlement services and to overcoming the significant heterogeneity within the legislative frameworks of European countries' (ECB/CESR press release, 25 October 2001).
15 See also the 1989 report of the Fédération Internationale Des Bourses de Valeurs (FIBV) on Improving International Settlement; IOSCO's 1990 Report of the Technical Committee on Clearing and Settlement; ISSA's 1992 Report on Cross-Border Settlement and Custody; Morgan Guaranty Trust Company of New York, Brussels Office's 1993 Report entitled 'Cross-border Clearance, Settlement and Custody: Beyond the G30 Recommendations'; the BIS 1993 Report on Central Bank Payment and Settlement Services with respect to Cross-Border and Multi-Currency Transactions; the 1996 FIBV Clearing and Settlement Best Practices; the 1996 IOSCO Report on Client Asset Protection; the G30/ISSA Status Reviews of 1997, 1998 and 1999; the 2001 CPSS/BIS Core Principles for Systemically Important Payment Systems and the 2001 standards prepared by the European Association of Central Counterparty Clearinghouses (EACH).

Consolidation

8.36 'The recent creation of the euro and longer-standing demographic and technological trends have stimulated demand from issuers and investors alike for integration of European capital markets.'[1] The major challenge which has been identified for the years ahead is the consolidation of the post trade infrastructure[2].

1 The DTCC *CCP White Paper*, p 7.
2 See The 1995 G30/ISSA Recommendations, pp 25, 26.

Current fragmentation of post-trade infrastructure

8.37 The European Commission's 1999 Financial Services Action Plan sets the objective of an integrated European capital market by 2005[1]. However, the process of market integration, particularly in the securities markets, is hindered by a fragmented post-trading infrastructure[2]. 'It is perhaps no exaggeration to conclude . . . that inefficiencies in clearing and settlement represent the most primitive and thus the most important barrier to integrated financial markets in Europe.'[3] The Lamfalussy Securities Market Report[4] discusses '. . . the excessive costs of cross-border clearing and settlement in the EU compared to the US, due to fragmentation'[5], and identifies potential annual savings of up to a billion euros[6]. The DTCC has added its voice to this debate, emphasising the need for an integrated post-trading infrastructure, and (like the ESF) highlighting clearing in particular[7]. The ESF emphasises the cost of numerous different European settlement systems[8], requiring separate IT links and resulting in high transaction costs[9]. The Giovannini Report identifies three types of cost associated with fragmentation[10], namely direct costs in the form of higher fees; indirect costs in the form of additional back office expenses; and opportunity costs associated with inefficient use of collateral, failed trades and trades foregone. It also identifies three types of barrier to efficient cross-border clearing and settlement[11]. These are: barriers relating to national differences in technical requirements/market practice[12]; barriers relating to national differences in tax procedures; and barriers relating to issues of legal certainty[13]. The European Commission suggests that perverse incentives may also bear some of the blame[14]. It is widely argued that the consolidation of clearing is the most urgent priority. 'A large part of the benefits to market participants that might accrue from fully integrating clearing and settlement across markets is realised by integrating CCPs alone.'[15]

The final shape that an integrated infrastructure will assume remains unclear[16].

1 The FSAP discusses current market fragmentation: 'Yet, the Union's financial markets remain segmented and business and consumers continue to be deprived of direct access to cross-border financial institutions' (p 3).

2 *Cross-Border Clearing and Settlement Arrangements in the European Union*, Brussels, November 2001 (The Giovannini Report), p 20:

> 'The existing infrastructure for the provision of clearing and settlement services in the European Union is the product of a fragmented securities market. Historically, the pattern of European securities trading has followed national lines, a pattern that was reinforced by the existence of different currencies (for a long time accompanied by exchange controls) and relatively basic technology.'

3 *Cross-Border Clearing and Settlement Arrangements in the European Union*, Brussels, November 2001 (The Giovannini Report), Foreword. See also p 20:

> 'The extent of fragmentation in the EU clearing and settlement infrastructure has been exposed by the increased demand for cross-border trading that is an inevitable consequence of financial integration . . . the additional cost and risk associated with this fragmentation represents a significant limitation on the scope for cross-border securities trading in the European Union. By extension, it also represents an important limitation on exploiting the economic benefits of the Internal market and the euro.'

4 The report comments dryly that 'Market infrastructure (exchanges and clearing and settlement systems) is not as efficient as it might be and the chances of delivering the FSAP on time are close to zero' (p 12) and'The Committee is convinced that further restructuring of clearing and settlement is necessary in the European Union' (p 16).

5 Lamfalussy Securities Markets Report, p 16. See also p 82:

> 'Managing the full web of bilateral linkages (which could amount to up to 650 bilateral links between the 26 existing settlement systems in the EU) is generally regarded as extremely cumbersome and a source of operational, some have said even systemic risk in itself.'

6 Lamfalussy Securities Markets Report, p 82.

7 See The DTCC *CCP White Paper*, p 4.
8 The Giovannini Report laments, notwithstanding existing consolidation, 19 CSDs and two ICSDs remain.
9 ESF Submission on ISD, p 10.
10 See section 4.
11 See section 5.
12 These comprise: national differences in information technology and interfaces; national clearing and settlement restrictions that require the use of multiple systems; differences in national rules relating to corporate actions, beneficial ownership and custody; absence of intra-day settlement finality; practical impediments to remote access to national clearing and settlement systems; national differences in settlement periods; national differences in operating hours/settlement deadlines; national differences in securities issuance practice; national restrictions on the location of (underlying) securities; and national restrictions on the activity of primary dealers and market makers.
13 Three in particular are identified as follows: the absence of an EU-wide framework for the treatment of interests in securities; national differences in the legal treatment of bilateral netting for financial transactions; and uneven application of national conflict of laws rules.
14 Commission Communication *Clearing and settlement in the European Union, main policy issues and future challenges*, 2002, COM(2002)257:

> 'However, the lack of progress may also be put down to perverse incentives among infrastructure owners, management and users. These arise either because the parties involved derive profit in some way from the current fragmented environment, or because those who would bear the costs of technical developments are not the ones who stand to gain the most from them.'

15 The DTCC *CCP White Paper*, p 2.
16 The Lamfalussy Securities Markets Report, p 82:

> 'Submissions to the Committee have highlighted the widespread differences as regards the optimal configuration of European clearing and settlement facilities.'

See also Joint work of the European System of Central Banks and the Committee of European Securities Regulators in the field of clearing and settlement, a call for contributions from interested parties, March 2002, p 4:

> 'The structure of the securities clearing and settlement industry in Europe has been hotly debated recently. An integrated market can be achieved via a number of routes, with concentration, interoperability and open access being the most obvious alternatives.'

Consolidation of settlement[1]

8.38 The cross-border settlement of fixed income securities was consolidated by the early establishment of the international settlement systems (known as international central securities depositories or ICSDs), Euroclear and Clearstream (formerly Cedel). Equity settlement remains fragmented[2]. Cross-border settlements in Europe are increasing not only because of the growth of cross-border trades, but also because of rights issues and other corporate actions in the context of cross-border takeovers. The CPSS/IOSCO Recommendations discuss channels of settlement for cross-border trades, and identify five:

- direct membership of the local CSD;
- use of local agent;
- use of global custodian;
- ICSDs; and
- links between CSDs[3].

The last option has been the focus of considerable industry activity in recent years. Important strategic alliances have been formed between existing systems[4]. The final goal is 'one-stop shopping', whereby membership of one settlement system permits the settlement of securities transactions in any European jurisdictions. However, 'The jury is still out as to whether full integration of Central Securities Depositories (CSDs) is required or whether technical linkages between existing entities will be sufficient.'[5] As for links between existing systems, two competing models for this are offered. By developing links to the national systems, the ICSDs (notably Euroclear) promote the 'hub and spoke' model. In the model, the ICSD serves as the hub of a notional wheel, of which the spokes are the national settlement systems. ECSDA has advocated an alternative model, known colloquially as the 'spider's web'. Instead of a central hub, this involves a series of bilateral links between national systems, together with a series of linked local hubs (also known as 'relayed links'). Whichever model emerges, it seems clear that the development of one-stop shopping remains a medium to long term project[6].

1 In July 2002 the merger of CREST and Euroclear was announced. See Chapter 9.
2 Giovannini Report, pp 20, 21:

> 'The capacity of the ICSDs to provide international clearance and settlement services for the bond markets has been helped by the comparative homogeneity in fixed-income securities and the extent to which they have been commoditised. Equities are more heterogeneous instruments and more complex to manage particularly with respect to corporate actions and insofar as they require continuous communication between the company that has issued the equity and its holder. In consequence, cross-border . . . settlement of equities . . . is particularly challenging.'

3 CPSS/IOSCO Recommendations, pp 44, 45.
4 Famous examples include the merger of Cedel and Deutsche Börse Clearing to form Clearstream, and the alliance between Euroclear and Sicovam to form Euroclear France.
5 Lamfalussy Securities Markets Report, p 82.
6 In the US, 'DTCC will develop plans for a combined, single settlement system to replace the two separate systems now in place at DTC and NSCC' (DTCC *T+1 White Paper*, p 4).

Consolidation of clearing and/or CCP services[1]

8.39 As indicated earlier, greater industry attention has recently focused on the integration of clearing than on that of settlement, because of the clear benefits offered by the consolidation of CCP services. To a greater extent than fragmented settlement, fragmented CCP services increase credit exposures and therefore tie up market participants' capital[2]. Beyond this, consolidation among CCPs offers commercial risk management and operational efficiencies[3]. Also, such consolidation makes '. . . the functioning of the market more resilient during a crisis, when replacement cost risk may increase sharply.'[4] The DTC has described the consolidation of CCP services as '. . . one of the most important developments shaping the global investment servicing industry over the next five to ten years.'[5] It is now generally accepted that the case for consolidation in Europe has been made. However, the commercial, operational and legal challenges cannot be underestimated, and the progress of consolidation has been disappointingly slow.

As with the consolidation of settlement, a number of alternative models for European consolidation are under discussion. The ESF is clear in its advocacy of a single EuroCCP[6], initially for equities and later for fixed income securities and derivatives. DTCC discusses the alternatives of the integrated clearer model (ie a CCP among CCPs); a joint venture model; and the use of common technology[7]. It comments that 'If the forces against consolidation are stronger than the forces for, many of the benefits may still be realised through cooperation.'[8] As an interim step, cross-margining agreements between CCPs may offer collateral netting efficiencies[9].

1 In July 2002 virt-x, LCH and x-clear announced a pan-European central counterparty.
2 See Lamfalussy Securities Markets Report, p 82.
3 The DTCC *CCP White Paper*, p 2.
4 DTCC *CCP White Paper*, p 9.

5 The DTCC *CCP White Paper*, p 3.
6 See ESF Blueprint, pp 23, 24.
7 The DTCC *CCP White Paper*.
8 DTCC *CCP White Paper*, p 11.
9 See CPSS/IOSCO Recommendations, p 48.

Underlying legal principles

8.40 The need for a legally robust basis for the post-trade infrastructure is beyond doubt. Challenges in achieving this include: the legal nature of property rights; the impact of insolvency; and the conflict of laws. The chief legal instrument of private sector arrangements (including clearing and settlement systems) is contract. However, a common feature of property rights, insolvency and the conflict of laws is that contractual provision is often ineffective to modify them. Therefore creating a legally robust post-trade infrastructure is largely dependent on national and international legislation. Very significant progress is being made by a number of law reform initiatives, discussed briefly below. Both the challenges and the initiatives that are designed to address them are discussed in turn below.

Property rights

8.41 It was indicated above that settlement involves the delivery of securities. To be more accurate, settlement involves the delivery of property rights in relation to securities. Property rights were very briefly considered in Chapter 1. While the legal nature of property rights is a matter of extensive academic debate[1], one essential feature of them is that they are enforceable against third parties[2]. There is a general principle that property rights should be public, as it would be unfair for third parties to be bound by rights, the existence of which they had no way of knowing. This general principle arguably explains a number of special rules which apply to property rights, including the requirement to register certain charges; certain formalities of transfer[3]; and the lex situs rule[4]. These special rules cannot in general be disapplied or modified by contract[5]. Because the application of these rules to electronic settlement may be inconvenient or uncertain, legislative support is generally required to create legally robust settlement systems. This slows down the reform of the post-trade infrastructure to the pace of the public sector. Moreover, these rules may differ from country to country, and therefore harmonised legislation may be needed[6].

1 Two of the authors' favourite discussions are Hohfeld *Fundamental Legal Conceptions* (1919, Yale University Press) and Gray 'Property in Thin Air' (1991) CLR 252.
2 Personal rights (eg such as those arising under a contract of sale) are enforceable only against the person who owes them (eg the seller). In contrast, property rights are generally enforceable against the world at large (with the possible exception of the good faith buyer of the assets subject to those rights without notice of them). This is why, after settlement, the buyer is generally able to assert its rights in purchased securities against the liquidator and creditors of the insolvent seller.
3 These also serve as anti-fraud measures. In the UK, see s 53(1)(c) and s 136 of the Law of Property Act 1925, discussed in Chapter 2.
4 This rule also serves the interest of commercial convenience, as discussed in Chapter 5.
5 This is because of course it would be unfair by a private contract to prejudice the rights of third parties.
6 As discussed in Chapter 5, the application of the lex situs rule to intermediated securities has presented a particular challenge, which a number of legislative initiatives seek to address.

Insolvency

8.42 Participant insolvency may have systemic implications for the post-trade infrastructure. In simple terms, it is important to ensure that the insolvency of one participant does not cause liquidity and/or credit problems for other participants, causing them to default in turn. Such consequential problems might arise for a range of reasons under the insolvency law of the defaulting participant. For example, payments and deliveries (in settlement of transactions or under collateralised lending arrangements) which the defaulting participant has made prior to the date of insolvency might be reversed under preference and other displacement rules. Also, payments and deliveries made by the defaulting participant after the moment of insolvency may be avoided as post-insolvency dispositions. As clearing and settlement systems may admit participants from many different countries, a particular concern is the widely varying provisions of the different national insolvency laws[1]. This lack of harmonisation has long been a major source of legal risk.

The treatment of the assets of an insolvent person is governed by the mandatory provisions of insolvency law. Any contractual provision which purports to modify such mandatory provisions is generally ineffective[2]. It is therefore necessary to ensure that the laws that would govern the insolvency of market participants do not conflict with the rules of the relevant clearing and settlement systems. Provisions contained in a number of EU measures, discussed in Chapter 5 and very briefly below, seek to address this risk. Two particular sensitivities are collateral and netting.

1 The Insolvency Regulation (1346/2000) refers, in Recital 11, to the 'widely differing substantive laws' of insolvency within the EU.

2 *British Eagle International Airlines Ltd v Compagnie Internationale Air France* [1975] 1 WLR 758, [1975] 2 All ER 390.

Collateral

8.43 The central premise of clearing is that the CCP is able to absorb credit risk without compromising its own financial stability. In order to achieve this, the CCP relies on a number of measures including, importantly, taking collateral from its members. Equally, settlement systems which assume credit exposures to their members seek to collateralise these exposures using the assets credited to members' accounts. The effect of successful collateral arrangements is to enable the CCP or settlement system to recover sums owed to it by disposing of the collateral assets, thus avoiding the need to prove as unsecured creditor in the member's insolvency. While helpful for the collateral taker, this of course involves a cost for the general creditors of the insolvent as it depletes the assets available to them. For this reason, insolvency law in each jurisdiction has wide powers to cut across collateral arrangements which are considered to be unfair to general creditors, as discussed in more detail in Chapter 4. The law reform initiatives very briefly discussed below seek to address this risk.

Netting

8.44 The netting of obligations is essential to clearing, both in day-to-day operations[1] and under default rules. In effect, the netting of obligations owed to and from a member involves the use of the member's rights against the CCP to meet its liability to the CCP. Like collateral, netting protects the CCP but involves a cost for the general creditors of an insolvent member, by depriving them of the benefit of the insolvent's netted rights. In order to avoid unfairness to general creditors, each system of insolvency law carefully defines the circumstances in which insolvency netting is permitted.

Interbank netting schemes were considered in detail in the 1990 Lamfalussy Netting Report[2]. Although the Lamfalussy Netting Report focused on private interbank netting schemes, it has served as a benchmark for the risk analysis of netting in the wider financial markets[3]. It recommends a number of minimum standards, the first of which is that 'Netting schemes should have a well-founded legal basis under all relevant jurisdictions.'[4] The call for legal certainty in netting has been stressed elsewhere[5]. Legally unreliable netting is worse than no netting, as it obscures the true measure of credit exposure[6]. Potential insolvency-related challenges to netting include the unavailability of insolvency set off[7]; insolvency displacement under preference or similar rules[8]; and zero hour rules[9]. (See Chapter 4 for a discussion of these terms, and Chapter 5 for a discussion of law reform initiatives which address these risk.)

1 In trade netting discussed above.
2 *Report of the Committee on Interbank Netting Schemes of the Central Banks of the Group of Ten Countries* ('the Lamfalussy Netting Report'). This followed and in part responded to Group of Experts on Payment Systems of the central banks of the Group of Ten countries, BIS *The Report on Netting Schemes* ('The Angell Report') of 1989.
3 Lamfalussy Netting Report, p 4. See also Hills et al 'Central Counterparty Clearing Houses and Financial Stability' (June 1999) *Bank of England Financial Stability Review* 124 at 125.
4 Lamfalussy Netting Report, p 17. See also p 11.
5 See 1995 G30/ISSA Recommendations, p 23.
6 See The Lamfalussy Netting Report, pp 2, 11.
7 Many sets of default rules rely on multi-lateral netting, which is not generally permitted under the normal principles of insolvency law, and requires special legislative support.
8 Which might displace previously netting positions.
9 See the Lamfalussy Netting Report, p 11.

The conflict of laws

8.45 These challenges are increased in the case of remote clearing and international settlement by the conflict of laws. The rules of domestic law on which CCPs and settlement systems rely differ from jurisdiction to jurisdiction. In a cross-border situation, therefore, the outcome of a dispute may depend on the rules for determining which of the potentially relevant systems of domestic law applies. These rules are called conflict of laws rules. The application of traditional conflict of laws rules to the post-trade infrastructure may be unclear[1]. This has hindered the achievement of legal certainty[2], particularly in relation to collateral[3] and netting[4]. However, the need to address this challenge in clearing[5] and settlement[6] has been stressed, and has generated a number of relevant law reform initiatives.

1 Unfortunately, the conflict of laws rules have traditionally also differed from jurisdiction to jurisdiction, so that the outcome of certain cross-border disputes has been highly dependent upon where they are heard; this has rendered them inherently unpredictable.
2 See Bank for International Settlements *Cross-Border Securities Settlement*, May 1994, Basle, and the ESF Submission on the ISD, p 2.
3 See the Lamfalussy Securities Markets Report, p 85.
4 See The Lamfalussy Netting Report, p 11. In the absence of harmonisation, the Lamfalussy Netting Report recommends that the legal basis of cross-border netting arrangements should be considered under '(a) the law of the country in which the counterparty is chartered and, if the counterparty is a branch of a foreign bank, then also under the law of the jurisdiction in which the branch is located; (b) the law that governs the individual transactions subject to the netting scheme; and (c) the law that governs any contract or agreement necessary to effect the netting' (p 18).
5 See the EU Commission's ISD Consultation Document, p 35.
6 See CPSS/IOSCO Recommendations, p 8.

Law reform initiatives

8.46 Many of the law reform initiatives discussed below relate directly or indirectly to insolvency. Historically, efforts to harmonise substantive insolvency law internationally have met with incomplete success. This is not surprising, because national insolvency laws reflect the policy priorities of each jurisdiction. Moreover, the insolvency sensitivities mentioned above are generally designed to protect general creditors of the insolvent, and reflect important policy concerns. However, securities settlement systems are often linked to wholesale payment systems, and the systemic propagation of liquidity and credit problems through settlement systems might pose a threat to the financial system[1]. For this reason, the policy case has been made to disapply some of the normal provisions of insolvency law in favour of major clearing and settlement systems, in order to address systemic risk.

1 See Recital 2 of the Settlement Finality Directive (discussed below).

The Settlement Finality Directive[1]

8.47 The Settlement Finality Directive ('SFD'[2]) was designed to reduce systemic risk in EU payment and securities settlement systems[3]. It displaces a number of the provisions of insolvency law that might otherwise disturb the smooth operation of such systems following the insolvency of a participant[4]. In order to benefit from the SFD, a system must be designated by a member state and notified to the Commission[5]. (Lawyers in London had speculated that some major custodians might apply to the FSA for recognition as a designated system for the purposes of the SFD, but the date of writing none have done so[6].) The SFD's provisions include the following. Transfer orders[7] and netting[8] will be binding and enforceable despite the insolvency of a participant[9], providing they occur before the moment of insolvency[10]. This is notwithstanding insolvency displacement rules[11]. Member states may provide for the defaulting participant's assets to be used to meet its settlement obligations on the day of insolvency[12]. Collateral giver insolvency shall not affect a collateral taker (being a central bank[13] or a participant taking collateral in connection with the system[14]).

While CCPs could benefit from the existing provisions of the Settlement Finality Directive, the Directive was not designed with CCPs in mind, and the ESF calls for revised provisions to cover, in particular, wider aspects of CCP default rules, and non-insolvency displacement[15].

1 Directive 98/26/EC of the European Parliament and of the Council of 19 May 1998 on settlement finality in payment and securities settlement systems.
2 98/26/EC.
3 Recital 1 indicates that the original inspiration of the SFD was the discussion of systemic risk in wholesale payment systems in the Lamfalussy Netting Report.
4 See Recital 4. In the UK, it builds on the pre-existing provisions of Pt VII of the Companies Act 1989.
5 Articles 1(a), 2(a) and 10. For the UK designation procedure, see Pt II of The Financial Markets and Insolvency (Settlement Finality) Regulations 1999 (SI 1999/2979).
6 As of that date, the FSA had not recognised CRESTCo as an approved system. It is understood that the delay was due, strangely enough, to the FSA's not being convinced that CRESTCo was a settlement system for the purposes of the Directive (notwithstanding the fact that the FSA in another capacity regulates CRESTCo).
7 'Transfer order' is defined to include instructions for the transfer of cash and securities: art 2(i).
8 Whether on default or otherwise: see art 2(k).
9 Article 3(1).
10 Or after but on the same day as the opening of insolvency proceedings, provided the settlement system can prove it was unaware of the opening of proceedings: art 3(1).

11 Article 3(2).
12 Article 4
13 Whether the central bank of a member state or the European Central Bank.
14 Article 9(1).
15 Submission on ISD, p 7.

Insolvency Regulation and Winding Up Directive

8.48 The Insolvency Regulation[1] provides[2] that the impact of insolvency on rights of and obligations to settlement systems is governed by the law of the system. In the Winding Up Directive[3] (which applies to credit institutions) art 27 protects transactions carried out on regulated markets; this will in turn protect clearing and settlement systems to which those markets are attached. Further, the Insolvency Regulation and the Winding Up Directive do much to harmonise the rules for insolvency jurisdiction and recognition in Europe, and clarify choice of law rules concerning the availability of set off and post-insolvency dispositions of (interests in) securities. See Chapter 5 for further discussion.

1 Council Regulation No 1346/2000.
2 In art 9. See also art 8 of the Settlement Finality Directive.
3 2001/24.

Financial Collateral Directive

8.49 The Financial Collateral Directive was discussed in Chapter 4. While the Directive's scope is not addressed primarily to the post trade infrastructure, it builds on the Settlement Finality Directive in addressing the legal risk associated with wholesale cash and securities collateral, primarily by harmonising and liberalising the provisions of national insolvency laws within the EU.

Hague Convention

8.50 The Hague Convention on the Law Applicable to Proprietary Rights in Indirectly Held Securities is discussed in Chapter 5. It builds on the Settlement Finality Directive by extending the concept of PRIMA to all dealings in intermediated securities.

European Securities Code

8.51 In its communication *Clearing and settlement in the European Union, main policy issues and future challenges*[1], the European Commission consults on the desirability of developing a European securities code[2]. In view of the challenges involved[3], the Commission suggests that this is not an option for the short term. The authors share the Commission's assessment that the challenges are considerable. However, the enviable levels of legal certainty achieved in the US securities markets have amply repaid the enormous effort that went into preparing and revising art 8 of the US Uniform Commercial Code. It is therefore hoped that a European Securities Code will be developed over the medium to long term[4].

1 2002, COM(2002)257.
2 *Clearing and settlement in the European Union, main policy issues and future challenges*, p 12:

> 'Given the substantial divergence in the legal treatment of securities across the EU, it has been suggested that the optimal solution would . . . require achieving a uniform legal treatment of securities across the EU. This implies creating a special legal regime for securities – a "uniform securities code"'.

See the European Securities Forum *Contribution on the Joint CESR/ECB Consultation on Clearing and Settlement*, 2002:

> 'One key area where a pan-EU instrument would serve is harmonisation of member states' diverse securities laws (ie property laws as they relate to securities) which have the effect of complicating all inter-member state securities activity involving EU securities and thus constitute barriers to a single market. Harmonisation needs to embrace payment finality laws, securities payment finality laws, bankruptcy laws and transfer of ownership laws. We understand that the US authorities solved some similar difficulties with a superordinate "universal security code" ' (ESF comment on consultation question 2.1).

3 *Clearing and settlement in the European Union, main policy issues and future challenges*, p 12:

> 'Such a regime would be far from easy to design, especially for equities, because of the many links with national property, company, succession and insolvency law in Member States.

4 Such a Code would complement the recently approved European Company Statute.

Chapter 9

UK settlement systems

CREST[1]

Introduction

9.1 CREST[2] is an electronic system for the paperless settlement of transactions[3] in registered securities in London[4]. CREST offers dematerialisation[5], payments by reference to central bank money for pounds sterling and euro, an assured payments system, and can handle corporate actions.

Use of CREST is in principle[6] optional both for issuers and investors, although this will depend on the terms of issue of the relevant shares or securities[7]. CREST is owned and operated by CRESTCo Limited ('CRESTCo'), which in turn is owned by Euroclear Bank SA/NV. The CREST system is operated by CRESTCo in accordance with The Uncertificated Securities Regulations 2001, SI 2001/3755 (the 'CREST Regulations') (which replace The Uncertificated Securities 1995, SI 1995/ 3272 (the '1995 Regulations') as amended by The Uncertificated Securities (Amendment) Regulations 2000, SI 2000/1682)[8].

The CREST system follows previous failures in London to dematerialise equity settlement[9].

1 The authors are grateful to Alastair FitzSimons and Maurits Talen of CRESTCo and (in relation to Euroclear) Diego Devos of Euroclear for kindly reviewing this chapter, although any errors are the authors' own.
2 The name is not an acronym.
3 Trade confirmation takes place outside CREST, although pre-settlement matching occurs within CREST. Types of transactions settled include transfers, securities loans and corporate actions.
4 Bearer securities are ineligible. However, securities which are bearer in paper form such as allotment letters may be dematerialised if a register is created: see CREST *The Business Description*, Bank of England, December 1994, p 14. UK shares and other securities are covered by the CREST Regulations (as defined at n 8), and equivalent regulations have been made in the Republic of Ireland Companies Act 1990 (The Uncertificated Securities Regulations) 1996 (SI No 68 of 1996) and such other regulations made under s 239 of the Companies Act 1990 (the 'Irish Regulations'), the Isle of Man (The Transfer of Securities Regulations 1996 and such other regulations made under s 28 of the Companies Act 1992 (the 'Isle of Man Regulations')) and Jersey (The Companies (Jersey) Law 1991 Companies (Uncertificated Securities) (Jersey) Order 1999 (the 'Jersey Order')) to provide for the transfer of securities issued in such jurisdictions through CREST. (Note that Guernsey securities are admissible to CREST provided there is appropriate provision in the articles of association of the issuing company, but that 'Guernsey shares are not participating securities as defined in the CREST Regulations'. See CREST Rule 8.) In addition, securities issued in other jurisdictions may be brought into CREST through depositary receipt schemes.
5 That is, the removal of the certificates and instruments of transfer which are otherwise generally necessary to permit UK registered securities to be evidenced and transferred. The Group of Thirty Securities Clearance and Settlement Study of 1989 ('the G30 Report') defines dematerialisation as:

'The elimination of physical certificates or documents of title which represent ownership of securities so that securities exist only as computer records'.

6 In practice, listed securities (other than certain types of listed debt securities and fixed income securities) are required to be capable of electronic settlement by the FSA Listing Rules (see para 9.39 of such Rules). This provision was introduced in September 1997.

7 Issuing companies may elect whether to make their securities eligible for CREST, and may also issue what the Regulations call 'wholly dematerialised securities', namely securities or shares the terms of issue for which provide that such instruments may only be held in uncertificated form and only transferred through CREST. Unless the securities are wholly dematerialised securities, investors in CREST-eligible securities may elect whether their securities should be held in uncertificated form in CREST, or in certificated form outside it, ie certificated securities may be brought into CREST, and uncertificated securities may be recertificated.

8 In this chapter, unless otherwise specified, any reference to a 'CREST Regulation' means a Regulation forming part of SI 2001/3755, and any reference to the CREST Rules, Reference Manual or Terms and Conditions, means the forms of such documents in effect and available on the CREST website as at 30 June 2002.

9 In 1979 the Stock Exchange introduced Talisman, an electronic system providing for automated settlement between stock jobbers (today's market makers). In Talisman, SEPON, the Stock Exchange Pool Nominee, acted as nominee custodian during settlement on behalf of member firms and their clients, who maintained SEPON accounts. Shares were registered in the name of SEPON, to whom certificates were not issued. Beneficial ownership of stock passed within Talisman by book entry. In 1981 the Exchange proposed to extend the system to the market as a whole, using a centralised database to maintain records of all shareholdings. The proposal was defeated by commercial registrars, who would have been put out of business.

The privatisation programme of the eighties led to a settlement crisis in 1987, and brokers' back offices were unable to cope with the unprecedented volumes of trades. The October crash and ensuing market chaos provided the impetus for change. In 1989 the Group of Thirty, a New York-based think tank for the securities industry, published its report, *Clearance and Settlement Systems in the World's Securities Markets*. Recommendations included delivery versus payment, three-day rolling settlement and dematerialisation. CREST was built by the Bank of England out of the ashes of Taurus, the proposed electronic settlement system that failed in 1993. In 1989, the same year as the G30 Report, the Exchange appointed the Securities Industry Steering Committee for Taurus ('SISCOT') with a brief to find a compromise solution that would prejudice no interest group. Registrars (again fearing redundancy) insisted that a central database be rejected in favour of a distributed system. Private client stockbrokers (fearing loss of shareholder entitlements) rejected SEPON-style pooling and insisted on direct ownership (investors names on registers). Plcs supported direct registration but, with a distributed network, feared that delay in identifying investors would increase vulnerability to takeovers. They were given a complex system-wide search facility. The result prejudiced none and failed all. Taurus collapsed under its own weight in March 1993 because it was over-complex. It would have cost too much, and taken too long to complete. Consequential losses were variously estimated as between GBP200 and GBP500 million. The Bank of England stepped into the breach and set up a broadly-based task force which proposed CREST in June 1993.

Core legal structure

Dematerialisation

9.2 Outside CREST, UK company legislation generally requires companies to issue share certificates[1] and to register transfers only on receipt of instruments of transfer[2]. Dematerialisation is based on the CREST Regulations[3].

1 Companies Act 1985, s 185.

2 Companies Act 1985, s 183.

3 SI 2001/3755, made under s 207 of the Companies Act 1989, which '. . . enable title to units of a security to be evidenced otherwise than by a certificate and transferred otherwise than by a written instrument . . .' (CREST Regulation 2(1)). CREST Regulation 14 expressly permits the electronic transfer of title. This is broadly comparable to the old statutory provision which permitted the dematerialisation of gilts within the CGO.

Interestingly, SI 2001/3755 is not limited to CREST and does not mention it by name. Accordingly, competing systems (including the continental settlement systems) are free to apply for recognition under SI 2001/3755 to settle UK shares and other registrable securities, and it may be argued that the form of SI 2001/3755 is thus beneficial in not stifling competition. The view has been expressed that, in practice, the need to handle the complex corporate actions associated with UK equities may keep such competition at bay, and another factor may be the continuing applicability of stamp duty and SDRT, and the need to take this into account when structuring systems (but see below in relation to the merger of CREST and Euroclear). For the sake of convenience, this chapter will refer to the system contemplated by SI 2001/3755 as CREST.

Legal and equitable ownership

9.3 Legal title to CREST securities is prima facie determined, both inside and outside the system, by registration[1]. The usual statutory requirements for written transfers are expressly disapplied[2]. The legal structure of CREST was closely modelled on that of the old Central Gilts Office (the 'CGO') which was originally operated by the Bank of England, then by CRESTCo and ultimately merged with CREST with effect from 3 July 2000).

1 See Companies Act 1985, s 361 and CREST Regulation 24.
2 Law of Property Act 1925, s 53(1)(c) and s 136 are disapplied by CREST Regulation 38(5).

Original structure

9.4 To begin with, under the 1995 Regulations, in the same way as with transfers using stock transfer forms, transfers of securities through the CREST system were followed by electronic notification through the CREST system to the registrar of the issuer of the securities. Thus, in addition to entries in the register of the issuer of the securities, CREST participants would have a record of their securities in accounts at CREST[1]. Registrars were required to register a CREST transfer within two hours of the corresponding change in the CREST records, and in order to protect the transferee from the credit risk of the transferor during this short interval, it was considered necessary to ensure that book entry transfer conferred on the transferee equitable ownership of the securities[2].

1 CREST securities accounts were regularly reconciled to the issuer's register under this system.
2 'The Government considers that this provision will provide the best possible level of protection for the transferee in the event of insolvency of the transferor after settlement but before registration' (HM Treasury Consultation Document on the Draft Uncertificated Securities Regulations, January 1995, p 71). Securities in the course of settlement were pooled without allocation to particular purchasers. As discussed at length in Chapter 3, there was some doubt at general law as to the validity of purported trusts over unascertained property ('the allocation question'), hence in order to address the allocation question in CREST, it was considered necessary to make express statutory provision. 'In the absence of statutory intervention, due to the unascertainability of the units, it is possible that if the transferor's name were not on the register, the buyer would not obtain a proprietary interest' (ibid, pp 93, 94). In the past, the allocation question was addressed in the CGO and Talisman by expressly providing for a tenancy in common. This reflects the solution probably implied by general law: see Chapter 3. However, the Treasury took a different approach with CREST. Instead of actual allocation through co-ownership (whereby all the securities in the pool are allocated to all the participants in the pool under a global trust), under the 1995 Regulations, Regulation 25 provided for notional allocation where there was no actual allocation. Regulation 25 of the 1995 Regulations provided that, at the time when the CREST system instructs the registrar of the issuer to register a transfer: '(1) . . . (a) the transferee shall acquire an equitable interest in the requisite number of uncertificated units of the security of the kind specified in the Operator-instruction in which the transferor has an equitable interest by virtue of this regulation, or in relation to which the transferor is recorded on the relevant register of securities as having title . . . (6) This regulation has effect notwithstanding that the units to which the Operator-instruction relates, or in which an interest arises by virtue of paragraph (1) . . . may be unascertained.'

Current structure

9.5 Currently[1], in relation to securities constituted under or governed by the laws of England and Wales, Northern Ireland or Scotland and admitted to CREST under the CREST Regulations ('UK Securities') (rather than, for example, the equivalent Jersey legislation) any interval between transfer across CREST accounts and corresponding updating of the register of title is avoided altogether by designating the records maintained by CREST as the register of legal title for UK Securities in dematerialised form which are held and transferred through CREST.

Under this structure, the CREST records constitute part of the register of title (the 'operator register (of securities)'): therefore a transfer from one CREST Account to another serves to transfer legal title (rather than an equitable interest followed by transfer of legal title when the register of title is updated). The relevant issuer is required to maintain a duplicate record of the CREST register of title (the duplicate record being known as the 'record (of securities)', as well as a register of holders of certificated securities (the 'issuer register'). (These arrangements apply to shares as well as registrable securities other than shares, and 'public sector securities'[2].)

The CREST Rules also reflect the electronic transfer of title[3]. The CREST Rules state that the operator register (ie the register of title maintained by CREST) for shares[4] consists of, effectively, the CREST Accounts of all CREST Members which record the relevant securities, and the Corporate Action delivery data[5].

The arrangements for registration of title to UK Securities raise certain interesting issues, some of which are discussed at para **9.75**.

1 Since 26 November 2001.

2 Defined to mean 'UK Government securities [securities "issued by Her Majesty's Government in the United kingdom or by a Northern Ireland department"] and local authority securities'. CREST Regulations, definitions (CREST Regulation 3)

3 It is important to note that currently these arrangements only apply to securities admitted to CREST pursuant to the UK CREST Regulations. Securities admitted under, for example, the relevant Irish legislation relating to CREST, are still subject to the two stage procedure for transfer of title, as explained in para **9.74**.

4 A similar definition is given in relation to other securities and public sector securities.

5 CREST Rule 14, Section 3:

> '. . . the records referred to below comprise the Operator register of members for a participating security which is a share:
>
> 3.1 the name and address of the member of a company who holds uncertificated shares in the company is determined by reference to the Participant Details relating to the Member;
>
> 3.2 the number of units of a participating security which is a share held by a member of a company is determined by aggregating the balance on the member's stock account(s) to which are credited units of the relevant participating security and, where the member initiated the delivery, the number of units of the relevant participating security comprised in the relevant Corporate Action delivery data (if any); and
>
> 3.3 the means by which each share or class of share is distinguished is determined by reference to the Security Details relating to the participating security.'

In this context, 'Corporate Action delivery data' means the Stock Postings Data which records system deliveries to the relevant Receiving Agent of securities which are the subject of a Corporate Action and which identify the Member who initiated such deliveries to the Receiving Agent.

(Note that in general the balance on a stock account in CREST will be the same as the number of securities recorded on the relevant operator record; but there are exceptions, for example in relation to certain corporate actions. See CREST Rule 14.)

Payments

9.6 For payments required to be made or received through CREST in connection with transactions settled through CREST, a CREST member has a cash memorandum account (in which associated obligations or entitlements are recorded) for each relevant currency, and the CREST member must have a settlement bank for each relevant currency[1]. The balance recorded in the cash memorandum account will change during the day, but at any one time shows the net amount which the CREST member is owed by its settlement bank (or owes to its settlement bank).

1 CREST Reference Manual, ch 6, Section 2, states that 'Each member can have only one settlement bank per designated currency, but could use the same bank as settlement bank for a number of designated currencies.'

REAL TIME GROSS SETTLEMENT

9.7 For payments in sterling and euro[1], settlement banks make payments to each other through their accounts with the Bank of England during the day on a real time basis as credits and debits are made to the CREST cash memorandum accounts for the CREST members for which the settlement banks provide services.

Under this arrangement, a CREST member making a transfer against payment through CREST still transfers securities from its CREST account in return for the creation of a payment obligation of the transferee's settlement bank[2]. However, the settlement bank's payment obligation will be satisfied not at the end of the day but at the same time as the CREST transfer. This happens by the creation of an irrevocable and unconditional undertaking by the Bank of England to credit the payment amount (the amount of the debit to the CMA, which is to be paid by the transferee's settlement bank) to the relevant account of the transferor's settlement bank. This means the Bank of England undertakes to credit the RTGS CREST settlement account of the transferor's settlement bank, and to make a corresponding debit to the RTGS CREST settlement account of the transferee's settlement bank. The undertaking given by the Bank of England in reality precedes the actual debits and credits to the RTGS CREST settlement accounts, but takes effect on the creation of the relevant debits, and because the undertaking is irrevocable and is given by the Bank of England (ie the UK central bank), the transferor in effect receives, in return for the transfer of legal title to securities, an enhanced claim against its settlement bank. This is because although it still has a claim against its settlement bank, such settlement bank now takes the credit risk of the Bank of England rather than credit risk on the transferee or its settlement bank. Consequently, the transferor is not exposed to the insolvency of the transferee or the transferee's settlement bank (although is still exposed to the insolvency of its own settlement bank). The Bank of England will make sure funds are available from each RTGS settlement bank to meet its obligations for CREST payments, and will earmark funds on the relevant settlement bank accounts (so that the settlement bank cannot remove such funds) in advance, but the undertaking from the Bank of England is 'entered into unconditionally and absolutely, and is not constrained to the value of funds earmarked' (CREST Reference Manual, ch 6).

New agreements were put in place between settlement banks and CREST (and between the Bank of England and the settlement banks) in relation to the RTGS payment process and the linking of CREST and RTGS systems, as well as consequential changes to the general CREST Terms and Conditions and CREST Manual.

Because settlement depends on the availability to the settlement bank of funds at the Bank of England, it is essential that settlement banks ensure they have sufficient funds or collateral with the Bank of England. Settlement banks can generate additional liquidity by transferring assets to the Bank of England under a repo transaction. In certain cases, the assets used for the repo can be the assets being purchased by the relevant CREST member in a 'self-collateralisation' procedure, where such CREST member enters into a repo with the settlement bank and the settlement bank uses the assets transferred under such repo to enter into a repo with the Bank of England on a back to back basis. The repo will be unwound when such assets are then sold on by the purchaser, as the CREST system will trigger a redelivery of the stock by the Bank of England and a simultaneous repayment to the Bank of England by the relevant settlement bank. In such cases, the repo is created and unwound automatically by CREST[3].

The self-collateralisation facility is only available for certain types of securities. CREST members will need appropriate documentation in place with their settlement banks for this purpose. This facility is available only where the relevant securities are held by the CREST member as principal or the underlying owner has consented to use of the securities in this manner. In addition, self-collateralisation will only apply to sterling transactions over the minimum value specified by the Bank of England.

1 Since 26 November 2001.

2 It would be impossible for all CREST participants to have accounts with the Bank of England: hence the transfer of legal title through CREST cannot literally take place against transfer to the seller of central bank money, ie the payment obligation created is still that of a settlement bank, not the central bank. It is arguable that this is in some respects an advantage for CREST participants, since there is a choice of providers for settlement bank services.

3 In a purchase of securities involving self-collateralisation, there is a transfer on the CREST accounts of the securities from seller to purchaser, and the creation of an obligation on the purchaser's settlement bank to make payment to the seller's settlement bank. The purchased securities will be transferred under a repo from the purchaser to its settlement bank, and the settlement bank makes a payment to the purchaser. The settlement bank in turn transfers the securities to the Bank of England and the Bank of England provides payment under the repo to the settlement bank by enabling the settlement bank to make payment to the seller's settlement bank. All such repos will be automatically unwound at the end of the day if they have not been unwound earlier when the relevant securities are sold or used as collateral in a DBV (delivery-by-value) arrangement. In a transfer of securities (for a sale or DBV) where the securities have been used in a self-collateralisation repo as described above, CREST will identify the transactions which require the stock and automatically return the securities to the relevant CREST member by procuring a redelivery by the Bank of England to the settlement bank, redelivery by the settlement bank to the CREST member, and delivery by the CREST member to the relevant purchaser, at the same time as repayment under the repo by the settlement bank to the Bank of England, repayment by the CREST member to the settlement bank, and payment (by debit and credit of CREST cash memorandum accounts) from the purchaser to the seller.

ASSURED PAYMENTS SYSTEM

9.8 CREST offers an assured payment system through the use of settlement banks. This system used to apply to all three currencies used for payments in CREST, but is now only relevant to payments in US dollars. The RTGS mechanism for payments in sterling or euro is discussed below. Every CREST participant is required to have appointed a settlement bank as a condition of admission into CREST[1] and must confirm this in the CREST Application Form. When book entry settlement takes place within CREST, the settlement bank of the transferee becomes irrevocably and unconditionally obliged to pay the purchase price to the settlement bank of the transferor[2].

The assured payment system was introduced because '... it was judged essential to have a payments system that would provide assurance of payment ...'[3] However, the system does not eliminate credit risk for the seller of securities. It merely replaces the credit risk of the buyer of securities with that of both the settlement bank of the buyer and the settlement bank of the seller[4].

The creation of the assured payment obligation (when the respective CMAs are debited and credited) discharges any payment obligation of the transferee. Inter-settlement bank payments are made through the CHAPS system outside CREST[5]. Payments between settlement banks and the CREST participants for whom they act are settled outside CREST as a commercial matter (usually by the operation of bank accounts associated with the relevant CMAs).

Under the assured payments system, settlement banks are exposed to each other's credit risk intra-day (but this is not the case under the real time gross settlement mechanism)[6]. Settlement banks may take charges over clients' assets within CREST: see paras **9.18–9.25**[7].

1 CREST Reference Manual, ch 6, Section 1.

2 The assured payments obligation is contained in the settlement bank agreement entered into bilaterally by each settlement bank and CRESTCo and also in the assured payments agreement entered into multilaterally by CRESTCo and all the settlement banks. New settlement banks are bound by the terms of the assured payments agreement under a deed of adherence. The assured payment obligation of the settlement bank is calculated by reference to the cash memorandum account of the member for which it acts, in which the payment obligations referable to the member's purchases are recorded.

> 'Each member will have a Cash Memorandum Account (CMA) which records all his payment obligations arising from receipts and sales. The CMA balance will also reflect cash movements not directly related to the transfer of securities, for example receipts of dividends paid through CREST. The balance (if negative) shows his use of intra-day credit . . . Each member will have one (or more) "real" bank accounts outside CREST to which the bank will post the member's final end of day cash position in CREST (ie the balance on his CMA) . . .' (Intra-day Credit and Caps in CREST, April 1995).

3 Gilt edged settlement. Phase 2 of the CGO Service, Bank of England Quarterly Bulletin, February 1987. (The CREST assured payments system was modelled on that used by the CGO.)

4 This assumes that the buyer's settlement bank does not agree to accept the risk of non-payment by the seller's settlement bank (such acceptance would be unusual). The arrangement is for the buyer's settlement bank to pay the seller's settlement bank, and for the seller's settlement bank in turn to pay the seller. If any link in this chain fails, the seller will not be paid. The seller's settlement bank's duty to pay is limited to sums it actually receives. The Bank has no obligation to stand behind a defaulting settlement bank. Moreover, if a settlement bank itself suffers loss due to the failure of another settlement bank, the member may be liable under an indemnity given by the member in the assured payment facility agreement (see s 4(1) and Sch 3, para (b) of the CREST Assured Payment Facility Agreement).

5 Inter-settlement bank obligations are discharged by net payments across accounts at the Bank of England: see Bank of England *CREST: The Business Description*, December 1994, p 49. While in practice settlement is on a multilateral net basis, the arrangements escape the rule in *British Eagle* [1975] 2 All ER 390 (broadly that contractual netting arrangements that purported to vary statutory insolvency netting are not effective) because the contractual payment obligations are calculated on a bilateral net basis, in accordance with r 4.90 of the Insolvency Rules 1986. These arrangements are akin to those in the CMO (and as used in the old CGO).

6 In the absence of RTGS, settlement banks can limit their exposures to their client members (under debit caps: see below) but not to each other. It is understood that the banks demanded a link to RTGS as a condition of acting as CREST settlement banks; in view of operational difficulties of providing this from the outset, CREST could only agree to offer RTGS as soon as practicable.

7 CGO settlement bank charges were protected under Pt VII of the Companies Act 1989 (as brought into effect by SI 1991/488 and SI 1991/878 and as modified by SI 1991/880 (the Financial Markets and Insolvency Regulations 1991)). Very broadly, this privileges such charges as 'market charges' by disapplying provisions of the Insolvency Act 1986 which would otherwise affect the effectiveness and enforceability of the charges in the administration or receivership of the chargor. (By way of background, it is understood that when the CGO was being set up, the settlement banks were uneasy with the limited liability involved in the assured payments system, and that this unease grew when the Insolvency Act 1986 restricted the value of a floating charge where the chargor goes into administration. In the circumstances, the banks desired the support of Pt VII as a quid pro quo for these exposures.) The equivalent protection for CREST settlement bank charges (referred to as 'system charges') appears in The Financial Markets and Insolvency Regulations 1996 (SI 1996/1469), as amended by the CREST Regulations (to reflect the changes from the 1995 Regulations). As with the old CGO arrangements, protections include (broadly) disapplication of restrictions on enforcement of security interests in the chargor's administration, the power of an administrator to deal with charged property and avoidance of property disposition.

DELIVERY VERSUS PAYMENT

9.9 CREST offers delivery versus payment or DVP[1]. In all forms of DVP, a settlement event is synchronised with a payment event. However, the important question is the exact nature of the settlement event and payment event. If the settlement event is not the passing of legal title but the passing of an equitable interest with legal title to follow, there is a risk that final settlement may not actually occur, for example if the transferor is insolvent. It is true that under the CREST procedure for requiring updating of the register within two hours of transfer across CREST accounts (see para **9.4**), there is less time for insolvency to arise and prevent registration, but it is nevertheless a potential issue. This issue does not arise where securities are subject to full electronic transfer of title as discussed above (see para **9.5**), such that legal title is transferred by debit to one CREST account and credit to another. (It should nevertheless be noted that a transfer can still be reversed in certain circumstances, for example where fraud is involved, and by operation of Insolvency Act 1986, s 88 and s 127.) Under the assured payment mechanism, the undertaking to pay by a buyer's settlement bank is irrevocable, but the transferor is still exposed to the credit risk of such settlement bank, or indeed its own settlement bank, and may not receive payment if either the buyer's settlement bank, or its own settlement bank, becomes insolvent[2].

1 See further discussion of DVP in Chapter 8.
2 Under the RTGS mechanism, exposure to the insolvency of another CREST member's settlement bank is removed, but exposure to the CREST member's own settlement bank still remains.

Regulation

CRESTCO

9.10 CRESTCo is regulated as a recognised clearing house ('RCH'[1]) by the Financial Services Authority (the 'FSA')[2]. In addition CRESTCo has been approved and is subject to supervision by the FSA as operator of CREST in accordance with the CREST Regulations[3] and, in respect of any non-clearing activities, is an exempt person for the purposes of the Financial Services and Markets Act 2000 ('FSMA')[4].

CRESTCo will not assist with the observance of US regulatory holding restrictions, but does have procedures regarding settlement discipline[5].

Custodians should monitor this exposure and ensure they have adequate indemnities in their customer documentation.

1 For the purposes of s 285 of the Financial Services and Markets Act 2000 ('FSMA').
2 Such recognition was necessary in order to settle Stock Exchange transactions. As a recognised investment exchange for the purposes of FSA 1986, s 36 the Stock Exchange is required under Sch 4, para 2(4) to clear transactions either itself or through an RCH.
3 Under Pt 2.
4 Under the Financial Services Act 1986 (Exemption) Order 1996 (SI 1996/1587), as amended by the CREST Regulations.
5 See CREST Rule 6, and CREST white booklet 'Settlement Discipline overview', April 2002.

CREST PARTICIPANTS

9.11 In general, participation in CREST does not of itself necessitate authorisation under FSMA. However, certain CREST members may require authorisation where they are providing sponsor or custody services:

- Persons acting as CREST sponsors (see the sections on custody accounts below) require authorisation for the purposes of FSMA[1].

- Irrespective of CREST, CREST members acting as custodians require authorisation to provide custody services for the purposes of FSMA[2].

1 See The Financial Services and Markets Act 2000 (Regulated Activities) Order 2001 (SI 2001/544), art 45.
2 See Chapter 7 in relation to regulatory issues for custodians.

SDRT

9.12 Stamp duty reserve tax, rather than stamp duty, is likely to be primarily the issue on a transfer of dematerialised chargeable securities within CREST[1].

1 Unless of course the transfer is itself exempt or zero rated. The following are indicative of CREST's approach to these issues (but see further in Chapter 10 in relation to the Inland Revenue approach):

> 'CREST incorporates functionality to allow stamp duty due to the UK or Irish tax authorities to be collected on transfers of chargeable securities occurring as the result of settlements in the system . . . CREST collects . . . SDRT on behalf of the UK authorities . . . from the purchaser (or his agent) on all transfers in CREST at the standard percentage rates of the stampable consideration . . . Certain securities (principally fixed-interest securities) are exempt from stamp duty. CREST will recognise these by means of exempt flags linked (by CREST) to their ISIN codes' (CREST Reference Manual, ch 8, Section 1).

> 'UK-registered securities held on behalf of exempt bodies such as charities should be held in one or more member accounts with an exempt member account tax status. Transfers into such accounts will be automatically exempted from duty. The Inland Revenue have stipulated that where two or more charities are pooled within a single member account, the designation of that account should begin "CH . . ." (where this is not possible for any reason, the member should notify the Inland Revenue). In addition, the Inland Revenue require the inclusion of charity reference numbers on the associated legs of transfers destined for charities, in particular where custodians acquire securities on behalf of charities' (CREST Reference Manual, ch 8, Section 2).

Custody accounts

9.13 Three options are available to custodians. The custodian's name (or that of its nominee) may appear on the register of title without any particular client designation (pooled accounts), or with a particular client designation (designated accounts). Alternatively, the client's name (or that of its nominee) may appear on the register (sponsored membership)[1].

1 It should be noted that if the client's name is on the register of title, technically the sponsor is not acting as custodian for those securities, because it is not holding on behalf of the client (although it may be acting as custodian of other securities, and providing administrative assistance).

Pooled accounts

9.14 In many cases, the securities of more than one client will be pooled[1] in a single account maintained by a custodian CREST member. A single debit cap (see explanation in para **9.19**) will permit efficiencies in the use of credit[2]. In the absence of effective trust arrangements between the custodian and its client, pooling may pose certain risks concerning the beneficial title of clients. A further risk is that a shortfall attributable to the business of client 1 may be borne by client 2.

1 See Chapter 3 for discussion of pooling generally.
2 So that clients who are net sellers of securities on any day can fund clients who are net purchasers.

Designated accounts

9.15 Individual designation may be desired by clients to avoid the above risks, or by the custodian for tax planning[1]. This is permitted within the holding of a CREST member by the use of separate accounts. CREST notes these different accounts against the name of the member in the operator register[2]. Also, it is possible for one person to have more than one CREST membership. Such designation[3] is considerably less expensive to the member than equivalent designation in the old CGO or the CMO, and accordingly clients may expect it. Greater levels of designation may also make corporate actions easier to handle, reducing the incidence of fractional entitlements.

However, even where a custodial trust is effective as against the custodian member and its liquidator, it will not be effective against CRESTCo, which will not assist any custody client in claims against a custodian member[4].

1 For example, to segregate different securities attracting different rates of SDRT.
2 'A designation may be an alphanumeric but should not give any indication of the identity of any beneficial owner . . . Where a member . . . has more than one member account, each member account is reflected on the register (and, in the case of UK Securities, the issuer's record). Member accounts can therefore be used to segregate one type of holding from another . . .' (CREST Reference Manual, ch 2, Section 5).
3 It is unclear how such designations in the register of UK shares accord with Companies Act 1985, s 360, which provides that 'No notice of any trust . . . shall be entered on the register'. Related provisions are included in CREST Rule 7, Section 2.9.2. The correct view may be that such designations are ineffective against the issuer (so that it is not fixed with notice of custody trusts) but are effective against the liquidator of the custodian (so that it cannot make the custody assets available to creditors of the custodian on the basis that any custody trust fails for want of certainty of subject matter). Independently of CREST, it has long been customary for company registrars to note special designations on the register beside members' names.
4 CREST Regulation 23(3) provides that 'No notice of any trust, expressed, implied or constructive, shall be entered on an Operator register of securities, or a part of such register, or be receivable by an Operator'.

Sponsored membership[1]

9.16 Certain custody clients may wish to have their names on the register of the issuer in place of the custodian, and may therefore wish to be sponsored members of CREST[2]. Sponsored members have CREST accounts in their own names[3] and are therefore the registered holders of CREST securities. However, their sponsor (the custodian) will maintain the electronic links with CREST and operate their CREST accounts on their behalf[4]. The arrangement is comparable to the administration by a custodian of certificated securities registered in the client's name through the use of a power of attorney. It protects the client from the custodian's insolvency but not from its fraud[5].

Sponsored members must appoint their own settlement banks[6], and custodians may be expected to arrange for this banking facility and prepare the documentation as part of the custody package. With separate settlement bank arrangements, sponsored members have separate debit caps[7]. The use of different debit caps for different custody clients may have the benefit of shielding one client from settlement gridlock attributable to excess purchases by another client; a disadvantage is that netting between one client's purchases and another's sales will not be available for the purposes of calculating headroom[8].

Sponsored members may not wish to handle their own corporate actions. Even though the client's name is on the register, the issuer could be instructed to direct any mailings to the address of the custodian on the client's behalf. However, this may be inconvenient for the custodian, who will be required to respond to any election separately for each sponsored member, and not once for a global holding.

The role of sponsor involves certain risks. A sponsor is obliged[9] to notify CREST immediately upon becoming aware of the occurrence of events affecting the sponsored member's ability to transfer title to CREST securities, although it is not clear that it would know of such an event[10]. In addition, similar concerns about confidentiality and risk arise for the sponsor as for the custodian member (see paras **9.18–9.25**). The drafting of the commercial agreement between the sponsor and its sponsored member (the terms of which are left to the parties to decide) is of great importance in limiting the risk of the custodian sponsor.

1 See CREST Reference Manual, ch 2, Section 2.

2 In practice, the sponsor may be the client's broker rather than its custodian; sponsored membership may be particularly attractive to pension funds.

3 Sponsored members must enter into an agreement (the CREST Terms and Conditions (which apply equally to members and sponsored members) and the CREST admission agreement) with CRESTCo (as well as a settlement bank agreement, and a commercial agreement with the sponsor). Where the sponsored member is a nominee, it may instead enter into a sponsored member (nominee) admission agreement (together with the CREST Terms and Conditions) which differs from the normal sponsored membership arrangements principally in that the CREST Terms and Conditions require undertakings and warranties to be given by the nominee's parent.

4 In CREST terminology, the sponsored member is a participant and the sponsor is a user.

5 Fraud risk may be reduced by specifying daily withdrawal limits.

6 Bank of England *CREST: The Business Description*, December 1994, indicates (at p 31) that 'A sponsored member will often be able to grant a charge over his assets in CREST for the benefit of the [settlement] bank, which should ensure that he will normally have no difficulty in obtaining an adequate amount of intra-day credit for his account to be operated within CREST.' However, it may not be able to give such a charge if it is itself subject to fiduciary or regulatory restrictions (eg if it is a pension trustee or insurance company).

7 In the case of private investors becoming sponsored members of CREST through their brokers, a zero debit cap is envisaged, on the basis that purchases are settled initially into the broker's CREST account, and then (after the client has put the broker in funds outside CREST) transferred free into the client's CREST account. See Bank of England *Sponsored Membership of Crest for the Private Investor*, April 1995, pp 9, 10, and CREST guidelines for personal members.

This approach may also be adopted by custodians, who may operate a settlement account with an adequate debit cap for the initial settlement of client trades, and then (following payment outside CREST) transfer securities nil paid to clients' sponsored member's accounts. This enables the custodian to concentrate credit in one account and keep control of the banking side of settlement.

8 See further discussion of debit caps and headroom at para **9.19**. It may not be feasible for custodians to take the alternative approach of deferring the settlement of the initial purchase until they are put in funds by clients, for the following reason. In settlement, the giver of both cash and securities can specify the priority of the trade and this will determine the order in which it is settled. A zero priority on securities will in effect freeze the transfer of securities until the priority is lifted. However, on the cash side of any transaction, at the end of the settlement day a zero priority is automatically raised. Thus, the securities side of a transaction can be frozen, but the cash side cannot. Therefore a custodian wishing to defer a purchase until it is put in funds by its client faces the problem that it is committed to the purchase as soon as the trade is matched. (The automatic raising of zero priorities on cash transfers was introduced in response to market consultation.)

Custodians may even be willing to transfer free to a sponsored member's account in advance of payment outside CREST, as they may be in a position to freeze securities in that account in exercise of any lien taken in their commercial documentation with the sponsored member (the sponsor's agreement does not require the sponsor to agree with CRESTCo that it will obey all instructions from the sponsored member). The same may be true for designated accounts.

9 Under section 8 of the sponsor's agreement.

10 The provision is included on the basis that it might. 'The obligations placed on the sponsored member to notify the Operator of anything which might give rise to a risk of a bad delivery or of any insolvency, is repeated in the Sponsor's Agreement, given that the sponsor may often be the first to learn of his client's situation' (Bank of England CREST Membership Agreements, July 1995, p 7).

Visibility

9.17 Concern has been expressed[1] at the extent of intermediation of the holdings of private investors and the consequent lack of 'shareholder visibility', ie the ability of issuers readily to identify investors in their shares[2].

While rapid rolling settlement may encourage the use of nominees, it has been argued that sponsored membership offsets this, and '. . . any net losses of visibility will be small'[3]. It should also be noted that in some cases there are commercial and practical arguments as to why lack of visibility can be useful; some clients of custodians may have legitimate and compelling reasons to wish to be invisible[4]. However, there has been growth in the use of personal membership (either directly or through sponsored membership) of CREST which, because of the fact that CREST is not a system based on immobilisation, means such persons are 'visible' as holders of securities.

1 By, among others, ProShare, a lobby group for small investors.
2 The development of CREST prompted a much-aired concern about loss of shareholder visibility, or the ability of issuers to identify investors by reference to the register. While investigation of beneficial ownership is possible under Companies Act 1985, s 212, this procedure is cumbersome. Ready identification of investors is more important to issuers in the UK than on the continent, because of the higher UK incidence of hostile takeovers. On the other hand, there is also concern about how the ultimate beneficial owner of shares can influence the exercise of the rights represented by the shares which it holds through a chain of intermediaries. This has been the subject of some attention in the White Paper 'Modernising Company Law' published July 2002 and the earlier steering group report 'Modern Company Law for a Competitive Economy: Final Report' published July 2001. The 2001 Report made various proposals, including increasing the rights of proxies at meetings of public companies, enabling a company to recognise the rights of persons other than the registered holder (including the right of such person to appoint a proxy), and making provision for secondary legislation which could require companies to recognise the rights of persons other than the registered holder of shares. However, the draft Companies Bill published 16 July 2002 currently only contains expansion of proxy powers but not any provision regarding the rights of beneficial owners. According to the 2002 White Paper, 'The Government is considering the practicality of' the proposed creation of a requirement for companies to recognise rights of persons other than the registered holder of shares. Recognition of such rights would of course raise additional issues, such as the questions of how to deal with conflicting instructions, and the evidence of beneficial interest which could be relied upon by the company receiving instructions.
3 Bank of England *CREST: The Business Description*, December 1994, p 93.
4 For example, high net worth individuals may wish to keep the extent of their wealth confidential for security reasons, and holders of shares in companies in sensitive areas may need to avoid pressure group action.

Risk

Credit

9.18 Credit may be a major risk issue for a custodian providing services in CREST, both in terms of the need to ensure sufficient credit or headroom is available promptly to settle clients' trades, and the need to control credit exposures to clients.

As a general point, if the settlement bank of a purchaser defaults, neither CRESTCo nor the vendor's settlement bank is obliged to make good the loss to the vendor[1]. Custodians should make it clear in the client documentation that, in the event of settlement bank default, they are not obliged to make good any shortfall, and that their only obligation is to account for sums actually received[2].

1 Section 5.2.1 of the CREST Terms and Conditions in effect excludes any duty on CRESTCo in relation to the risk of the default of other CREST members or settlement banks.
2 Where inter-settlement bank payments are made on a net basis, allocating cash shortfalls to particular clients may be a complex matter. It is not necessarily the case that shortfalls can be allocated pro rata between clients.

HEADROOM

9.19 Through the payment mechanisms, the settlement bank of a purchaser of securities will assume personal liability for the payment of the purchase price. The CGO settlement banks were generally collateralised (where the participant owned the securities in its account) by taking security over the assets within the CGO system. Generally, CREST securities can be charged in the same way[1], permitting collateralised capped assured payments ('CCAP')[2]. However, because of the significant legal difficulties which arise where custodians seek to charge assets beneficially owned by their clients, CCAP may not be available to custodians[3].

Settlement banks may control their CREST exposures by imposing debit caps, ie limits on the volumes of net purchases they will permit a participant to settle on any day[4]. Such caps are not the norm in settlement systems, and raise certain concerns[5]. A member is in practice free to delay the settlement of a purchase by ensuring that it has insufficient headroom to settle it. Moreover, the possibility of gridlock must be present. At times of volume surge (following privatisations or in market crashes) such caps might lead to the very settlement backlogs that, in the mid-80s, prompted the search for a better settlement system[6]. CREST does not monitor the exhaustion or withdrawal of credit caps; where headroom is exhausted, back-ups will simply occur, prompting members to seek to resolve the problem amongst themselves (although its document 'Settlement Discipline' indicates that CRESTCo may monitor and enforce timely settlement). Because of the interdependencies of settlement credit and the fact that CRESTCo does not regulate the matter, the ability of the system to function depends on each member taking a responsible approach.

Custodians must also consider the risk that heavy buying by one client may affect its ability to settle purchases for another client[7].

1 CREST provides facilities for the maintenance of margin, ie the monitoring of the value of securities charged as collateral in relation to a settlement bank's exposures.

2 See CREST Reference Manual, ch 6, Section 3.

3 Briefly, the custodian is not empowered to charge the assets without the consent of the client. Under the rule *nemo dat quod non habet* (none can give that which it does not own), where a security interest is purportedly given without the consent of the beneficial owner of the charged assets, the chargee may have a valid security interest if it can show that it acted as bona fide purchaser of the legal estate for value without notice of the lack of consent. A chargee can be treated as a purchaser for this purpose, but only if it takes a legal security interest. A charge is always equitable, so that the settlement banks cannot be protected by this doctrine, and will always be vulnerable if the true owners did not consent to the charge. For example, the client may not be free to give such authority because of fiduciary, regulatory or constitutional restraints on it, particularly if it is an insurance company or a pension fund. In addition, where the assets of more than one client are held together in one CREST account, the granting of a charge would result in one client's assets being used to secure exposures referable to the business of another client. It is hard to envisage authority properly being given for a charge to be granted in such circumstances.

4 'Every member must have at least one cap. Each cap is set by only one settlement bank and relates to only one member. The same cap can cover a number of CMAs [cash memorandum accounts within CREST] in different designated currencies and payment types belonging to the same member, provided that the same settlement bank is associated with each CMA and has specified the base currency of that cap . . . The cap allows a settlement bank to control the amount of intra-day credit available to a member. The cap represents the maximum cumulative net debit position on his CMA(s) that a member can run during the settlement day. A zero cap is possible' (CREST Reference Manual, ch 6, Section 3).

'Transactions which would cause a member's total net payments to exceed his cap (credit limit) will be queued until sufficient sales have settled to create headroom under the limit. "Circles" processing will help to resolve potential gridlock' (*The Business Description*, p 17). For a discussion of circles, see CREST Reference Manual, ch 5, Section 6.

'CREST will ensure that the cap is not breached. Banks may be willing to provide more credit if the customer can provide more collateral . . . Those with inadequate credit will be more likely to have settlement delays and fails . . .' (Intra-day Credit and Caps in CREST, April 1995).

The ability to alter debit caps is frozen while the circles process is operating: CREST Reference Manual, ch 6, Section 3.

5 See Bank for International Settlement *Cross-Border Securities Settlement*, Basle, March 1995, pp 18, 19.

6 On the other hand, it might be argued that the problem is not peculiar to CREST, as insufficient credit within a market will always impede settlement in practice. A CREST publication, 'Intra-day Credit and Caps in CREST', April 1995, takes a positive view, indicating that 'The normal cap does not have to be large enough to cope with an exceptional intra-day credit need. A member and his bank can agree and rapidly implement a temporary increase in the cap, in advance or during the day, to allow an exceptional trade to settle. The "circles" process will settle dependent deliveries. This may reduce the need for intra-day credit for CREST members who aim to end each day more or less flat.'

7 Unless the custodian opens separate designated client accounts and negotiates separate debit caps for them, all clients will share the same cap (see the CREST Reference Manual, ch 6, Section 3). Custodians may wish to address this in the custody agreement by imposing volume limits on clients, and making express disclosures about the possibility of delays.

CREDIT EXPOSURES TO CLIENTS

9.20 Outside CREST, credit arrangements with clients may be undocumented, with informal overdrafts arising in the course of settlement[1] and credit limits being unadvised to clients. However, the involvement of settlement banks and debit caps in CREST precludes such an informal approach. Where custodians operate pooled accounts, they cannot rely on the debit cap effectively to control credit exposures to *particular* clients[2]. Internal credit controls, based on the custodian's own books and not merely on the pooled accounts of CREST, will be necessary.

However, provided custody documentation grants custodians effective security interests over their clients' securities, these exposures may be effectively collateralised by virtue of DVP within CREST.

1 The custodian might simply pay the purchase price on behalf of its clients and then seek to be put in funds to the extent of any overdraft.

2 This is because where client A is a net buyer and other clients are net sellers, an overall debit cap will not prevent client A in effect buying securities with the proceeds of the other clients' sales, nor relieve the custodian from the obligation of repaying to the other clients those proceeds of sale.

Bad deliveries and fraudulent transfers

9.21 It is not suggested that dematerialisation increases fraud or bad deliveries. Paper based fraud has occurred in the City, and CREST arguably provides a more secure environment. However, the custodian and its clients should note the types of CREST transfers that are permitted to fail by the CREST system, as well as the types that are allowed to proceed.

BAD DELIVERIES[1]

9.22 For UK Securities other than those subject to the electronic transfer of title arrangements described at para **9.5**, the major protection against bad deliveries in CREST is the fact that the transfer between CREST account transfers legal title or that legal title will be granted within two hours of the transfer across CREST accounts[2] and, in the case of electronic transfer, the two-hour risk window no longer exists. A further protection is that securities being dematerialised and transferred into CREST will not be credited to a member account until registered[3]. However, the risk cannot be excluded that some CREST settled trades will not proceed to registration, for example where the securities in question are affected by a court order[4] or insolvency[5]. Note that the Bank of England will not stand behind a transferee's rights in relation to gilts[6], and the Bank of England has the right to reject any transfer unless it is furnished with such evidence as it may require of the transferor's right to make the transfer (Government Stock Regulations 1965 (SI 1965/1420, as amended by the CREST Regulations), reg 5). CREST Regulation 28 contemplates and permits bad deliveries, in the sense that the general requirement of participating issuers to register book entry transfers is disapplied in certain circumstances.

Where custody client A purchases securities, it may expect to be able to sell them immediately they are credited to the custodian's CREST account. If electronic transfer of title does not apply, such sale may occur in advance of registration. The risk is therefore present that if the first transfer fails after A has on-sold the securities, a shortfall will arise[7]. If the account also contains the securities of clients B, C and D, these clients bear A's shortfall (in effect, the custodian has lent the securities of B, C and D to A). In order to avoid breach of duty to its clients, the custodian should disclose these risks to B, C and D[8]. It should also consider collateralising the exposure to A.

Custodians face further risk (in relation to bad stock held for their clients) under the CREST Terms and Conditions, which provide[9] in effect that CREST may take action to seek to avert a bad delivery at the risk of the member and with the benefit of an indemnity from the member.

1 '. . . a transfer of title from one member's uncertificated holding to another member's uncertificated holding which cannot be effected on the register in response to an RUR' (CREST Rule 12). Note that this cannot apply to securities where the entity on the member's CREST account itself constitutes title to the securities. In CREST Rule 12 it is stated that the bad delivery rule 'applies to securities which have been admitted to CREST pursuant to the Irish Regulations, Isle of Man Regulations or the Jersey Order and to CREST Guernsey securities, as defined in CREST Rule 8. It may also (at CRESTCo's discretion) be applied to securities admitted to CREST pursuant to the UK Regulations if it were to become necessary to rectify an Operator register of securities.'

2 CREST also seeks to reduce the risk of bad deliveries by providing (in CREST Rule 7, Section 2.9) that the constitutional documents of issuers of CREST eligible securities must not permit notice of trusts to be entered on the register. This is presumably intended to reduce tracing claims by reducing notice of beneficial interests.

3 *The Business Description*, p 61.

4 That is, a charging order, stop order or stop notice.

5 CREST Regulation 31(8) states that the provisions of CREST Regulation 31 do not take effect to confer a proprietary interest if to do so 'would otherwise be void by or under an enactment or rule of law'. (Arguably, this was necessary because s 207(4) of the Companies Act 1989 provides (broadly) that regulations to be made under s 207 shall leave unchanged 'so far as practicable' rights and obligations in relation to uncertificated securities.) It should be noted that no direct financial criteria are imposed on CREST members in order to reduce the risk of member insolvency. 'In principle, anyone can be a member of CREST . . . CREST will not itself impose a criterion of, or tests for, financial soundness on potential members' (*The Business Description*, pp 8, 14). It may be that the obligation to appoint a settlement bank will operate indirectly to exclude bad credit risks from membership. In any case 'CRESTCo does not owe the Member any duty in relation to the admission of any person as a system-member . . .' (CREST Terms and Conditions, Section 5.2.1).

6 In such circumstances the Bank is protected from liability by provision in reg 3 of the Stock Transfer (Gilt-edged Securities) (CGO Service) Regulations 1985 (SI 1985/1144) as amended, that a CGO credit is not a representation that the member has title to the securities.

7 A potential source of bad deliveries is the indication in the note to CREST Rule 7, Section 2.4 that securities which are not freely transferable may be admitted to CREST in exceptional circumstances. 'In such cases CRESTCo does not supervise compliance with the limitations', so non-compliant transfers (possibly subject to reversal by court order or even ineffective under the articles of the issuer) will be permitted. The CREST Terms and Conditions seek to limit risk by requiring the member to warrant, represent and undertake that it will not bring into CREST any securities if it is aware of any defect in its title (Section 9.1.2). If the member becomes aware of a stop notice or court order, or if other circumstances occur that might affect the member's ability to transfer securities through CREST it is required immediately to notify CREST under Section 15 of the CREST Terms and Conditions. There will be a shortfall if A's account does not contain additional securities sufficient to absorb the debit.

8 In practice, the custodian would look to A immediately to eliminate the shortfall and, if A failed to do so, would buy securities in the market to make good the account, looking to A to repay the

purchase price, but the issue is that there is a risk that A is insolvent and therefore cannot make good the shortfall. It should be noted that the current FSA Rules try to draw attention to this type of problem arising in relation to the pooled assets, by requiring custodians to tell clients if assets will be held on a pooled basis, and to warn private clients of what this means.

9 In Section 14.2.

FRAUDULENT TRANSFERS

9.23 The dematerialisation of forged securities should not give rise to bad deliveries because securities are not credited to CREST accounts until registered in the name of the CREST transferee[1]. In the case of UK Securities, following the delivery of a dematerialisation notice, the issuer is required to delete the relevant entry from the issuer register of securities and CREST will subsequently enter the name of the relevant system-member on the relevant CREST account which constitutes the register of title for this purpose.

While the circumstances in which the CREST Regulations permit issuers to omit to register CREST transfers include (very broadly) notice of fraud against a participant or a sponsored member, and in the case of UK Securities CREST may refuse to register for similar reasons[2], the relevant circumstances do not include notice of fraud against an indirect beneficial owner of CREST securities. There is no protection for frauds outside the system. The difficulty with this is that the system reduces the issuer's ability to respond to such fraud. Even if an issuer's registrar had actual notice of such a fraud against a custody client, it would apparently have to register the fraudulent transfer or, if UK Securities, would have no opportunity to notify CRESTCo not to register the transfer (subject to the possibility of obtaining a court order)[3]. Clients may therefore be particularly exposed to custodian fraud in such circumstances[4]. Equally, custodians bear the risk of fraudulent transfers affecting their client securities[5].

1 See para **9.22** in relation to absence of bad deliveries for UK Securities.

2 CREST Regulations 27(4)(d) and 35(5)(a)(i)–(iii).

3 While issuers could in effect escape liability for complying with their registration requirements in respect of instructions affected by fraud against the operator, a participant or a sponsored member under Regulation 29(4) and (7) of the CREST Regulations, this now does not apply to UK Securities but only securities where the CREST account does not constitute the record of title. Even in relation to non-UK Securities, the limitation of liability does not extend to circumstances where indirect beneficial owners are defrauded, and for UK Securities there is still the question of what liabilities may apply to the issuer in respect of the actions of CREST (see para **9.76**).

This may leave issuers exposed to claims from defrauded custody clients, where the issuer or CREST knowingly registered a fraudulent transfer because it was required to do so under the Regulations. (In practice it is perhaps less likely that CREST could be shown to have made such a transfer with knowledge of the relevant issue.)

Where an issuer has actual notice of such a fraud, it may decide to seek a court order against itself or CREST forbidding registration; CREST is required to refuse to register where prohibited by a court order under CREST Regulation 27(2)(a).

Rectification of registers in relation to uncertificated securities are only permitted, pursuant to a court order or with the consent of CRESTCo. CREST Rule 11, Section 4 indicates that consent will not be given where, after consultation, any affected member objects to the proposed rectification. This consultation process can take five business days in accordance with CREST Rule 11, Section 6.

CREST Regulation 36 imposes certain compensation obligations on the operator of CREST for losses in certain circumstances, but these are limited to £50,000 for 'each such forged dematerialised instruction, induced amendment to an Operator register of securities or induced Operator instruction' (CREST Regulation 36(6)) and do not affect the liability of any other person for losses associated with CREST (CREST Regulation 36(8)).

4 Where they become aware of such a fraud, their only option may be to seek a court order to prevent registration; this may be difficult if little time is available. Unless compelled by a court order, no assistance may be available from CREST, as it is not bound by notice of any trusts and need therefore not recognise the rights of custody clients: CREST Regulation 40(3).

5 Section 9.1.1 of the CREST Terms and Conditions requires the member to represent (broadly) that any form of transfer presented by it bringing stock into and out of CREST will be validly executed. Where such transfers are executed by clients or third parties, the custodian may not be in a position to confirm this.

UNSCRAMBLING BAD DELIVERIES

9.24 CREST Rule 12 makes provision for the unscrambling of bad deliveries[1]. Depending on the circumstances, bad deliveries will be (a) reversed, (b) replaced or (c) addressed by tracing:

(a) Reversals: broadly speaking, where sufficient securities remain in the account of the transferee, CREST will reverse the bad delivery at the price for which it was made[2]. Reversals raise the following exposures in relation to the return of the purchase price. Reversal is dependent on the availability of sufficient 'headroom' in the cash memorandum account of the original transferor, which is placed under an absolute obligation to increase this if necessary[3]. This raises concerns for the custodian. If transfers through CREST from the custodian's clients fail, the custodian may be absolutely required to obtain additional credit and therefore unable to resist commercially unreasonable terms from its settlement bank. Even where the custodian acts as its own settlement bank, the CREST Rules may require it to return the purchase price even if its clients have spent it, exposing it to their credit. If transfers through CREST to the custodian's clients fail, the custodian's ability to recover the purchase price for its clients will depend on the debit caps of the transferor[4].

In cases where the original purchase price cannot be determined[5] CRESTCo seeks to unscramble the securities side of the transaction without assisting the transferee in getting its money back[6]. This may expose the custodian to other CREST members, unless this credit risk can be transferred to the custodian's clients by provision in the custody agreement.

(b) Replacement: in cases where insufficient securities remain in the transferee's account to reverse the book entry, 'The Original Transferor shall procure the free delivery (if necessary from a third party) to the Original Transferee of the relevant amount of registrable securities within two hours of being notified by CRESTCo of the bad delivery'[7]. Custodians may need to consider their operational ability to comply with the strict time limits, and may wish to take express indemnities from their clients in respect of this exposure.

(c) Tracing: the above techniques depend in some measure on participant co-operation and therefore may fail to resolve the bad delivery[8]. In these cases, tracing may be necessary for the following reasons. Where A transfers securities to B through CREST, B may also transfer those securities to C before the first transfer is registered (other than where electronic transfer of title applies) or rejected by the registrar and hence the potential arises for the 'domino effect', considered in CREST Rule 12, Section 2.2.2[9]. CREST securities are fungible[10] and there is therefore a need for rules for allocating bad deliveries across accounts, akin to the equitable tracing rules. CREST Rule 12, Section 7 specifies a tracing methodology[11].

A member who was not the source of the bad stock may be required to make good the shortfall, if the burden is allocated to it. While this measure of systemic risk may be inevitable in any clearing system, custodians may wish to ensure that it is borne, not by them, but by their clients, through adequate disclosure in the custody agreement[12].

1 Bad deliveries are CREST transfers that do not proceed to registration: see discussion at para **9.22**.
2 CREST Rule 12, Section 1.3.2.

3 CREST Rule 12, Section 8.3.1.
4 Custodians should consider expressly disclosing this risk to clients.
5 The original price would only be undeterminable in rare cases involving 'complex deliveries', eg corporate actions involving the transfer of more than one parcel of stock against a cash payment. In such cases, it may not be possible to determine how much of the cash was attributable to a particular parcel of stock.
6 CREST Rule 12, Sections 4 and 6.
7 CREST Rule 12, Sections 5.3 and 6.4.
8 For example, CREST Rule 12, Sections 5.3 and 6.4. contractually require the original bad transferor to provide replacement stock. As the major source of bad deliveries may be transferor insolvency, new securities may not be forthcoming under these Rules when they are needed.
9 See also CREST Rule 12, Sections 5.2 and 6.2.
10 CREST Rule 7, Section 2.7: 'All units of the security must be in all respects identical . . .' and Section 2.8: 'The units of the security must not be numbered or otherwise identifiable individually'.
11 Based on transaction order and size. It represents a departure from normal equitable tracing Rules.
12 CREST Rule 12, Sections 5.4 and 6.4. require CRESTCo, if new securities are not forthcoming from the original 'bad transferor' within two hours, to notify 'the members affected' of the bad delivery 'so as to enable them to make such applications (whether to the court or otherwise) as they think fit'.

Custody agreements

9.25 Should custodians offering services through CREST include specific drafting in their custody agreements? In the old CGO membership agreement, a CGO participant holding assets on behalf of another was required to obtain from its client an acknowledgment and authority in a prescribed form[1]. Because of the operational difficulty in obtaining the positive consent of existing clients to new terms, custodians usually prefer to minimise the introduction of new provisions for existing customers[2]. It may be possible effectively to bind existing customers with new provisions concerning CREST by unilateral notice in cases where the notice of new provisions is given to the client before the custodian begins providing services in CREST[3].

In any case, new drafting is recommended for custodians for a number of reasons. First, the custodian owes duties of confidentiality to its clients both as banker and as fiduciary. General law relieves these duties of confidentiality where there is a legal duty of disclosure. However, many of the disclosure provisions in the CREST agreements binding the custodian member are wider than this. Therefore, in order for the custodian not to be in breach of its duties of confidentiality to its clients, its disclosure obligations under the CREST agreements should be drawn to clients' attention, and their consent obtained in the custody agreement.

Second, special risks associated with CREST (and discussed in this section) should be disclosed to clients, and their consent to them obtained, in order to protect the custodian from liability for client losses attributable to such risks. While the CREST Regulations relieve trustee participants from liability associated with the absence of DVP within CREST[4], other CREST risks may involve the custodian in liability to clients suffering loss in consequence of them. A custodian's ability to recover any damages from CRESTCo is extremely limited by provision in the CREST Terms and Conditions[5]. Special provision in the custody agreement would be appropriate to protect the custodian from liability to its clients in connection with the use of CREST.

In addition, specific drafting is arguably necessary in order to discharge a custodian's contractual obligations to CRESTCo. The CREST Terms and Conditions require[6] the custodian member (broadly) to obtain the consent of clients to aspects of CREST that may affect the clients[7]. The better way of complying is to give express disclosure of relevant risks and to obtain a signed acknowledgment and consent to such risks. In addition, the CREST Terms and Conditions oblige the custodian 'so far as it is able' to prevent clients making adverse claims against transferred securities so as to prevent registration[8]. It is not clear how this can be achieved otherwise than by express contractual provision binding clients.

As all members (including custodians) are obliged to indemnify CRESTCo in respect of (broadly) the member's CREST business[9], a corresponding indemnity should be taken by the custodian from the client. This indemnity should also expressly cover the liability of the custodian member to make good any shortfalls in CREST accounts[10] and the potential liability of the custodian associated with its warranty that all CREST transfers it settles can take place free of third party claims[11]. In addition, custodians should consider whether their collateral arrangements are sufficient in view of the personal liabilities they may bear as CREST members. Where custodians access CREST through nominees (ie the nominee rather than the custodian is the CREST member), care should be taken to ensure that any indemnities and collateral arrangements provided to the custodian also cover liabilities of the nominee.

1 See para **9.77**.
2 The original draft Membership Agreement (July 1995) prescribed specific wording which custodian members were to be required to include in their custody agreements (adopting the approach of the CGO and the CMO). Custodian institutions resisted this obligation and wished to be able to confine themselves to writing to clients in relation to CREST without obtaining client responses. Also, it might be hoped to rely on clients' general consent in existing documentation to the custodian using clearing systems on the terms of those systems. However, this approach is not recommended for the reasons discussed below. (It is interesting to note that following the merger of the CGO into CREST, it was not uncommon for custodians to require clients to sign up to a new copy of the wording formerly required for CGO purposes but this time referring to *all* securities transferred through CREST, rather than only the instruments formerly held through the CGO, even though technically such wording is no longer required.)
3 On the basis that services provided through CREST are a new addition not envisaged in existing documentation, and that the client, by permitting the custodian to use CREST on the disclosed basis, has accepted the new terms by conduct. However, this question must be considered on a case by case basis.
4 For non-UK Securities and USD assured payment: CREST Regulation 40.
5 See Sections 2.1.2, 5.1.2, 5.2.1–5.2.6, 6.5, 6.6, 7.2–7.6, 8.1, 8.2, 11.1, 12.2, 12.3, 13.3, 14.2, 16.5, 17.1–17.14. As indicated above, CREST Regulation 36 provides for compensation orders to be made against CRESTCo in relation to (broadly) fraudulent CREST instructions, but limitations on the quantum of compensation (GBP50,000 maximum) and the circumstances in which it is available reduce the value of this provision.
6 CREST Terms and Conditions, Section 5.2.6.
7 Enforcing the commercial argument that such provision is necessary to protect the custodian.
8 CREST Terms and Conditions, Section 10.1.2. Since this may be clients' only effective recourse in the case of fraud, it may be hard to obtain their consent to such provision in the custody documentation. The custodian's obligation to CREST is not limited by reasonableness, and (where custody clients have suffered fraud) may cut across the custodian's commercial relationship with its clients.
9 CREST Terms and Conditions, Section 17.11.
10 CREST Terms and Conditions, Section 11.1.2.
11 CREST Terms and Conditions, Section 10.1.1.

Cross-border issues

9.26 As discussed in Chapter 5, it is a general rule of private international law that formalities necessary for the transfer of assets are determined by the law of the place where the assets are situated (*lex situs*). Lex situs of registered securities is generally the law of the jurisdiction in which the principal register is located[1]. Because a UK statutory instrument cannot alter foreign law, the CREST Regulations cannot dematerialise foreign securities.

One method of bringing foreign securities into CREST is to seek local legislation achieving the same result as the CREST Regulations, as discussed below. A pragmatic alternative is to turn foreign securities into UK securities, by repackaging them under English law depositary receipt ('DR') programmes[2]. The taxation of DRs in CREST is an important issue[3].

1 See Chapter 5.
2 Special provisions relating to DRs are included in CREST Rule 9, requiring inter alia the maintenance of a register in the UK, Ireland, Isle of Man or Jersey, as appropriate. Alternatives to DRs are Depositary Interest ('DI') programmes (similar to the CREST CDI structure described at para **9.27**, but involving the relevant registrar as issuer of the DIs) or use of ETF (exchange-traded fund) structures.
3 See Chapter 10.

International securities[1]

9.27 At the time of writing, the only securities which are eligible for transfer through CREST are registered securities constituted under the laws of England and Wales, Scotland or Northern Ireland, the Republic of Ireland, the Isle of Man, Jersey or Guernsey[2]. This is because relevant legislation has been enacted in each case[3]. Securities created under other legal systems can be transferred through CREST if repackaged as securities constituted under appropriate law[4], or if held through CREST by use of the links between CREST and other settlement systems[5].

Securities which would not otherwise be eligible for transfer through CREST may be held by a CREST member through CREST if the relevant securities can be held in a settlement system with which CREST has a link. The precise details of settlement through links with other systems (including the types of securities which can be transferred via the link, and whether transfers can only occur free of payment) will depend on the nature of the relevant linked system and the way the link has been set up. Broadly speaking, the arrangements for the acquisition of an international security by a CREST member from a counterparty who is not a CREST member operate as follows[6].

The international securities are transferred into the account of the relevant CREST nominee[7] in the other settlement system, and the nominee holds its rights to such securities on behalf of CREST Depository Limited. CREST Depository Limited issues dematerialised depository interests (CDIs) representing its interest in the underlying securities. CDIs are securities constituted by a Deed Poll governed by English law and are eligible for holding and transfer in CREST. The relevant CREST member's holding of CDIs is recorded in such CREST member's CREST account, which constitutes the register of title for such CDIs.

In each such case, the relevant CREST nominee or its sub-custodian will hold assets in the settlement system subject to such system's terms of participation. If the CREST nominee is using a sub-custodian, the nominee will be subject to the relevant terms on which the sub-custodian holds assets in the settlement system on behalf of the CREST nominee. The CREST nominee holds its rights to assets under an English law trust for CREST Depository Limited, and CREST Depository Limited issues the CDIs, and holds the relevant rights against the CREST nominee on trust, subject to an English law trust as described in the Global Deed Poll.

Generally, CDIs are only issued in uncertificated form, are not treated as different from the underlying securities for the purposes of listing, and have the same ISIN (as well as size and price) as the underlying securities.

Where participants in a linked settlement system wish to hold CREST-eligible securities, such securities can be transferred from the relevant transferring CREST member into the CREST account of the settlement system, and such system will then hold those securities for the participant in such system subject to its usual terms[8].

1 For further details see the CREST White Book, 'The International Legal Framework', July 2001, and the section of the CREST Manual entitled 'CREST International Manual').
2 See para **9.1**, n 4, for the Irish Regulations, the Isle of Man Regulations and the Jersey Order.
3 Except for Guernsey. See para **9.1**, n 4.
4 For example, an English law depositary receipt established in accordance with The Uncertificated Securities Regulations 2001. See CREST Rule 9.
5 At the time of writing such links exist with the following central securities depositories: SIS SEGAIntersettle AG ('SIS') in Switzerland, the Depository Trust Company in the US, and Euroclear Bank in Belgium. These arrangements allow CREST members to hold and settle securities issued under the laws of the following countries (although in certain cases only in restricted circumstances). Austria, Belgium, Canada, Denmark, Finland, France, Germany, Greece, Italy, Luxembourg, the Netherlands, Norway, Portugal, Spain, Sweden, Switzerland and the US. Many of these jurisdictions are available as a result of the sub-custodian network of SIS. CREST also has links with Nederlands Centraal Instituut Voor Giraal Effectenverkeer BV, 'NECIGEF' (now part of Euroclear), the Värdepapperscentralen VPC AB ('VPC') in Sweden, and SIS, which allow CREST members to deliver and receive certain CREST securities to and from participants in these settlement systems.
6 Further details can be found on the CREST website: see in particular the CREST International Manual and the International Service Description.
7 CREST International Nominees Limited or CIN (Belgium) Limited (these entities and CREST Depository Limited are wholly owned subsidiaries of CRESTCo).
8 NECIGEF, VPC and SIS only.

Collateral and securities lending

9.28 An important use of CREST eligible securities (whether shares or other securities, including public sector securities such as gilts) is to serve as collateral, whether for securities lending or for other exposures. The involvement of custodians in collateral arrangements is discussed in Chapter 4.

CREST securities may serve as collateral in a variety of ways, both under arrangements within and outside the CREST system. However, in all cases it is important to appreciate that CREST does not create security interests (or outright collateral transfers); it merely facilitates delivery for the purposes of creation of security interests (although certain functions are designed particularly to facilitate creation of security interests, such as arrangements for escrow balances, securities lending and repos, and DBVs, as discussed below). Any security interest (or outright collateral transfer) in CREST securities must be created by documentation[1] between the parties.

1 Or, in some circumstances, by operation of law.

Security interests

9.29 As discussed in Chapter 4, a wide range of security interests are available under English law, varying in the degrees of formality involved and the robustness of the protection given to the security holder.

LEGAL MORTGAGES (CREST TRANSFERS)

9.30 Under a legal mortgage, legal title to assets is transferred by way of security, with the mortgagor retaining only the equity of redemption (ie the right to have the assets back free from the security interest upon the discharge of the secured obligations).

SDRT does not arise in respect of a legal mortgage effected by a delivery through CREST, but fixed rate stamp duty of £5 will be payable in connection with the procedure required[1].

1 'The Inland Revenue have explained that a "transfer by way of security for a loan" can be executed through the CREST system using flag 5 provided the transfer is accompanied by a letter of direction which is duly stamped with £5 fixed duty. CREST transaction flag 5 applies to this and certain other transfers on which stamp duty at a fixed rate would apply to transfers in materialised form' (CREST Reference Manual, ch 8, Section 2, penultimate paragraph of 'Data flags' sub-section). (See further discussion at para **10.23**.)

EQUITABLE MORTGAGE (ESCROW BALANCE)

9.31 Prior to CREST, much of the security that was given over English equities was by way of an equitable charge, which arose upon the deposit with the chargee of share certificates and signed but undated transfer forms. With dematerialisation in CREST, this is not possible, and a need arises for the functional equivalent of an equitable mortgage of shares, ie a rapid and informal method of using shares as security which does not involve re-registering them.

This is offered by the escrow balance, an arrangement which involves blocking securities in a sub-account of the security giver's account, where they are subject to the order of the security taker[1]. Mortgagors are subject to the fraud risk of mortgagees who improperly dispose of the mortgaged securities, within CREST as outside it. The movement of securities to an escrow balance does not appear on the register of the issuer.

The crucial question is whether the interest of the security taker over securities in the escrow balance would be enforceable in the insolvency of the security giver. Broadly speaking, it will if the interest is proprietary, and will not if it is merely contractual[2]. Placing of securities in the escrow balance of itself probably does not confer a property interest in the escrow agent[3]. It is therefore important to document any security interest using the escrow balance carefully, to ensure that a proprietary security interest is conferred.

A further issue arises in the insolvency of the CREST member granting security over its assets. In such case, there will normally be an automatic freezing of CREST accounts imposed by CRESTCo, in which case the chargee will be unable to exercise its control over the escrow balance until the relevant liquidator has been appointed and taken control of the insolvent entity's CREST accounts. This could present significant problems for a chargee who needs to enforce quickly[4].

The CREST Terms and Conditions (see Section 12) place responsibility on the custodian member for the suitability and adequate use of the escrow balance. In practice, this may mean ensuring that no client fails to take effective security through the escrow balance. This is a very wide responsibility, in view of the possibility that the collateral agent's interest may be merely contractual.

An obvious limitation of the escrow balance is that CREST securities can only be encumbered in this way in favour of CREST participants. The corollary is an opportunity for CREST participants to act as security agent for non-CREST lenders who wish to take security over dematerialised securities.

1 See CREST Reference Manual, ch 7, Section 3. CREST refers to the mortgagee as an 'escrow agent'. (Note that escrow accounts are also used for other functions, such as processing corporate actions).
2 Because of the restriction in Insolvency Act 1986, s 127 on dispositions of a company's property after the commencement of winding up.
3 The escrow balance is also used for corporate actions, in which case no property is conferred.
4 But see special procedure for settlement bank taking security: CREST Reference Manual, ch 6, Section 7.

CHARGES

9.32 CREST members (and their clients) are free to charge their interests in CREST members' accounts in the ordinary way (subject to any negative pledge given to a settlement bank to support a settlement bank charge). If charged securities remain in the chargor's account, a floating charge may be created; floating charges created by UK corporates are registrable[1].

1 Under Companies Act 1985, s 395.

PLEDGES

9.33 A pledge involves the transfer of possession of a tangible asset, and therefore cannot be given in respect of shares, which are intangible. Although share certificates were capable of pledge, with dematerialisation, the pledge is irrelevant for dematerialised securities.

Securities lending and repos[1]

9.34 Provisions are available in CREST to facilitate the use of dematerialised securities in securities lending or repo transactions as loaned securities or securities collateral[2].

1 See CREST white paper 'A guide to stock lending and collateral transfers in CREST', October 2000 (note this pre-dates the creation of the Global Master Securities Lending Agreement 2000).

2 'While CRESTCo believes that the functionality has been designed to be consistent with the principles of the Global Master Securities Lending Agreement (2000), CREST does not monitor or enforce compliance with the terms of that or any other agreement or with any other applicable regulatory or other requirement . . . Stock lending functionality may also be used in the context of a sale and repurchase agreement ("repo") executed, ordinarily, pursuant to the terms of the TBMA/ISMA Global Master Repurchase Agreement. As with stock loans, CRESTCo does not monitor compliance with the terms of this agreement' (CREST Reference Manual, ch 7, Section 1: chapter 7 uses the term 'stock loan' to refer to both repos and securities lending transactions.) CREST facilitates the settlement of bilateral securities lending (or repo) arrangements entered into (independently of CREST) between participants. This contrasts with securities lending (or repo) arrangements in Euroclear and Clearstream, where the clearers are involved in arranging securities lending programs between participants.

CASH COLLATERAL

9.35 Where securities are transferred within CREST by way of a stock loan, and the transfer is made against payment within CREST, the payment obligation constitutes the cash collateral.

Where CREST transfers are identified as stock loans, special facilities are available to handle automatic redeliveries[1] and the margining of cash collateral[2].

1 While there is no need for the lender to give instructions for the return, the automatic return instruction is given zero priority so that the borrower will need to intervene to lift the priority to permit settlement. (See CREST Reference Manual, ch 7, Section 1.)

2 Reference Manual, ch 7. In CREST these margin adjustments are automatically made through the payments system.

SECURITIES COLLATERAL: DELIVERY BY VALUE (DBV)

9.36 Where CREST securities are to be delivered as collateral[1], automatic collateral selection is available by using the delivery by value (DBV) facility. A member may instruct CREST to transfer securities from its account by way of collateral to another member's account. The aggregate value of the collateral to be delivered is specified, but not the individual securities, and the CREST system selects the securities to be delivered[2]. Where CREST securities are provided by a DBV, the securities are registered in the name of the collateral taker[3].

DBV securities are automatically 'redelivered'[4] in the next business day[5]. New DBV collateral must be put up by the borrower daily; the amount of daily DBV collateral will need to be adjusted to reflect the margining requirements of the securities lending arrangement.

It may be operationally convenient to have a separate DBV account, although this is not necessary[6].

1 In practice, a sequential combination of cash and securities collateral may be used, as follows. Following a request from a borrower for securities, a broker may obtain the securities from a lending institution. The securities will be transferred from the account of the lender to that of the broker, and then on into the account of the borrower. In respect of each of these transfers, the payment obligation of the transferee will serve as cash collateral. During the currency of the loan, the borrower may wish to use the cash that has been provided by way of collateral to the broker. The brokers may be willing to release this money against the provision of further collateral. Outside CREST, this further collateral may be provided in the form of Stock Exchange short-term certificates or other securities. Within CREST, it may be provided by DBV (the assured payment for the DBV constituting the return of the cash). DBV is only provided once daily towards the end of the settlement process. Intra-day, borrowers may rely on cash collateral. Towards the end of the day, the borrower can recover the cash by substituting securities through DBV.

2 Although the parties must specify the DBV Class (the category of securities to be included in the DBV, for example FTSE 100, FTSE 250, all British Government Securities, Eurotop 300, US Securities, etc), and each DBV will exclusively relate to one category; also, DBVs may optionally be subject to a 10 per cent concentration restriction and DBV takers may exclude certain securities which they are prevented from holding. See the CREST Reference Manual, ch 7, Section 2.

3 This was not the case in the CGO but was introduced with the original two-hour registration time frame in CREST (as opposed to the old three-day cycle in the CGO). Moreover, whereas transfer of title in CGO was based on contract, the basis of transfer of title in CREST is statutory (CREST Regulation 24) and (unlike in the old CGO) linked to registration.

The collateral taker is exempted from the requirements of the Companies Act 1985 relating to the disclosure of interests in shares by the Disclosure of Interests in Shares (Amendment) Regulations 1996.

4 Strictly, the 'redelivery' is not of the same securities but of equivalent securities; DBV securities are delivered outright and not by way of security.

5 Unless countermanding instructions are given by the collateral taker wishing to enforce the collateral.

6 It might be argued that the placing of DBV securities in a special account exposes the arrangement to the risk of recharacterisation as a charge (which might in turn be void for want of registration) as opposed to an outright transfer. However, provided there is no obligation on the DBV recipient to use a special account, and no restriction on its freedom to take the securities out of that account or to block their 'redelivery', this should not be a problem, as it does not imply any retained property in the DBV securities by their provider by way of a charge.

Corporate actions[1]

9.37 CREST may be used to execute corporate actions[2]. Whether or not to use this functionality is the choice of the issuer and its agent, but where companies do choose to make use of the CREST facilities, CRESTCo requires that the relevant specified procedures should be followed in order to achieve a standard approach in the CREST system. Corporate action details provided by the issuers or their agents are held in the CREST system and a range of special transaction types are available for use in corporate actions[3]. However, compliance with the terms of a stock event (for example, deadlines for acceptance) is not the responsibility of, and not monitored or enforced by, CRESTCo.

For further details see CREST Reference Manual ch 7, Section 4.

1 See CREST Reference Manual, Section 4.

2 It was here that TAURUS came to grief, and it has been argued that the need to handle complex stock

events (together with stamp duty) has deterred the continental European clearers from competing for the settlement of UK equities.

3 These are: complex deliveries, unmatched stock events, registrar's adjustment, transfers to escrow, transfers from escrow and escrow account adjustment.

Central counterparty

9.38 The central counterparty arrangements were launched on 26 February 2001 and concern trades by members of the London Stock Exchange on SETS (the London Stock Exchange electronic order book)[1]. A trade on SETS, once registered by the London Clearing House ('LCH') as a matched trade, automatically constitutes an agreement by the relevant parties to make a sale or purchase, as the case may be, of the relevant securities with LCH as the counterparty, on the basis that settlement will take place through CREST between the CREST accounts of the LCH and the CREST accounts of the selling and purchasing parties (or their custodians or nominees). LCH becomes the central counterparty to the SETS trades when the parties execute the trades (rather than replacing one party by novation of an existing contract), and the trade information is automatically transferred into CREST which then creates the settlement instructions (rather than waiting for separate input of matched instructions by LCH and the relevant CREST members). CREST members using this service are able to access through CREST on an ongoing basis information such as details of open positions, margin, historical prices and securities eligible for this service.

Since LCH has exposure as principal to the counterparties to the trades, LCH requires such counterparties to provide collateral (both initial margin and variation margin) in accordance with the relevant LCH terms.

Initially, the central counterparty settlement service operated on the basis that the trades settled on an 'as dealt' or 'gross' basis, but in due course the option of settlement netting was introduced[2].

1 The CREST system already provides settlement generally for trades on the London Stock Exchange, the Irish Stock Exchange and virt-x. A new initiative has also been announced by LCH, virt-x and x-clear (the Swiss clearing house) which is to be launched in March 2003, whereby trades on virt-x may be cleared by x-clear or LCH, and settled through Euroclear, CREST or SIS SEGAIntersettle, at the option of the transaction parties.

2 Optional settlement netting launched 1 July 2002.

Gilts

9.39 The paperless settlement of gilt-edged securities[1] takes place through CREST in essentially the same way as other CREST-eligible securities, removing the need for stock certificates and stock transfer forms necessary to evidence and transfer gilts outside CREST. Outside CREST written instruments are required for the transfer of government stock[2]. Dematerialisation is based on the Stock Transfer (Gilt-Edged Securities) (CGO Service) Regulations 1985, SI 1985/1144 ('the 1985 Regulations') made under the Stock Transfer Act 1982, as amended, although holding and transfer are subject to the CREST Regulations.

Gilts are registered debt securities, denominated in sterling, issued by the Bank of England on behalf of the UK government. Market liquidity is provided by gilt-edged market-makers ('GEMMs') who continuously quote two-way prices for gilts. GEMMs deal with each other electronically on a no-names basis through inter-dealer brokers. For a discussion of stock lending and repos in the gilts market, see below[3].

Ninety per cent of gilts are held in dematerialised form. CREST's payments systems provides for the payment of the cash consideration for transfers through settlement banks. Dividends are paid outside CREST to registered holders. Although all gilts are eligible for CREST settlement, investors may elect to hold their gilts in certificated form[4] unless, as discussed earlier, pursuant to the CREST Regulations the relevant instruments have been issued in wholly dematerialised form[5].

1 The UK registered securities of the European Bank for Reconstruction and Development can also be settled in CREST (under SI 1991/340).
2 The Government Stock Regulations 1965 (SI 1965/1420), as amended by the CREST Regulations, permit government stock to be transferred either by written instrument according to the Stock Transfer Act 1963, or through a system operated pursuant to the CREST Regulations.
3 Formerly, dematerialised gilts settled through the Central Gilts Office (the 'CGO'), an electronic system established in 1986 as a joint initiative by the Bank and the London Stock Exchange, then operated by CRESTCo in 1999 and finally merged into CREST with effect from 3 July 2000, although the Bank continues to maintain a register for all gilts (whether held in paper form or through CREST). See CREST Regulation 21.
4 Unless issued on a wholly dematerialised basis, certificated gilts may be dematerialised in CREST, and uncertificated gilts may be recertificated.
5 Gilt strips are wholly dematerialised; it is understood that HMT intends that in due course gilts should all be issued on a wholly dematerialised basis.

Transfer of title

9.40 Transfer of legal title and payments in relation to gilts are handled by the CREST system in the same way as other CREST eligible securities. (See paras **9.5–9.9**.) Although the register of title is now constituted by the relevant CREST account records, the corresponding record of register entries is still maintained by the Bank[1].

1 CREST Regulation 21(3).

Stamp duty and SDRT

9.41 Transfers of gilts (within and outside CREST) are exempt from stamp duty and SDRT[1].

1 See further para **10.6** for the exemption from stamp duty for transfers of gilts, and para **10.21** with respect to SDRT.

Gilt title finance (stock lending and repos)

RESTRICTED AND FREE MARKET

9.42 Until January 1996 the rules of the London Stock Exchange prohibited gilt repos and restricted gilt stock lending to GEMMs[1] and Stock Exchange Money Brokers (SEMBs) serving GEMMs[2]. The purpose of permitted borrowing was limited to the filling of a short position.

In January 1994 the Bank developed arrangements for supplying liquidity in the banking system through the use of gilt repos between the Bank and market counterparties[3].

On 2 January 1996 an open gilt stock lending and repo market was introduced by changes in the Stock Exchange rules[4]. GEMMs continue to be obliged to quote continuous two-way prices on gilts, but now any market participant is free to engage in stock lending or repos of gilts with any counterparty for any purpose.

1 And discount houses for stock up to seven years' maturity.
2 GEMMs incur short positions in the course of their market making. To cover these short positions, they must borrow stock. Until January 1996, they were only permitted to borrow from SEMBs who in turn borrow stock from Inland Revenue approved institutional lenders. The restrictions meant in effect that only GEMMs could go short in gilts, and that therefore only they could make a market in gilts.
3 Back-to-back repos between the Bank's counterparties and other gilt holders were also permitted.
4 The ability to borrow gilts ceased to be confined to GEMMs; the permitted purpose of borrowing ceased to be limited to covering a short position and gilt repo transactions were permitted.

STOCK LENDING

9.43 The former restriction of gilt stock lending to GEMMs and SEMBs has now been relaxed, and the role of SEMBs has dropped away[1]. However, GEMMs continue to dominate gilt stock lending.

The borrowed stock is transferred in each case through CREST. Certain institutional lenders may prefer to hold securities to cash for investment and risk management reasons[2]. They therefore often require alternative collateral in the form of DBVs. In addition, GEMMs may have surplus gilts but not surplus cash, preferring to 'borrow back' the cash collateral and substitute gilts through the DBV system. A DBV against payment provides for the return of the cash collateral.

As DBVs are automatically returned on the next business day, it is necessary to 'roll over' or redeliver DBVs on a daily basis during the currency of the loan.

1 The Stock Exchange Rules no longer refer to this category and the CREST Reference Manual does not. The firms that used to make it up are seeking a wider intermediary role, while many participants in gilt stock lending enter into their transactions direct, without using intermediaries.
2 In the past, certain institutional lenders faced tax problems with cash collateral, but these are largely historic.

REPOS

9.44 Certain enhancements to the old CGO system were introduced to assist the new repo market. The Bank issued a gilt repo code of best practice for use by market participants[1].

1 Current version is August 1998.

Unit Trusts/OEICs

9.45 Since April 1999, CREST has provided facilities in relation to the issuance and redemption of units in unit trusts and OEICs, where the product provider and the relevant holder of units are both CREST members (if either party is not a CREST member, these CREST facilities are not available). The CREST Courier and Sorting Service processes paperwork, and instructions and payments can be transmitted through CREST and its assured payments system. At present units in OEICs and unit trusts are not eligible for transfer through CREST (although in contrast exchange traded funds can take the benefit of dematerialised settlement in CREST).

Moving towards a dematerialised securities market[1]

9.46 A working party involving CREST and certain broker and registrar entities has taken the analysis of electronic registration of title one step further by considering how it may be possible to reduce still further the role of paper in the holding[2] and transfer of shares, and the processing of dividends, rights issues and takeover acceptances[3]. Consideration is given to the fact that any proposed solution could not be complex or impose high costs on shareholders. One theory is that shareholders holding shares outside CREST already bear higher costs than CREST members because brokers will charge more for processing a transfer using share certificates and stock transfer forms. In addition shareholders should be able to retain legal title rather than being required to become a CREST member or to use some form of intermediary.

The working party's principal ideas are that all UK or Irish nominees and all CREST members should have to hold and transfer CREST eligible securities through CREST, and that share certificates should either be replaced with 'share statements' where the shares can then transferred by using a stock transfer form or giving a specific reference number or a broker (or registrar) to transfer the shares (or record a transfer), or that a central entity should maintain records of all shareholders and transfers would be made in its records.

In the case of the 'share statement' proposal, a shareholder would have its name on the register of title but would have the option to have no share certificate but instead a Shareholder Reference Number allocated by the registrar for each shareholding. The Shareholder Reference Number would be given by the shareholder to its broker when instructing the broker to transfer all or part of the shareholding to which such Shareholder Reference Number relates. A new Shareholder Reference Number would be allocated once the shares had been transferred on the register of title. The intention is that a transfer could be made simply by providing the Shareholder Reference Number or, if preferred, by producing a signed Stock Transfer Form together with the Shareholder Reference Number. The broker would send an instruction to the registrar through CREST to update the register, and the register would move the relevant shares to the broker's clearance account in CREST for the broker to make onward delivery to the relevant transferee (the broker is thus making a deposit of the relevant securities into CREST by using the Shareholder Reference Number rather than a stock transfer form and share certificate).

Given the significance of the Shareholder Reference Number in this structure, it is extremely important to consider what security measures would be taken to ensure that the Shareholder Reference Number provided by the registrar is only obtained by the relevant shareholder, and that when such information is provided to the broker it is not misused by the broker. In order to meet security concerns, the alternative proposal was made of a central entity which would issue security numbers for all shareholders, but this would require considerably more infrastructure to support this approach. In either case, legislative change would be required, and it is unclear in practice whether shareholders would be willing to accept such changes of approach.

1 CREST consultation document, produced July 2001

2 Broadly, large numbers of shareholders hold shares in certificated form although such shares constitute a small proportion of the value of shares and are not traded very often ('around 85% of UK issued share capital is held by shareholders in secure dematerialised form within the CREST system' but of an estimated 'over 10 million shareholders in the UK and over 25 million shareholdings . . . around 90% are retail and certificated' and 'these shareholders only account for 15% of the market value' (CREST consultation document, July 2001).

3 However, it was also noted that the issues involved are 'complex and political and to propose a single mandatory solution . . . [is] . . . unrealistic', and that 'Any new model(s) should be optional for investors, although such model(s) might lay the foundations for a future move by Government to mandatory dematerialisation.' It is useful to bear in mind that The Uncertificated Securities (Amendment) Regulations 2000 introduced the provision stating that it was not necessary for a relevant system (eg CREST) to enable system participants to convert uncertificated securities into certificated securities if the terms of issue of such securities provide that such securities 'may only be held in uncertificated form and title to them may only be transferred by means of a relevant system'.

Conclusions

9.47 The legal aspects of CREST were drafted with a light hand. An early consultative paper stated, 'the government wishes to rely as far as practicable on the existing legal framework affecting shareholdings'. The deliverable was not law reform, but an effective settlement system. One result of this approach is that key legal aspects of the system were left to the contractual provisions to be developed between different players involved in CREST. For custodians, the negotiation of sponsorship and custody agreements, together with the terms of settlement bank facilities, is of primary importance. Another important point is that the CREST system was not intended to provide solutions to all possible issues from the outset, but by starting with a fairly simple model with which the market was familiar, it has been possible to develop additional functions over time with appropriate consultation with CREST participants, leading to significant developments such as electronic transfer of title, the RTGS payments arrangements and the proposed electronic proxy voting[1].

1 Intended to go live in January 2003.

The Central Moneymarkets Office

Introduction

9.48 The Central Moneymarkets Office ('the CMO') is a depositary and electronic settlement system for sterling money market bearer securities such as bills and certificates of deposit[1]. As will be discussed below, because of the different nature of the instruments held and settled through the CMO, the structure and operational procedures of the CMO are considerably different from CREST (and the old CGO) where securities are in registered form. The CMO was designed to facilitate rapid issuance and transfer of short term bearer negotiable debt instruments, typically traded over the counter for same day settlement, and used for short term funding and investment, and developed from the idea of depositing physical instruments with the CMO as depositary[2].

Lodging of issues into the CMO is done by the appropriate issuer or its agent, rather than controlled centrally by the system (as in CREST).

The CMO was originally operated by the Bank of England ('the Bank')[3] but is now operated by CRESTCo, although any physical securities held in the CMO are still immobilised in a vault at the Bank which acts as Depository for the CMO service.

As with CREST, securities are transferred between CMO members electronically by debiting the account of the transferor and crediting the account of the transferee[4]. Associated payment instructions are notified daily to members' settlement banks for payment. Unlike CREST the CMO does not operate an assured payments system (see further discussion below).

The CMO has facilities for the automatic presentation of matured securities to CMO member issuers[5], and CMO securities may be withdrawn from the CMO and subsequently relodged[6].

1 The CMO Service allows settlement of the following types of sterling and euro money market instrument: Treasury Bill, Local Authority Bill, Eligible Bank Bill (defined in the Glossary of the CMO Reference Manual as 'A bank bill accepted by a bank whose acceptances are eligible for discount at the Bank of England.'), Ineligible Bank Bill, Trade Bill, Bank Certificate of Deposit, Building Society Certificate of Deposit and Commercial Paper (CMO Reference Manual, Section A, 3.1).

All instruments held in the CMO must be payable at maturity by a CMO member or at the office of a CMO member and where the liability arises under an acceptance, the acceptance must be general (in accordance with s 19 of the Bills of Exchange Act 1882) (CMO Reference Manual, Section F.1.2).

2 But see paras **9.58–9.61** in relation to subsequent dematerialisation

3 The CMO was launched by the Bank in 1990 following a failure by market participants to establish their own system, and was transferred to CRESTCo in September 1999.

4 A transfer between CMO members operates in the following broad stages: (a) transfer instructions (the transferor gives instructions for the transfer via its CMO terminal); (b) transferee acceptance (the transferee gives instructions for acceptance of the transfer via its CMO terminal); and (c) book entry (the securities are debited from the transferor's CMO account and credited to the transferee's CMO account). These stages correspond with the first three stages of a transfer within CREST. However, unlike the CMO transfer, a CREST movement transfers legal title because the CREST account is in effect the register of title. There is no equivalent to this in the CMO, as CMO securities are bearer and not registered, but in practice transfer across a CMO account of a dematerialised instrument achieves a similar result.

5 CMO Reference Manual, Section A.3.7.

6 CMO Reference Manual, Section I.2.24.

Core legal structure

Possession

9.49 While the operational provisions of the CMO and CREST are similar, their legal structures are fundamentally different. In contrast with CREST, the proprietary aspects of the CMO have no statutory basis and rest on general law concepts derived from common law possession. This reflects the fact that the securities represented in CMO accounts are tangible instruments[1].

These concepts are bailment[2] and attornment[3]. The Bank in its capacity as Depository holds the instruments in the CMO as bailee for the participants to whose accounts they are credited[4]. The effect of a book entry transfer within the CMO is an attornment by the Bank to the transferee[5].

There are provisions for the use of CMO securities as collateral[6], and these are referred to in the CMO Reference Manual as involving a pledge. Pledge is the common law method of giving security by transfer of possession.

Dematerialisation affects the availability of these possession-based concepts (see below).

1 Except, of course, in the case of dematerialised securities (see below). CREST securities are registered and therefore intangible.

2 Bailment is a common law relationship of safekeeping based on the transfer of physical possession of a tangible asset.

3 Attornment is an undertaking whereby a bailee acknowledges that it holds property for a third party.

4 CMO Reference Manual, Section H.1.2, Section K.2.5. See also form of Deed Poll as set out in Section H (entered into by the Bank of England on 20 September 1999 (the date CRESTCo took over operation of the CMO from the Bank of England) to constitute the Bank as bailee of the CMO instruments in its possession).

5 See form of Deed Poll (Clause 2.1); also CMO Reference Manual Section I.5.3, and Section R.3.11.

6 See paras **9.62–9.67**.

Negotiability

9.50 The secondary markets in bearer securities have traditionally benefited from the doctrine of negotiability. As discussed in Chapter 2, a negotiable instrument has two attractive features. First, it is transferable without formalities. Second, honest acquisition confers good title (even if the transferor did not have good title), ie the holder in due course takes free from prior equities and defects in the title of the transferor.

Instruments held within the CMO are intended to be negotiable. There is no legal difficulty in characterising CMO transfers of physical securities as negotiations[1] but, as the CMO definition[2] suggests, dematerialisation affects the negotiable status of CMO instruments (see below).

1 Negotiation involves the delivery of an instrument by transfer of possession. The fact that CMO instruments are immobilised is not problematic, as possession for this purpose includes constructive possession; attornment is the transfer of constructive possession.
2 The Glossary to the CMO Reference Manual defines 'CMO Instrument' as 'A negotiable bearer instrument or a Dematerialised Instrument of a description for the time being specified in the CMO Manual as capable of being held or, as the case may be, created and issued within or into the CMO Service'.

Payments

9.51 As with CREST, each CMO member is required to appoint a settlement bank as a condition of membership. Electronic transfers of securities within the CMO automatically generate payment instructions to the settlement bank of the transferee member which instruct the bank to make a payment to the transferor's settlement bank equal to the purchase price. These payment instructions are synchronised with the change of ownership of the securities on book entry transfer. Payments are made between the settlement banks at the end of the day through the RTGS accounts at the Bank of England.

In contrast to the payments systems in CREST, payments in the CMO are not assured, and settlement banks can reverse payments[1]. In the event that payment is reversed, the associated transfer is not affected[2].

1 See CMO Rules, Section 4, 4.2, 4.3.
2 See CMO BIS/IOSCO disclosure information on the CREST website.

Custody accounts

Client documentation

9.52 Where the CMO member acts as custodian, the membership agreement requires it to obtain from its client an acknowledgment and authority in prescribed form[1]. Because of the special risks discussed below, ideally additional risk disclosure wording should also be included by the custodian in its custody terms, and specific risks to the custodian should be addressed with an express indemnity and possibly collateral arrangements.

1 See para **9.78**.

Segregation

9.53 While separate CMO accounts may be opened for individual custody clients, such arrangements are expensive. Moreover they may be unnecessary. This is because the CMO operates on an allocated basis. When instruments are lodged at the CMO, each is mechanically stamped with a distinctive number, which is quoted in every subsequent transfer and withdrawal of the instrument. The segregation of the assets of one client from another may be achieved without separate CMO accounts, provided the records of the custodian allocate particular securities to particular clients.

Recognition by the Bank/CRESTCo

9.54 The Bank and CRESTCo do not recognise any trusts[1], even in the case of designated nominee accounts[2].

1 CMO membership agreement. See also section F.1.5 of the CMO Reference Manual.
2 However, where the Bank and CRESTCo have actual notice of trusts (for example where a trust is indicated in an account title) there must be doubt as to the effectiveness of contractual provisions in the membership agreement in defeating the proprietary claims of third party beneficiaries. Some of this doubt may be addressed by the requirement in Section 7.15.1(b) of the CMO membership agreement, which overcomes the problem of privity by requiring the CMO custodian member to include in its custody agreement with clients an acknowledgment from the client that CRESTCo and the Bank do not generally recognise trusts; however, this would not of course address the risk of claims of beneficial owners other than the direct clients of the custodian. Similar concerns do not arise in CREST as the exclusion of notice of trusts has statutory backing.

Risk

Credit

9.55 There is no assured payment system in the CMO. Because settlement banks are able to revoke payment instructions (see above), the system does not offer true delivery versus payment.

Defects in title to securities

9.56 A major legal issue is the risk that securities held in the CMO may be forged, stolen or otherwise subject to adverse claims from third parties. A credit entry in a CMO account does not mean that the account holder has title to the relevant securities. Rather, it indicates that, whatever interest the Bank has in the securities by virtue of possession, it holds as bailee for the account holder[1]. In other words, CMO members and not the Bank (or CRESTCo) bear the risk of defects in title.

Certain provisions are included in the CMO documentation to reduce the risk of defects in title. If CRESTCo receives notice of adverse claims in respect of CMO securities it may freeze or withdraw those securities and if a member receives such notice it must inform the CMO system[2]. Further, there are restrictions on lodgement. Whereas any CGO member may bring stock into the system, securities may be lodged in the CMO only by the issuer (or acceptor) or their agent[3] because only they can guarantee the validity of the instruments[4]. (Accordingly, custodians wishing to settle transfers into the CMO will have to act as agent of the issuer or acceptor. This will in turn entail entering into a lodging agency agreement with the issuer, and executing a lodging agent's undertaking in favour of CRESTCo[5].)

However, some aspects of the system increase risk. Securities are credited to CMO accounts before they are lodged and checked[6], and there is provision for the lodging of non-security printed instruments[7]. In addition, exposure to adverse claims is possibly increased by the non-negotiable status of dematerialised securities (see below).

1 CMO Reference Manual, Section H.1.2; also Deed Poll, Section 2. A credit entry in a CMO account indicates a bailment (ie the relationship between the Bank and the member) but does not indicate title (ie the relationship between the member and the issuer of the securities).
In this respect the position of a CMO member is weaker than that of a CGO member; a credit balance in a CGO account constitutes a representation by the Bank that prima facie evidence of title in the member has been produced.
2 CMO membership agreement Section 4.4.2.

3 CMO Reference Manual, Section I.1.4.
4 Lodging members must replace any defective instruments lodged by them: see CMO Reference Manual, Section I.
5 CMO Reference Manual, Sections I.2.5 and I.2.6.
6 CMO Reference Manual, Section I.2.17 and I.2.22.
7 Such instruments must carry a statement in bold capitals on their face that 'This Certificate is valid only when stamped by Bank of England, as Depository for the CMO Service, with an identifier number' (CMO Reference Manual, section I.4.2).

Liability of custodians[1]

9.57 As indicated above, there may be significant risks associated with defects in title to securities within the CMO. The liability of the Bank for such risks is extremely limited[2].

In contrast, the liabilities of CMO members in relation to fraudulent securities are onerous. Lodging members[3] are obliged to make good any shortfall arising on the discovery of bad stock[4]. Moreover, any member (whether it introduces stock or not) must indemnify CRESTCo and the Bank in respect of any adverse claims to any CMO securities[5]. Custody members are required to indemnify the Bank and all other CMO members against adverse claims from their clients in respect of dematerialised securities[6]. Thus, where the CMO member is a custodian, it must (in effect) guarantee the validity of its customer's securities (and those of its nominees' customers)[7]. This may be a very significant exposure, and a custodian would normally wish to ensure that any indemnity or similar comfort provided by a client covered this exposure.

1 This section considers the liability of members acting as custodians. Significant liabilities are also imposed on members who act as lodging agents, including liability for fraud by or through customers. Both the lodging agent and the custodian are required to assume risks that they are unable to control. While it might be argued that the lodging agent who introduces bad paper into the system should properly bear the cost of it, it is less clear why a custodian should be exposed if its clients buy bad paper through it.
2 The Bank and CRESTCo exclude liability as a result of defective instruments in the CMO membership agreement. See also CMO Reference Manual, Sections I.2.4 and K.1.6 and the Deed Poll.
3 That is, members introducing stock into the CMO, such as custodians settling client transfers into the system. If defects in title cause loss to another CMO member, it may sue CRESTCo or the Bank. The Bank's liability is contractually extremely limited (see above). However, there may be some risk that the limitation provisions are ineffective. If so and if CRESTCo or the Bank suffers substantial liabilities, the indemnity in favour of CRESTCo and the Bank may represent an important exposure.
4 CMO Reference Manual, Section I.2.10.
5 CMO membership agreement. If defects in title cause loss to another CMO member, it may sue the Bank or CRESTCo.
6 See dematerialisation agreement.
7 Because a member is liable for its nominees (see above).

Dematerialisation

Generally

9.58 Since September 1994 it has been possible for sterling certificates of deposit to be issued into the CMO system in dematerialised form[1]. Dematerialised securities[2] may be withdrawn from the CMO; on withdrawal of a dematerialised security, the original lodging member is required to make available a security printed instrument at the CMO counter[3].

1 That is, without any paper instrument. See Section I.4.6 of the CMO Reference Manual. For example, according to the CREST newsletter for June 2001, approximately 90 per cent by value of instruments in the CMO were in dematerialised form.
2 The CMO uses the term 'dematerialised instrument'; however an instrument is necessarily physical.
3 CMO Reference Manual, Section K.2.3 and the deed of covenant (see below).

Documentation

9.59 As a precondition of CMO membership, all members must enter into a dematerialisation agreement[1]. In addition, a precondition of issuing dematerialised CMO securities is the execution by the issuing member of the CMO deed of covenant[2]. These documents ('the dematerialisation documentation') are drafted to provide that the dematerialisation does not affect the rights of CMO members to whose accounts dematerialised securities are credited ('holders')[3]. However, it is not clear that this objective is achieved for the following reasons.

1 An agreement for the dematerialisation of CMO instruments between the Bank and CMO members was executed in 1994, and was replaced by a similar agreement between CRESTCo and each CMO member when CRESTCo took over operation of the CMO. Persons becoming CMO members after the date of the agreement are bound by the terms of the dematerialisation agreement by an agreement of adherence, a form of which is scheduled to the dematerialisation agreement. The requirement to enter into the dematerialisation agreement as a condition of membership is referred to in Section B.1.5 of the CMO Reference Manual and the dematerialisation agreement.
2 See the dematerialisation agreement and CMO Reference Manual, Section I.4.6. This is a deed of covenant made in favour of the members for the time being of the CMO. The purpose of the deed of covenant is to evidence the rights of members to whose accounts dematerialised securities are credited.
3 See the dematerialisation agreement and the deed of covenant.

Negotiability

9.60 Physical instruments held in the CMO are regarded as negotiable instruments[1], and the dematerialisation documentation is drafted with a view to replicating contractually the benefits of negotiability. In the deed of covenant, issuers agree and acknowledge that holders shall have the same rights as against them (the issuers) in respect of dematerialised securities as if the holders held the security in physical form. Dematerialised securities cannot be negotiable[2]. The chief benefit of negotiable status under the law merchant is (broadly) that the holder in due course of a negotiable instrument takes it free of adverse claims from the issuer[3] or third parties[4].

Holders of dematerialised securities are contractually protected against claims from issuers (by the deed of covenant) and from other CMO members[5]. However, not all third party claims are excluded. For example, if CMO custodian A fraudulently sells securities belonging to its clients to CMO member B, B might be sued by A's clients[6]. Because the basis of the CMO is merely contractual and not statutory it cannot affect the rights of third parties who are not contractually bound. For this reason, the full benefits of negotiability cannot be replicated[7].

In some circumstances protection from such claims may be available from the rules of equity if not under the doctrine of negotiability[8]. However, it is important for the CMO custodian to appreciate that, to the extent that there are increased risks of adverse claims from its custody clients, it bears them personally under an indemnity it is required to give to CRESTCo, the Bank and other CMO members.

1 See para **9.50**.
2 Negotiability is based on the physical possession of a tangible instrument.
3 For example, in respect of sums owed to the issuer by previous holders.

4 For example, previous holders claiming to be the true owners because an earlier transfer was fraudulent.
5 See the dematerialisation agreement.
6 In such circumstances A would be contractually bound to indemnify B under the dematerialisation agreement.
7 The dematerialisation agreement provides that the CMO Rules may make provision that a holder of dematerialised securities has rights equivalent to those of a holder in due course of a physical instrument and shall accordingly acquire a title to a dematerialised instrument which is free of equities. However, this can only take effect in respect of persons bound by the CMO Rules.
8 A CMO transferee may have a defence against adverse claims as a bona fide purchaser of the legal estate without notice of the adverse claim. However, the availability of this defence depends on all the circumstances.

Formalities of transfer

9.61 As indicated above, the CMO documentation provides that the legal basis of CMO transfers is attornment by the Bank as bailee. The provision that the Bank holds CMO instruments as bailee cannot apply to dematerialised securities, for two reasons. First, bailment requires a tangible subject matter[1]. Second, it is not clear that the Bank holds the intangible securities at all, for they are issued straight on to the screen[2]. Whereas, in the case of physical securities, the CMO involves intermediation (by the Bank) there is no intermediation in the case of dematerialised securities.

Section 136 of the Law of Property Act 1925, which requires legal assignments of choses in action to be (inter alia) in writing[3], does not apply to physical instruments in the CMO as these are deemed by the law merchant to be documentary intangibles and choses in possession, requiring no formalities for their transfer. However, this is not true of dematerialised securities. It is therefore arguable that these are subject to the restrictions in s 136. Because the requirement for a written assignment is not satisfied by book entry transfers in the CMO, it may be that CMO transfers of dematerialised securities cannot be effective in law and can only take effect in equity.

Section 53(1)(c) of the Law of Property Act 1925 requires dispositions of equitable interests to be in writing; purported dispositions subject to but not complying with the section can take effect only in contract. The CMO does not benefit from statutory disapplications of these provisions[4]. There may therefore be some risk that transfers of dematerialised securities within the CMO may be unwound in the insolvency of a transferor.

1 The express provision that the Bank holds securities as bailee in the membership agreement only relates to physical instruments.
2 The Bank maintains the database whereby ownership of the securities is recorded, but this role is akin to registrar and not custodian.
3 More accurately, it exempts such assignments complying with its terms from the general common law prohibition of the assignment of claims.
4 Unlike CREST (and the old CGO).

Collateral, repos and securities lending

Collateral

9.62 Investors may wish to use CMO securities as collateral. Special facilities are available within the CMO for this purpose (the pledged-out memorandum account). Alternatively, CMO securities may be put up as collateral independently of the CMO.

PLEDGED-OUT MEMORANDUM ACCOUNT

9.63 Collateral may be delivered within the CMO using the CMO pledged-out memorandum account. Collateral securities appear as pledged out in the account of the collateral giver and as collateral in the account of the collateral taker[1]. The collateral giver cannot use the securities for any purpose; the collateral taker is free to 'on-pledge' the securities[2] but is not generally otherwise free to deal with them. There is no automatic return of collateral. Exchanges of collateral require positive acceptance by the collateral taker.

Although the Reference Manual describes these arrangements as a pledge, it goes on to provide that the status of collateral delivered in this way depends entirely upon the arrangements between the parties, which do not necessarily constitute a pledge[3]. However, the Reference Manual indicates that, as far as CRESTCo and the Bank are concerned, all CMO collateral pledges constitute outright transfers, as CRESTCo and the Bank will not recognise any residual right (or equity of redemption) in the collateral taker[4].

Irrespective of what CRESTCo and the Bank will or will not recognise, it is not clear that, as a matter of law, these arrangements can constitute outright transfers. The restrictions on the freedom of the collateral taker to deal with the collateral securities may be incompatible with full title.

When collateral is delivered using this facility, it is crucial to establish that the interest of the collateral taker over the securities would be enforceable in the insolvency of the collateral taker. Broadly, it should be enforceable if it is proprietary, and will not be if it is merely contractual[5]. Although the position taken by CRESTCo and the Bank (ie the outright transfer provisions) may assist in showing that property has passed, this will not be conclusive. Therefore it is important to document carefully any security interest using the pledged-out account to ensure that a proprietary security interest is conferred.

1 CMO Reference Manual, Section L.1.6.
2 See CMO Reference Manual, Section L.1.8, 1.9, 2 and 3.
3 CMO Reference Manual, Section L.1.2.
4 '. . . CRESTCo and the Depository act upon instructions in relation to a CMO instrument only from the CMO member to whose account it is credited in the CMO System and do not recognise any proprietary or equitable interest or other right in respect of the instrument other than an absolute right in that CMO member to the entirety of the instrument' (CMO Reference Manual, Section L.1.4). As indicated above, pledged-out securities are credited to both the account of the collateral giver and that of the collateral taker; however, since CRESTCo and the Bank accept the instructions only of the collateral taker in relation to such securities, the above provisions should presumably be taken to mean that only the interest of the collateral taker will be recognised.
5 This is because of the restriction in s 127 of the Insolvency Act 1986 on dispositions of a company's property after the commencement of winding up.

INDEPENDENTLY OF THE CMO

9.64 For instruments outside the CMO, a legal security interest may be created under a legal mortgage or pledge, by transferring (respectively) legal title or possession by way of security. As legal title in bearer instruments passes by possession, both a legal mortgage and a pledge may be created by transfer of possession; the intention of the parties (recorded in security documentation) determines which type of legal security interest was created.

Because CMO securities are immobilised or dematerialised within the CMO, the CMO member cannot pledge them to a third party independently of the CMO; it may be able to do so through a CMO transfer, but the position is highly uncertain. However, where the CMO member is a custodian, the beneficial owner may pledge CMO securities (other than dematerialised securities) to the custodian.

It might be possible for a CMO member to create a legal mortgage in favour of a third party through a CMO transfer; however, there may be some danger that the outright transfer provisions contained in the CMO documentation[1] may cut across the equity of redemption of the chargor.

It is not clear that an equitable mortgage can be created in CMO securities, as this form of security interest traditionally involves the delivery of physical documentation. Possibly, the only type of equitable security interest that can be created in CMO securities is an equitable charge, which may be registrable[2].

Thus, the placing of instruments in the CMO may reduce the options for their use as collateral.

1 CMO Reference Manual, Section F.1.5.
2 Pledges are not registrable. Charges created by UK corporates may be registrable under s 395 of the Companies Act 1985 if, inter alia, they are charges over book debts or floating charges. Charges over CMO instruments should not constitute charges over book debts, as CMO instruments would be recorded in the books of the chargor as securities and not as book debts. Very broadly speaking, the defining characteristic of a floating charge is that the chargor retains the freedom to deal in the charged assets. This may well be the case with CMO securities, unless they are removed from the account of the chargor.

DEMATERIALISATION

9.65 The dematerialisation of securities in the CMO renders them ineligible to be pledged, as a pledge can only relate to a tangible subject matter. Purported pledges will probably take effect as charges. Care should be taken to ensure the registration provisions of the Companies Act 1985 are complied with. Where a custodian or other intermediary takes a security interest from investors, it may be necessary to place restrictions on the investors' freedom to deal in the securities in order to avoid the creation of a registrable floating charge.

Repos

9.66 CMO securities can be delivered under repurchase transactions through the CMO. However, there are no special facilities for automatic returns or in relation to collateral margining. Both the initial delivery of the securities, and the redelivery of equivalent securities, must be input by the parties as separate outright transfers[1].

1 CMO Reference Manual, Section J.2.2.

Securities lending

9.67 It is not customary for CMO instruments to be loaned under securities lending arrangements. However, such instruments are used as collateral for securities loans. Standard securities lending documentation[1] provides for the outright transfer of collateral. It is customary for this collateral to be delivered through the pledged-out account.

1 That is, the documentation produced under the auspices of the International Securities Lenders Association (ISLA).

Tax

9.68 The withholding tax position on interest paid by an issuer of securities held in the CMO follows general principles. There may be additional considerations where the security is a certificate of deposit, the interest on which is beneficially owned by an individual, but these are not addressed in this discussion.

If the interest on the CMO security has a UK source and is short interest (broadly speaking, payable on a security with a term of 364 days or less) the interest will be payable without withholding or deduction for or on account of tax. In other circumstances, the interest will be paid under deduction of tax at the lower rate (currently 20 per cent) unless a specific exemption is available, for example if the interest is paid by a bank in the ordinary course of its business[1].

No stamp duty will be payable on the transfer of securities within the CMO. First, it is likely that the CMO security will constitute exempt loan capital, the transfer of which is exempt from stamp duty[2]. The transfer across CMO accounts by book entry of bearer securities, the transfer of which would be exempt if physically delivered, will also not attract stamp duty (on the basis that no instrument of transfer will be brought into existence). Stamp duty reserve tax will likewise not be payable on an agreement to transfer CMO securities, the transfer of which is exempt from stamp duty[3].

1 For discussion of loan capital which constitutes exempt loan capital, see para **10.5**.
2 For discussion of withholding tax see paras **10.36–10.42**.
3 See further discussion in Chapter 10 and in particular para **10.2**, n 1 and **10.21**.

The future of the CMO

9.69 Following the merger of the CGO into CREST, the next logical step in the process of consolidating settlement structures in the UK is to merge the CMO into CREST too, but this presents more difficult issues than the CGO/CREST merger. The CGO, like CREST, settled transfers of registered instruments and (unsurprisingly, given that CREST was developed largely from the same model as the CGO) the two systems operated in broadly similar ways. In contrast, the CMO processes issuances and transfers of what are essentially bearer instruments, subject to the dematerialisation process discussed at paras **9.58–9.61**. Following various consultations and discussion papers[1], and analysis by the Money Markets Working Group[2], the current proposal is that, after publication of a detailed explanation of the new structures in the autumn of 2002[3], arrangements will be made for the transfer of money market instruments ('MMIs') through CREST, beginning in July 2003. The intention is that the CMO will be closed down by the end of July 2003 at the latest. Inevitably, in order to merge the CMO into CREST there will need to be various changes to the way in which the CMO operates.

Equally, in view of the way in which the underlying market rationale of the CMO differs from CREST, it is important that the merger of CMO into CREST should not remove the particular benefits offered by the CMO to the relevant market sectors.

1 See in particular the CREST consultation paper 'Money Market Instruments in CREST' produced in January 2001, and the Bank of England interim report 'The Future of Money Market Instruments' produced at the same time.
2 Consisting of representatives from the CMO user base, the Bank of England, APACs, the LMMA and the BBA.
3 Migration plans and trialing will take place in March/April 2003, followed by the production of the relevant legislation in June 2003; see further the Money Markets Working Group Paper dated 31 May 2002 and related publications, accessible on the CREST website (www.crestco.co.uk). Amendment of the CREST Regulations will be necessary and will probably be done pursuant to the same power used for the creation of the 1995 Regulations, namely s 207 of the Companies Act 1989 which permits the making of 'regulations for enabling title to securities to be evidenced and transferred without a written instrument'.

Paper-interface and negotiability

9.70 As explained above, a useful aspect of physical bearer instruments is the concept of negotiability. This is not relevant to registered instruments (or dematerialised issuances in the CMO system)[1]. Under the new proposals, no physical MMIs may be lodged with CREST. Issuances for settlement through CREST can only be in fully dematerialised form[2]. It will of course still be possible to issue and hold physical instruments outside CREST, and holders may be able to deposit physical instruments in exchange for dematerialised instruments held through CREST, but this will be dealt with by and at the option of the appropriate Issuing and Paying Agent for the relevant instruments rather than by the central CREST service.

The Issuing and Paying Agent is a new type of CREST Participant to be introduced by CREST in connection with MMIs. It will be responsible for the input of an issuance of MMIs into the CREST system, in a similar way to lodging agents currently in the CMO. The idea is that, as in the CMO, the issuer's agent will have control over the issuance of MMIs through the CMO: hence the issuance, allocation of an ISIN number, and transfer to third parties can happen very rapidly through CREST[3], rather than applications for admissions of securities to CREST being processed centrally within CREST as happens for gilts and equities. The record of title to MMIs all be maintained by CREST, in the same way as for equities, but the administration in connection with such register will be handled by the relevant Issuing and Paying Agent, not CRESTCo.

1 The Bank of England and CRESTCo consulted leading counsel (Mr Richard Sykes, QC) on the effect of the loss of negotiability for MMIs (see The Bank of England Consultation Paper 'The Future of Money Market Instruments', published November 1999, and in particular Appendix II). Mr Sykes was of the view that a holder of a dematerialised MMI through CREST was not in a worse position than the holder of a negotiable instrument, not least on the basis that reg 29 of the Uncertificated Securities Regulations 1995 has the result that where a transfer follows a properly authenticated dematerialised instruction, such transfer cannot be reversed even if it can be shown that the relevant authenticated dematerialised instruction was in fact forged or unauthorised. It is therefore arguable that transfer of dematerialised MMIs through CREST at the least provides better protection than transfer of dematerialised MMIs through the CMO because there is the benefit of statutory provision rather than just contractual arrangements (see discussion at para **9.60**). However, there is also the argument that the CREST arrangements do not necessarily give the same protection as exists for transfer of negotiable instruments. For further discussion of the CMO issues, see ch 9 of J Benjamin *Interests in Securities* (2000, OUP).

2 Currently in the CMO only CDs can be issued in dematerialised form. The MMIs which will be eligible for issuance and settlement through CREST will be Treasury Bills, Certificates of Deposit, Commercial Paper, Guaranteed Commercial Paper and Bank Bills, but not Trade Bills (bills of exchange accepted by a company which is not a bank) or Letters of Credit. In practice this may not be a major concern since, although technically Trade Bills, Local Authority Bills and Letters of Credit can settle through the CMO, it is rare. 'During 1999, the value of assets held daily in the CMO was £143 billion. This represented 9,000 issues made up of just under 60,000 individual instruments. The bulk of the MMIs held are Certificates of Deposit, totalling almost 90% by value. The remaining 10% is made up of Bills of Exchange, Treasury Bills and Commercial Paper' (CREST consultation paper 'Money Market Instruments in CREST', January 2001). According to the CREST website, as at the end of June 2002, there were 5,729 bank CDs in issue (nominal value £125,927,780,000) and 1,197 eligible bank bills (nominal value £10,277,689,550.91), as well as 486 building society CDs (nominal value £5,298,650,000), three ineligible bank bills (nominal value £4,753,623.19) and 20 Treasury Bills (nominal value £16,450,000,000).

3 Very important given the fact that large numbers of issues are lodged each day: according to the Bank of England Interim Report 'The Future of Money Market Instruments' (June 2001), an average of 200 new issues are lodged in the CMO each day.

Fungibility

9.71 A further consequence in the change in nature of MMIs in CREST is that such instruments will be issued not as separate identifiable instruments but as issuances of fungible instruments[1]. This is significant for any person holding MMIs on behalf of another, because it will no longer be possible to identify the particular instruments held for a particular client but only that a proportion of an undivided whole is held[2]. This may not necessarily be of concern to a custodian, depending on how it holds assets for its client, but may be relevant if clear identification is important to the custodian or its clients. It should be noted that the usual CREST account facilities will be available in relation to MMIs: therefore, if necessary, MMIs can be held through designated accounts or sponsored member accounts[3]. This contrasts with the CMO arrangements, where a CMO member maintains omnibus accounts, although can maintain separate accounts under different nominee names.

1 CREST consultation paper, 'Money Market Instruments in CREST' (January 2001).
2 See further discussion of issues arising in Chapter 3.
3 See paras **9.13–9.17**.

Collateral

9.72 An important use of MMIs is as collateral. The arrangements within the CMO allow for what is referred to as a pledge of CMO instruments[1]. Outright transfer is also possible, but in that case the CMO system simply records a transfer of assets, and the underlying agreement to create some form of a security interest will depend on contractual arrangements outside the CMO. The benefit of a CMO pledge arrangement is that the collateral taker does not have freedom to deal with the collateral (although is able to on-pledge it within the CMO). For MMIs in CREST, the collateral arrangements will be similar to those which apply currently to all CREST eligible securities[2], and will therefore involve outright transfer of MMIs. If this is a concern for entities providing or taking MMIs as collateral, it would be necessary to try to impose additional restrictions by contract (see discussion of escrow balance arrangements at para **9.31**), or another option would be to pledge physical instruments outside CREST (but this is unlikely to be appealing because it would reintroduce the administration issues of dealing with paper).

1 See para **9.63**.
2 See paras **9.28–9.36**.

Settlement and payment

9.73 A major change for transfers against payment in the CMO will be the application of real time gross settlement to MMIs[1]. The payment mechanism in central bank funds for sterling and euro will be available for MMI transfers, and the USD currency assured payment facility will also be available. Since the current CMO payment arrangements do not involve assured payment this will mean similar exposure for settlement banks as currently exists in CREST; therefore settlement banks providing services in connection with MMI transfers through CREST may well need to reconsider debit caps accordingly.

1 See discussion at para 9.9.

CREST – the future

9.74 With the continuing concern to speed up settlement and make systems more efficient, a major area of concern is how the current fragmented arrangements consisting of many different systems will change in the future. Views on the way forward vary: for example, both Euroclear and Clearstream have a large number of system links but increasingly have focused on joining forces with existing systems as far as possible, whereas CREST has historically concentrated on creating cross-border links with other systems (see discussion at para **9.26**). Whichever approach is preferred, the central idea is to increase efficiency by reducing administration and effectively maintaining one point of access to a central system through which the participant can access settlement for as wide a variety of securities as possible. In this context, it is useful to consider the merger of CREST and Euroclear[1] and the potential issues involved.

According to various publications on the merger[2], although CRESTCo is now part of the Euroclear group[3], the CREST system has in effect become another service available from the Euroclear stable of services. The challenge of merging different systems created under different systems of law is of course quite considerable, particularly when, as indicated above, the underlying basis of settlement differs. The international service provided by Euroclear under Belgian law involves the holding by Euroclear of a variety of securities, which may be issued under and subject to the law of many different jurisdictions. Euroclear holds the relevant securities pursuant to Belgian law[4] in an arrangement akin to a trust under English law, so that effectively a person holding securities through Euroclear has exchanged rights under the laws governing the underlying security for a repackaged asset (a type of securities entitlement) in the form of a Belgian law interest in the securities held by Euroclear. This 'interest' (under Belgian law, a form of co-ownership right in the pool of fungible securities recorded in the books of Euroclear) is subject to the relevant Belgium legislation as well as the contractual terms of participation in Euroclear entered into with Euroclear ('Terms and Conditions governing the use of the Euroclear System' and related documentation which are governed by Belgian law). How can such arrangements 'merge' with a system based on English or French law where the system participant has direct title under local law, rather than a co-ownership right to securities held by a settlement system?

The answer seems to be that the Euroclear group has not attempted a radical change to existing ownership structures. Although the ultimate aim is for a system participant to have one securities account, one interface with the system and one payment or settlement relationship, essentially the same services as provided independently by CREST and the other relevant systems should remain available. The discussion paper[5] notes specifically that 'European consolidation of settlement will be successful only if it offers the full range of services already enjoyed by customers without diminution of service provision' and that 'A single platform which operated a single, rigid, settlement and custody service would not meet the needs of all its customers.' Consequently, system participants will be able to obtain what is termed a 'domestic service' by signing up to terms governed by, for example, French law for the service from Euroclear France, and English law for the service from what is currently CRESTCo. This will at least mean that the arrangements with the relevant local central securities depositary for holding direct title to securities issued in France or the UK will be governed by the appropriate local legal system[6] as well as the applicable regulatory requirements of the local regulator. It is also the intention that specific services which are unique to a particular system will remain available (where required in the relevant market), such as the DBV arrangements in CREST[7]. In addition to the domestic services, participants can obtain the 'full service' provided under Belgian law which, as discussed above, is based on the concept of Euroclear holding relevant rights in securities for participants subject to Belgian law.

It should be noted that any local restrictions on participation will still apply[8]. It remains to be seen how the merged settlement service provider (in the first phase, to be referred to as the 'single settlement engine') will cope with the significant difference between the respective approaches by CREST and Euroclear to admission of participants. Historically Euroclear has restricted participation to, broadly, large financial institutions[9], whereas CREST has, broadly, permitted participation by any individual or institution which is able to comply with the relevant operational and fee arrangements[10]. Presumably to the extent that a participant in one area or entity in the Euroclear group is unable to meet the requirements relating to a service provided by another section of the group, it may not be permitted to receive such service.

As a system development, this merger should be of assistance to participants who can deal with what is effectively one system entity using one account (or set of accounts). However, it will present some interesting issues regarding the interrelation of the different agreements governed by different laws but which are entered into with the same system (or what are in practice different entities within the system), particularly if issues arise in the event of insolvency or fraud (see discussion in Chapter 5). It will also be necessary to consider how local regulatory requirements may affect these arrangements, since they are likely to have an impact on the domestic holdings of securities. In principle, these issues already exist, whether an entity participates in a number of different systems, or in systems all brought beneath one umbrella, and in practice it may be easier to reach conclusions or at least some pragmatic solution in the event of conflicting claims, given that the arrangements will be intra-group if not with the same system entity. Nevertheless it will be interesting to see how such systems will work together in practice and evolve over time.

1 On 4 July 2002, the boards of Euroclear and CRESTCo announced that the terms of the proposed merger had been agreed, and this was approved by shareholders at meetings on 14 and 16 August 2002. The merger proposal was reviewed in accordance with the UK Fair Trading Act 1973, but the Secretary of State for Trade and Industry decided not to refer the merger to the UK Competition Commission, and subsequently at the UK High Court hearing on 19 September 2002 the scheme was sanctioned by the court. The merger completed on 23 September 2002.

2 See in particular CREST/Euroclear press release dated 4 July 2002, CREST Press Release dated 18 July 2002 and the paper published in July 2002 by CREST and Euroclear entitled 'Delivering a domestic market for Europe'.

3 CRESTCo has become a wholly owned subsidiary of Euroclear Bank SA/NV.

4 The Belgian Royal Decree No 62 of November 1967, as amended (and most recently by the law of 2 August 2002 on the oversight of the financial sector: art 133).

5 'Delivering a domestic market for Europe', July 2002.

6 Note that the merger of CRESTCo into Euroclear will cover the CREST service for all CREST-eligible securities as described at para **9.1**, n 4, such as Irish, Jersey, Guernsey and Isle of Man securities.

7 Apparently it has not yet been decided whether the current links between CRESTCo and other systems, or the CDI service, will remain available through the CREST domestic service, or whether the holding of non-CREST eligible securities via intermediation will only to be handled through Euroclear subject to the Belgian law regime.

8 Broadly, only credit institutions and inter-professional institutions (eg clearing houses and foreign CSDs) are permitted to participate in Euroclear Netherlands (formerly Necigef).

9 Euroclear requires participants to meet its criteria in relation to matters such as financial resources, technological ability, system requirements, and market reputation.

10 Arguably, the process of vetting potential CREST participants ends up in the hands of the CREST settlement banks (or, possibly, sponsors where relevant), since a person cannot become a CREST member without appointing a settlement bank, and a bank will in practice not enter into an agreement with such person without going through its normal counterparty and credit checks. It should of course be remembered that while a settlement bank may choose to provide services on the basis of the protection provided by the settlement bank charge, this is no guarantee that the relevant person is creditworthy or a reputable counterparty, and CRESTCo takes no responsibility for this.

Further issues for consideration in relation to CREST

Operator register of title, record of title and issuer register

9.75

(a) An issuer of UK Securities maintains a register of holders of shares in certificated form, but in relation to uncertificated shares only has a duplicate record of the register of title maintained by CREST. The public cannot examine the CREST records: therefore this presents potential problems for due diligence[1].

(b) Under CREST Regulation 24, although the operator register or issuer register is prima facie evidence of 'any matters which are by these Regulations directed or authorised to be inserted in it', this is not true for the issuer register to the extent that it is inconsistent with the operator register. Consequently, although the issuer register in theory governs title to certificated shares, if the CREST register records a different position, it would not do so (and this would not be obvious to anyone looking at the issuer register). In principle, it is difficult to see why there would be an inconsistency given that the issuer register records only certificated shares, but there could be difficulties in some cases, for example where shares were being transferred from certificated to uncertificated form, or vice-versa. Again, this could cause difficulties for persons inspecting the issuer register but unaware of inconsistencies with the operator register.

(c) Also in CREST Regulation 24, it is stated that a person's name in the issuer register will not be prima facie evidence that such person is a member of the company unless the issuer register shows such person to be a holder of certificated shares, or the operator register shows such person to be a holder of uncertificated shares, or such person is deemed to be a member of the company (as discussed at (e) below).

(d) It is unclear what the position is where the CREST register and the company's duplicate record are inconsistent[2]. Note that Sch 4, para 5(2) of the CREST Regulations requires that the issuer record should be 'regularly reconciled with the Operator register of members' unless 'it is impracticable to do so by virtue of circumstances beyond its control'. There is no reference in the CREST Regulations as to what is meant by 'regularly reconciled' (although see CREST Registrar Service Standards and the standard Registrar Agreement), but para 5(3) has the effect that, provided the issuer record is 'regularly reconciled' with the operator register, the company will not be liable for any action taken on the assumption that the record details 'accord with' the operator register details[3].

(e) Where there is a transfer of uncertificated shares to a person who will hold in certificated form, the relevant entry on the operator register will be deleted and an appropriate entry made on the issuer register in due course. There will in principle be a period during which there is no record of the ownership of the relevant shares on either the operator register or the issuer register (although presumably the transferring party will still (briefly) appear in the issuer record until the issuer register is updated). CREST Regulation 31 provides that, until the transferee is entered on the issuer register, the transferor will retain legal title but the transferee acquires (at the time of the deletion from the operator register) an equitable interest in the relevant securities being transferred. In CREST Regulation 32, which relates to the conversion of shares from uncertificated to certificated form (ie shares come out of CREST but are held by the same person) it is specifically stated that 'During any period between the deletion of any entry in an Operator register of securities . . . and the making of the entry in an issuer register of securities . . . the relevant system-member shall retain title to the units of the security . . . notwithstanding the deletion of any entry in the Operator register of securities; and . . . where those units are shares, the relevant system-member shall be deemed to continue to be a member of the company'[4]. These are important exceptions to current company law (Companies Act 1985, s 22) where a person is only a member of a company if entered on the register of that company.

(f) CREST Regulation 33 relates to the conversion of securities into uncertificated form. Again there appears to be a potential timing issue regarding register entries. The relevant issuer is required to give a dematerialisation notice to CREST in the circumstances specified in this CREST Regulation (including where a system-member requests conversion of securities from certificated to uncertificated form), and upon doing so, to delete the relevant securities from the issuer register. The operator is required to enter the relevant system-member in the operator register, but the only obligation regarding notification to the relevant issuer is to notify whether or not the registration has been made on the operator register 'within 2 months of receiving a dematerialisation notice'. In principle, the issuer could check the register at an early stage, and presumably in practice the relevant system-member would be aware quite quickly whether or not the relevant securities were recorded in its CREST account, but this information will not be available to the public, except to the extent that the issuer's record notes this[5]. This is a potential issue where the making of an entry on the register is time critical[6].

(g) CREST Regulation 33 has wording similar to CREST Regulation 32 in that it states that the relevant system-member will 'retain title to the units of the security specified in the dematerialisation notice notwithstanding the deletion of any entry in any issuer register of securities' and in relation to shares shall 'be deemed to continue to be a member of the company'[7].

1 The company and its registrar do have the right to inspect CREST's register, and could therefore be required to certify as to the accuracy of the duplicate record, but arguably this does not give the same protection as an independent examination of the register. In addition, as discussed in relation to CREST Regulations 31 and 32 below, there may be intervals where shares are not registered in either the operator register or the issuer register (such shares may still appear in the issuer record but, as noted, this is not a record of title).

2 The idea is that the company should be subject to the same obligations and liabilities in relation to the maintenance of the duplicate record of uncertificated shares as apply to the maintenance of the register of certificated shares, but if a problem is caused by CREST, is there any recourse? For example, if the CREST register shows more securities than are actually in issue, is the company required to issue more securities to remove the shortfall? The normal position under English law is that a company is liable for statements on the register, and is generally regarded as estopped from arguing that the number of shares shown in the register as being in issue is wrong; therefore the company is required to issue more shares to eliminate any shortfall. There is no indication that this normal rule would not apply: therefore in principle an issuer accepts the same liability for CREST as maintainer of the operator register in this respect as it does in relation to the actions of itself (or its registrar) in relation to maintaining the register of certificated shares.

3 In wording comparable to s 354 of the Companies Act 1985, an issuer with more than 50 members is required to maintain a single record of when people become, or cease to be, members, whether they hold shares in certificated or uncertificated form (CREST Regulations, Sch 4, para 7(1)).

4 CREST Regulation 32(6).

5 Although presumably the issuer's record will only be updated once it is confirmed that the relevant securities have been registered on the operator register.

6 Note also CREST Regulation 34(1), where CREST's obligation to enter names on the register of securities is subject to the rules of CREST, which raises similar issues.

7 Note that, unlike under CREST Regulation 31 (transfer from uncertificated to certificated form), the transferee where securities are being converted and received in uncertificated form following a transfer does not receive equitable title, and the transferor remains the relevant holder until the transferee's name is entered on the operator register.

Capacity and liability of registrar

9.76

(a) Is CREST maintaining part of the register as agent of the company?[1] CREST Regulation 20 states that in relation to shares issued by a company participating in CREST 'there shall be (a) a register maintained by the participating issuer . . . and . . . a register maintained by the Operator'. It is also stated that 'References in any enactment or instrument to a company's register of members shall, unless the context otherwise requires, be construed in relation to a company which is a participating issuer as referring to the company's issuer register of members and Operator register of members.' However, there is no clear indication whether the company ceases to be responsible for the functions to be carried out by the operator, or whether the operator is maintaining the register as agent of the company.

(b) It should be noted that in Sch 4 of the CREST Regulations it is stated that s 352 of the Companies Act 1985 (obligations to maintain register) does not apply[2] to a company which is a participating issuer. As a result, if an issuer has any securities in uncertificated form, its obligations regarding maintenance of the register will be under the CREST Regulations rather than the Companies Act 1985. The same is true for certain other parts of the Companies Act 1985, eg s 353 (location of register).

CREST will not be subject to the same liability for failure to maintain the register correctly as the company, given the extent of the exclusions of liability by CREST[3]. It should also be noted that the CREST Terms and Conditions (which all members sign up to) state that CREST will only be liable if negligent, fraudulent or in wilful default (and such limitation is intended to apply to all claims in contract, tort, misrepresentation, breach of any other duty imposed by law or in any other way), but the maximum liability for all claims (not just claims from an individual CREST member) arising from the same event is capped[4]. Therefore, in practice, if there were ever a major problem and many claimants, each claimant might well recover very little.

1 The primary obligation to maintain the whole register under the Companies Act 1985 is disapplied, but it is unclear if the company may have liability for CREST if CREST does not maintain the register properly; although see para **9.75**, n 2. See also CREST Regulation 23(1)(b).

2 Section 352(5) will apply in the sense that the company and its officers may still face a fine for non-compliance with obligations in relation to maintenance of the register, although such obligations arise under Sch 4, para 2, rather than s 352.

3 For example, CREST Regulation 23: 'The obligations of an Operator to maintain and to keep and enter up, any register of securities, imposed by these Regulations . . . shall not give rise to any form of duty or liability enforceable by civil proceedings for breach of statutory duty.' However, Sch 4, paras 18 and 19 indicate that certain fines for failure to maintain the Operator register properly will apply to CREST and its officers. Commentary notes in the HM Treasury consultation paper 'Modernising Securities Settlement' (produced in connection with the first draft of the present Regulations) indicated the intention that CREST should still be liable for its own fraud or negligence without limitation, but this is not clear from CREST Regulation 23.

4 At the time of writing the cap was £40,000,000 (or £20,000,000 where liability of CRESTCo arises out of an act, omission or event prior to 3 July 2000) (see CREST Terms and Conditions, Section 17 and Sch 5).

Extract from old CGO membership agreement

9.77 Clause 3(16):

'If and whenever the CGO Member acts or proposes to act as nominee or agent for another person ('a principal') in relation to stock held or to be held on, or transactions over, CGO Accounts of the CGO Member, to obtain from that principal before beginning to act as nominee or agent for that principal:

(a) an acknowledgment that the holding of stock for the account of that principal on the CGO Accounts of the CGO Member and all transactions over those CGO Accounts or otherwise in relation to facilities relating to the CGO Member's membership of the CGO Service will be subject to all of the provisions of this Agreement and to the CGO Rules and in particular (but without limiting the generality of the foregoing):
   (i) that the stock is to be introduced into the CGO only if it has been purchased or is held on terms authorising the holder to deal with it free from any proprietary or equitable interest of any other person and in particular free from any unpaid vendor's lien; and
   (ii) that the Bank of England and its servant, and agents, with certain limited exceptions expressly provided for in this Agreement, are exempt from liability caused directly by or indirectly by the provision or operation of the CGO Service or any part thereof, or by any loss, interruption or failure in the provision or operation of the CGO Service or any part thereof, and entitling the Bank of England without liability to act without further enquiry on instructions or information or purported instructions or information received through the CGO Service or otherwise in accordance with the CGO Manual; and

(b) an authority for the CGO Member on behalf of that principal to do all such acts and things and execute all such documents as may be required to enable the CGO Member fully to observe and perform its obligations under this Agreement and the CGO Rules, and enter into any arrangement which the CGO Member considers proper for the purpose of facilitating clearance of or settlement of transactions effected on behalf of the principal through the CGO.'

The terms of Clause 3(16)(a)(i) were compatible with custody arrangements, as they provided, not that the stock was free from third party equities, but that it could be dealt free from such equities.

Extract from CMO Rules

9.78 Rule 7.15:

'If and whenever the CMO member acts or proposes to act as nominee or agent for another person (a "principal") in relation to CMO Instruments held or to be held on, or transactions over, CMO Instruments Accounts of the CMO member, it will obtain from that principal before beginning to act as nominee or agent for that principal –

(1) an acknowledgment (expressed to be in favour of CRESTCo, the Depository and the Bank) that the holding of CMO Instruments for the account of that principal on a CMO Instruments Account of the CMO member and all transactions over such a CMO Instruments Account or otherwise in relation to facilities relating to the CMO Member's membership of the CMO Service will be subject to all of the provisions of the CMO Membership Agreement, the CMO Manual and the CMO Service Rules and in particular (but without limiting the generality of the foregoing);

(a) that instruments are to be lodged with the CMO Service only if they have been purchased or are held on terms authorising the holder to deal with them free from any proprietary or equitable interest or other right of any other person;

(b) that except as required by law, neither CRESTCo nor the Depositary is bound by or compelled to recognise any proprietary or equitable interest in or any other right in respect of any CMO Instrument other than an absolute right to the entirety of that CMO Instrument in the CMO member to whose CMO Instruments Account that CMO Instrument is for the time being credited or for whose account that CMO Instrument is otherwise held for the time being, and that the principal will not assert or permit any person claiming under or through him to assert any such proprietary or equitable interest or other right against CRESTCo or the Depository;

(c) that CRESTCo, the Depository and the Bank, with the limited exceptions expressly provided in this Agreement, are exempt from liability caused directly by or indirectly by the operation or failure or loss of the CMO Service;

(d) that CRESTCo and the Depository, with the limited exceptions expressly provided in this Agreement, are entitled without further enquiry to execute or act upon any instruction or information or purported instruction or information received through the CMO Service or the network provided by the Network Services and any instruction or information or purported instruction or information received in accordance with the CMO Manual or the CMO Service Rules otherwise than through the CMO Service (including without limitation any instruction with respect to the lodgement or withdrawal of CMO Instruments) notwithstanding that it may afterwards be discovered that such instruction or information was not genuine or was not initiated by the CMO Member or any other person entitled to give it or was not initiated through the Equipment operated by the CMO Member or the like apparatus or equipment operated by any other such person;

(e) that CRESTCo and the Depository have made their own arrangements as described in the CMO Manual and CRESTCo and the Depository may from time to time make additional or substitute arrangements, for the provision of a network to enable each of them to receive electronic messages from and send any messages to the other which network and associated equipment, software and other systems form part of the CMO Service and are not provided under the Network Service;

(f) that CRESTCo and the Depository shall be entitled without further enquiry to execute or otherwise act upon instructions or information or purported instructions or information received from the network referred to in Clause 7.15.1(e) of the CMO Membership Agreement and instructions or information or purported instructions or information received in accordance with the provisions of the CMO Manual or the CMO Service Rules otherwise than through the said network notwithstanding that it may afterwards be discovered that such instructions or information were not genuine or not initiated by CRESTCo or, as the case may be, the Depository;

(2) an authority for the CMO Member on behalf of that principal to do all such acts and things and execute all such documents as may be required to enable the CMO Member fully to observe and perform its obligations under the CMO Membership Agreement and the CMO Requirements, and enter into any arrangement which the CMO Member considers proper for the purpose of facilitating clearance of or settlement of transactions effected on behalf of the principal through the CMO Service.'

Similar provisions were also required in respect of the CGO except for 7.15.1(b) which is unique to the CMO and reflects the lack of statutory basis for the Bank's exclusion of notice of trusts. In addition, the dematerialisation agreement (see below) requires custodian members, in section 4.1 to '. . . obtain from . . . [the custody client], before beginning to act as nominee or agent . . . an acknowledgment (expressed to be in favour of CRESTCo and of every CMO member for the time being) that the holding of Dematerialised Instruments for the account of that principal on a CMO Instruments Account of the CMO Member and all transactions over such a CMO Instruments Account or otherwise in relation to facilities relating to the CMO Member's membership of the CMO Service affecting Dematerialised Instruments will be subject to all the provisions of this Agreement, the CMO Membership Agreement, the CMO Manual and the CMO Service Rules.' Equivalent procedures are in place to allocate distinctive numbers to dematerialised securities.

Chapter 10*

United Kingdom taxation

Introduction

10.1 This chapter is intended to outline some of the main United Kingdom tax considerations which may arise in the context of custody arrangements.

It should perhaps be stressed that a global custodian may, depending upon the precise circumstances, be subject to taxation liabilities and/or compliance obligations (such as information reporting requirements) in more than one jurisdiction with respect to securities held by the custodian. The focus here is solely on United Kingdom tax law as it is likely to relate to custody assets (rather than, for example the direct tax position of the global custodian itself). Although not dealt with here, a global custodian will need to consider its own direct tax position and to familiarise itself with the taxation regime in each of the jurisdictions which may seek to impose a taxing right with respect to assets which it holds in custody.

Stamp duty and each charge to tax are examined in turn to give a brief overview of how stamp duty or each tax is levied, in order that some specific practical issues which arise can then be addressed. The discussion is not comprehensive, but it is hoped that it will serve to highlight certain areas where difficulties can arise.

Tax treatment is essentially parasitic on underlying legal relationships and property rights. Whether, for example, a document is chargeable to duty, a payment is liable to deduction of income (ie withholding) tax, or a custodian is directly assessable for income tax as an agent/trustee of an investor can depend (as appropriate) upon the legal effect of a document, the nature of a payment and the precise circumstances in which a custodian is acting. Difficulties associated with the interpretation of tax law and Inland Revenue practice apart, the precise nature of the rights and obligations enjoyed by and owed to participants in the financial markets forms an essential foundation for any tax analysis. Shortage of space prevents a detailed analysis of how all these pieces may be fitted together, but it is important to keep in mind that the taxation aspects covered in this chapter cannot be understood outside the context of the legal analysis in the other chapters of this book.

In order to avoid unnecessary confusion, it is worth noting that a word or phrase may have a precise meaning in the context of a particular duty or tax which differs from the meaning accorded to that word or phrase in other contexts. With regard to the terminology used in other chapters of this book, references are made to a 'clearance' service (and clearing systems) which are described as settlement systems[1]. However, in the context of charges to United Kingdom stamp duty and SDRT, which are discussed below, a clearance service (such as Clearstream, Euroclear or DTC) is regarded by the Inland Revenue as a system for holding securities and settling transactions, whereas they characterise an entity such as CREST as a settlement system through which transfers of securities are settled[2]. Consequently, the use of the term 'settlement' and 'clearing' by the Inland Revenue in the context of these stamp duty and SDRT charges differs from the customary market use of such terms; the latter simply equates settlement with delivery, and clearing with the pre-settlement of credit exposure, usually by the use of a central counterparty (as discussed in Chapter 9).

* This chapter was written by Gerald Montagu, solicitor in the international tax group at the London office of Clifford Chance LLP, to whom Joanna Benjamin and Madeleine Yates are grateful. Gerald would like to thank Peter Elliott, Tom Hawes and Sarah Squires, Partners, and Helen Tse in the international tax group of the London office of Clifford Chance LLP for, in Peter's case, gamely reading a draft, and in Tom, Sarah and Helen's case, assisting with aspects of this chapter; any errors are his alone.

It has been assumed for the purposes of this chapter that, notwithstanding various provisions of the Finance Act 2002 referred to in this chapter are intended to come into force on different dates, all the provisions of the Finance Act 2002 are in full force and effect.

1 See Chapter 9.

2 See further para **10.12**.

Stamp duty

10.2 Stamp duty is a duty on instruments[1] (rather than a tax on transactions). An instrument is within the charge to duty if it is executed in the United Kingdom, or relates (wherever it is executed) to any property situated in, or any matter or thing done or to be done in the United Kingdom[2]. There is, as a matter of tax law per se, generally no obligation to pay duty, as the payment of duty is not generally enforceable as a debt due to the Crown[3]. In practice, however, duty must be paid if a document is to be registered in the United Kingdom[4] or if an instrument is to be produced in evidence, or available for any purpose whatever, in civil proceedings in the United Kingdom[5]. If duty is not paid within 30 days of an instrument being executed, interest runs at a rate set periodically[6]. Additionally, a penalty is payable if an instrument is not presented for stamping within thirty days of execution (if an instrument is executed in the United Kingdom or (wherever executed) relates to land in the United Kingdom), or is not so presented within 30 days of the day on which the instrument is first received into the United Kingdom (if an instrument is executed outside the United Kingdom and does not relate to land in the United Kingdom). If an instrument is presented for stamping within one year of the end of the thirty-day period the penalty is the lesser of £300 and the amount of duty due; thereafter the penalty is the higher of £300 and the amount of duty due[7].

Stamp duty is charged under various heads; in the context of the financial markets (and hence situations likely to be regularly encountered by custodians), the following heads of charges are particularly relevant.

1 It follows that where a book entry system is in use (eg in the context of a settlement system like CREST, or a clearance system such as Clearstream) no stamp duty should be chargeable on a transfer as no stampable instrument is produced; see further para **10.17**, n 1.

2 Stamp Act 1891, s 14(4). 'The provision . . . speaks of an instrument "relating to" certain subjects. There is no expression more general or far reaching than that', per McNaughton J in *IRC v Maple & Co (Paris) Ltd* [1908] AC 22.

3 If, however, duty chargeable under Finance Act 1999, Sch 15, para 2 on stock constituted by or transferable by means of a bearer instrument is not paid on the first transfer of such stock in the United Kingdom, each person in the United Kingdom who transfers the stock by means of the instrument or is concerned as broker or agent in any such transfer is jointly and severally liable to the Crown for the duty chargeable, interest on the unpaid duty from the date of the transfer in question until the date

on which duty is paid, and severally liable to a penalty not exceeding £300 and the amount of the duty chargeable (Finance Act 1999, Sch 15, para 23).

4 If an instrument is not duly stamped, a person whose office it is to enrol, register or enter in or upon any rolls, books or records an instrument is liable to a penalty (Stamp Act 1891, s 17).

5 Stamp Act 1891, s 14(4). In August 2001, the Professional Standards Committee of the Bar Council, after consultation with the Chancery judges, announced that a 1956 Bar Council ruling under which it had been unprofessional (other than in revenue cases) for a barrister to take a stamp duty objection, was obsolete. There is therefore now no longer any rule of practice or conduct that it is unprofessional for an advocate to take a stamp objection.

6 Stamp Act 1891, s 15A(3). The rate is set by the Treasury using powers under Finance Act 1989, s 178; on 6 November 2001 the rate was reduced to 6.5 per cent (being 2.5 per cent above the average base rate of six high street banks) in respect of duty paid late (Taxes (Interest Rate) Regulations 1989 (SI 1989/1297), reg 3). Interest under £25 is disregarded and is not payable; where interest is payable it is rounded down to the nearest £5: Stamp Act 1891, s 15A(4).

7 Stamp Act 1891, s 15B as amended by the Finance Act 2002.

Bearer instrument[1]

10.3 Duty is chargeable (at the rate of 1.5 per cent) on:

(a) the issue of a bearer instrument in the United Kingdom and on the issue of a bearer instrument outside the United Kingdom by or on behalf of a UK company[2]; and

(b) (if there is no charge on issue under (a)) on the first transfer in the United Kingdom of stock constituted by or transferred by means of a bearer instrument if either duty would be chargeable on a conveyance or transfer on sale if the transfer were effected by means of an instrument other than a bearer instrument, or the stock constituted by or transferable by means of a bearer instrument consists of units under a unit trust scheme[3].

In practice, payment of duty under this head of charge is rarely encountered with respect to issues of debt securities. An exemption is available, for example, if either the stock constituted by or transferable by means of a bearer instrument falls within the statutory definition of loan capital[4], or stock is expressed in a currency other than sterling[5]. Duty is, therefore, likely to be an issue only where a sterling denominated bearer instrument does not qualify as loan capital[6].

1 The evolution of this charge to duty shadows the withering of exchange control. For the use of bearer securities and how their increased popularity was a consequence of the rolling back of exchange control in 1963 and its abolition in 1979, see J Benjamin *Interests in Securities: A Proprietary Law Analysis of the International Securities Markets* (2000, Oxford University Press), p 32, n 6. For a narrative treatment against a broader canvass, see also David Kynaston *The City of London: IV A Club No More 1945–2000* (2001, Pimlico), pp 98–9, 562, 581, 600.

2 A 'UK company' is defined as a body corporate formed or established in the United Kingdom: Finance Act 1999, Sch 15, para 11.

3 Finance Act 1999, Sch 15, paras 1–2.

4 Finance Act 1986, s 79(2); loan capital is defined to mean (s 78(7)):

'(a) any debenture stock, corporation stock or funded debt by whatever name known, issued by a body corporate or other body of persons (which here includes a local authority and any body whether formed or established in the United Kingdom or elsewhere);

(b) any capital raised by such a body if the capital is borrowed or has the character of borrowed money, and whether it is in the form of stock or any other form; and

(c) stock or marketable securities issued by a government of any country or territory outside the United Kingdom'.

5 Finance Act 1999, Sch 15, para 17.

6 The exemption provided for foreign loan securities by Finance Act 1999, Sch 15, para 13 is not often relied upon in practice, as it is a requirement (in addition to the loan being expressed in a currency other than sterling) that a bearer instrument (a) is not offered for subscription in the United Kingdom,

or (b) offered for subscription with a view to an offer for sale in the United Kingdom of securities in respect of the loan. Such restrictions are clearly incompatible with the marketing of many securities traded on the international capital markets.

Transfer or conveyance on sale

10.4 Duty is chargeable (at the rate of 0.5 per cent in the case of stock or marketable securities, and otherwise at a rate not exceeding 4 per cent) on a transfer or conveyance on sale of property for stampable consideration[1].

1 Finance Act 1999, Sch 13, paras 1–4. Stampable consideration takes the form of cash, stock, marketable securities and debt: Stamp Act 1891, ss 55, 57. The amount of duty payable is rounded up to the nearest £5: Finance Act 1999, s 112.

Exempt loan capital

10.5 Duty is not chargeable on the transfer of a bearer instrument by delivery provided that, as one would expect to be the case, no documentary transfer is produced[1]. There is an exemption from all stamp duties for an instrument which transfers exempt loan capital. A security will qualify for this exemption if it is loan capital (within the scope of the statutory definition[2]) and is therefore essentially 'vanilla' debt without any (equity-like) disqualifying features[3]. If an instrument transfers an interest in securities, and the securities themselves are within the loan capital exemption, that instrument is also exempt from all stamp duties[4]. There is also an exemption for an instrument which transfers stock in accordance with a repo or stock loan where the arrangement is effected on an EEA Exchange and the stock is regularly traded on that exchange[5].

1 A physical bearer instrument should by its nature be transferable only by delivery, depending of course on all the circumstances. It is, however, conceivable that a document characterised as an instrument transferring or conveying an immobilised or dematerialised bearer security (or conveying or transferring such a security in contemplation of the sale of that security (Finance Act 1965, s 90)) could be stampable as a transfer or conveyance on sale.

2 See para **10.3**, n 4.

3 An instrument will not qualify as exempt loan capital which 'at the time the instrument is executed, carries a right (exercisable then or later) of conversion into shares or other securities, or to the acquisition of shares or other securities, including loan capital of the same description' (Finance Act 1986, s 74(5)), or (s 79(5)):

'. . . at the time the instrument is executed or any earlier time, carries or has carried:

(a) a right to interest the amount of which exceeds a reasonable commercial return on the nominal amount of the capital,

(b) a right to interest the amount of which falls or has fallen to be determined to any extent by reference to the results of, or of any part of, a business or to the value of any property, or

(c) a right on repayment to an amount which exceeds the nominal amount of the capital and is not reasonably comparable with what is generally repayable (in respect of a similar nominal amount of capital) under the terms of issue of loan capital listed on the Financial Services Authority's Official List.'

Finance Act 1986, s 79(7A) (introduced by the Finance Act 2000) provides that an instrument is not regarded as falling within (b) above by reason only that loan capital carries a right to interest which (i) reduces in the event of the results of the business or part of the business improving, or the value of any property increasing, or (ii) increases in the event of the results of a business or part of a business deteriorating, or the value of any property diminishing. Notwithstanding this legislation, however, the Inland Revenue appear to continue to take a generally very expansive view of the meaning of (b), with the result that a limited recourse security is generally treated as not qualifying as exempt loan capital.

4 Finance Act 1987, s 50.

5 Finance Act 1986, s 80C.

Call options

10.6 It should be noted that a call option is also chargeable to duty under this head of charge, because such an option is treated as a transfer or conveyance of property in its own right[1]. Care should therefore be taken that an issuer's right to redeem securities is a term of debt securities rather than a separate option (as the latter could constitute a chargeable document on the day on which it is granted). The type of difficulties which can arise in this area have been attested by the discussions which took place between the Inland Revenue and the Financial Services Authority before the launch in September 2002 by the Stock Exchange of a covered warrants market under Chapter 24 of the Financial Services Authority's Listing Rules. In the course of those discussions the view was put forward that the issue of such global warrants might give rise to a stamp duty charge under the *Wimpey* principle[2]. However, the Inland Revenue is understood to have given the Financial Services Authority sufficient reassurance that no stamp duty should be chargeable with respect to the issue of a global covered warrant listed under Chapter 24 for the Stock Exchange to launch the new market.

1 *George Wimpey & Co Ltd v IRC* [1975] 1 WLR 995, [1975] 2 All ER 45.
2 Financial Times (18 September 2002), p 2.

Other exemptions

10.7 In addition to the exemption for exempt loan capital referred to above, a transfer of shares in government or parliamentary stocks or funds or strips of such stocks or funds, and a renounceable letter of allotment, letter of rights or other similar instrument where the rights under the letter or other instrument are renounceable not later than six months after its issue, are each exempt from duty under the transfer or conveyance head of charge[1].

1 Finance Act 1999, Sch 13, para 24.

Depositary receipts

10.8 No *ad valorem* stamp duty is in practice usually paid on a transfer of a depositary receipt, as a depositary receipt is usually represented by a book entry maintained by a depositary, with the register being kept, and any transfer documents executed and kept, outside the United Kingdom. Notwithstanding that in practice this is often the position, it is arguable that a depositary receipt in respect of a security issued by a United Kingdom incorporated company can be said to relate to property situate in the United Kingdom. As trading in a depositary receipt ultimately determines title to an economic interest (and, in a customary depositary receipt structure, constitutes a transfer or conveyance of an equitable interest) in the underlying securities, it is conceivable that, if circumstances were to arise in which a depositary receipt holder wished to prove title to an underlying security, a documentary record of an instruction to a depositary to transfer a depositary receipt might need to be produced in evidence before a court in the United Kingdom. In such a case it may be arguable[1] that that instruction, or a print-out of the depositary's records, could be a stampable document (as, respectively, a transfer or conveyance on sale, or as a memorandum of a transfer or conveyance on sale)[2]. A well advised depositary will try to ensure, in the unlikely event that the intermediation structure of which it forms part were to unravel in such a fashion (for example in circumstances in which a depositary's customer sought to acquire the actual underlying security to which a depositary receipt related), that any stamping is undertaken by others.

1 Much will depend upon the precise nature and legal effect of the documentation; cf, for example, para **10.17**, n 1.
2 Under what is sometimes called the 'memorandum rule' a memorandum of an agreement which is brought into existence to implement the transfer or conveyance of property which that instrument purports to record is stampable as if it were an agreement to transfer or convey that property: *Lord Braybook v A-G* (1861) 9 HL Cas 150; *Wigan Coal and Iron Co Ltd v IRC* [1945] 1 All ER 392; *Associated British Engineering Ltd v IRC* [1941] 1 KB 15; *IRC v Clarkson-Webb* [1933] 1 KB 507; *Horsfall v Hey* (1848) 2 Exch 778; *Garnett v IRC* (1899) 81 LT 633.

Transfer or conveyance of any other kind

10.9 Fixed duty of £5 is payable on a transfer or conveyance of any other kind (ie otherwise than on sale)[1]. Some examples of where this duty may be payable include where the consideration for a sale does not comprise stampable consideration[2], and where legal title alone is transferred.

In particular, if an instrument transfers securities of a United Kingdom incorporated company to a United Kingdom resident company, the business (or part of the business) of which is exclusively that of holding shares, stock or other marketable securities as nominee or agent for a provider of clearance services, to another company which fulfils the same requirements, £5 fixed duty (rather than *ad valorem* duty at the rate of 1.5 per cent under the clearance service charge to duty – see further below) is payable[3]. A similar provision operates in respect of an instrument which transfers relevant securities from one nominee or agent of an issuer of depositary receipts to another such nominee or agent of the issuer of depositary receipts: such an instrument is chargeable with fixed duty of £5 (rather than *ad valorem* duty at the rate of 1.5 per cent under the depositary receipt charge to duty)[4].

There is also an exemption which provides that stamp duty is not chargeable on an instrument which effects a transfer of securities if the transferee is a member of an electronic transfer system (eg a system such as CREST which enables title to securities to be transferred and evidenced without a written instrument in accordance with the Uncertificated Securities Regulations 2001). For the exemption to apply, an instrument must be in a form which will, in accordance with the rules of that system, ensure that securities are changed from being held in certificated form to being held in uncertificated form so that title to them may become transferable by means of that system[5].

1 Fixed duty was 50 pence for instruments executed prior to 1 October 1999.
2 See para **10.4**, n 1.
3 Finance Act 1986, s 70(9).
4 Finance Act 1986, s 67(9).
5 Finance Act 1996, s 186. See also *Stamp Office Manual* (March 2002) paras 10.36–10.40.

Contract or agreement chargeable as a conveyance on sale

10.10 An agreement for the sale of an interest in securities is stampable as a conveyance or transfer on sale, unless (i) the securities qualify as stock[1] or marketable securities[2], or (ii) the securities constitute property situated outside the United Kingdom, and (in either case) the agreement is for the sale of legal and equitable title to those securities[3].

1 For the definition of 'stock' see Stamp Act 1891, s 122: 'stock' includes –

> '. . . any share in any stocks or funds transferable at the Bank of England or at the Bank of Ireland, any strip [within the meaning of Finance Act 1942, s 47] of any such stocks or funds, and any share in the stocks or funds of any foreign or colonial state or government, or any capital stock or funded debt of any county council, corporation, company, or society in the United Kingdom, or of any foreign or colonial corporation, company or society'.

2 For the definition of 'marketable security' see Stamp Act 1891, s 122: 'marketable security' means 'a security of such a description as to be capable of being sold in any stock market in the United Kingdom'. This phrase has been glossed as referring to securities which are capable 'according to the use and practice of stock markets, of being there sold and bought', per Shand J in *Texas Land and Cattle Co Ltd v IRC* (1888) 16 R 69 (see also *Speyer Bros v IRC* [1908] AC 92, HL). If a security could be admitted to trading on a stock exchange, but is not so admitted, this should not prevent that security constituting a marketable security. In order to be a security an instrument must also create an obligation (*Brown Shipley & Co v IRC* [1895] 2 QB 598) and whether a certificate for registered debenture stock constitutes a marketable security depends upon whether a contract between the debenture holder and the company issuing the debenture are enshrined within the certificate; a contract was so enshrined in *Re Dunderland Iron Ore Co Ltd* [1909] 1 Ch 446 but not in *Noakes v IRC* (1900) 83 LT 714). Hypothecation is not necessary for a security to constitute a marketable security (*Speyer Bros v IRC* [1907] 1 KB 246 (where there was no hypothecation); *Deddington Steamship Co Ltd v IRC* [1911] 2 KB 1001 (where there was hypothecation).

3 Finance Act 1999 Sch 13, para 7.

Depositary receipts

10.11 There is a charge to duty (at the rate of 1.5 per cent) on an instrument which transfers the securities of a company incorporated in the United Kingdom to certain persons, including a person whose business is exclusively that of holding relevant securities as a nominee or agent for a person whose business is or includes issuing depositary receipts[1]. This charge, however, does not bite on the issue of a security to a depositary (although there may be a charge under the bearer instrument head of charge). This charge on the transfer of securities to a depositary at triple the usual 0.5 per cent rate of duty was introduced to compensate the Exchequer for the loss of duty (or SDRT) which would, in the absence of the issue of depositary receipts, have been chargeable on future transfers of the underlying securities to which the depositary receipts relate.

A transfer of exempt loan capital, which is exempt from all stamp duties, is exempt from this charge. Irrespective of whether the loan capital is available, no chargeable instrument should be produced if a bearer instrument is transferred by delivery to a depositary prior to the issue of depositary receipts. This charge is, therefore, only likely to be in point where depositary receipts are issued in respect of the registered securities of a United Kingdom incorporated company which do not benefit from the loan capital exemption.

1 Finance Act 1986, s 67.

Clearance service[1]

10.12 There may be a charge to duty (at the rate of 1.5 per cent) on an instrument which transfers shares in stock, or marketable securities of a company incorporated in the United Kingdom to certain persons, including a person whose business is exclusively that of holding shares, stock or other marketable securities as a nominee or agent for a person whose business is or includes the provision of clearance services for the purchase and sale of shares, stock and marketable securities[2]. The Inland Revenue take the view that CREST is not a clearance service for the purposes of this charge to duty (or the equivalent charge to SDRT). The Inland Revenue's *Stamp Taxes Manual* states that CREST is a settlement system and not a clearance service (and that it is not a trading exchange, a custodian or a clearance service)[3]. The rationale for drawing this distinction is that a clearance service is a system for holding securities and settling transactions in those securities by book entry and 'the securities may be held indefinitely within the system despite changes in beneficial ownership and are held either by the company operating the clearance system or its nominee'[4]. Most European settlement systems (other than in the United Kingdom, Ireland and the Nordic states) operate on an intermediated basis, as discussed in Chapter 9.

1 See para **10.1** in relation to the distinction between the terminology used in relation to stamp duty and the terminology used elsewhere in this book.
2 Finance Act 1986, s 70.
3 Stamp Office Manual (March 2002), para 10.16.
4 Stamp Office Manual (March 2002), para 14.10.

One-off charge

10.13 Where applicable, there is a one-off charge on the issue or transfer to a clearance service at triple the usual 0.5 per cent rate of duty that was (like the depositary receipt charge) introduced to compensate the Exchequer for the loss of duty (or SDRT) which would, in the absence of transfer by clearing system book entries, have been chargeable on future transfers of the underlying securities which have been placed in a clearing system. Indeed, the drive for the introduction of the clearance service charge came, in large part, from market players seeking to create a level playing field between issuers of depositary receipts and operators of clearing systems[1].

1 See further para **10.29**, n 2.

Election to pay stamp duty or SDRT

10.14 The operator of a clearance service may, however, elect that instead of the clearance service charge applying, stamp duty (or, more probably, SDRT) will be charged on any agreement to transfer of securities[1]; the Board of the Inland Revenue may require, as a condition for approving such an election, that the operator makes and maintains such arrangements as the Board considers necessary for the collection of duty in respect of such transfers[2]. If such an election is made, no charge to duty is made under the clearance service charge (nor under the sister charge to SDRT in respect of a transfer to a clearance service)[3]. Furthermore, if an election is made, there should be no charge to duty on the issue of securities into the clearance service; and the better view is that any instrument transferring a security to the depositary/nominee for the operator of a clearance service will not be chargeable with *ad valorem* stamp duty (as no economic interest moves to the nominee for the clearing system, there is no 'sale' of a security), but is chargeable with fixed duty of £5.

1 As discussed at para **8.6**, where securities are immobilised or dematerialised transfers are made through book entries in the accounts maintained by the system for its participants. Consequently, where a security is held in a clearance system there is not likely to be any documentary transfers of those securities when secondary market trading takes place between investors. No dutiable instrument may be created in the course of executing such trades, but SDRT is likely to arise in respect of an agreement to transfer chargeable securities: see further below.
2 See further para **10.31**, n 2.
3 Finance 1986, s 97A(3).

Exempt agreements to transfer

10.15 A transfer of exempt loan capital, which is exempt from all stamp duties, is exempt from this charge and, where the exemption for such loan capital is not available, no chargeable instrument should be produced if a bearer instrument is transferred by delivery to the provider of a clearance service. This charge is, therefore, only likely to be in point where registered securities of a United Kingdom incorporated company which do not benefit from the loan capital exemption are transferred to a nominee for a clearance system.

Investors

10.16 Generally speaking, stamp duty is likely to be principally of concern to a person wishing to prove title to securities: in many cases this will be the investor[1]. An issuer and the arranger/lead manager in respect of an issue of securities usually co-operate to ensure that no duty is payable on the issue of a security and that the characteristics of a security are such that an investor can trade in the security, or in interests in that security, without duty necessarily being payable. Thus, for example, a written instruction to transfer an American depositary receipt issued in respect of a registered equity share of a company which is incorporated in the United Kingdom (and where the register is in the United Kingdom) may well be within the charge to stamp duty as it relates to property, namely a share, situated in the United Kingdom. Provided, however, that the share to which the depositary receipt relates remains with the depositary and an investor trades the depositary receipt in respect of the share and is not obliged to prove title before a court in the United Kingdom, duty need not be paid on a written instruction to transfer a depositary receipt. Any duty payable on the transfer of such a share to a depositary (or a clearing system) should as a commercial matter be borne by the issuer of the securities; as an indemnity in respect of stamp duty may be void[2], a depositary (or clearing system) should customarily seek a covenant from the issuer that the issuer will ensure that a stampable document is duly stamped.

1 Note, however, the rules in relation to bearer instrument duty: see para **10.2**, n 2.
A person whose business is or includes the provision of clearance services for the purchase and sale of relevant securities incorporated in the United Kingdom must notify the Commissioners of the Inland Revenue within one month of first providing such clearance services; a person whose business includes holding relevant securities as nominee or agent for the operator of a clearance service is under a similar notification duty and this duty must be fulfilled within one month of first holding such securities as nominee or agent for such purposes.
A company incorporated in the United Kingdom which becomes aware that the operator of a clearance system, or the agent or nominee for such a person, holds shares in that company must also notify the Commissioners within one month of becoming aware of such a fact. If an operator, or an agent or nominee for such an operator fails to comply with this duty, the operator, agent or nominee is liable for a penalty not exceeding £1,000; in the case of a company the penalty for non-compliance may not exceed £100. See Finance Act 1986, s 71.

2 Stamp Act 1891, s 117.

Custodians

10.17 A custodian needs to be sensitive to stamp duty considerations as it may hold stampable documents and may, indeed, if it issues depositary receipts or 'custody receipts' (as such instruments are sometimes referred to in the United States) be liable to pay a depositary receipt charge. In certain circumstances a custodian's clients may be concerned to understand a custodian's operating procedures in order to ascertain whether a custodian's operating procedures might involve the unnecessary production of documentation which would be stampable and, if so, whether the production of such documentation can be avoided. Generally speaking, however, other than in the case of an instrument liable to duty under the bearer instrument head of charge, a custodian should not itself directly incur liability for the stamping of instruments in its custody[1]. A custodian in the United Kingdom is, however, obliged to satisfy itself in registering title to property that an instrument of transfer is duly stamped; otherwise it will infringe s 17 of the Stamp Act 1891 on entering on a register a transfer to which an unstamped instrument relates[2].

1 Whether a document is stampable depends upon the precise contents of that document; for example:
(a) it should be the case that an instruction from a client to make the appropriate entries under a book entry system pursuant to an agreement which that client has reached with another party to transfer an interest in securities represented by account entries, should not be stampable. Such an instruction, if in writing, represents a contractual request to the custodian – it does not transfer property, nor should it be regarded as a memorandum of agreement to transfer property (since it was not produced for the purposes of recording the agreement and bringing it into effect as between the parties, but merely between an account holder and the custodian); and
(b) a written transfer of registered securities is stampable.
Stamp Act 1891, s 5 provides that 'all the facts and circumstances' affecting the chargeability of an instrument must be fully and accurately set forth in that instrument; otherwise a person who executes an instrument or is concerned with its preparation with an intent to defraud the Crown incurs a penalty not exceeding £3,000 (see also *Parinv (Hatfield) v IRC* [1996] STC 933; affd [1998] STC 305, CA; Inland Revenue, Press Release (August 1997)).
2 The penalty may not exceed £300.

Evidence

10.18 A custodian should also be concerned to ensure that it will not be obliged to have to pay duty in order to have an instrument by which it is appointed stamped, so that such an instrument can be produced in evidence in civil proceedings before a court in the United Kingdom[1]. Although one would normally expect a custodian's clients, rather than a custodian, to wish to stamp an instrument (or to have it stamped) to prove title to property which is held in custody by the custodian, circumstances could arise where a person providing custody services wishes for its own purposes to produce a document before a court: such circumstances could include the enforcement of covenants given to the custodian or where a custodian (eg if the custodian is a trustee) seeks a declaration from the court as to its duties with respect to the custody assets. Although an indemnity for stamp duty may be void under s 117 of the Stamp Act 1891, a covenant to ensure that duty is paid may be enforceable and a covenant of this type is often included in documents[2]. A custodian may obtain further comfort that the instrument by which it is appointed is not stampable if, as in many capital market transactions, lawyers for the issuer or the arranger give a written opinion to the effect that transaction documents (including the instrument of appointment) are not stampable (and the trustee is an addressee of such an opinion).

1 An instrument of appointment, such as a custody agreement, should not be stampable with ad valorem duty provided that it does not contain:
(a) a transfer of beneficial ownership (or an equitable interest in) property;
(b) an agreement to transfer beneficial ownership of (or an equitable interest in) property;
(c) an option to transfer beneficial ownership of (or an equitable interest in) property; or
(d) an agreement to grant an option.
2 If, for example, a trust deed is only stampable with fixed duty (£5) (ie it does not constitute a transfer or conveyance on sale, but is a simple transfer of legal title to property) a custodian trustee may be content to rely on a right to recover expenses (including duty) from trust property (this right should

be expressly contained in a well drafted trust deed, but if no express right is included a right to to recover properly incurred expenses is implied under Trustee Act 2000, s 31). Note that industry standard custody agreements allow the custodian to collect amounts to cover their expenses out of the custody assets, as discussed at para **6.20**, n 1.

Reform of stamp duty

10.19 Although in many respects the main pillars of the stamp duty regime have remained in place for some three hundred years, significant reforms to the stamp duty charge were heralded by the publication of a consultation document to coincide with the Budget delivered by the Chancellor of the Exchequer in April 2002, and legislation is expected to be introduced in the Finance Bill 2003[1]. Notwithstanding that a major impulse behind the proposed changes is the desire to modernise the stamp duty charge in relation to land in preparation for the introduction of electronic conveyancing of registered land under the Land Registration Act 2002, certain aspects of the consultation document may merit notice by global custodians of financial assets. The stated intention is that at least in some respects the status quo will not be altered, as the consultation document sternly affirms that reform will 'not disturb the scope and impact of the main SDRT charge and of stamp duty as it applies to share transfers'[2]. However, it is proposed that (shares and securities apart) the stamp duty charge will be restricted to transactions involving land and buildings in the United Kingdom. Other types of asset, such as receivables, will be removed from the scope of stamp duty and the Inland Revenue anticipate that this will remove a charge which currently may affect debt factoring and the securisation of debts[3].

1 *Modernising Stamp Duty on land and buildings in the UK*, April 2002.
2 In certain cases, a stamp duty relief or exemption currently offers the only way of avoiding a liability to SDRT (ie an SDRT charge is cancelled if a transfer or conveyance is duly stamped as being exempt from stamp duty) because the stamp duty exemptions are not all mirrored under the SDRT legislation. It remains to be seen how this reform will work in practice and whether transactions which are in effect currently exempt from stamp duty (and on which the SDRT charge is cancelled) become chargeable to SDRT.
3 A transaction may currently be structured as an offer for sale on the part of an originator which a receivables trustee or special purpose company may accept by conduct in such a way that no stampable instrument is produced.

Stamp duty reserve tax (SDRT)

Chargeable securities

10.20 SDRT (unlike stamp duty) is a tax on transactions and is enforceable as a debt due to the Crown. SDRT is chargeable in relation to chargeable securities[1]. Chargeable securities are defined as[2]:

(a) stocks, shares, or loan capital[3];
(b) interests in, or in dividends or other rights arising out of, stocks, shares or loan capital;
(c) rights to allotments of or to subscribe for, or options to acquire[4], stocks, shares, or loan capital; and
(d) units under a unit trust scheme[5].

1 There is a distinction between the person who is liable for SDRT in the case of each charge to tax, and the 'accountable person' who may be obliged to account to the Inland Revenue within set time

limits (with respect to the principal charge to SDRT (other than where securities are in CREST, as to which see para **10.23**)), normally the seventh day in the month after the month in which an agreement which is chargeable to SDRT is made) for the SDRT. For a list identifying accountable persons and the time limits within which tax must be paid (without interest or penalties becoming payable) and other rules relating to the collection and enforcement of SDRT, see the Stamp Duty Reserve Tax Regulations 1986 (as amended).

2 Finance Act 1986, s 99(3).

3 'Loan capital' is 'capital raised which is borrowed or has the character of borrowed money' (*A-G v South Wales Electrical Power Distribution Co* [1920] 1 KB 552, CA) or 'funded debt' (*Reed International v IRC* [1976] AC 336, [1975] 2 WLR 622, [1975] 1 All ER 484).

In the South Wales case the Court of Appeal offered guidance as to what constitutes capital raised which is borrowed or has the character of borrowed money. That case concerned the issue by a company of 'warrants' in lieu of interest which had fallen due on debenture stock issued by that company (such that warrants bore interest and fell due after a specified date). In holding that such warrants did not constitute capital raised which is borrowed or has the character of borrowed money, Atkin LJ stated that 'this case is really determined by a consideration of the nature of the transaction' (at 557) (see similarly the tone of Younger LJ's judgment at 560 and Lord Sterndale MR at 555). The Inland Revenue take the view that the definition of loan capital is intended to cover 'any loan, for a specific period, however short'.

There is no statutory definition of 'funded debt'. Lord Wilberforce expressed the view in *Reed International v IRC* [1976] AC 336 at 361B that:

> 'It may be that no precise definition can be given, but I think that at any rate a debt is funded if it has some degree of permanence or long term character and some other indicia such as would be expected by a creditor, repayment of whose debt is to be postponed. Amongst such indicia would be payment of stipulated interest, a premium on redemption, security through a sinking fund or periodical drawings, or by a charge on specific revenues, the assignment of a definite order of priority as compared with other debts, the possibility of transfer in separate amounts.'

The other members of the Judicial Committee which heard *Reed* agreed with Lord Wilberforce, and Viscount Dilhorne added the observation that 'something more is needed in addition to the debt being permanent or semi-permanent or long term for it to be regarded as funded'.

4 This can embrace a warrant which carries a right to acquire a security which is not itself a chargeable security. Whether a warrant will be regarded as an 'option to acquire' will depend upon the rights enjoyed by the owner of that option. For example, an 'American style' warrant under the terms of which an investor may, on exercise, demand physical settlement is likely to be a chargeable security. A warrant which is treated as a chargeable security as an 'option to acquire' is also likely to be chargeable to stamp duty on issue under the principle outlined by the House of Lords in *George Wimpey & Co Ltd v IRC* [1975] 2 All ER 45: see para **10.6**.

5 Prior to amendments made by the Finance Act 1987 to s 57 of the Finance Act 1946 which brought the definition of 'unit trust scheme' into line with that in the Financial Services Act 1986, there was a concern that global and immobilised securities could be regarded as unit trusts and therefore qualify as chargeable securities.

This point was of concern in an SDRT context as a unit trust is structured as issues and redemptions of units in order to avoid stamp duty on secondary market transactions (transfers to a manager are subject to special provisions in Finance Act 1999, Sch 19). No stamp duty arises on the transfer of a dematerialised security (as it is a duty on instruments) but the principal charge to SDRT which arises on agreements to transfer chargeable securities could apply if a dematerialised security were a chargeable security. Historically, unit trust instrument duty was chargeable on the creation of a unit trust scheme and, prior to the abolition of this duty in 1988 (and the alteration of the definition of unit trust scheme in 1987), there was therefore a concern that a global and/or immobilised security could give rise to unit trust instrument duty.

Prior to the 1987 amendments Finance Act 1946, s 57(1) had defined 'unit trust scheme' to mean 'any arrangements made for the purpose, or having the effect of providing, for persons having funds available for investment, facilities for the participation by them, as beneficiaries under a trust, in any profits or income arising from the acquisition, holding, management or disposal of any property whatsoever'. The current definition in Finance Act 1999, Sch 19, para 14 tracks the definition of 'unit trust scheme' in Financial Services and Markets Act 2000, s 237(1) which replaced the Financial Services Act 1986 provision. This definition provides that 'unit trust scheme' means 'a collective investment scheme under which the property is held on trust for the participants'.

Immobilised and global securities do not per se generally fall within the Financial Services and Markets Act 2000 definition. Firstly, it is arguable that arrangements for immobilised securities and global securities do not satisfy this primary definition of a unit trust scheme, as the purpose and effect of such arrangements is not participation in and receipt of profits or income. Although that may be the purpose and effect of investment in the underlying issue, the purpose and effect of interposing an intermediary to create immobilised securities or global securities is the achievement of settlement efficiencies and (where securities are to be offered for sale to US persons) compliance with US securities restrictions. Secondly, immobilised global securities are taken out of the definition by Financial Services and Markets Act 2000, s 235(2) which provides that 'the arrangements must be such that the persons who are to participate ("participants") do not have day to day control over the management of the property in question . . .'

Excluded securities

10.21 Certain securities, including the following are excluded from being chargeable securities:

(a) securities which are exempt from all stamp duties (this includes exempt loan capital and gilts (irrespective of whether a transfer of gilts is within CREST)[1];
(b) securities issued or raised by a body corporate[2] not incorporated in the United Kingdom, where the securities are not registered in a register kept in the United Kingdom by or on behalf of the issuer, or in the case of shares which are not paired with shares issued by a body corporate incorporated in the United Kingdom[3];
(c) a depositary receipt for stocks or shares[4]; and
(d) a UK depositary interest in foreign securities[5];
(e) a unit under a unit trust scheme, if either –
  (i) all the trustees of the scheme are resident outside the United Kingdom and the unit is not registered in a register kept in the United Kingdom by or on behalf of the trustees of the scheme, or
  (ii) under the terms of the scheme the trust property can only be invested in exempt instruments[6].

1 Finance Act 1986, s 99(5).
2 On the meaning of 'body corporate', see G F H Montagu 'Is a foreign state a body corporate?' British Tax Review (2001) vol 6, as reissued with minor (albeit not quite complete) corrections in 2002 to more closely reflect the final proofs, pp 421–48.
3 Finance Act 1986, s 99(4).
4 Finance Act 1986, s 99(6). A 'depositary receipt for stocks or shares' is an instrument acknowledging:
(a) that a person holds stocks or shares or evidence of the right to receive them, and
(b) that another person is entitled to rights, whether expressed as units or otherwise, in or in relation to stocks or shares of the same kind, including the right to receive such stocks or shares (or evidence of the right to receive them) from the person mentioned in (a) above.
However, a 'depositary receipt for stocks or shares' does not include an instrument acknowledging rights in or in relation to stocks or shares if they are issued or sold under terms providing for payment in instalments and for the issue of the instrument as evidence that an instalment has been paid. See Finance Act 1986, s 99(7).
5 Finance Act 1999, s 119 and The Stamp Duty Reserve Tax (UK Depositary Interests in Foreign Securities) Regulations 1999 (SI 1999/2383 as amended by SI 2000/1871 and SI 2001/3997). A UK depositary interest is a depositary interest which is issued in the United Kingdom or registered in a register kept in the United Kingdom. A 'depositary interest' is defined as a security which –
(a) consists of the rights of a person in or relating to securities of a particular kind which, or entitlements to which, are held on trust for the benefit of that person by another person, and
(b) under the terms of its issue, can only be transferred in accordance with regulations under Companies Act 1989, s 207 (transfer of securities without written instrument) or by means of a transfer within Finance Act 1996, s 186(1) (transfer of securities to a member of electronic transfer system).
'Foreign securities' are securities within Uncertificated Securities Regulations 2001, reg 3(1) which –
(a) are issued or raised by a body corporate that is not incorporated, and whose central management and control is not exercised, in the United Kingdom;
(b) are not registered in a register kept in the United Kingdom by or on behalf of the body corporate by which they are issued or raised;

(c) are not units or shares in, or do not otherwise represent rights relating to, a collective investment scheme; and
(d) are of the same class in the body corporate as securities which –
  (i) are listed on a recognised stock exchange, or
  (ii) would have been treated as so listed immediately before 28 November 2001.

6 Finance Act 1986, s 99(5A). An investment is an exempt investment if (s 99(5B)):
(a) in the case of an interest under a collective investment scheme, ad valorem stamp duty would not be chargeable on the transfer of the instrument and the investment is not a chargeable security;
(b) in the case of an interest under a collective investment scheme, the scheme is an authorised unit trust scheme or an open-ended investment company and under the terms of the scheme property cannot be invested otherwise than to give rise to income taxable under Sch D, case III and can only be invested in exempt investments; and
(c) in the case of a derivative, it relates wholly to one or more exempt investment.

Charges to SDRT

10.22 There are three charges to SDRT.

Principal charge

10.23 This charge arises where a person (A) agrees with another person (B) to transfer chargeable securities (whether or not to B) for consideration in money or money's worth[1]. Tax is chargeable at the rate of 0.5 per cent of the consideration in money or money's worth. Person B is liable for SDRT chargeable under the principal charge[2]. However, where chargeable securities have been dematerialised within CREST, CRESTCo, as operator of a 'relevant system' for the purposes of the Stamp Duty Reserve Tax Regulations 1986, is generally required on or before the accountable date, except where different arrangements are authorised by the Board of the Inland Revenue, both to notify the Inland Revenue of each charge to tax which has arisen and to pay the tax due[3].

1 Finance Act 1987, s 87.
2 Finance Act 1986 s 91(1).
3 Stamp Duty Reserve Tax Regulations 1986, reg 4A. CRESTCo may, on making a claim, be relieved of its liability to account for and pay tax (and any interest on that tax) if it proves to the Board of the Inland Revenue's satisfaction that it has taken without success all reasonable steps to recover from the person liable for the tax in respect of which CRESTCo is obliged to account under reg 4A: reg 7.
For an outline of the Inland Revenue's approach to administering SDRT through CREST see the *Stamp Office Manual* (March 2002) paras 10.21–10.35 and see also the CREST Reference and Procedures Guidance Manual and the 'blue' book published by CRESTCo in September 1999.
SDRT is charged, and exemptions from SDRT are generally given effect to, by means of a 'transaction stamp status ("TSS") flag' or 'exception flag' which is inputed by a CREST participant with respect to each transaction. The main flags are:

'P'	0.5% *ad valorem* SDRT	
'R'	1.5% *ad valorem* SDRT	
'O'	no SDRT	On a transfer between nominees, or between a nominee and a beneficial owner, without a transfer of beneficial ownership
'S'	no SDRT	On a transfer to an exempt charity
'T'	no SDRT	SDRT paid inside CREST on another CREST transaction
'U'	no SDRT	Stamp duty paid outside CREST on a physical document (including a form 169); or SDRT payable outside CREST on corporate action
'W'	no SDRT	Issuing house exemption on new issue

'3'	no SDRT	Intra-group transfer entitled to relief from stamp duty under s 42 of the Finance Act 1930 (as amended), a letter of direction having been executed (see further Finance Act 1986, s 88(1B))
'4'	no SDRT	Stock loan return or transfer of delivery by value (DBV) (see para **9.36**) collateral relating to loans
'5'	no SDRT	A letter of direction having been issued (eg pension scheme merger, purchase of life insurance policy, or transfer by way of security for a loan)
'6'	no SDRT	Merger of authorised units, or the conversion/amalgamation of authorised unit trusts/OEICs
'7'	no SDRT	Stamp duty liability outside the United Kingdom

A CREST participant is obliged to keep evidence to support an exemption when it inputs an exemption flag. In an unusual case where one of the flags is not suitable and a statutory exemption is available, either (where a paper transfer attracts fixed stamp duty) use of a paper transfer (rather than settling the transfer through CREST) should be considered, or a repayment of SDRT can be sought from the Inland Revenue.

Where a repayment is claimed, the CREST Transaction ID, individual SDRT claim amount, trade date, and relevant repayment code must be submitted to the Inland Revenue's SDRT Operations Unit. For the Inland Revenue's practice with respect to reclaims of SDRT, see Stamp Taxes' *Customer Newsletter* – SDRT, No 1 (July 2002).

EXEMPTIONS

10.24 There are a number of exemptions from the principal charge. For example, these include exemptions which apply to:

(a) certain repos and security loans[1];
(b) intermediaries[2];
(c) an agreement to transfer a non-UK bearer instrument[3];
(d) an agreement to transfer a UK bearer instrument where (amongst other things):
  (i) the agreement is not made in contemplation of, or part of, an agreement for a takeover of the body corporate which issued the instrument;
  (ii) a chargeable security (or a depositary receipt for the chargeable securities)[4] are listed on a recognised stock exchange[5].

There is also an exemption from the principal charge for an agreement which gives rise to a charge to SDRT under the depositary receipt charge or the clearance service charge (discussed below), or where when an agreement is made and the Board of the Inland Revenue is satisfied that chargeable securities are held for the purpose of a business which consists of holding stock, shares or marketable securities as nominee for a clearance service provider, or when an agreement is for the transfer of a depositary receipt for chargeable securities[6]. An agreement to transfer securities to a body of persons established for charitable purposes, or certain other categories of exempt persons, is also exempt[7].

1 Finance Act 1986, s 89AA. The exemption applies where a person (P) has entered into an arrangement with another person (Q) under which Q is to transfer chargeable securities of a particular kind to P or his nominee, and chargeable securities of the same kind and amount are to be transferred by P or his nominee to Q or his nominee and certain conditions are fulfilled. The conditions are that (i) the agreement is effected on an EEA exchange or a recognised foreign exchange, (ii) securities of the kind concerned are regularly traded on that exchange, and (iii) the chargeable securities are transferred to P or his nominee and Q or his nominee in pursuance of the arrangement.

In order to be effected on an EEA exchange, an agreement must be subject to the rules of the exchange and reported to the exchange in accordance with the rules of that exchange (with respect to securities admitted to trading on the London Stock Exchange, see The Rules of the London Stock Exchange, especially chs 2 and 8). The Inland Revenue indicate, in the context of the

Intermediaries exemption from SDRT (Finance Act 1986, s 88A), which uses similar terminology to the repo exemption, that they regard a security as being regularly traded on an exchange provided that it is listed or admitted to trading within art 21 of the Investment Services Directive and the security is not an illiquid security.

The Inland Revenue accept that a security which has just been admitted to listing or trading by an exchange with which the Inland Revenue has entered into arrangements is 'regularly traded' as, in such a case, the rules an infrastructure of the exchange provide a mechanism for transactions in a security to be regularly carried out under the oversight of an exchange and subject to an exchange's rules of conduct, trade publication and transparency (Inland Revenue's *Stamp Taxes Manual* (March 2002), para 12.9).

An arrangement does not fall within the exemption if it is not such an agreement as would be entered into by persons dealing with each other at arm's length, or under the arrangement any of the benefits or risks arising from fluctuations before the transfer to Q or his nominee takes place in the market value of the chargeable securities accrues to, or fall on, P.

2 Finance Act 1986, s 88A(1) exempts from the principal charge to SDRT any agreement to transfer securities of a particular kind to B or his nominee if: (a) B is a member of an EEA exchange, or a recognised foreign exchange, on which securities of that kind are regularly traded; (b) B is an intermediary and is recognised as an intermediary by the exchange in accordance with arrangements agreed with the Board of the Inland Revenue; and the agreement is effected on the exchange.

Finance Act 1986, s 88A(2)–(3) similarly exempts any agreement to transfer securities of a particular kind to B or his nominee if: (a) B is a member of an EEA exchange, or a recognised foreign options exchange; (b) options to buy or sell securities of that kind are regularly traded on that exchange and are listed by or quoted on that exchange; (c) B is an options intermediary and is recognised as an options intermediary by that exchange in accordance with arrangements approved by the Board of the Inland Revenue; and (d) the agreement is effected on an EEA exchange, or a recognised foreign options exchange, on which securities of that kind are regularly traded or the agreement is effected on such an exchange pursuant to the exercise of the relevant option and options to buy or sell securities of that kind are regularly traded on that exchange and are listed by or quoted on that exchange.

An 'intermediary' (or an options intermediary) is essentially a person who carries on a bona fide business of dealing in chargeable securities and does not carried on an excluded business. Excluded businesses include a business which consists wholly or mainly of making or managing investments, insurance business, managing or acting as trustee in relation to a pension scheme, or operating or acting as trustee for a collective investment scheme (Finance Act 1986, s 88A(4)–(5)). The equivalent stamp duty exemptions are in Finance Act 1986, s 80A.

There are also exemptions, made by the Treasury using powers conferred by the Finance Act 1991 (s 116 with respect to stamp duty, and s 117 with respect to SDRT), which prevent multiple charges arising due to the mechanics of particular exchanges where a transaction is entered into by a recognised intermediary on an exchange and that intermediary has entered into appropriate arrangements with the Inland Revenue. The relevant exchanges are the London Stock Exchange (Stamp Duty and Stamp Duty Reserve Tax (Investment Exchanges and Clearing Houses) (The London Stock Exchange) Regulations 2001 (SI 2001/255)); virt-x (Stamp Duty Reserve Tax (Tradepoint) Regulations 1995 (SI 1995/2051 as amended by 2001/2267); LIFFE (Stamp Duty and Stamp Duty Reserve Tax (Investment Exchanges and Clearing Houses) Regulations 1997 (SI 1997/2429)); OMLX (The Stamp Duty and Stamp Duty Reserve Tax (Investment Exchanges and Clearing Houses) (OM London Exchange Limited) Regulations 1999 (SI 1999/3262)); NASDAQ Europe and JIWAY (The Stamp Duty and Stamp Duty Reserve Tax (Investment Exchanges and Clearing Houses) (Jiway Limited) Regulations 2000 (SI 2000/2995)).

3 Finance Act 1986, s 90(3)(a).

4 See para **10.27**, n 1 (Finance Act 1986, s 90(6)).

5 Finance Act 1986, s 90(3A)–(3F).

6 Finance Act 1986, s 90(4)–(6).

7 Finance Act 1986, s 90(7).

DOUBLE CHARGE

10.25 Although it is possible in certain circumstances for there to be a double charge, to SDRT under the principal charge and to stamp duty under the transfer or conveyance on sale head of charge, such a result is often avoided by the cancellation of an SDRT charge (and the refund of any SDRT which has been paid) if an instrument is executed pursuant to an agreement to transfer chargeable securities and that instrument is duly stamped[1].

1 Finance Act 1986, s 92.

10.26 Where an instrument is not chargeable to stamp duty on the dematerialisation of chargeable securities by virtue of s 186 of the Finance Act 1986[1], any SDRT which has been paid may be reclaimed (within the relevant time limits) and if SDRT has not been paid the principal charge to SDRT charge is cancelled[2].

1 See para **10.9**.
2 Finance Act 1986, s 88(1A).

Depositary receipt charge

10.27 There is a charge to SDRT where in pursuance of an arrangement a person (a 'Depositary') whose business is or includes issuing depositary receipts for chargeable securities[1] has issued or issues a depositary receipt for chargeable securities; chargeable securities of the same kind and amount are transferred or issued to the Depositary or a person (a 'Custodian') whose business is or includes holding chargeable securities as nominee or agent for the Depositary; and chargeable securities are appropriated towards the eventual satisfaction of the entitlement of the receipt holder to receive chargeable securities[2]. The rate of SDRT applicable is 1.5 per cent[3]. If *ad valorem* stamp duty is payable on an instrument effecting the transfer of securities, then the amount of SDRT payable is reduced by the amount of stamp duty[4]. The person liable for the SDRT is the person who issues depositary receipts, but if that person is not resident in the United Kingdom and does not have a branch or agency in the United Kingdom, the person to whom the securities are transferred is liable for the tax[5].

1 A 'depositary receipt for chargeable securities' is an instrument acknowledging (a) that a person holds chargeable securities or evidence of the right to receive them, and (b) that another person is entitled to rights, whether expressed as units or otherwise, in or in relation to chargeable securities of the same kind, including the right to receive such chargeable securities (or evidence of the right to receive them) from the person mentioned in (a) above. However, a 'depositary receipt for chargeable securities' does not include an instrument acknowledging rights in or in relation to chargeable securities if they are issued or sold under terms providing for payment in instalments and for the issue of the instrument as evidence that an instalment has been paid. See Finance Act 1986, s 94(1).
2 Finance Act 1986, s 93(1)–(3).
As at October 2001, according to an unpublished Inland Revenue practice, SDRT was asserted (subject to an exemption applying) against transactions involving:

System	**Nominee/recipient**
Guarantee Nominees (ADRs)	Guarantee Nominees Ltd
BNY Nominees (ADRs)	BNY (Nominees) Ltd
HSBC Bank (DRs)	HSBC Issuer Services Depository Nominees (UK) Ltd

For this practice, see M J Quinlan *Sergeant and Sims: Stamp Duties* (13th edn), para A13. The author is grateful to Michael Quinlan for clarifying the source of the authority for this information.
3 Finance Act 1986, s 93(4).
4 Finance Act 1986, s 93(7).
5 Finance Act 1986, s 93(8)–(9).

EXEMPTIONS

10.28 There are various exemptions from the depositary receipt charge. There is no charge to tax:

(a) on a transfer by, or to, a company which is an agent for the depositary and is a UK resident company[1];
(b) on a transfer, issue, or appropriation of a UK bearer instrument except in the case of[2]:
 (i) a renounceable letter of allotment which is exempt from stamp duty[3], or
 (ii) a non-sterling bearer instrument which does not raise new capital[4] and is not issued in exchange for an instrument raising new capital[5];

(c) on an issue by a company (X) of securities in exchange for shares in another company (Y) where either[6]:
   (i) X has control of Y, or
   (ii) X will have control of Y due to the exchange or an offer, as a result of which the exchange is made and the shares in Y are held under a depositary receipt scheme;

(d) on the transfer or issue of certain replacement securities[7].

For practical purposes, the exemption at (b) is the most frequently in point. Effectively, that exemption confines the depositary receipt charge in respect of bearer securities to the issue of depositary receipts for certain non-sterling bearer instruments issued by United Kingdom incorporated companies[8]. The logic appears to be that where a bearer instrument benefits from an exemption from stamp duty under the bearer instrument head of charge it would not be appropriate to impose an SDRT charge on the issue of depositary receipts. The somewhat gothic nature of the provisions, which are designed to ensure that the issue of depositary receipts for such foreign currency denominated bearer securities only escape a charge to duty if the securities represent genuine loan capital, is attributable to some arrangements which certain United Kingdom incorporated companies employed in the past to minimise stamp duty/SDRT by means of using foreign currency denominated bearer securities in the context of mergers and acquisitions.

1 Finance Act 1986, s 95(1).
2 Finance Act 1986, s 95(2)–(2D).
3 Finance Act 1999, Sch 15, para 16.
4 An instrument which raises new capital includes an instrument issued in connection with relevant securities which are subscribed for only in cash. A 'relevant security' is a security the holders of which have a right to a dividend at a fixed rate (but no other right to share in profits), or loan capital (as defined in Finance Act 1986, s 78), and which does not carry any rights by which securities which are not relevant securities may be obtained.
5 For example, an instrument issued in conjunction with the issue of relevant securities by a company in exchange for relevant securities issued by another company and immediately before exchange an instrument would have been regarded as raising new capital.
6 Finance Act 1986, s 95(3)–(5).
7 Finance Act 1986, s 96(2). Tax is charged on a percentage, where securities are issued, of their price when issued; or where securities are transferred for consideration in money or money's worth of the amount or value of consideration; and in any other case, the value of the securities.
8 Note that, for these purposes, the definition of chargeable securities is narrowed so as to exclude from the definition (and hence from the depositary receipt charge and clearance system charge) any capital raised by a company not incorporated in the United Kingdom: Finance Act 1986, s 99(10).

TRANSFERS BETWEEN RECEIPT AND CLEARANCE SYSTEMS

10.29 There is no charge under the depositary receipt charge in relation to a transfer between a depositary receipt system and a clearance system[1]. Note, however, that if chargeable securities remain in a clearing system and a depositary receipt is issued in respect of chargeable securities it would appear that a depositary receipt charge could arise (even if a clearance service charge had already arisen in respect of the chargeable securities)[2].

1 Finance Act 1986, s 97B. This section does not apply to a transfer from a clearance system if at the time of the transfer an election for the alternative system of charge under Finance Act 1986, s 97A is in force.
2 Any such harsh result may be attributable to the history of the depositary receipt charge and the clearance service charge. The depositary receipt charge was originally mooted to protect the Exchequer from the perceived loss of revenue when American depositary receipts ('ADRs') were issued in respect of multiples of securities issued by United Kingdom companies and subsequently transferred without there being a transfer of the underlying securities. The clearance service charge

was introduced so as to create a level playing field between issuers of ADRs into the American market and distribution to investors in the European markets, where it is more usual to trade interests in underlying securities held through the medium of a clearing system than to trade depositary receipts.

Clearance service[1]

CLEARERS

10.30 There is a charge to SDRT where in pursuance of an arrangement a person (a 'clearer') whose business is or includes the provision of clearance services for the purchase and sale of chargeable securities has entered into an agreement to provide such services for another person, and in pursuance of that arrangement, chargeable securities are transferred or issued to the clearer or a person whose business is or includes holding chargeable securities as nominee for the clearer. The mechanics of the clearance service charge are similar to those of the depositary receipt charge. Thus, the rate of SDRT applicable is 1.5 per cent[2]. If *ad valorem* stamp duty is payable on an instrument effecting the transfer of securities, then the amount of SDRT payable is reduced by the amount of stamp duty[3]. The person liable for the SDRT is the clearer but, if that person is not resident in the United Kingdom and does not have a branch or agency in the United Kingdom, the person to whom the securities are transferred is liable for the tax[4].

1 See para **10.1** in relation to the distinction between the terminology used in relation to SDRT and the terminology used elsewhere in this book.
2 Finance Act 1986, s 93(4).
3 Finance Act 1986, s 96(5).
4 Finance Act 1986, s 96(6)–(7).

EXEMPTIONS

10.31 The exemptions from the clearance service charge to SDRT are also similar to those which are available in respect of the depositary receipt charge[1]. However, as an alternative to such exemptions, the operator of a clearance system may, with the approval of the Board of the Inland Revenue, elect for an alternative system of charge to apply[2]. If an election is made[3], the clearance service charge to SDRT will not apply when a security is issued or transferred into the clearance system, but the principal charge will apply to an agreement to transfer the chargeable securities[4] (although the better view is that no tax is actually payable under the principal charge in respect of the agreement to transfer a security to a depositary/nominee for a clearing system, on the basis that such an agreement is not an agreement to transfer a chargeable security for consideration in money or money's worth)[5]. Both Euroclear[6] and Clearstream are understood to have made an election under s 97A[7]. As discussed above, there is no charge under the depositary receipt charge in relation to a transfer between a depositary receipt system and a clearance system[8].

1 Finance Act 1986, ss 97, 97AA.
2 Finance Act 1986, s 97A. The details of any such arrangement will depend on the particular circumstances, but the Inland Revenue take the view (*Stamp Taxes Manual*, March 2002, para 14.14) that significant issues which will be considered include:
(a) comparability with the procedures for accounting for SDRT through CREST;
(b) ensuring that all chargeable transactions are reported and tax paid;
(c) considering how higher rate charges and any reliefs would be administered;
(d) ensuring a flow of information for audit purposes that is accessible in the United Kingdom;
(e) preventing participants operating clearance services under cover of the arrangement; and
(f) the need for an overseas clearance service to appoint a UK fiscal representative.

3 The Inland Revenue, as of October 2001, took the view that the following systems were unelected clearance services:

System	Nominee/recipient
DBC (Germany)	Vidacos Nominees Ltd (Citibank)
Sicovam (France)	Vidacos Nominees Ltd (Citibank)
Clearstream (Luxembourg)	Vidacos Nominees Ltd (Citibank)
Amsterdam Stock Exchange	Askas Nominees (Kas Associates)
VPC (Swedish CSD)	VPC
Necigef (Netherlands CSD)	Necigef

For this practice see M J Quinlan *Sergeant and Sims: Stamp Duties* (13th edn), para A12. The author is grateful to Michael Quinlan for clarifying the source of the authority for this information.

For the position in relation to Euroclear (which has elected for the alternative system of charge to apply in respect of certain securities) see n 6 below.

4 Finance Act 1986, s 97A(3) disapplies the exemption from the principal charge to SDRT in s 90(5).

5 Note that the stamp duty clearance service charge is also disapplied if an election for the alternative system of charge is made.

6 Euroclear made an election for the alternative system of charge in 1999 for certain uncertified equity securities which are, in Inland Revenue parlance, 'settled' through CREST. As at 20 May 2002 only 11 such securities were held by Euroclear outside the election and subject to the 1.5 per cent charge.

With effect from 7 June 2002, as part of the rationalisation of Euroclear France market links, Euroclear Bank introduced a more general policy with regard to accepting CREST-eligible UK equities subject to the SDRT 1.5 per cent clearance service charge. By default the alternative system of charge (ie under the s 97A election will continue to apply) and Euroclear will identify securities accepted under the s 97A election by using an ISIN number and a first Common Code. It is, however, possible for a participant in Euroclear to submit a request that the alternative system of charge should not apply: in such a case securities will be identified by a second Common Code only. In addition to identifying the applicable SDRT regime by reference to the ISIN/Common Code, Euroclear will add the applicable SDRT rate to the name of the security. Separate accounts are used by Euroclear to enable a participant to hold and transfer UK equities under the 1.5 per cent charge or the alternative system of charge (and, apparently, to convert from one regime to the other when dealing with a counterparty which uses a different regime from that used by a participant). Where the 1.5 per cent regime applies, SDRT is charged to a participant and Euroclear communicates this to a participant by means of a corporate action notification (DACE notice). See further *Euroclear Newsletter 2002-N-03* (20 May 2002) and the 'United Kingdom' section in Euroclear's *Participant User Guide: Market Links* (20 May 2002).

7 It appears that whether an election is acceptable to the Board, and the extent of any such election which is accepted, will depend in each case upon the circumstances. However, the Inland Revenue has indicated that some of the main issues to be considered in this context are (*Stamp Taxes Manual* (March 2002), para 14.14):

- comparability with the procedures for accounting for SDRT through CREST;
- ensuring that all chargeable transactions are reported and duty paid;
- considering how higher rate charges and any reliefs would be administered;
- ensuring a flow of information for audit purposes that is accessible in the UK;
- preventing participants operating clearing services under cover of the arrangement;
- the need for an overseas clearance service to appoint a UK fiscal representative; and
- noting that s 97A enables the Inland Revenue to terminate the election on notice.

8 Finance Act 1986. s 97B. This section does not apply to a transfer from a clearance system if at the time of the transfer an election for the alternative system of charge under s 97A is in force.

Settlements and direct assessment

10.32 Although settlements rarely arise in practice, care needs to be taken to ensure that a settlement does not arise for income tax [1], capital gains tax [2], or inheritance tax [3] purposes.

A person in the United Kingdom, such as a custodian, may be assessable for income tax (a) as a trustee or agent under s 59 of the Income and Corporation Taxes Act 1988, or (b) if he is a United Kingdom representative of a person who is not resident in the United Kingdom and carries out a trade, profession or vocation through the custodian, under provisions in the Finance Act 1995.

1 An income tax settlement should not arise unless a trust is established by virtue of any act of bounty (*Bulmer v CIR* [1967] Ch 145, [1966] 3 WLR 672, [1966] 3 All ER 801; *IRC v Plummer* [1979] STC 793). If a settlement were to arise, the trustees of the settlement would be assessable at the rate applicable to trusts (34 per cent at the time of writing), or at the Sch F trust rate in respect of, Sch F type income (25 per cent at the time of writing) (Income and Corporation Taxes Act 1988, s 686(1)–(2)). Sch F type income, in relation to trustees, includes income chargeable under Sch F (distributions from United Kingdom companies), equivalent foreign income chargeable under Case V of Sch D, stock dividends, and a qualifying distribution by a company on the redemption, repayment or purchase by a company of its own shares or on the purchase by a company of rights to acquire its own shares (Income and Corporation Taxes Act 1988, ss 686(5A), 686A).

2 A capital gains tax settlement will not arise provided that property is held under a 'bare trust' (Taxation of Chargeable Gains Act 1992, s 68). Property is held under a bare trust only if the beneficiary is 'absolutely entitled' against the trustee; if there is more than one beneficiary, the beneficiaries must be 'jointly . . . absolutely entitled' against the trustee (Taxation of Chargeable Gains Act 1992, s 60(1)). There are four leading cases on the meaning of 'jointly absolutely entitled' in this context: *Kidson v McDonald* (1973) 49 TC 503; *Stephenson v Barclays Bank Trust Co Ltd* (1974) 50 TC 374; *Booth v Ellard* (1980) 53 TC 393; and *Jenkins v Brown* (1989) 62 TC 226. These form a unified line of authority; each decision followed and applied each of the previous ones:
(a) 'absolutely': beneficiaries must be entitled together to put an end to the trust and call for a transfer of the trust property; and
(b) 'jointly': interests must be 'concurrent' (ie not successive) and 'in common' (ie must relate to a common pool of property); the interests must be 'the same', meaning 'a similarity of interests in quality, not equality in quantity . . . each has, pro rata to the size of his . . . holding, the same sorts of rights'.

The rate of capital gains tax in respect of gains accruing to trustees of a settlement in a year of assessment is equivalent to the rate for that year applicable to trusts under Income and Corporation Taxes Act 1988, s 686 (Taxation of Chargeable Gains Act 1992, s 4(1AA)).

3 Although the prospect of a capital markets issue of securities giving rise to inheritance tax can initially induce incredulity, it is possible to create such a settlement as, despite the name of the tax and associations with the death of individuals, inheritance tax is a tax which may arise on chargeable transfers of value from an individual's estate both during life and on death. An inheritance settlement will be created (Inheritance Tax Act 1984, s 43) if property (other than excluded property falling within s 48):
(a) is held in trust for persons in succession or for any person subject to a contingency;
(b) held by a trustee on trust to accumulate the whole or part of any income of the property or with power to make payments out of that income at the discretion of the trustee or some other person, with or without power to accumulate surplus income; or
(c) charged or burdened (other than for full consideration paid to the settlor) with the payment of any annuity or other periodical payment payable for a life or any other limited or terminable period.

If such a settlement is a non-interest in possession settlement, inheritance tax is chargeable on settled property in certain circumstances including, where a transfer of value is made out of the settlement and, at the rate of 10 per cent, on the tenth anniversary of the date on which the settlement commenced and subsequent ten-yearly intervals (Inheritance Tax Act 1984, s 64).

Income and Corporation Taxes Act 1988, s 59

10.33 Section 59 of the Income and Corporation Taxes Act 1988 provides that income tax is chargeable under Sch D, and payable by, a person who receives or is entitled to income which is chargeable to tax under the Income Tax Acts. Tax is chargeable on such a person as the representative of the beneficial owner of the income[1]. At current tax rates, a custodian can be assessed to tax at a number of different rates depending upon the nature of a security in respect of which income arises and the identity of an investor[2]. It is, however, arguable that given all the layers of intermediation which may occur between a custodian and the ultimate investor in securities a strict operation of this section would not be feasible, as in many cases a custodian would not have knowledge, and would not have any means to gain knowledge, as to the beneficial owner of each security in a custody portfolio. In reality, if a custodian were chargeable under s 59, the basis on which a custodian should comply with the rules governing self assessment for income tax and a practical basis upon which tax is or may be assessed should be discussed with the Inland Revenue.

The forerunner of s 59 dates back to the Taxes Act 1842, long before the rise of global electronic securities markets. In the context of a security trust arrangement (where a secured asset is held on trust for a class of collateral takers), a security trustee is not thought (in leading counsel's view) to be assessable under s 59 prior to the enforcement of the security. Whether a party in a depositary receipt structure is treated as receiving or entitled to income will depend upon the nature of the transaction and the drafting of the documentation: the position is not always so clearcut and the Inland Revenue are known to have taken the view that in certain circumstances a depositary receipt structure can involve a separate and independent obligation owed by a depositary trustee to the recipient holder, which may give rise to a charge to tax under s 59. This is an area in which professional advice should always be sought.

1 See *Williams v Singer* [1921] 1 AC 65, where Viscount Cave said that a trustee needed 'actual receipt and control' of income if it were to be chargeable to tax in respect of that income; *Reid's Trustees v IRC* (1929) 14 TC 512; *Kelly v Rogers* (1935) 19 TC 692. The Inland Revenue's Centre for Non-Residents has issued guidance stating that a bare trustee is not obliged to complete a self-assessment return, http://www.inlandrevenue.gov.uk/cnr/nr_trusts.htm#13

2 A person assessable in a representative capacity is generally assessable (subject, arguably, to the provisions of any applicable double taxation treaty or Finance Act 1995, s 128 which limits the income tax chargeable on certain types of income to which a person resident outside the United Kingdom is beneficially entitled) at the basic rate (currently 22 per cent), except in relation to 'savings income' which is assessable at the lower rate (currently 20 per cent). 'Savings income' basically includes (Income and Corporation Taxes Act 1988, ss 1(2), 1A), subject to certain exceptions:

(i) income chargeable under, Sch D, Case III (eg UK source interest, annuities, annual payments and discounts),

(ii) 'equivalent foreign income', being income which would otherwise have been within (i) but which arises from securities or possessions outside the UK, and

(iii) any dividend or distribution from a United Kingdom tax resident company chargeable under Sch F.

Where securities are beneficially owned by a person within the charge to corporation tax (ie a United Kingdom tax resident company or a company which carries on a trade through a branch or agency in the United Kingdom and the securities are used by, or held for, the branch or agency) a person in the United Kingdom who receives or is entitled to such income is not liable to assessment under s 59 to income which is within the charge to corporation tax by virtue of Income and Corporation Taxes Act 1988, ss 6(2) and 59(4).

If, as generally should not be the case in relation to a custodian operating in the financial markets, income is to be accumulated by or payable at the discretion of a custodian or any other person, the rate applicable to trusts, currently 34 per cent, will apply, other than in respect of income to which the Sch F trust rate applies. The Sch F trust rate (currently 25 per cent) applies in respect of a distribution from the United Kingdom tax resident company on the purchase or redemption by such a company of its own shares or the purchase by such a company of rights to acquire its own shares. See Income and Corporation Taxes Act 1988, ss 686–686A.

Finance Act 1995

10.34 A UK representative of a person who is not resident in the United Kingdom and conducts a trade, profession or vocation in the United Kingdom through a branch or agency can be subject to obligations and liabilities in respect of income tax, corporation tax and chargeable gains tax[1]. Generally speaking, a custodian should not be liable to assessment as a United Kingdom representative of a person who is not resident in the United Kingdom and who conducts a trade, profession or vocation in the United Kingdom through such a custodian. Section 128 of the

Finance Act 1995 provides that income received by a United Kingdom representative of such a person is, in many cases, excluded income and therefore exempt from income tax. Excluded income includes income chargeable under Schedule D, Case III (United Kingdom source interest, annuities, annual payments, discounts and income from public securities payable out of public revenues of the United Kingdom or Northern Ireland) and income chargeable under Schedule F (dividends and distributions paid by United Kingdom resident companies)[2].

There is also a special exemption in s 127, which provides that a person in the United Kingdom who acts as an investment manager for a person who is not resident in the United Kingdom is not to be treated as a United Kingdom representative of such a non-resident. If a custodian, in addition to providing custody services, offers investment management services, professional advice should be sought with a view to ensuring, if possible, that in performing such management services the custodian's activities fall within the scope of the investment manager exemption. The requirements necessary to fall within this exemption are complex and the Inland Revenue have issued *Statement of Practice 1/01* setting out their approach to the treatment of investment managers and their overseas clients[3].

1 Finance Act 1995, s 126(1), Sch 23.
2 Finance Act 1995, s 128(3)(a).
3 See S J Squires 'Something old, something new . . .' *The Tax Journal* (9 April 2001), pp 12–14.

Enforcement in the United Kingdom of tax assessed under the laws of another jurisdiction

10.35 It has long been an established principle of English law that the courts in England and Wales will not enforce a foreign revenue law, either directly or indirectly[1]. Similarly, an English court will not permit an action to be brought before it to collect the taxes of a foreign country[2]. Consequently, a custodian has for the most part not needed to be concerned as to whether enforcement proceedings could be taken against assets in its care in respect of unpaid foreign tax. Inroads into this principle have, however, been made by the EU. Initially, the EU assault related only to value added tax and certain other indirect taxes sought by the tax authorities in other member states of the European Union and enabled such a tax to be recovered as if it were a debt due to the Crown[3]. However, the Finance Act 2002[4] implements a new 'Mutual Assistance Recovery Directive'[5] which aims to 'improve'[6] existing procedures for recovery of indirect taxes under an older Directive[7] and extends the mutual assistance provisions to cover direct taxes (income tax, corporation tax, capital gains tax and petroleum revenue tax)[8]. Under the legislation introduced by the Finance Act 2002, the United Kingdom tax authorities may, pursuant to United Kingdom law and after consultation with the EU member state seeking to recover tax in the United Kingdom, allow a debtor time to pay or authorise payment by instalments[9]. This legislation might have an impact on a custodian operating from an EU member state other than the United Kingdom, if it had not paid tax it owed on its own account in such a member state (and equivalent legislation should cause the provisions of the New Directive to be enacted into the national law of each of the EU member states so that, for example, tax unpaid in the United Kingdom could be enforced against a custodian's own assets in another EU member state). Equally, however, a custodian may need to be aware of the possibility that, although assets held in the United Kingdom cannot be subject to enforcement proceedings in the

United Kingdom to collect tax which a custodian's client has not paid under the laws of a non-EU jurisdiction, such assets may be subject to enforcement proceedings in the United Kingdom where a client has not (or is alleged not to have) paid tax in the relevant non-EU jurisdiction.

1 *Rossano v Manufacturers' Life Insurance Co* [1963] 2 QB 352.
2 *Government of India, Ministry of Finance (Revenue Division) v Taylor* [1955] AC 491, [1955] 2 WLR 303, [1955] 1 All ER 292; *QRS 1 Aps v Frandsen* [1999] STC 616.
3 Finance Act 1977, s 11 implementing Directive 76/308/EEC.
4 Finance Act 2002, s 31, Sch 38 (Recovery of taxes etc due in other member states).
5 Directive 2001/44/EC (the 'New Directive').
6 Press Release IR/CE1, 17 April 2002.
7 Directive 76/308/EEC (the 'Old Directive').
8 Article 7 of the New Directive states that a revenue authority of another EU member state may address a request to recover unpaid tax to the relevant UK tax authority and such a request must be accompanied by an official or certified copy of the instrument permitting its enforcement, issued in the EU member state and, if appropriate, by the original or a certified copy of other documents necessary for recovery. The Old Directive provided guidelines (preserved under the New Directive) on the procedures the EU member state must undertake to recover the tax. Article 7(2)(a) and (b) of the Old Directive provide that the EU member state may not make a request for recovery unless the claim and/or the instrument permitting its enforcement are not contested by the relevant UK tax authority and the EU member state in which the liability has arisen has applied appropriate recovery procedures which have not resulted in the payment in full of the unpaid tax.
9 Note that interest will be charged for late payment under the laws, regulations and administrative provisions in force in the United Kingdom and shall be remitted to the EU member state seeking to recover the tax.

Withholding tax

10.36 There is no generic definition of withholding tax in United Kingdom tax law. A withholding tax may be said, in United Kingdom tax law terms, to constitute the imposition on a person making a payment or collecting a receipt, of a liability to deduct or account for income tax (which represents the liability, or part of the liability, to income tax of the person beneficially entitled to the payment or receipt). In recent years United Kingdom withholding[1] has been significantly simplified by the abolition with respect to payments made and receipts collected on or after 6 April 2001 of the paying and collecting agent rules which applied to foreign dividends paid or received by agents in the United Kingdom[2]. Withholding has (under pressure, at least in part, to find a political comprise acceptable both to European Union institutions and the City of London to perceived tax evasion in respect of savings income)[3], in many respects (other than in respect of United Kingdom source[4] annual[5] interest[6] or annual payments[7]) given way to information reporting.

Legislation has traditionally maintained a distinction between withholding tax imposed on payers and paying agents on one hand and that imposed upon collecting agents on the other hand[8]. This distinction remains important (notwithstanding that it seems unlikely to play a role in the proposed EU Savings Directive on the taxation of savings income). The following analysis is divided into a section on payers and paying agents and a section on collecting agents. Although a global custodian is more likely to be a collecting agent, an awareness of the rules governing payers and paying agents may also be relevant to a global custodian.

1 Simplification has also resulted from the abolition of advance corporation tax in respect of distributions made on or after 6 April 1999 and the consequent disappearance of complex provisions dealing with the credit which used to arise in respect of advance corporation tax ('ACT') paid by companies within the charge to United Kingdom corporation tax. For United Kingdom tax purposes

ACT represented an advance payment in respect of a company's corporation tax liability which was, subject to certain limitations, creditable against that company's liability to mainstream corporation tax.

2 Broadly speaking, these rules applied to the payment or receipt by a person in the United Kingdom of a dividend, interest, annual payment or annuity paid by a body of persons established outside the United Kingdom or out of funds outside the United Kingdom. The paying and collecting agent rules, which enjoyed their final statutory incarnation under provisions enacted by the Finance Act 1996, dated back to the nineteenth century when provisions applied to what were then known as 'foreign and colonial dividends'.

3 Other influences have also been at work. The (phased) introduction of payment on account of corporation tax for accounting periods ending on or after 1 July 1999 has reduced the cashflow advantage to the Exchequer which was represented by withholding in respect of foreign dividends.

4 Whether interest has a United Kingdom source is determined by reference to a 'basket' test. The characteristics of each borrowing are considered to determine whether a sufficiently strong nexus with the United Kingdom is formed for an interest payment to be regarded as having a United Kingdom source. Unfortunately, case law in this area is somewhat obscure and it is difficult in certain respects to reconcile it with Inland Revenue guidance: *Westminster Bank Executor and Trustee Co (Channel Islands) Ltd v National Bank of Greece SA* (1970) 46 TC 472; *Tax Bulletin*, November 1993, p 100; Inland Revenue's *Inspector's Manual* (May 2002), para 3940. Important factors include: where a debt may be enforced, the location of any security or collateral, the source of funds from which interest and principal will be paid and the currency of a debt. Thus, although interest paid by a United Kingdom incorporated company will have a United Kingdom source, it is thought that if interest is paid by a company incorporated outside the United Kingdom under a borrowing secured on assets (such as land), or out of funds, situated in the United Kingdom, such interest should also be regarded as having a source in the United Kingdom for United Kingdom tax purposes.

5 Interest is 'annual' interest for these purposes if is payable with respect to a borrowing with a term of a year or more. This is a factual test and turns on the intention of the parties. Consequently, if for example a borrowing has a term of less than a year and there is provision for it to be rolled over beyond a year, or the parties contemplate that the loan will not be repaid within the year, then interest will be treated as annual interest. In this context, care should to be taken in the context of putting in place a programme for issuing interest bearing commercial paper.

6 There is no statutory definition of interest for UK tax purposes, although the meaning of the word has been considered in a number of cases. The classic description, by Rowlatt J in *Bennett v Ogston* (1930) 15 TC 374 at 374 is 'payment by time for the use of money'. More recently, Megarry J in The *Euro Hotel (Belgravia) Limited* (1975) SITC 293 at 301I–302B) said:

> 'It seems to me that running through the cases there is the concept that as a general rule two requirements must be satisfied in order for a payment to amount to interest, and a fortiori to amount to "interest of money". First, there must be a sum of money by reference to which the payment which is said to be interest is to be ascertained. The payment cannot be "interest of money" unless there is the requisite "money" for the payment to be said to be "interest of". Plainly, there are sums of "money" in the present case. Second, those sums of money must be sums that are due to the person entitled to the alleged interest; and it is this latter requirement that is mainly in issue before me. I do not, of course, say that in every case these two requirements are exhaustive, or that they are inescapable.'

Payment of a premium is treated as interest for UK taxation purposes, although a discount is not treated as interest (and is, therefore, not subject to withholding) (*Lomax v Peter Dixon* (1943) 25 TC 353). Note also, for example, that payment of a price differential under a repo agreement, while not interest, is deemed to be a payment of interest on a deemed loan for the purposes of the Taxes Acts (Income and Corporation Taxes Act 1988 s 730A) and such interest may, accordingly, be subject to withholding.

7 An annual payment is a payment which is:
(a) an income and not a capital payment;
(b) pure income profit in the hands of the payee;
(c) made under a legally binding obligation; and
(d) capable of recurrence.

8 There is no generally applicable statutory definition of a paying or collecting agent, although the (repealed) paying and collecting agent rules included detailed provisions by reference to which it was possible to ascertain whether in performing a particular function a person was regarded for the purposes of that legislation as acting as a paying or collecting agent. Typically, however, a paying agent is appointed by an obligor to make payments on the obligor's behalf and a collecting agent is appointed by a payee, lender, or investor. A collecting agent may, of course, make payments to its customer, but the function it performs (in the capacity of agent or trustee) is to ensure that payments are received (or assets realised) on behalf of its customer.

Payers and paying agents

10.37 Where a payment of UK source annual interest is paid, otherwise than in a fiduciary or representative capacity, by a company (other than a building society) or a local authority[1], or by or on behalf of a partnership of which a company is a member, or by any person to another person whose usual place of abode is outside the United Kingdom, the payer is obliged to deduct income tax at the lower rate (20 per cent at the time of writing)[2], unless an exemption applying a direction to make gross payment is obtained from the Inland Revenue's Centre for Non Residents[3], or these rules are disapplied by provisions introduced by the Finance Act 2001 (as amended by the Finance Act 2002).

1 The meaning of 'local authority' for these purposes is defined by Income and Corporation Taxes Act 1988, s 842A.
2 Income and Corporation Taxes Act 1988, s 349(2).
3 The Centre for Non-Residents (known prior to April 2001 as part of FICO) is charged with administering the Board of Inland Revenue's power under the Double Taxation Relief (Taxes on Income) (General) Regulations 1970 to issue a direction authorising gross payment where a recipient of interest is entitled to relief under a double taxation agreement in respect of that interest.

Eurobonds

10.38 In the context of the global custody business, the exemption which has most relevance is that for interest paid in respect of quoted Eurobonds[1]. For payments made on or after 6 April 2001[2], this exemption applies to payments made in respect of a security issued by a company which carries a right to interest and is (and continues to be) listed on a recognised stock exchange[3]. This position reflects changes introduced by the Finance Act 2000 and amounts to significant deregulation, as it removes difficulties previously associated with reconciling on the one hand the requirement (abolished by the Finance Act 2000 with effect from 6 April 2001) that, for the quoted Eurobond exemption to apply in respect of a payment, a security had to be in bearer form with, on the other hand, US tax and regulatory requirements that a security should not be in bearer form. Along with the need for a quoted Eurobond to be in bearer form, certain administrative requirements have also been abolished. These requirements concerned the location of paying agents; stated that in certain instances an investor should be tax resident outside the United Kingdom in order to receive gross payment (and should produce a declaration to evidence the same) and specified the recognised clearing systems[4] in which a quoted Eurobond could be held.

1 Income and Corporation Taxes Act 1988, s 349(3)(c). A 'recognised stock exchange' is currently defined as the Stock Exchange and any stock exchange outside the United Kingdom which is designated as a recognised stock exchange by an order made by the Board of the Inland Revenue (Income and Corporation Taxes Act 1988, s 841). Under an Inland Revenue interpretation (see Inland Revenue *Press Release*, 28 November 2001), securities which are listed on a stock exchange in a country which is a member of the European Union or which is part of the European Economic Area will satisfy this requirement if they are listed by a competent authority in that country and are admitted to trading on a recognised stock exchange in that country; securities which are listed in any other country will satisfy this requirement if they are admitted to trading on a recognised stock exchange in that country.
2 The modified rules apply to payments made on or after 6 April 2001, even if a security was issued prior to that date.
3 Income and Corporation Taxes Act 1988, s 349(4).
4 Euroclear, Clearstream (Luxembourg) and the Depositary Trust Company were 'recognised clearing systems'. The abolition of the concept of a recognised clearing system has opened the way for a gross paying quoted Eurobond to be cleared (viz: 'settled' as used in other chapters of this book; see para **10.1** for an explanation of this terminology) through other clearing systems (such as Monte Titoli, SICOVAM).

Disapplication

10.39 Section 85 of the Finance Act 2001 introduced further provisions, subsequently extended by the Finance Act 2002, which cumulatively disapply the obligation to withhold or deduct income tax from certain payments of United Kingdom source annual interest (and annual payments) by a company or local authority to a person who:

(a) the payer has a reasonable belief beneficially owns the income[1], and
(b) either is –
  (i) a company which is tax resident for United Kingdom tax purposes in the United Kingdom[2];
  (ii) a company not so resident which carries on a trade in the United Kingdom through a branch or agency and income which that payment constitutes income in that person's hands which is chargeable to corporation tax as part of the profits of that branch or agency[3];
  (iii) certain other entities[4]; or
  (iv) a partnership every member of which falls within (i) to (ii) (or certain entities within (iii) above)[5] or the European Investment Bank[6].

The effect of these provisions on global custodians is expected to be limited initially (as a custodian has not generally been obliged to withhold or deduct income tax from receipts of United Kingdom source interest, as in many cases it receives interest but it is not a person through whom a payment of interest is made) and is examined below under 'collecting agents'[7].

1 Income and Corporation Taxes Act 1988, s 349A(1).
2 Income and Corporation Taxes Act 1988, s 349B(1)–(2).
3 Income and Corporation Taxes Act 1988, s 349B(2).
4 The other categories of entity referred to in (iii) above include (Income and Corporation Taxes Act 1988, s 349B(3)–(5)):
(a) specified tax-exempt bodies. A local authority, a health service body, a public office or department of the Crown, a charity, certain scientific research organisations, the United Kingdom Atomic Energy Authority, the National Radiological Protection Board, an administrator or trustees of certain pension schemes;
(b) a nominee or manager of a tax-exempt personal equity plan or individual savings account; and
(c) a society or institution which receives the payment in respect of a tax-exempt special savings account.
5 Income and Corporation Taxes Act 1988, s 349B(1)(6)(a). The entities which may not be included in a partnership, if such a partnership is to be entitled to receive gross payments, are (a) a nominee or manager of a tax-exempt personal equity plan or individual savings account, and (b) a society or institution which receives the payment in respect of a tax-exempt special savings account.
6 Income and Corporation Taxes Act 1988, s 349B(6)(b)–(7).
7 The possible application of this legislation is not assisted, from the perspective of a paying agent, by Income and Corporation Taxes Act 1988, s 349(A)(5) which states that reference to 'the company by which a payment is made' does not include 'a company acting as agent or trustee for another person'. Although one might suspect that it would be logical for a paying agent to be able to form a reasonable belief as to the entitlement of a payee to receive gross payment, the effect of this subsection appears to cast some doubt as to whether a paying agent would be entitled to pay gross if it formed a reasonable belief that the payee was entitled to gross payment.

Collecting agents

10.40 As a result of the repeal by the Finance Act 2000 of the collecting agent rules with respect to receipts collected on or after 6 April 2001, there is no liability upon a collecting agent in the United Kingdom to withhold or deduct United Kingdom income tax from a receipt it receives in its capacity as collecting agent.

Although the rules in s 349(2) of the Income and Corporation Taxes Act 1988 which apply to a payer (or a paying agent) making a payment of United Kingdom source annual interest do not apply to a collecting agent, changes made by the Finance Acts 2000, 2001 and 2002 may have an indirect impact on the business of some custodians.

Eurobonds

10.41 The lifting of the requirement that a quoted Eurobond be in bearer form for a payment of interest made in respect of a quoted Eurobond to be made gross, removes at a stroke the difficulties which custodians had previously faced in satisfying the requirement that a security be in bearer form for United Kingdom tax purposes, while at the same time (eg if the security were to be offered for sale to United States persons) qualifying as a registered security for the purposes of the Tax and Equity Fiscal Responsibility Act 1993 for United States purposes.

'Reasonable belief' test

10.42 Furthermore, s 85 of the Finance Act 2001 introduced further provisions, subsequently expanded by the Finance Act 2002[1], which may apply where the financial asset in custody is not a quoted Eurobond, and these new provisions may in the future have an impact on the manner in which a custodian performs services where the payer has a reasonable belief that the person beneficially entitled to that payment is entitled to gross payment[2]. In introducing a 'reasonable belief' test, rather than an objective set of conditions, these provisions break new ground. It is understood that part of the Inland Revenue's preference for a reasonable belief test was due to their desire to give a payer some flexibility in the manner in which it satisfies itself that the conditions for gross payment are met; rather than a direct representation or warranty from an investor as to its status and the manner in which it holds a financial asset a payer may be able to form a reasonable belief based upon an assurance given to it by an investor's custodian/collecting agent. It is not entirely clear precisely in what circumstances, in the Inland Revenue's view, a payer will be able to form a reasonable belief that gross payment is appropriate[3]. Market reaction is also likely to influence the extent to which custodians are prepared to become involved in helping a payer to form a reasonable belief. As a payer is usually obliged as a matter of contract to pay gross unless required by law to deduct tax, an investor who can supply sufficient information to a payer for that payer to form a reasonable belief that the conditions for gross payment are fulfilled would appear (unless a payer is to risk breach of contract) to be in a position to compel a payer to pay gross. With the many layers of intermediation common in the capital markets it seems unlikely that as a practical matter these provisions will generally find wide application (as, for example, a depositary for a global bond is extremely unlikely to have any information as to the identity of the ultimate beneficial owner of an interest in that security), although where a registrar keeps a register of holders of securities it may be (if a registrar has the benefit of an appropriate representation from a holder of its status and as to its beneficial ownership of a security) that a registrar can assist a borrower (and, if appropriate, its paying agent) in arriving at a reasonable belief that payment should be made gross[4].

1 Income and Corporation Taxes Act 1988, ss 349A–349D.
2 Income and Corporation Taxes Act 1988, ss 349A(1), 349B. For the categories of payee entitled to gross payment see para **10.39**.

3 On 30 March 2001 the Inland Revenue issued some initial guidance to accompany the publication of clause 83 of the Finance Bill 2001 (this clause, as enacted, became s 85 of the Finance Act 2001). Subsequently, in the *Tax Bulletin* (August 2001), the Inland Revenue issued further guidance. This guidance indicates that what constitutes grounds for 'reasonable belief' will vary depending upon the relationship between the payer and the payee. The Revenue suggest that where a payment is made between associated companies, the payer is in a good position to know whether the payee meets the conditions for gross payment. Conversely, where the payer and payee are not known to each other, a payer may want to obtain documentary evidence of the payee's status. Such evidence may take the form of a statement signed by an appropriate officer of the payer company containing either confirmation that the payee meets the conditions for gross payment or, if the payee is a nominee, confirmation that the beneficial owner of income meets the conditions for gross payment. The Revenue state that if a payer is in any doubt as to the accuracy or trustworthiness of such evidence, the payer will not have reasonable grounds for believing the payee is entitled to receive payment gross and should deduct tax from a payment to that payee. It remains to be seen whether the Revenue will accept that if evidence supplied is inaccurate (eg there is a typographical error or the wording of such a confirmation does not precisely track the statute) but a payer has no reason to suspect bad faith on the payee's part, a payer can be regarded as having the requisite reasonable belief to make gross payment. The Revenue have also stressed that they are willing to work with market operators in drawing up guidance for specific markets. For the Revenue's mission to 'be seen to enable as well as to regulate', see Sir Nicholas Montagu 'The Reality of Today's Revenue' *The Tax Journal* (29 July 2002) pp 4–6.

4 In March 2001 the Inland Revenue undertook a consultation exercise as to whether, where a collecting agent is involved in a chain of payments and it is necessary to seek the tax which should have been deducted, the tax could be sought from the collecting agent (if resident in the UK) instead of from the payer: Inland Revenue Press Release, *REV BN13*, 7 March 2001. The Revenue asked: 'Would such a system be an advantage?' The results of this consultation exercise have not been published at the time of going to press. It is, however, worth noting that, unless a collection mechanism were optional and suitable protection was built in for a collecting agent, such a change could amount to an extension of the obligation to withhold United Kingdom tax to collecting agents (whereas this obligation currently, as observed above, only applies to paying agents). As the Finance Act 2002 extended the legislation originally introduced by the Finance Act 2001, but did not provide for the introduction of such a system, it seems likely that, at least for the moment, the Inland Revenue has concluded against taking any steps to introduce such a regime.

Manufactured overseas dividends ('MODs')

10.43 A manufactured overseas dividend is a payment, made under a contract or other arrangements for the transfer of overseas securities[1], which is representative of a dividend on those overseas securities[2].

Despite the restriction in the scope of the manufactured overseas dividend rules in 1996 to apply only to overseas equities (whereas the rules had previously applied equally to overseas debt securities)[3], and the simplification which has followed the abolition in April 2001 of the paying and collecting agent rules with which the MOD rules interacted in a particularly complex manner, this is still a difficult area and professional advice should always be sought. In broad terms, the effect of the MOD rules is to treat a manufactured payment as an annual payment and to require a person who makes (or where a so called 'reverse charge' applies, receives[4]) a manufactured payment withhold tax at the basic rate (at the time of writing, 22 per cent)[5] subject to specific rules which apply in certain circumstances, various exemptions and rights of set off[6].

In the context of custody arrangements covered in other chapters of this book, it will suffice to highlight two features of the MOD regime.

1 An 'overseas security' is defined as 'shares, stock, or other securities issued by a government or public or local authority of a territory outside the United Kingdom or by any other body of persons not resident in the United Kingdom': Income and Corporation Taxes Act 1988, Sch 23A, para 1(1).

2 Income and Corporation Taxes Act 1988, Sch 23A, para 4(1). Examples of a manufactured payment include where a loan of overseas securities is outstanding over a dividend date and the borrower makes a payment to compensate the lender of the securities for a dividend paid on the dividend date, or a buyer of securities under the outward leg of a repo makes a payment to the seller of the securities representing a dividend which the buyer receives in respect of the securities.
3 Income Tax (Manufactured Overseas Dividends) Regulations 1993, reg 2B.
4 The reverse charge applies where there is a United Kingdom recipient (a person who is tax resident in the United Kingdom or a non-resident carrying on a trade in the United Kingdom) of a manufactured payment and a manufacturer is not United Kingdom resident and does not make the payment in the course of a trade carried on in the United Kingdom through a branch or agency: Income and Corporation Taxes Act 1988, Sch 23A, para 4(3).
5 Income and Corporation Taxes Act 1988, Sch 23A, para 4(2).
6 The Inland Revenue's initial response to manufactured payments was to regulate such payments extremely closely. Over time this approach has become more pragmatic and the Inland Revenue have used AUKI and AUKCA (see below) to police the rules. Even after these reforms, however, the MOD legislation is not straightforward.

Underlying security

10.44 The first feature is that for those purposes where a security is held in a depositary and a depositary receipt issued, the Inland Revenue look through the depositary receipt to the underlying security. Consequently, any payment made under arrangements for transferring a depositary receipt which is representative of a dividend on the underlying overseas securities is regarded as a manufactured payment[1].

1 *Inland Revenue Manufactured Payments on Overseas Securities Guidance Notes: April 2001*, para 3.12, p 8.

Manufacturers

10.45 The second feature is that only a person who is acting as principal (ie not as an agent) is regarded as a manufacturer[1]. This means both that a tax liability will generally only arise if an intermediary acts as principal (such a liability can be managed by setting-off tax suffered against that person's tax liability in respect of the dividend received[2]) and also that an entity acting as agent will need to demonstrate that it is not acting as principal in a particular transaction. Liability can, however, arise for an intermediary acting as agent if the reverse charge applies and that agent carries on a trade in the United Kingdom on behalf of an overseas principal[3], or in certain circumstances if an overseas dividend is paid to either an approved UK intermediary ('AUKI'[4]) or an approved UK collecting agent ('AUKCA'[5]) by a manufacturer who is not an AUKI and is resident in the United Kingdom (or if not so resident makes the payment in the course of a trade carried on in the United Kingdom) and the manufacturer receives the real overseas dividend which the manufactured payment represents, or a manufacturer who is not an AUKI makes a payment to an AUKI or AUKCA without deducting tax from a manufactured payment[6]. An AUKI or AUKCA may, however, issue a notice authorising another AUKI or AUKCA to pay gross, so that there can be a chain of intermediaries[7].

1 *Inland Revenue Manufactured Payments on Overseas Securities Guidance Notes: April 2001*, para 3.14, p 9.
2 Income Tax (Manufactured Overseas Dividends) Regulations 1993, regs 9, 9A.
3 Income and Corporation Taxes Act 1988, Sch 23A, para 4(3).
4 An AUKI is an overseas dividend manufacturer who is resident in the United Kingdom, or if not so resident, carries on a trade in the United Kingdom through a branch or agency, and has obtained

approval from the Board of the Inland Revenue: Income Tax (Manufactured Overseas Dividends) Regulations 1993, reg 2(1).

5 An AUKCA is a person who is a collecting agent and who is resident in the United Kingdom, or if not so resident, carries on a trade in the United Kingdom through a branch or agency and has obtained approval from the Board of the Inland Revenue: Income Tax (Manufactured Overseas Dividends) Regulations 1993, reg 2(1).

6 Income Tax (Manufactured Overseas Dividends) Regulations 1993, reg 4(3). An AUKI or AUKCA need not deduct tax if (reg 5) either:
(i) an intermediary has entered into arrangements with the Board of the Inland Revenue entitling it to make payments gross without deducting tax under the Double Taxation Relief Regulations (Taxes on Income) (General) Manufactured Overseas Dividends) Regulations 1993 (and it has received a form MOD1 or MOD2 from the recipient of the dividend), or
(ii) the so called 'domestic to domestic' rule applies.
Under the 'domestic to domestic' rule, if a payment is made to an individual or a company beneficially entitled to that payment who is not tax resident in the United Kingdom (and, in the case of a company, centrally managed and controlled outside the United Kingdom) and the security is issued by a government, public/local authority or a resident of that territory, tax is deducted at the rate which would have applied to a real dividend paid to that recipient in respect of those securities. The 'domestic to domestic' rule is inapplicable if a tax treaty between the United Kingdom and the overseas territory contains an 'other income' article.

7 Income Tax (Manufactured Overseas Dividends) Regulations 1993, reg 5(2)(b)(iii).

Information reporting requirements

10.46 In the March 2000 Budget the United Kingdom Government took a policy decision, subsequently enshrined in the Finance Act 2000, that a system of information reporting should replace the paying and collecting agent rules (the abolition of which has been referred to above)[1]. The broad rationale behind this approach is that the tax base can be protected, and tax be paid by the individual who is the beneficial owner of income, if the fiscal authority with jurisdiction to charge the beneficial owner income possesses information that such income has been received by that individual; in such a case there is, consequently, no need to impose an obligation on a third party (the payer, a paying or a collecting agent) to deduct income tax (which effectively represents tax payable by the beneficial owner of the income) from a payment or receipt.

Under the information reporting regime any person by or through whom interest[2] is paid (irrespective of whether tax is deducted from that payment) and any person by whom any such interest is received must notify the Inland Revenue of certain information in relation to that payment (this information includes the amount of the payment, the name and address of the person (the 'investor') whom interest is paid to or on whose behalf interest is received)[3]. These provisions apply irrespective of whether an investor is resident in the United Kingdom for United Kingdom taxation purposes. Where an investor is not resident in the United Kingdom, the details provided to the United Kingdom Inland Revenue may, in certain cases, be passed by the United Kingdom Inland Revenue to the tax authorities of the jurisdiction in which an investor is resident for taxation purposes.

There are a number of circumstances in which information need not be supplied to the Inland Revenue. The most important of these is where there is a payment to, or a receipt for, a person who is not an individual (in whatever capacity the individual concerned is acting)[4]. Another significant exclusion relates to a payment in respect of a payment plan such as a personal equity plan or an individual saving account[5]. (There is also no requirement to report where a person passively collects interest: for example, where a bank does no more than clear a cheque or arranges for a cheque to be cleared, but takes no step to secure the payment of monies). The Inland Revenue have published guidance notes indicating how they intend to approach the implementation of the new reporting requirements[6].

1 A recent instance of this emphasis upon information exchange may be found in art 27 of the double taxation agreement between the United Kingdom and the United States of America which was signed on 24 July 2001. The treaty (which at the time of going to press is still subject to ratification) provides that information relating to persons who are not resident in either the United Kingdom or the United States may be exchanged (art 27(1)). Information may be exchanged even where the contracting state providing the information does not require the information for its own tax purposes (art 27(2)). If specifically requested to do so by the competent authority of a contracting state, the competent authority of the other contracting state will provide information in the form of authenticated copies of unedited original documents (art 27(4)).

2 'Interest' is defined for these purposes as any dividend in respect of a share in a building society, any amount to which a person holding a relevant discounted security (as defined by Finance Act 1996, Sch 13, para 3) is entitled on the redemption of that security and any foreign dividend (a 'foreign dividend' is any annual payment, interest or dividend payable out of, or in respect of, the stocks, funds, shares or securities of a body of persons that is not resident in the United Kingdom or a government or public or local authority of a country outside the United Kingdom): Taxes Management Act 1970, s 18(3E)–(3G). These provisions do not apply to payments or receipts representing redemption proceeds in respect of relevant discounted securities or foreign dividends (not including foreign interest) made or received prior to 6 April 2003 (Income Tax (Interest Payments) (Information Powers) Regulations 1992, reg 3(4)(a)–(b)), repo interest, or manufactured payments.
Although, as a technical matter, it may be arguable that payments in respect of a guarantee do not constitute 'interest', it is thought that for compliance purposes it may be prudent to regard a payment made in respect of a guarantee as being within these provisions.

3 Taxes Management Act 1970, s 18(1), (3B)–(3C); Income Tax (Interest Payments) (Information Powers) Regulations 1992 (as amended by SI 2001/405). A person who has responsibility for reporting, may report payments/ receipts in respect either of all individuals or of individuals with an address in a fully reportable country. Fully reportable countries, at the time of writing, are Anguilla, Australia, Austria, Belgium, Bermuda, British Virgin Islands, Canada, Cayman Islands, Denmark, Finland, France, Germany, Greece, Guernsey, Ireland, Isle of Man, Italy, Japan, Jersey, Luxembourg, Montserrat, Netherlands, New Zealand, Norway, Portugal, South Korea, Spain, Sweden, Turks & Caicos Islands, the United Kingdom and the United States of America.

4 Income Tax (Interest Payments) (Information Powers) Regulations 1992, reg 3(4)(c).

5 Income Tax (Interest Payments) (Information Powers) Regulations 1992, reg 3(4)(h).

6 *Savings Income –TMA 1970, s 18 Return Guidance Notes*, July 2001. The Inland Revenue will normally require an annual return to be submitted, and a return must be made as directed in the notice (a notice must usually be submitted by whichever is the later of 30 June following the end of the tax year to which a notice relates, or four months after the issue of the notice).

Proposed European Union Directive on the taxation of savings income

10.47 On 13 December 2001 the European Commission published a revised draft of a proposed EU Directive on the taxation of savings income, which is designed to secure that at least a minimum effective rate of tax is paid on all interest and similar savings income earned by individuals who are residents of EU member states. The Directive is not expected to come into effect before 2004. The proposals are not yet final, and they may be subject to further amendment and/or clarification.

It is proposed that where a 'paying agent' established in any EU member state makes payments of interest, discount or premium to an individual resident in another member state, the tax authorities of the paying agent's member state will be required to supply details of the payment to the tax authorities of the other member state. For these purposes, the term 'paying agent' is widely defined to include both the principal obligor under a debt obligation; a paying agent in the normal sense of that term; and an agent who collects interest, discounts or premiums on behalf of an individual beneficially entitled to such interest, discount or premium[1].

1 Note that the use of the terms 'paying agent' in this context is much broader than under current United Kingdom tax law: see para **10.37**.

Transitional provisions

10.48 During a transitional period of not more than seven years from the coming into effect of the Directive, certain member states (expected to be confined to Austria, Belgium and Luxembourg) may, instead of supplying information on savings income to the tax authorities of other member states, operate a withholding tax. In such cases 'paying agents' established in the relevant member states must withhold tax from any interest, discount or premium paid to an individual resident in another member state. The withholding tax will be levied at a rate of 15 per cent during the first three years of the transitional period, and at a rate of 20 per cent during the remaining four years. The withholding tax will not be levied if the individual authorises the disclosure of details of the income to the tax authorities of his state of residence, or if he presents a certificate obtained from the tax authorities of his state of residence confirming that those authorities are aware of the payment due to the individual.

Exemptions

10.49 Eurobonds and other negotiable debt securities which are issued before 1 March 2001, or are issued under a prospectus certified by a competent authority before that date, will be exempt from the withholding tax provisions of the Directive even if interest, discounts or premiums on such securities are paid through a 'paying agent' established in a member state which adopts the transitional withholding tax regime. Securities issued on or after 1 March 2002 will be fully within the scope of the Directive when it comes into force. However, there will be no requirement for the Directive to be applied to payments made in respect of securities issued before 1 March 2001, or to payments in respect of securities issued before 1 March 2002 and fungible with securities issued before 1 March 2001[1].

1 It is proposed that where securities are issued after 1 March 2002 by a government or a 'related entity' which are fungible with securities issued prior to 1 March 2001, both the new (post 1 March 2002) and the old (pre March 2001) securities will be subject to the Directive (ie none of the relevant securities will be grandfathered).

A list of 'related entities' (none of which are in the United Kingdom) was agreed by ECOFIN in March 2002; see *Press Release 11 March 2002* (6596/02).

Euroclear and Clearstream have announced that where securities are not issued by a government or a related entity, they will only treat securities issued after 1 March 2002 as fungible with an earlier issue of securities if the closing date for the first issue was on or after 1 March 2001 and the issuer, or its agent, represent that no competent authority approved any original issuing prospectus before 1 March 2001.

Conditional adoption

10.50 It is expected that the Directive, which can be adopted only by unanimous agreement amongst the member states, will also be conditional on the adoption of equivalent measures in countries with significant financial centres (including the USA and Switzerland) and in dependent or associated territories of certain of the EU member states.

Value added tax

10.51 A taxable person[1] who makes taxable supplies in the United Kingdom must account to HM Customs & Excise for value added tax in respect of supplies of goods and services which that person makes. If, in an accounting period, the amount of supplies made by a taxable person (outputs) exceeds the taxable supplies received by that person (inputs) and attributable to those outputs, a sum equal to the amount by which the outputs exceeds inputs must be paid to HM Customs & Excise. Where, however, inputs which are attributable to outputs exceed those outputs for an accounting period a sum equal to the excess may be reclaimed from HM Customs & Excise. The rate at which tax is chargeable depends upon the nature of a particular supply; a supply can be exempt, zero rated, taxable at 5 per cent or taxable at 17.5 per cent. For the financial services industry (including providers of custodian services), where supplies are often exempt, a recurrent difficulty is that inputs attributable to exempt outputs are not recoverable from HM Customs & Excise.

1 A taxable person is a person who is, or is required under the Value Added Tax Act 1994 to be, registered (VATA 1994, s 3). A person becomes liable to be registered if the value of its taxable supplies in the past year exceeds £55,000 or there are reasonable grounds for believing that the value of its taxable supplies in the following 30 days will exceed £55,000 (VATA Sch 1, para 1(1)).

Scope

10.52 Before considering whether a supply of financial services is exempt or standard rated, it is necessary to check whether a supply is within the scope of United Kingdom value added tax. The place of supply rules are complex, but the starting point for general purposes tends to be that services are supplied where the supplier is established (and will be supplied in the United Kingdom if a supplier has a business establishment in the United Kingdom with which the supplies are connected). However, in certain cases (this is known as the 'reverse charge') supplies are treated as being supplied where received and may therefore be outside the scope of United Kingdom value added tax if supplied to a recipient who is outside the United Kingdom. Banking, financial and insurance services are types of services to which the reverse charge applies[1].

1 Value Added Tax Act 1994, Sch 5.

Exemptions

10.53 The services which a custodian provides are likely to be exempt or standard rated. A supply of financial services is exempt if it falls within one the categories set out in Group 5 of Value Added Tax Act 1994, Sch 9. This Group includes:

(a) the issue, transfer or receipt of, or any dealing with, money, any security for money or any note or order for the payment of money. The grant of credit does not include the management of credit[1];

(b) the issue, transfer or receipt of, or any dealing with, any security or secondary security, being shares, stocks, bonds, notes (other than promissory notes), debentures, debenture stock or shares in any oil royalty, certain bearer documents and letters of allotment;

(c) the provision of intermediary services in relation to (a)–(b) above by a person acting in an intermediary capacity: intermediary services consist of the bringing together, with a view to the provision of financial services, of persons who are or may be seeking to receive such services and persons who provide financial services.

HM Customs & Excise have agreed with the British Bankers' Association an extensive taxonomy of financial services which sets out the appropriate treatment for many types of service[2]. Following the refusal of HM Customs & Excise's application to seek permission to appeal to the House of Lords in *First Data Resources Ltd v CCE*[3], HM Customs & Excise have conceded that United Kingdom law relating to the classification of financial services is out of step with European law. HM Customs & Excise consider that the decision in *First Data Resources* has made clear the circumstances in which clearing house type services are exempt supplies, and they take the view that this does not affect the fundamental point that credit management by someone other than the credit provider, data preparation, authorisation services, account maintenance services etc are taxable. HM Customs & Excise have, nonetheless, indicated that in the light of *First Data Resources* the border between exempt and standard rated services relating to financial services under United Kingdom law needs to be 'redrawn' so as to allow exemption from value added tax where a transfer between accounts is the predominant or core element in the supply[4].

A custodian can, as a practical matter, insulate itself with regard to the risk that value added tax must, or will in future, be payable in respect of its fees or that (where supplies are not exempt) the rate of value added tax may alter. This is achieved by including an express statement in an agreement regulating the custodian's remuneration that fees and amounts expressed to be payable to a custodian are exclusive of any value added tax which may be chargeable (and that, if value added tax is due, an amount equal to the value added tax due in respect of a supply will be paid when the fees or other amounts fall due).

1 Notes 2A–2B provide that credit checking, valuation, authorisation services, taking decisions relating to a grant or an application for a grant of credit, or creating and maintaining records relating to the grant or an application for credit on behalf of a credit provider, and the monitoring of a creditor's payment record or dealing with overdue payments are subsumed within the management (rather than the granting) of credit.

2 The *Blue Book*, which is updated periodically in line with changes to the law and practice.

3 *First Data Resources Ltd* (LON/95/2887). First Data Resources Limited ('FDR') provided credit card transaction processing services to banks. These services include the production and issue of cards, transaction authorisation, anti-fraud checks, transaction processing, debt settlement and the preparation and issue of customer and merchant statements and FDR has been likened to a 'clearing house' service for card transactions. Customs took the view that the services were taxable at the standard rate and FDR claimed, successfully, that the supplies were exempt supplies under art 13B(d)(3) of the EC Sixth Directive.

4 *Business Brief 10/2001*, 16 July 2001.

Chapter 11

Conclusions

Preceding chapters

11.1 This work has sought to provide a clear legal analysis of global custody and related securities arrangements. Chapter 1 gave an overview of the global custody industry and the legal context in which it operates, introducing fundamental operational and legal concepts. Chapter 2 discussed electronic intermediation in the securities markets and considered the impact of this on the legal nature of traditional securities. It argued that the asset of the investor in the electronic intermediated environment comprises equitable, indirect co-proprietary rights, which are called by the authors 'interests in securities'.

Chapter 3 considered the custody relationship in the electronic environment. It argued that, with respect to client cash accounts, the custodian bank is generally a debtor and that, with respect to client securities accounts, the custodian is generally a trustee. In relation to global client accounts, a valid trust may be established in favour of clients generally, preferably using express wording, but shortfall risk remains. Chapter 4 related to the use of the custody portfolio as collateral, considering in turn the collateralisation of the global custodian's own exposures to the client, and those of third parties. Different legal collateral structures were considered, together with the particular legal sensitivities associated with each. Recent industry and law reform developments were discussed.

Cross-border questions were discussed in Chapter 5, with special reference to sub-custodian insolvency and cross-border collateral arrangements. Chapter 6 considered the global custodian's duties, looking in turn at the use of limitation clauses; contractual, tortious and trustee duties; liability for third parties; particular clauses; indemnities for breach of duty; and corporate actions. The UK and international regulatory regime in which global custodians operate was discussed in Chapter 7.

Chapter 8 surveyed the post-trade infrastructure, giving an overview of developments in clearing and settlement; considering risk management in the industry; the process of consolidation; and underlying legal principles. CREST and the CMO were discussed in Chapter 9, and Chapter 10 considered certain UK taxation aspects of global custody.

Managing legal risk

11.2 A priority for all those involved in the global custody industry, and more generally in the international securities markets[1], is managing legal risk. It is important to be able to determine, with as much certainty as possible, the rights, duties and liabilities of global custodians, their clients and counterparties, and all those dealing with them, including collateral takers. This work has sought to make some progress towards that objective.

Two challenges in particular have been encountered. Firstly, practice has moved ahead of settled law, with the computerisation of the securities markets. This has cut across traditional legal analysis. It has been argued that computerised interests in securities cannot be negotiable instruments (Chapter 2) and that the lack of a tangible subject matter takes custody beyond the scope of bailment (Chapter 3). Secondly, international portfolios of securities raise complex conflict of laws issues. A particular sensitivity is intermediation, where the asset of the client corresponds to a number of different account entries maintained by the international chain of intermediaries through whom the client's asset is held. This is discussed in Chapter 5.

1 Including their regulators. See the discussion of proposals for regulatory capital weighting for operational risk (including legal risk) in Chapter 7.

Interests in securities

11.3 This work has indicated that legal analysis must follow contemporary operational practice. As indicated in Chapter 3, the client's interest in the securities making up the investment portfolio is characteristically unallocated and indirect. Rather than owning particular securities, the client has commingled rights in a fungible bulk, often held on a cross-border basis through one or more intermediaries. She cannot in general enforce these rights directly, but only through the global custodian. However, her rights are protected in the insolvency of the global custodian, and in this sense they are proprietary. These rights have been referred to as 'interests in securities'. Although interests in securities confer the same economic benefits and burdens[1] as direct and allocated ownership of the underlying securities, they are legally distinct from them. This distinction is significant in relation to the rights of the client against the custodian[2], to priorities[3], and to collateral structures[4], particularly cross-border collateral structures[5].

1 For example, the client owning interests in securities suffers a capital loss when the value of the underlying securities drops.
2 Which arise under a trust relationship and not a bailment. See Chapter 2.
3 The client's interest is equitable; equitable interests generally suffer weaker priority than competing legal interests. See Chapter 4.
4 An equitable asset cannot be subject to a legal security interest. See Chapter 4.
5 See the discussion of PRIMA in Chapter 5.

Investment Securities Code

11.4 The above analysis also informs the concept of securities entitlements, introduced in the US by the revised art 8 of the Uniform Commercial Code[1]. With both English law interests in securities, and US securities entitlements, the interest of the investor is enforceable only through the intermediary, ring-fenced in the intermediary's insolvency and generally located, for conflict of laws purposes, in the jurisdiction of the intermediary. The practical advantages of this approach are clear. The investor is protected from custodian credit risk, and the legal analysis of cross-border collateral is simplified. It is argued in this work that the position achieved by statute in the US is available under the general principles of English law.

However, in order to put the matter beyond doubt, and also to address and clarify important issues of priority, security of transfer and perfection, work has started in London to produce an Investment Securities Code, as briefly mentioned in Chapter 1. It is hoped that this work will enhance the competitive position of London as an international financial centre, by providing a solid legal foundation for the law of global custody and investment securities generally.

1 See the discussion in J S Rogers 'Policy Perspectives on Revised UCC Article 8' UCLA Law Rev, June 1996, p 1431; the concept of securities entitlements relates inherently to custody: '. . . the indirect holding system rules in Revised Article 8 come into play only with respect to the custodial function' (p 1495).

The future?

11.5 As has been indicated, the global custody industry is a moving target. The underlying systems and operational arrangements, as well as the legal and regulatory framework, are constantly changing. Existing trends that seem likely to continue include: straight through processing (notwithstanding the temporary shift of emphasis from STP to disaster recovery after September 11); prime brokerage; outsourcing by fund managers; web-based automation, including corporate-action management (with an increased confidence regarding security issues); and the consolidation of the trading and post-trading infrastructure, particularly within Europe. The ideal of one central counterparty to service all European markets may be highly desirable in view of the potential netting benefits (particularly in the equity markets, where mixed participation involves a wide range of credit exposures). However, the consolidation of clearing predicates a measure of legal and regulatory consolidation. Because of the number of different legal and regulatory regimes involved, this will be a greater challenge in Europe than it is in the US. In due course, a single European Investment Securities Code may provide the way forward.

Any entity providing or receiving services in these markets needs to keep up to speed with new initiatives in order to remain competitive. Awareness of the legal and regulatory implications of operational changes, together with changes in the applicable legal and regulatory regimes, must be an integral part of this process, and not merely an afterthought. An exhaustive analysis and resolution of legal issues in the global custody industry would not be realistic. To attempt to eliminate legal risk altogether may even be undesirable, if it would serve to stifle innovation. However, it is important that those involved in managing legal issues have a sound working model for the legal analysis of this industry. It is hoped that this work may serve that purpose.

Bibliography

Adams, D, *Corporate Finance: Banking and Capital Markets* (2002) Jordans
Austen-Peters, A O, *Custody of Investments* (2000) Oxford University Press
Bank for International Settlements *Central Bank Payment and Settlement Services with respect to Cross-Border and Multi-Currency Transactions* (1993)
— *Collateral in Wholesale Financial Markets: Recent Trends* (March 2001)
— *Cross-Border Securities Settlement* (May 1995)
— *Delivery Versus Payment in Securities Settlement Systems* (1992)
— *The New Basel Capital Accord* (January 2001)
— *Report of the Committee on Interbank Netting Schemes of the Central Banks of the Group of Ten Countries* ('Lamfalussy Netting Report') (1990)
— *Report on Netting Schemes* ('The Angell Report') (1989)
— *Settlement Risk in Foreign Exchange Transactions* (1996)
Bank for International Settlements and CPSS *Core Principles for Systemically Important Payment Systems* (2001)
Bank for International Settlements and IOSCO *Disclosure Framework for Securities Settlement Systems* (1997)
Bank of England *CREST: The Business Description* (December 1994)
— *The Future of Money Market Instruments* (November 1999)
— *Sponsored Membership of CREST for the Private Investor* (April 1995)
Beaves, A, 'Global Custody – A Tentative Analysis of Property and Contract' in Palmer and McEndrick (eds) *Interests in Goods* (2nd edn, 1998) LLP
Benjamin, J, *Interests in Securities* (2000) Oxford University Press
— 'Custody: an English Law Analysis' (1994) 9 JIBFL 121
— 'Negotiability and Computerisation' (1995) 10 JIBFL 253
— 'Recharacterisation and Conflict of Laws' in *Butterworths Journal of International Banking and Financial Law* (December 1997)
Bernasconi, C, *The Law Applicable to Dispositions of Securities Held through Indirect Holding Systems*, Hague Conference on Private International Law (January 2001)
Birks, P, 'Mixtures' in Palmer and McKendrick (eds) *Interests in Goods* (2nd edn, 1998) LLP
Birks, P (ed) *English Private Law* (2000) Oxford University Press
— *Overview: Tracing, Claiming and Defences, Laundering and Tracing* (1995) Clarendon
Black, J, *Rules and Regulators* (1997) Clarendon
Blackstone *Commentaries*, Book II
Brown, J, 'Recovery wakes up to extreme risk' *Euromoney* (November 2001)
Collins, L (ed) *Dicey and Morris on the Conflict of Laws* (13th edn, 2000) Sweet & Maxwell

CMO Reference Manual
CPSS/IOSCO Joint Task Force *Recommendations for Securities Settlement Systems* (2001)
CREST Reference Manual
DTCC *Central Counterparties: Development, Cooperation and Consolidation* (October 2000)
Encyclopedia of Banking Law (1994) Butterworths
Euroclear *Comments from Euroclear to the Basel Committee on Banking supervision on the New Basel Capital Accord* (31 May 2001)
— *Participant User Guide: Market Links* (20 May 2002)
European Commission *Clearing and settlement in the European Union; Main policy issues and future challenges* (May 2002)
— *Final Report of the Committee of Wise Men on the Regulation of European Securities Markets* (15 February 2001) ('Lamfalussy Securities Market Report')
— *Financial Services: Implementing the Framework for Financial Markets: Action Plan*, COM (1999) 232
European Securities Forum *Contribution on the Joint CESR/ECB Consultation on Clearing and Settlement* (2002)
— *EuroCCP; ESF's Blueprint for a Single Pan-European Central Counterparty* (2000)
Ewart, J S, 'Negotiability and Estoppel' (1900) 14 LQR 135
Fédération Internationale Des Bourses de Valeurs *Clearing and Settlement Best Practices* (1996)
— *Improving International Settlement* (1989)
Financial Services Authority *Handbook*
Finn, P D, *Fiduciary Obligations* (1977) Law Book Co, Sydney
— *The Fiduciary Principle, Equity, Fiduciaries and Trusts* (1989) Carswell
Fletcher *Insolvency in Private International Law* (1999) Clarendon
— 'International Insolvency: Recent Cases' (1997) JBL 471
Giovannini Group *Cross-Border Clearing and Settlement Arrangements in the European Union* (November 2001)
Goode, R M, *Legal Problems of Credit and Security* (2nd edn, 1988) Sweet & Maxwell
— 'Ownership and Obligation in Commercial Transactions' (1987) 103 LQR 433
— 'The Nature and Transfer of Rights in Dematerialised and Immobilised Securities' (1996) 10 JIBFL 162
Gray, K, 'Property in Thin Air' (1991) CLJ 252
Group of 30 *Clearance and Settlement in the World's Securities Markets* (1989)
Guest, A G (ed) *Chitty on Contracts* (27th edn, 1994) Sweet & Maxwell
Guiliano and Lagarde Report on the Rome Convention
Guynn, R, *Modernising Securities Ownership, Transfer and Pledging Laws* (1996) IBA
Hayton, D J, *Underhill & Hayton on the Law relating to Trusts and Trustees* (15th edn, 1995) Butterworths
— 'Developing the Law of Trusts for the Twenty-First Century' (1990) 106 LQR 87
— 'The Irreducible Core of Trusteeship' [1996] JTCP
— 'Uncertainty of Subject-Matter of Trusts' (1994) 110 LQR 335
Hayton, D J and Marshall *Cases and commentary on the law of Trusts and Equitable Remedies* (11th edn, 2001) Sweet & Maxwell
Hayton, Kortmann and Verhagen (eds) *Principles of European Trust Law* (1999) Kluwer

HM Treasury *Domestic and International Initiatives Concerning Conflict of Law Issues Relating to Securities: Consultation Document* (July 2001)
Hills et al 'Central Counterparty Clearing Houses and Financial Stability' (June 1999) *Bank of England Financial Stability Review* 124
Hohfeld *Fundamental Legal Conceptions* (1964) (first printed 1919) Yale University Press
Inland Revenue *Inspector's Manual* (May 2002)
— *Manufactured Payments on Overseas Securities Guidance Notes* (April 2001)
— *Stamp Office Manual* (March 2002)
— Stamp Taxes' *Customer Newsletter* – SDRT, No 1 (July 2002)
— *Tax Bulletin* (August 2001)
International Organisation of Securities Commissions *Client Asset Protection* (1996)
— *Report of the Technical Committee on Clearing and Settlement* (1990)
International Society of Securities Administrators *Report on Cross-Border Settlement and Custody* (1992)
Jowitt's Dictionary of English Law, (2nd edn, 1985) Sweet & Maxwell
Kennett, W, 'The Brussels I Regulation' (2001) ICLQ 725
Kirby, A, 'Global Straight-Through Processing is this Year's Imperative for Custodian Banks and their Clients' (6 January 2000) www.gstpa.org
Kynaston, D, *The City of London: IV A Club No More 1945–2000* (2001) Pimlico
Law Commission *Fiduciary Duties and Regulatory Rules* (1995) Law Com No 236
— *Registration of Security Interests: Company Charges and Property other than Land* (2002) Consultation paper No 164
Lee, R, *What is an Exchange? The Automation, Management, and Regulation of the Financial Markets* (1998) Oxford University Press
London Business School *Custodianship and the Protection of Client Property* (July 1994)
Megarry and Wade *The Law of Real Property* (6th edn) Sweet & Maxwell
Micheler E, 'Farewell Quasi-Negotiability; Legal Title and Transfer of Shares in a Paperless World' (2002) JBL 358
Mokal, R J, 'Priority as Pathology: The Pari Passu Myth' (2001) 69(3) CLJ 581
Montagu, G F H, 'Is a foreign state a body corporate?' (2001) *British Tax Review*, vol 6
Montagu, N, 'The Reality of Today's Revenue' *The Tax Journal* (29 July 2002)
Mooney, C W, 'Beyond Negotiability' (1990) 12 Cardozo LR 305
Morgan Guaranty Trust Company Report *Cross-Border Clearance, Settlement and Custody: Beyond the G30 Recommendations* (1993)
Myners, P, *Institutional Investment in the United Kingdom, A Review* (4 March 2001)
Palmer, N E, *Bailment* (2nd edn, 1991) Sweet & Maxwell
— *Liability of Bankers as Custodians of Client Property* (1979)
Palmer, N and McKendrick, E (eds) *Interests in Goods* (2nd edn, 1998) LLP
Pollock, F, *An Essay on Possession in the Common Law* (1888) Clarendon
Potok (ed) *Cross Border Collateral: Legal Risk and the Conflict of Laws* (2002) Butterworths
Prime, T, *International Bonds and Certificates of Deposit* (1990) Butterworths
Quinlan, M J, *Sergeant and Sims: Stamp Duties* (13th edn)
Rogers, J S, 'Policy Perspectives on the Revised UCC Article 8' (1996) 6 UCLALR 1413
Rogers, W, *Winfield and Jolowicz on Tort* (16th edn, 2002) Sweet & Maxwell
Rogerson, P J, 'The Situs of Debts in the conflict of Laws – Illogical, Unnecessary and Misleading' (1990) CLJ 441

Ryan, R, 'Taking Security Over Investment Portfolios held in Global Custody' (1990) 10 JIBL 404
Schwarcz, S L, 'Intermediary Risk in a Global Economy' (2001) 50 Duke LJ 1541
Smart, P, *Cross-Border Insolvency* (2nd edn, 1998) Butterworths
Snell's Principles of Equity (30th edn, 2000) Sweet & Maxwell
Squires, S J, 'Something old, something new . . .' *The Tax Journal* (9 April 2001)
Tennekoon, R C, *The Law and Regulation of International Finance* (2000) Butterworths
Tsien, P, 'Present Problems and Future Possibilities for Central Counterparties' in Marcus Evans Conference Proceedings *Trading in Europe: Assessing the Future for Central Counterparties* (1 and 2 October 2001)
Turing, D, 'The EU Collateral Directive' (2002) 5 JIBFL 187
Valdez, S, *An Introduction to the Global Financial Markets* (2nd edn, 1997) Macmillan
Virgos, M and Schmit, E, *Report on the Convention on Insolvency Proceedings* (1996)
Wood, P, *Comparative Financial Law* (1995) Sweet & Maxwell
Worthington, S, *Personal Property Law; Text and Materials* (2000) Hart Publishing
— *Proprietary Interests in Commercial Transactions* (1996) Clarendon
— 'Shares and Shareholders: Property, Power and Entitlement, Part 1' (2001) Comp Law 22(9)
— 'Sorting out ownership interests in a Bulk: Gifts, Sales and Trusts' (1999) JBL 1
Youdan, T G (ed) *The Fiduciary Principle, Equity, Fiduciaries and Trusts* (1989) Carswell

Index